Collective Memory of Political Events

Social Psychological Perspectives

Collective Memory of Political Events
Social Psychological Perspectives

Edited by

James W. Pennebaker
Southern Methodist University

Dario Paez
University of the Basque Country, Spain

Bernard Rimé
University of Louvain, Belgium

 LAWRENCE ERLBAUM ASSOCIATES, PUBLISHERS
1997   Mahwah, New Jersey

Lawrence Erlbaum Associates, Inc., Publishers
10 Industrial Avenue
Mahwah, New Jersey 07430

Cover design by Jennifer Sterling

Library of Congress Cataloging-in-Publication Data

Collective memory of political events : social psychological
    perspectives / edited by James W. Pennebaker, Dario Paez, Bernard
    Rimé.
        p.   cm.
    Includes bibliographical references and index.
    ISBN 0-8058-2182-1 (c : alk. paper).
    1. Memory—Social aspects. 2. Autobiographical memory. 3. Social
psychology. I. Pennebaker, James W. II. Páez, Darío. III. Rimé,
Bernard.
    BF378.S65C65   1997
    153.1'3—dc20   96-29389
                                                                              CIP

Books published by Lawrence Erlbaum Associates are printed on acid-free paper,
and their bindings are chosen for strength and durability.

Printed in the United States of America
10 9 8 7 6 5 4 3 2 1

Contents

Introduction

James W. Pennebaker
Southern Methodist University

Families, neighborhoods, cities, regions, and entire cultures are bound together by a shared set of beliefs, experiences, and memories. These shared histories cement individuals' identities with the groups to which they belong. Some of the historic memories are fixed events that were experienced by virtually all members of the group—an accident, a natural disaster, a birth, or a death. Other shared memories are not memories at all, but rather shared *presumed* memories or histories—for example, the group's members assume that their ancestors fought for a particular cause several generations earlier.

Powerful collective memories—whether real or concocted—can be at the root of wars, prejudice, nationalism, and cultural identities. For example, in the United States, citizens "remember" how they single-handedly defeated the Germans in World War II. Not surprisingly, Russians, British, and French nationals remember the defeat of Germany in very different ways. The assassination of John F. Kennedy was initially thought to be the act of a lone gunman who desperately sought the attention of others. Thirty years later, a majority of Americans "remember" Kennedy's assassination as the result of a conspiracy—perhaps with the complicity of the U.S. government. No overwhelming evidence exists to support either memory. Where do these memories come from and how do they exert such remarkable power over a culture? Further, how do these collective cultural memories remain alive across generations—often in the face of contradictory evidence?

The purpose of this book is to explore the creation, maintenance, and distortions of collective memories of societal events from several social psychological perspectives. What makes this volume unique is that each chapter focuses on political upheavals within and across several cultures. Authors from several countries analyze the psychological, social, and developmental features of cultural upheavals within their own shifting societies. Wars, kidnappings, torture, scandals, assassinations, personal and cultural tragedies and victories are the stuff of history. In this volume, we attempt to explore some of the social psychological dynamics that result from these events.

THE LIFE OF COLLECTIVE MEMORIES

We have divided the study of collective memory into three overlapping domains. Part I is devoted to the creation and maintenance of collective memories over time. Although hundreds of events make headlines each year, only a fraction will be remembered by the culture in subsequent years. What factors contribute to making an enduring collective memory? Empirical studies on political upheavals in the United States (Pennebaker & Banasik, chapter 1) indicate that we remember events that change the course of the lives of a large segment of the population and that are also associated with high levels of talking. Monuments are built and movies are made at predictable times after the upheavals occur.

Work in autobiographical memory (Conway, chapter 2) as well as sociological surveys of historical events (Schuman, Belli, & Bischoping, chapter 3) indicate that cultural upheavals maximally affect people between the ages of 15 and, perhaps, 30. Collective memories, then, are often cohort memories. Further, members of a given cohort who have been affected by a large-scale event will be the very people who subsequently write the event's history and influence the collective memories for succeeding generations (Igartua & Paez, chapter 4). Art and literature are only two of the mechanisms that help to keep collective memories alive. People naturally commemorate events in their own or their culture's past. The social and psychological bases of commemoration reveal the building blocks of collective memory (Frijda, chapter 5).

SOCIAL AND EMOTIONAL PROCESSES
OF COLLECTIVE MEMORIES

Broad-based collective events derive much of their potential power by inciting strong emotional feelings and provoking active discussion. In Part II, we analyze the intertwined roles of emotional and interpersonal processes that shape collective memories. Both laboratory and real world investigations have long demonstrated that it is difficult, if not impossible, to experience intense emotions without sharing them with others. Within the context of collective memory, political turmoil arouses a shared sense of anxiety and fear. The more intense the personal emotions, the more likely that people will talk with others about them. Further, those who later hear about the emotional experiences from others will, themselves, share the events with yet others. These cultural events can be positive or negative and can be associated with virtually all emotions (Rimé & Christophe, chapter 6). In addition, the degree of social sharing within a country about the nation's unwanted past can be related to a positive emotional climate, if open discussions are encouraged—or a negative emotional climate, if repressive governmental forces are at play (Paez, Basabe, & Gonzalez, chapter 7).

Note also that emotional experiences linked to political upheavals can be brief (as in hearing a shocking announcement) or prolonged (as with a series of smaller events that gradually unfold resulting in significant political changes). Brief emotional experiences tied to specific political events can result in vivid flashbulb memories among those people whose identities are most closely tied to the events (Gaskell & Wright, chapter 8). Further, these flashbulb memories are empirically linked to the degree to which they incite surprise rather than negative emotion per se (Finkenauer, Gisle, & Luminet, chapter 9). Other, more lingering emotions, such as nostalgia, are associated with a broader sense of the social order (Bellelli & Amatulli, chapter 10). Whereas flashbulb memories tied to political events can bond a cohort of individuals together, resulting in a highly specific collective memory, feelings of nostalgia about a place or time are related to individuals' attempts to relive an earlier identity by embracing collective memories of the past.

THE CONSTRUCTION, DISTORTION, AND FORGETTING OF COLLECTIVE EXPERIENCES

Although some would deny it, most psychologists and sociologists are intrigued with collective memories because they are so often distorted. Part III examines how collective histories are gradually constructed, reconstructed, and on occasion forgotten. In chapter 9, Lira offers a striking case study of the transition of her country, Chile, from a democracy to the 1973 military coup and then, 17 years later, to a democracy once again. She points to the fascinating and deeply disturbing dilemmas faced by those who were tortured or suffered during the dictatorship and those who escaped relatively unscathed. Part of her culture demands a public acknowledgment and open commemoration of the past horrors. Other segments of Chilean society seek to "get on with life" and avoid thinking of the past. Lira adroitly points to emerging collective memories and, at the same time, collective forgetfulness.

Whereas the Chilean tension between a military dictatorship and democracy is still alive, collective memories of the Spanish Civil War over a half century ago are less vivid and accurate among today's Spanish students. Today's collective memories suggest that history has been reconstructed to suggest a more orderly view of the past which, ultimately, helps to legitimize the present (Íñiguez, Valencia, & Vázquez, chapter 12). Comparable transitions in collective memories are apparent among Portuguese students in explaining the Portuguese Colonial War which lasted from 1961 until 1974 (Marques, Paez, & Serra, chapter 13). Adding to the distortions and reconstruction of memories in Chile, Spain, and Portugal were the respective governments' official denials of reality concerning the various incursions.

Why do governments and entire populations reconstruct history to such an impressive degree? Certainly, as many authors acknowledge, governmental leaders are motivated to avoid responsibility in the commission of heinous, embarrassing, or incompetent acts. Cultures, not unlike individuals, seek to make themselves look good, honest, and honorable. When incomprehensible events occur, we construct coherent and flattering narratives to preserve our identities. Basic social psychological processes that have traditionally been examined in highly controlled laboratory settings are apparent on a societal level (Baumeister & Hastings, chapter 14).

Taken as a whole, the emerging research topic of collective memory brings together a wide range of ideas across several disciplines in psychology, sociology, anthropology, and political science. Part of our understanding can be traced to traditional cognitive and memory processes (e.g., Bartlett, 1932) or to more recent information processing models (e.g., Neisser, 1982). Psychodynamic and personality processes are also implicated (e.g., Freud, 1920/1966; Fromm, 1955). Whereas psychologists have typically been more interested in memory from an individual perspective, sociological theorists have been particularly influential in emphasizing the social and cultural bases of shared memories. Karl Mannheim (1928/1952) and, perhaps most importantly, Maurice Halbwachs (1950/1992) provided initial evidence to indicate that memories were ultimately social and were passed from generation to generation.

This volume celebrates and extends many of the early contributions surrounding the idea of collective memory. The research methods employed by the authors range from natural observation to controlled laboratory investigations. Despite the striking differences in methodological approaches, the various contributions point to the importance and relevance of thinking about memory, perception, and history from a social perspective.

REFERENCES

Bartlett, F. C. (1932). *Remembering: A study in experimental and social psychology.* New York: Macmillan.

Freud, S. (1966). *Introductory lectures on psychoanalysis.* New York: Norton. (Original work published 1920)

Fromm, E. (1955). *The sane society.* New York: Rinehart.

Halbwachs, M. (1992). *On collective memory.* Chicago: University of Chicago Press. (Original work published 1950)

Mannheim, K. (1952). *Essays on the sociology of knowledge.* London: Routledge & Kegan. (Original work published 1928)

Neisser, U. (Ed.). (1982). *Memory observed: Remembering in natural contexts.* San Francisco: Freeman.

Part I

THE LIFE OF
COLLECTIVE MEMORIES

On the Creation and Maintenance of Collective Memories: History as Social Psychology

James W. Pennebaker
Southern Methodist University

Becky L. Banasik
University of Chicago

In 1973, Kenneth Gergen ushered the deconstruction movement into social psychology by arguing that the theories and findings within social psychology were dependent to a large degree on the prevailing culture. Further, because the field was generating culture- and time-dependent scientific results, these findings should be considered as historical data points or records. Social psychology, in his view, was a form of history. At the time, Gergen implied that history itself was an impartial truth with social psychological findings serving as archival reminders of the ways people thought and behaved at the time the studies were conducted. Although this chapter agrees with many of Gergen's assumptions, it is important to appreciate that history itself is highly contextual. Indeed, social psychological processes help to define history. The ways people talk and think about recent and distant events is determined by current needs and desires (see also Tetlock, Peterson, McGuire, Chang, & Feld, 1992). Just as the key to the future is the past, the key to the past is the present.

In the United States over the last half century, most adults would agree that a relatively small number of national events have profoundly affected Americans' collective memories: World War II, the assassination of John F. Kennedy, the peace movement/anti-Vietnam/Woodstock period, Watergate, and, perhaps, the explosion of the Challenger space craft. This is not to say that other extremely important events did not occur—such as the Korean War, the Bay of Pigs in Cuba, the election of Ronald Reagan, and the Persian Gulf War. However, this second group simply did not have the same psychological impact as the first. Why does society tend to spontaneously recall the first set of events rather than the second? What distinguishes an event that yields a broad-based collective memory from one that does not? By the same token, in whom are these collective memories instilled and what maintains them over time?

The creation and maintenance of a collective or historical memory is a dynamic social and psychological process. It involves the ongoing talking and thinking about the event by the affected members of the society or culture. This interaction process is critical to the organization and assimilation of the event in the form of a collective narrative.

ELEMENTS OF COLLECTIVE MEMORY

The recent resurgence of the term *collective memory* can be traced back to the French sociologist Maurice Halbwachs (1992) and the Russian psychologist Lev Vygotsky. Each questioned the assumption that memory resides in the individual. Halbwachs addressed the topic of collective memory, and Vygotsky presented a theory of the mind allowing others to theorize about it (Wertsch, 1985). Halbwachs asserted that all memories were formed and organized within a collective context. Virtually all events, experiences, and perceptions were shaped by individuals' interactions with others. Society, then, provided the framework for beliefs and behaviors and recollections of them. Vygotsky's assumptions were similar in noting that adult memory is dependent on society or community. The social mechanism guiding memories was language—the primary symbol system that defines the framework for individuals' memories (Bakhurst, 1990). By extension, people's ways of remembering the past should be dependent on their relationship to their community (Radley, 1990).

In stark contrast to the assumptions of collective memory, most traditional laboratory-based memory research has attempted to understand memory as a context-free, isolated psychological process. This laboratory-based strategy has yielded some important findings about what individuals can and do remember. For example, memories for events, objects, or facts (declarative memory) are most likely to be remembered if they are unique, provoke emotional reactions, are actively rehearsed, and are associated with subsequent changes in behaviors or beliefs (e.g., Craik & Lockhart, 1986). It is particularly important to appreciate that unique emotion-provoking events requiring no psychological adaptation are not necessarily memorable. Moreover, while individuals are psychologically adapting, they may be more likely to remember events that occur during that time (Pillemer, Rhinehart, & White, 1986).

One interesting subset of memories is the phenomenon of *flashbulb memories* (Brown & Kulik, 1977). Flashbulb memories are an example of a mixture of personal circumstances and historical events in memory. When people hear the news about a shocking significant event, like the fall of the Berlin Wall, they not only remember details about the event, but also their personal circumstances when they heard about it. Therefore, almost everyone who was at least 12 years old at the time of the tearing down of the Wall can tell their story (their narrative) of what they were doing when they heard the news.

Strangely enough, these flashbulb memories, which are reported with confidence, are often inaccurate (e.g., Bohannon & Symons, 1992). This is understandable because all memories fade or are reconstructed. Neisser (1982) hypothesized that flashbulb memories are not established at the moment of the event, but after the event when the significance of the event to society or to the individual has been established, leaving more room for error. People have such a vivid, long-lasting recollection when it comes to flashbulb memories because they allow individuals to place themselves in the historical context, and when relaying their personal flashbulb memories to others, they are able to include themselves in the event.

These event features that are important for individual memories should, by definition, be necessary for collective memories as well. Specifically, a society should embrace and/or collectively remember those national or universal events that affected their lives the most. Interestingly, this suggests that massive national situations that ultimately did not affect the course of history should not be part of the national psyche to the same degree as events that signaled important institutional or historical changes.

Consider, for example, the four most recent wars fought by the United States: World War II, the Korean War, the Vietnam War, and the Persian Gulf War. Each provoked tremendous national discussions, and was associated with the loss of life and huge consumption of resources. Only two, however, appear to have had any long-term psychological consequences: World War II and Vietnam. Surprisingly, winning versus losing does not appear to affect collective memory. Rather, these two wars were important turning points for American self-views. With World War II, the United States emerged as a dominant military and economic force for much of the world. Vietnam changed this egocentric perspective, thereby producing a new generation who questioned the role of the United States in the world.

A critical initial step in understanding both individual and collective memories, then, is that the long-term impact of events themselves help to determine the memories. Studies on individual memories, for example, demonstrate that people tend not to recall common events or objects that have no personal impact or adaptive importance (e.g., Bruce, 1985). By the same token, a war may give the impression of changing the course of history at the time. However, if no institutional and/or personal effects are apparent once the war is over, there will be very few collective memories. Citing the powerful social memory of the execution of Louis XVI in France in 1793, Connerton (1990) demonstrated that previous murders of French kings were ultimately unimportant because the basic dynastic succession remained. With the French revolution and the death of Louis XVI, however, the basic structure of government changed forever.

RESHAPING COLLECTIVE MEMORIES FOR THE PRESENT

Significant historical events form stronger collective memories, and present circumstances affect what events are remembered as significant. Fentriss and Wickham (1992) argued that memory plays an important social role. In their view, individuals invent or redefine the past to fit the present. Evidence that current events affect the ways a society remembers them can be seen in the commemorative symbols the society constructs (e.g., Connerton, 1990; Schwartz, 1991).

Schwartz (1982) documented the people and events commemorated in the paintings, statues, murals, frescoes, reliefs, and busts displayed in the U.S. Capitol. There are congressional procedures that commission artworks for the Capitol building that encourage diverse views of what should be commemorated. Schwartz noted that this effort to reflect the nation's diversity did not result in an evenhanded display of the important events in American history. Instead, he found that certain historical periods were disproportionately represented and people or events that were not deemed important to the people living in the time period depicted were often "picked up" by later generations. For example, the early colonists commemorated John Cabot as a major explorer. But with the rise of anti-British sentiment came an interest in Columbus, who subsequently became the most celebrated explorer in the United States.

Schwartz (1991) also observed a similar phenomenon with regard to Abraham Lincoln's reputation and how it changed after his death. Prior to his assassination, Lincoln was neither overwhelmingly popular nor a national hero. After his death, however, there was a 14-day funeral procession by rail passing through most of the largest cities in the country that was witnessed by millions of people. The combination of the funeral procession and the high emotions of the country surrounding the end of the Civil War started a trend in transforming Lincoln's popularity that eventually elevated him to a status akin to George Washington. According to Schwartz, Lincoln's image was further bolstered by a shifting national sentiment that believed in the common man rising to lead the people.

THE ROLE OF LANGUAGE IN AFFECTING
COLLECTIVE MEMORIES

Translating events or images into language affects the ways they are thought about and recalled in multiple ways. Typically, if not always, language is a social act. When an event is discussed, its perception and understanding is likely to be affected by others in the conversation. On a more psychological level, talking about an event is a form of rehearsal. Further, the act of rehearsing the event through language can influence the way the event is organized in memory and, perhaps, recalled in the future.

Talking as a Memory Aid: Rehearsal

On an individual level, objects or events are most likely to be consolidated in memory if they are rehearsed (e.g., Baddeley, 1986). In laboratory settings, the most common ways by which events are rehearsed are that they are thought about in verbal form. Repeating a 9-digit number over and over again—either subvocally or out loud—helps the person to retain the number for seconds, minutes, or, on occasion, longer.

Most memories for events are quite different from phone numbers or lists of nonsense words in that they have a social component. As noted earlier, Halbwachs argued that virtually all memories are collective—in large part because they are discussed with others. Indeed, for societies to exist at all, the societal members must share a very high percentage of their experiences to increase the cohesiveness of their memories. Indeed, Shils (1981) claimed that for a society to exist over time, its communications must be said, said again, and reenacted repeatedly.

When a large-scale event affects an entire region or society, a common response is for people to openly talk about it. In two related studies on a natural disaster (the San Francisco Bay Area earthquake of 1989) and responses to the Persian Gulf War, the degree of self-reported talking and thinking about these events was startling (Pennebaker & Harber, 1993). In both of these studies, weekly or semiweekly samples of residents of San Francisco (for the earthquake project) and of Dallas, Texas (for the war project), were interviewed using random-digit dialing sampling methods immediately after the war or quake through at least 3 months later. Among the questions that both groups of samples were asked was "How many times in the last 24 hours have you talked with someone about the quake (or war)?" Similar questions asked the number on times subjects thought and heard about the quake or war.

As can be seen in Fig. 1.1, the degree of social sharing and ruminating about these events was remarkably high during the first 2 weeks following the quake and the onset of the war. Clearly, the raw ingredients for shared

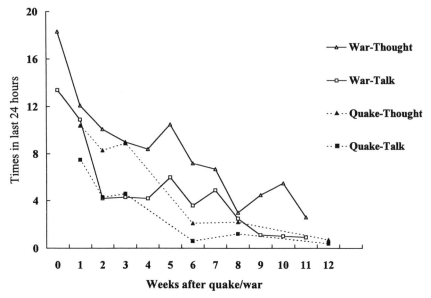

FIG. 1.1.   Thoughts and conversations about war/quake.

experiences and memories were being laid down. Not only were people discussing these events to a high degree, but they were bombarded with features of the events via the media. In other words, most residents received similar information from television and newspapers, which in turn was talked and thought about. Given these basic ingredients, it would be difficult for people not to have similar memories of the experience, that is, collective memories.

Talking as a Forgetting Aid: Cognitive Organization

Just as talking about an event is a form of rehearsal that may aid memory, talking or translating an experience into language can help to organize and assimilate the event in people's minds (cf. Horowitz, 1976). An emotional experience, by definition, provokes talking because those who are affected by it are attempting to understand and learn more about it (Rimé, 1995). Language, then, is the vehicle for important cognitive and learning processes following an emotional upheaval. Talking about an event may successfully organize and assimilate it, which will allow the person to move past the upheaval. Ironically, once an event is cognitively assimilated, individuals no longer need to ruminate about it and, once it is out of their minds, they may actually forget about it.

   An intriguing example of how cultures forget important events can be seen in the case of the Persian Gulf War. As noted earlier, the degree to which people talked about the Persian Gulf War in the United States in the first weeks after its beginning was remarkable. Extrapolating from these numbers, it seems that Americans would have a clear memory for the major features of it. However, if talking about an event helps individuals to organize and forget about it, those who talked most about the war would be the ones with the poorest memories in the years following the war.

As a test of this theory, 76 university students who completed weekly questionnaires in classrooms about the degree to which they talked about the war during the time the war was ongoing were contacted 2½ years later (Crow & Pennebaker, 1996). In the 2½-year follow-up, the participants were asked a series of factual questions about the war, including: Who did we fight? [Iraq] Who was the leader of the opposing force? [Saddam Hussein] How many United States soldiers were killed? [148]. Astonishingly, most people's memories for the war were extremely poor. It is interesting to note that two factors predicted poor long-term historical memory for the war: degree of talking and negative emotions surrounding the war. Basically, those who talked the most and for those who the war aroused the most negative emotions were the ones whose memories were the worst 2½ years later.

CORRELATES OF COLLECTIVE MEMORIES

An intriguing feature of a large-scale event that evokes collective memories is that it can also bring about collective behavioral responses to the event. For example, in the mid-1970s, the wife of the president of the United States, Betty Ford, was diagnosed with breast cancer. Within days of this announcement, clinics around the country reported a large surge in the number of women seeking breast exams.

Particularly revealing from a psychological perspective are cases where large groups of people respond to an event in similar ways that, on the surface, do not appear to be related to the collective memory-related event. This phenomenon was first discovered when studying the psychological and health effects of the assassination of John F. Kennedy in Dallas. By way of background, Kennedy was assassinated in Dallas, Texas, on November 22, 1963. Two days later, his assassin was murdered by an angered nightclub owner. At the time, the entire country was thrown into shock. Kennedy was viewed as young and vigorous, and no other president had been assassinated since the turn of the century.

Oddly, many Americans immediately blamed the city of Dallas for the assassination. Dallas residents were discriminated against when they traveled and became the victims of harsh media criticism. As a city, Dallas responded by pretending nothing had happened. It became the city of the future and, at the same time, the city without a past. Dallas residents quickly embraced this new image. Compared to other cities with equivalent economic bases, Dallas experienced a tremendous growth in the 3 years after the assassination; dozens of dramatically large buildings and skyscrapers were built. A disproportionate amount of city funds, as compared to other Texas cities, was directed toward making the city cleaner after the assassination. Similarly, Dallas residents themselves donated more money to worthy causes, such as the United Way. All of these positive effects were most apparent between 1964 and 1968. In fact, in 1968, attention was shifted away from Dallas because of the assassinations of Martin Luther King and Robert F. Kennedy. In an odd way, most collective behaviors that distinguished Dallas ceased at this time (Pennebaker, 1990).

Beneath these positive features of the assassination on Dallas were a number of consequences indicating that the city experienced a great deal of stress during this time. For example, deaths due to heart disease (the major cause of death at the time) increased 4% over the 4 years after the assassination, as compared with an overall 2% decline in the rest of the United States and other Texas cities. Murder and suicide rates increased significantly in Dallas in the 2 years following the assassination compared to control cities as well. In short, health and crime statistics indicated that the failure to admit to the psychological effects of the assassination was ultimately unhealthy.

THE COLLECTIVE MEMORY OF SILENT EVENTS

A silent event is one where people actively avoid talking about a major shared upheaval. This failure to talk can be imposed by a repressive government following a coup or other authoritarian institution such as a religion. By the same token, an event can be considered so guilt worthy or shameful that most affected people refuse to talk about it, as in the case of Dallas residents following Kennedy's assassination. In many ways, silent events may be the most potent in the development of collective memories for several reasons.

Recent studies indicate that when people attempt to suppress unwanted thoughts, they typically fail. Wegner (1989), for example, found that when people were told to avoid thinking of an object, they subsequently thought about it at rates comparable to control conditions where people were explicitly told to think about the object. In short, when people are told to avoid talking or even thinking about an important event, that event becomes more deeply ingrained in memory.

Even in studies of the Persian Gulf War and the San Francisco Bay Area earthquake, evidence was found to suggest that people quickly develop norms to not talk about the relevant events beginning 2 to 3 weeks after the war/earthquake began. It was at this precise time that individuals were most likely to dream about the war or earthquake. In other words, when people are blocked from talking about an important psychological event for whatever reason, they continue to process it in their sleep. Indeed, in both studies, over 30% of those people who were randomly selected to be interviewed reported dreams about the quake or war in the 3 to 6 weeks after the beginning of the event—a number much higher than the 10% who had comparable dreams in the first 2 weeks after the quake or war, or in the periods following the 6-week interview period.

Just as the diminution of talking about an event is correlated with increased dreaming, it is also associated with tension, hostility, and violent crimes. In the 2 to 6 weeks after the earthquake, aggravated assault rates increased 10% over the previous year in San Francisco (Pennebaker, 1992). A comparable jump in assaults was apparent in Dallas 2 to 6 weeks after the war started. More startling is what happened approximately 2 weeks after the war ended. Recall that the Persian Gulf War was declared to be a striking victory 6 weeks after it started. However, within a week of its conclusion, it became quite apparent to most Americans that the Iraq government was essentially unchanged and the brutal treatment of Kurdish residents was, if anything, intensified. The surveys indicated that people simply no longer wanted to hear or think about the war. It was at this time that aggravated assaults jumped 70% above the previous year (Pennebaker & Harber, 1993).

When people do not want to or cannot openly talk about an important event, they continue to think and even dream about it. They are also more likely to display aggression and initiate fights with friends and acquaintances. Ironically, then, actively trying not to think about an event can contribute to a collective memory in ways that may be as powerful if not more so than events that are openly discussed.

THE LIFE OF COLLECTIVE MEMORIES: THE PSYCHOLOGY OF LOOKING BACK

Ultimately, the importance and interest of collective memories is that they persist for years or even generations. What fuels these memories? This question may be addressed by looking at various indicators of popular culture within the United States. Much of this work was the outgrowth of the Kennedy assassination project. In the years following the assassination, there was very little open acknowledgment that Kennedy's death took place within Dallas itself. Virtually no landmarks were erected. Unlike most other cities in the United States, there were no schools, streets, or buildings named after Kennedy. Oddly, a similar phenomenon occurred in Memphis, Tennessee, the city where Martin Luther King was assassinated in 1968. In Memphis, there were no schools, buildings, or streets named after King. (But Dallas has several buildings or streets named after King and Memphis has schools or streets named after Kennedy.)

Approximately 25 years after the assassination, Dallas opened an elaborate museum/exhibit acknowledging Kennedy's murder in the downtown area. Earlier attempts to open exhibits in the city had been met with tremendous opposition. Likewise, approximately 25 years after the assassination of King, Memphis opened a large exhibit commemorating the death of the famous civil rights leader. Also, the Vietnam Memorial Wall, commemorating people who fought in Vietnam, was opened in 1982, almost 25 years after the first Americans died in the war. Moreover, in the late 1970s, the Vietnam War was not an acceptable theme for mainstream movies, yet by 1986, *Platoon* and approximately 12 other Vietnam-themed motion pictures were released (Adams, 1989).

Is this 25-year lapse between a traumatic experience and the building of a moment real or coincidental? To test this idea, a study sought to find monuments that had been erected within the previous 100 years in the United States commemorating a single discreet event (e.g., disaster, battle, or similar event—either positive or negative). The time between the event and the erection of the monument was then computed. As can be seen in Fig. 1.2, monuments tend to be erected either immediately after an event, or in 20- to 30-year cycles thereafter. Interestingly, whether the event

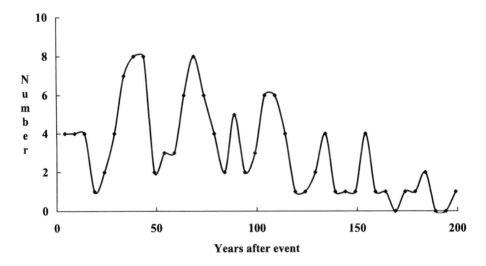

FIG. 1.2.   Number of monuments built as a function of the number of years after the commemorating event (5-year rolling average).

that is commemorated is positive or negative does not make a tremendous difference.

Two related questions arise in examining Fig. 1.2. The first concerns why it takes 20 to 30 years to build a monument in the first place. Similarly, why does monument building appear to go in 20- to 30-year cycles? On a certain level, the erection of monuments is a complex coordinated social activity. For example, there usually must be some consensus and very little overt opposition among residents to build a monument in the first place. Typically, numerous committees must be coordinated to acquire funding for an artist and the land on which the monument is to be built. Whether the building of a monument reflects the enthusiasm of the builders or the lack of opposition to the monument is unknown.

One way by which to establish the generality of this looking-back phenomenon is to consider other forms of expression that could reflect a society's interest or need to collectively remember an earlier event. The second project was to study when movies depicting historical events were made and released. In the study, a random sample of 1,400 popular movies from a pool of over 20,000 made from 1920 to 1990 were coded for date of release and the era that the movie depicted. Not surprisingly, the majority of movies depict the present (i.e., the time period when the movie was released). However, as can be seen in Fig. 1.3, movies not depicting the present tend to take place about 20 to 25 years earlier. This pattern

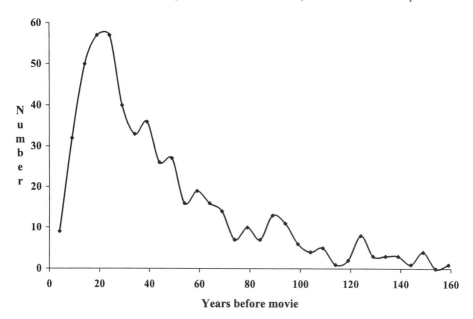

FIG. 1.3. Time that movies depict.

is actually stronger for top grossing movies (in terms of ticket sales) than movies in general. U.S. film watchers, and probably those elsewhere around the world, seek to remember what was happening 22 years earlier.

Groups of individuals and entire societies collectively look back at specific times. During these times of looking back, people openly talk about and acknowledge the relevance of these events to their own personal development. What accounts for the emergence of the 20- to 30-year cycle in looking back? There are probably at least three interrelated processes at work. The first concerns the idea that people have a critical period in life in which national events are most likely to affect their identity. The second, which overlaps with the first, concerns a generation argument; specifically, monuments are built and movies are made when one has the power to create them. The third explanation concerns the role of time gradually removing the pain of recalling negative events. Each of these hypotheses is briefly examined.

The Critical Period Hypothesis

Certain national events are more impactful for people at certain ages than others. Events that occur between ages 12 and 25 should be some of the most long lasting and significant of a person's life. This hunch is based on personal experience and theoretical speculation. In this relatively short time span, most people fall in love, form and leave very tight social bonds (e.g., secondary school, gangs, college), marry, and have children. For at least the last two generations in the United States, most people seem to like listening to music that was popular when they themselves were 12 to 25 years old. Movies depicting this time period are also held in special reverence. This is a highly social time, then, in which collective memories have the potential to be formed.

Other researchers have also pointed to the importance of this general life period. According to Erikson (1950), for example, the task of people between the ages of 12 and 19 is to work toward and adopt an integrated, single identity. Beginning around age 20, the next task is to develop close friendships and establish intimate relationships with others. Afterward in Erikson's view (as well as in the thinking of Levinson, Darrow, Klein, Levinson, & McKee, 1978), most life transitions are more individualistic and, perhaps, subtle (see also Conway's chap. 2).

Research dealing with autobiographical memories suggests that people tend to spontaneously recall memories that were formed between the ages of 12 and 25. In a fascinating review of his and other studies, Rubin and his colleagues (Rubin, Wetzler, & Nebes, 1986) described the results of memory experiments with individuals who were between the ages of 50 and 70 years old. In the studies, participants were asked to recall a series of memories in response to various cued words. Although subjects were likely to be reported that had occurred between the ages of 11 and 20, and second most likely to be recalled if they had originated between ages 21 and 30 (note that the ages were aggregated by decade so that more refined evaluations of ages were not possible).

This has also been born out for memories of national and world events. Schuman and Scott (1989) found that when people of varying ages were asked what historical changes or events seemed especially important to them, they disproportionally refer to events that occurred in their late teens and early twenties. So, national events are most likely to create profound social/collective memories on a cohort of society rather than on all members of society.

The reasons why this age period is most likely to result in salient long-term memories are still under debate. In addition to the forming of one's identity and first intimate relationships, it is also a time of tremendous emotional and physiological variability—all dimensions independently related to memory formation and recall. (For a cogent discussion of these issues, see Conway, 1990.) Moreover, memories of large-scale events may be stronger for those who experienced them in their late teens and early twenties because they are more disruptive to those who are experiencing the significance of major events for the first time, or as Mannheim (1968) put it, these events constitute a "fresh" experience.

Obviously, the fact that events affect young people more than those who have more established views probably would not apply to a situation wherein an entire society was completely devastated. It would also suggest that any writers, biographers, historians, or even psychologist studying collective memory would overemphasize the impact of events that occurred during the times that they were between the ages of 12 and 25. It should be noted that when the first author was between the ages of 12 and 25, Kennedy was assassinated, Vietnam started and ended, Watergate occurred, and the Beatles and the Rolling Stones sang some of the best songs in history.

The Generational Resource Hypothesis

Allied with the critical period hypothesis is that events are commemorated when people have the economic resources and social or political power to do so. Immediately after an upheaval, for example, people often devote their energies and finances to dealing with the upheaval itself. If a war starts, a natural disaster hits, or a leader is assassinated, members of society must immediately cope with the event rather than worry about building a monument. Months or years might elapse before people are able to stand back and commemorate the event.

If the critical period hypothesis is true, the people who are most invested in ultimately building monuments and looking back in general are the younger members of the society. Soon after a potentially memorable event, this group does not have the economic or political clout to establish monuments. Around 25 years later, when the affected cohort is, on average, over 40 years of age, they are now in the position to openly acknowledge their own past by building monuments, investing in movies, or writing and publishing books. Note also that when individuals pass the 40-year mark, they become progressively interested in looking back and validating their own lives (cf. Erikson, 1975).

The Psychological Distance Hypothesis

It is well established that immediately after a traumatic experience, individuals tend to distance themselves from it. Any reminders of the trauma can arouse anxiety and distress (e.g., Horowitz, 1976). This phenomenon helps explain why people often avoid building monuments soon after an emotional upheaval. The monument simply prolongs the pain of the event itself.

   This problem is exacerbated when looking at a group of people rather than separate individuals. In coping with a trauma, people tend to employ different defense mechanisms. In Dallas after the assassination of Kennedy, for example, some individuals sought to openly discuss the event. Others increased their donations to worthy causes (perhaps a form of sublimation). Yet others murdered, committed suicide, or died quietly from heart disease. Statistically, then, a community or culture can show a number of seemingly inconsistent patterns following an unwanted tragedy.

   Based on the Dallas example, a sizable minority of a society will support the building of a monument and a separate group will vehemently oppose it. One groups seeks to remember, the other to forget. Interestingly, the impact of these two forces changes over time in very different ways. The desire to look back slowly increases as people begin to acknowledge the event's effects on their own lives and on that of their society. The members of society who initially oppose the building of a monument do so because the event arouses too much anxiety and distress. These negative emotions, however, tend to dissipate over time. The driving emotional force of the opposition to any monument, then, quietly diminishes. The net effect is that society builds a consensus for the erection of a monument and an acknowledgment of the importance of the given collective memory.

**SUMMARY AND IMPLICATIONS
FOR UNDERSTANDING COLLECTIVE MEMORIES**

Very few empirical studies have attempted to understand when and why cultures develop collective memories. This chapter has pointed to some of the dynamics that can contribute to the building and maintenance of these memories. The basic findings can be summarized as follows:

• Collective memories are most likely to be formed and maintained about events that represent significant long-term changes to people's lives. A massive political upheaval (e.g., the 1848 revolutions in Europe, the Korean War, the Persian Gulf War) that results in virtually no major institutional alterations are much less likely to become part of a society's collective memory.

• Memories are most likely to be formed if people actively talk and think about events to a high degree. The social sharing of the events also helps in shaping people's perceptions of the events such that a consensus narrative emerges. If, however, an event does not change the course of history, talking about it should help people to organize, assimilate, and ultimately forget the event.

• Emotionally charged events about which people actively avoid talking will continue to affect individuals by increasing their rate of thinking and dreaming about the events. Political repression of speech about an occurrence, then, will have the unintended consequence of consolidating collective memories associated with the repressed event.

• Events that have a collective psychological impact will result in collective individual behaviors. Following significant cultural events, changes in crime, suicide, physical health, and even prosocial behaviors can be expected to change.

• Major national events will affect people of different ages in significantly different ways. In general, those between the ages of 12 and 25 will be most affected. The national events occurring during this age bracket will typically have the greatest impact on this cohort's self-views and collective memories.

• Over time, people tend to look back and commemorate the past in cyclic patterns occurring every 20 to 30 years. Monuments are erected, movies made, and books are written about national events for a number of reasons.

This chapter has addressed a small number of issues surrounding collective memories. However, some of the findings make clear predictions about how countries such as Chile will deal with the turbulent upheavals it experienced between 1973 and the present. Similarly, the ongoing changes in Russia and the countries that were once part of the Soviet Union should create collective memories that we will likely see for generations. Indeed, it will be quite revealing to learn more about the mass destruction of monuments that have taken place in several parts of the former Soviet Union. How, if at all, will the 75 years of communism be commemorated in future generations? Shils (1981) and Connerton (1989) argued that social or collective memories and, indeed societies themselves, are maintained by rites and tradition. With the elimination of monuments and traditions, social memories should be profoundly altered. On the other hand, the present findings dealing with the time course of collective memories hint that a resurgence of positive collective memories will begin to surface no earlier than two decades from now.

Finally, collective memories are powerful meaning-making tools both for the community and the individuals in the community. Individuals partly define themselves by their own traits, but also by those groups to which they belong, as well as by their historical circumstances. Collective memories provide a backdrop or a context for much of people's identity (cf. Baumeister, 1986). History defines us just as we define history. As our identities and cultures evolve over time, we tacitly reconstruct our histories. By the same token, these new collectively defined historical memories help to provide identities for succeeding generations.

ACKNOWLEDGMENTS

Part of the research was supported by grant SBR94-11674 from the National Science Foundation and MH52391 from the National Institutes of Health to James W. Pennebaker.

REFERENCES

Adams, W. (1989). War stories: Movies, memory, and the Vietnam War. *Comparative Social Research, 11,* 165–189.

Baddeley, A. D. (1986). *Working memory.* Oxford, England: Oxford University Press.

Bakhurst, D. (1990). Social memory in Soviet thought. In D. Middleton & D. Edwards (Eds.), *Collective remembering.* London: Sage.

Baumeister, R. F. (1986). *Identity: Cultural change and the struggle for the self.* New York: Oxford University Press.

Bohannon, J. N., & Symons, V. L. (1992). Flashbulb memories: Confidence, consistency, and quantity. In E. Winograd & U. Neisser (Eds.), *Affect and accuracy in recall* (pp. 65–91). New York: Cambridge University Press.

Brown, R., & Kulik, J. (1977). Flashbulb memories. *Cognition, 5,* 73–99.

Bruce, D. (1985). The how and why of ecological memory. *Journal of Experimental Psychology: General, 114,* 78–90.

Connerton, P. (1989). *How societies remember.* Cambridge, England: Cambridge University Press.

Conway, M. A. (1990). *Autobiographical memory: An introduction.* Philadelphia: Open University Press.

Craik, F. I. M., & Lockhart, R. S. (1986). CHARM is not enough: Comments on Eich's model of cued recall. *Psychological Review, 93,* 360–364.

Crow, D. M., & Pennebaker, J. W. (1996). *The Persian Gulf War: The forgetting of an emotionally important event.* Manuscript submitted for publication.

Erikson, E. (1950). *Childhood and society.* New York: Norton.

Erikson, E. (1975). *Life history and the historical moment.* New York: Norton.

Fentriss, J., & Wickham, C. (1992). *Social memory.* Cambridge, England: Blackwell.

Gergen, K. J. (1973). Social psychology as history. *Journal of Personality and Social Psychology, 26,* 309–320.

Halbwachs, M. (1992). *On collective memory.* Chicago: University of Chicago Press.

Horowitz, M. (1976). *Stress response syndromes.* New York: Aronson.

Levinson, D. J., Darrow, C. M., Klein, E. B., Levinson, M. H., & McKee, B. (1978). *The seasons of a man's life.* New York: Knopf.

Mannheim, K. (1968). *Essays on the sociology of knowledge.* London: Routledge & Kegan Paul. (Original work published 1952)

Neisser, U. (1982). *Memory observed: Remembering in natural contexts.* San Francisco: Freeman.

Pennebaker, J. W. (1990). *Opening up: The healing power of confiding in others.* New York: Morrow.

Pennebaker, J. W. (1992). Inhibition as the linchpin of health. In H. S. Friedman (Ed.), *Hostility, coping, and health* (pp. 127–139). Washington, DC: American Psychological Association.

Pennebaker, J. W., & Harber, K. (1993). A social stage model of collective coping: The Persian Gulf and other natural disasters. *Journal of Social Issues, 49,* 125–145.

Pillimer, D. B., Rhinehart, E. D., & White, S. H. (1986). Memories of life transitions: The first year in college. *Human Learning, 5,* 109–123.

Radley, A. (1990). Artifacts, memory and a sense of the past. In D. Middleton & D. Edwards (Eds.), *Collective remembering.* London: Sage.

Rimé, B. (1995). Mental rumination, social sharing, and the recovery from emotional exposure. In J. W. Pennebaker (Ed.), *Emotion, disclosure, and health* (pp. 271–292). Washington, DC: American Psychological Association.

Rubin, D. C., Wetzler, S. E., & Nebes, R. D. (1986). Autobiographical memory across the life span. In D. C. Rubin (Ed.), *Autobiographical memory* (pp. 202–221). Cambridge, England: Cambridge University Press.

Schuman, H., & Scott, J. (1989). Generations and collective memory. *American Sociological Review, 54,* 359–381.

Schwartz, B. (1982). The social context of commemoration: A study in collective memory. *Social Forces, 61,* 375–402.

Schwartz, B. (1991). Mourning and the making of a sacred symbol: Durkheim and the Lincoln assassination. *Social Forces, 70,* 342–364.

Shils, E. A. (1981). *Tradition.* Chicago: University of Chicago Press.

Tetlock, P. E., Peterson, R. S., McGuire, C., Chang, S., & Feld, P. (1992). Assessing political group dynamics: A test of the groupthink model. *Journal of Personality and Social Psychology, 63,* 403–425.

Wegner, D. M. (1989). *White bears and other unwanted thoughts.* New York: Viking.

Wertsch, J. V. (1985). *Vygotsky and the social formation of mind.* Cambridge, MA: Harvard University Press.

Chapter 2

The Inventory of Experience: Memory and Identity

Martin A. Conway
University of Bristol, U.K.

In his definitive essay, "The Problem of Generations" (1952), Mannheim commented that "[the] inventory of experience which is absorbed . . . from the environment in early youth often becomes the historically oldest stratum of consciousness, which tends to stabilize itself as the natural view of the world [for each particular generation]" (p. 328). Indeed, Mannheim thought that the process of "absorption" was complete and the basis of experience more or less fixed by about 25 years of age. Current evidence from the study of autobiographical memory (AM; reviewed later) suggests that Mannheim was right. The concept of an "inventory of experience" does not, however, simply refer to individuals' memories for the events of their life. Rather, Mannheim used this concept in a surprisingly contemporary way to encompass all types of knowledge a person might acquire, that is, conceptual knowledge of word meanings, world knowledge, skills, as well as memories.

Memory researchers have often found it useful to make distinctions between different types knowledge in long-term memory. For instance, Tulving (1972, 1983, 1985) outlined three general classes of knowledge: *episodic*, *semantic*, and *procedural*. Episodic knowledge, or AM, refers to memories for experienced events; semantic knowledge refers to the meanings of words, numbers, and general factual knowledge (i.e., Paris is the capital of France); and procedural knowledge refers to skills such as driving a car, typing, and even whistling. These three types of knowledge may be represented in different ways in long-term memory (cf. Schacter & Tulving,

1994) in partly separate memory systems. This chapter is concerned primarily with AM and how this supports generational identity, particularly Mannheim's concept of generational identity. The contribution of semantic memory to identity is also considered. Although semantic memory is arguably a critically important source of self-defining knowledge, and the question of differences in conceptual knowledge across generations a fascinating one, there is comparatively little research into this aspect of conceptual knowledge and, consequently, little that can be stated firmly. Procedural memory will not be considered, again because of a paucity of relevant research. Before considering any findings in detail, the nature of AM, role of the self, and Mannheim's view on the location of generations are first reviewed.

WHAT IS AUTOBIOGRAPHICAL MEMORY?

It might be thought that the answer to the question, "What is autobiographical memory?" is self-evident: AM is, surely, memory for the events of one's life. The problem with this definition lies in the word "events." Consider individuals who when asked to recall an event from their childhood respond by saying: "I remember I went to a little nursery school, quite close to the house we then lived in. This would be when I was between 3 and 5 years old." Is this an event? Compare it to an account of another childhood memory reported by a colleague:

> My own memory for the declaration of the second world war, from September 1939, occurred when I was age 6 years and 6 months. I have a clear image of my father standing on the rockery of the front garden of our house waving a bamboo garden stake like a pendulum in time with the clock chimes heard on the radio which heralded the announcement. More hazily, I have an impression that neighbors were also out in the adjoining gardens listening to the radio and, although my father was fooling around, the feeling of the memory is one of deep foreboding and anxiety. I have never discussed this memory with anyone and very rarely thought about it. (G. Cohen, personal communication, 1994)

Clearly, both these accounts are drawn from autobiographical knowledge, but only the latter would be classed as a memory of an event. Autobiographical knowledge takes a number of forms and at least three different types or layers of autobiographical knowledge have been identified so far: lifetime periods, general events, and event-specific knowledge (ESK; cf. Conway, 1992, 1996a, 1996b, 1996c; Conway & Rubin, 1993). *Lifetime periods* refer to lengthy periods of time typically measured in years and represent the goals, plans, and themes of the self during particular periods. Goals, plans, and themes are reflected in knowledge of significant others, records of goal attainment, and general knowledge of actors, actions, and locations characteristic of the period. The second layer, *general events*, is more specific and consists of records of extended and repeated events that occurred over periods of weeks and months. General events contain knowledge that can be used to access ESK sensory-perceptual details. In addition, general events may themselves be further organized into small sets of thematically related events (see Robinson, 1992). General events can be accessed by knowledge contained in lifetime periods and, in turn, knowledge contained in general events accesses or indexes ESK. *Event-specific knowledge* consists of images, sensations, smells, and other sensory-perceptual features associated with an experience.

Layers of autobiographical knowledge are represented in knowledge structures in long-term memory and organized by thematic and temporal knowledge. Figure 2.1 depicts this scheme graphically for two general themes, a work theme and a relationship theme. The knowledge structures shown in Fig. 2.1 are hierarchical and terminate in an unorganized undifferentiated pool of ESK details. This "pool" of knowledge can only be accessed by specific cues held in general events and lifetime periods. Notice that there are no specific representations of memories with this model. That is to say that memories are not represented in the model as "holistic" or discrete units. Rather, memories are compilations of knowledge at different levels of specificity. Thus, in the previous example of a memory about hearing the news of the outbreak of World War II a lifetime period is specified (When I was 6) with associated details characteristic of the period (father, neighbors, radio, etc.). The general event is playing in the garden and ESK details are also described (the swinging bamboo stake, clock chimes, and the feeling of anxiety). In contrast, the earlier example of the nursery school memory contains only lifetime period knowledge (when I was age 3 to 5 years, a nursery school).

The central proposal of this constructivist account of AM is that memories are transitory mental representations constructed by a centrally mediated complex retrieval process (Anderson & Conway, 1993; Conway, 1996a, 1996b; Conway & Rubin, 1993). When a memory is to be constructed, the retrieval process repeatedly samples the knowledge base starting with a cue that is first elaborated to provide initial access, and then proceeds by evaluating accessed knowledge with respect to current task demands. For instance, a person asked to retrieve a memory to a cue word such as "bicycle" might elaborate this into an internally derived cue, such as "when did I ride a bicycle a lot?" and then search the highest level of autobiographical knowledge for a lifetime period that contains bicycle as a characteristic feature of that period. Imagine that the rememberer accesses the lifetime period "When I lived in Cambridge" and knowledge held at this level contains cues that index general events relating to cycling. These can then

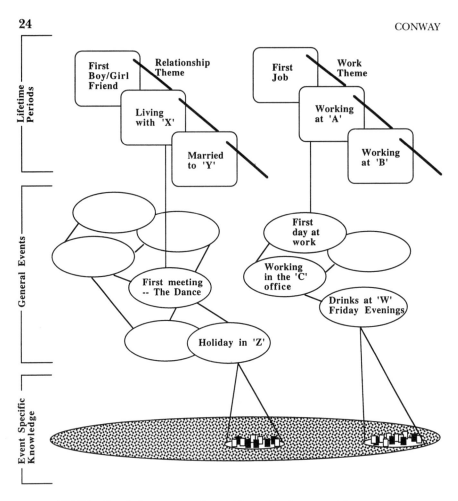

FIG. 2.1.   Knowledge structures in autobiographical memory (after Conway, 1992).

be accessed and, eventually, ESK knowledge will be activated. At this point, a whole stable pattern of activation has been established in long-term memory and this, together with some record of the process of retrieval, represents a specific AM in that episode of retrieval (see Conway, 1992, for a fully worked account of an AM constructed to this cue). Memories are not then like books in a library that we can pull down, open up, and read. Instead, they are complex transitory patterns of activation across a layered and structured knowledge base. Sometimes they will include ESK and records of the minutiae of experiences. On other occasions, for the same or different memories, they will not include such details. In all cases, however, memories encompass lifetime period knowledge that frames accessed autobiographical knowledge in the context of the individual remember's own life.

THE SELF AND THEMES OF THE SELF

Lifetime period knowledge, general events and ESK, are not encoded randomly into long-term memory nor are they represented in a disorganized or unsystematic way. One of the main influences on the encoding and structure of autobiographical knowledge is the self; indeed, autobiographical knowledge might be thought of as a resource of the self (Robinson, 1986). It is in this sense that Salaman (1970) described the use of AM by immigrants, refugees, and victims of war, as a record of times when the self was not threatened or stressed and when the goals and plans of the self ran smoothly and were attainable. Consulting this record can sustain the self during periods of stress, threat, and alienation. In the constructivist account of AM, the self is conceived as part of the central control processes that initiate and modulate the operation of more automatic processes, such as the spread of activation through long-term memory structures (Anderson & Conway, 1993; Conway, 1992, 1996a, 1996b; Conway & Rubin, 1993). Central control processes have not usually been considered in this way and instead have often been viewed as devices that synchronize, by activation or inhibition, the outputs from other processing modules (e.g., Norman & Shallice, 1980). However, there are good grounds for suggesting that control processes must contain and use some set of plans and these clearly must entail personally relevant goals. Thus, it is assumed that at any given time there is an active set of plans and goals and these reflect the current themes of the self (Conway, 1992): In a sense, this might be thought of as a "working" self and may be part of the central executive of working memory (Baddeley, 1986). The themes of the self (represented in memory control processes as plans and goals) arise in response to discrepancies between the current or working self-concept and some desired or even feared self and, as such, are the affect-laden central meaning constructs of the self. This characterization of themes is based, in part, on Higgins' (1987) self-discrepancy theory, which proposes that discrepancies between different self states—for example, the actual self and the ideal self—generate motives and affective experience. However, the concept of themes as used here is also closely related to Oatley's (1992) account of the plan-based structure of emotions. Briefly, in Oatley's model, a plan consists of a goal (e.g., some set of constraints or preconditions), a set of actions, and a set of effects. Obviously, few plans are this simple and most plans in human cognition take multiple goals, are structured (hierarchically or in some other way), and are dynamic in the sense that plan implementation is conditional on the outcome of subgoals within the whole plan structure (see Oatley, 1992, pp. 24–36; Oatley & Johnson-Laird, 1987). Emotions arise at junctures in plans, when goals are achieved, or when a plan is frustrated. According to the plan-based model of affect, emotions signal the need for the reevaluation of goals and plans, and facilitate processes that mediate such reevaluations. Within this general view, themes are generated in response to self-discrepancies and, when active, are instantiated in complex dynamic plan structures that have evolved to effect changes to the (current) self-themes might be thought of as the semantic content of emotions.

Themes directly influence the encoding of autobiographical memories and when a theme becomes inactive (i.e., it is no longer associated with currently active self-discrepancies), it is then primarily represented by the autobiographical memories with which it was originally associated. Indeed, Strauman (1990) observed that cues based on self-discrepancies are particularly potent in eliciting related childhood memories (see also Conway, 1996c, for an account of the relation between plans, goals, and flashbulb memories).

Undoubtedly, the area where thematic aspects of AM have been of most concern is in psychotherapy, and particularly in psychoanalysis. Indeed, Freud's (1914) account of repression assumes that one of the aims of analysis is to bring to consciousness memories of events and fantasies that, due to their affective qualities, are no longer directly accessible. One interesting account of the mechanisms of repression is due to Kris (1956/1975), who described what he called the *personal myth.* Kris found that some of his patients could provide very detailed and fluent accounts of their lives, almost as though they had, as it were, carefully rehearsed their life story. During the process of therapy, Kris discovered that often these personal myths were in fact incorrect, and contained carefully edited sections in which whole lifetime periods had been omitted. For instance, for one of his patients who claimed to have left home at age 16, it later transpired that he had in fact left when he was 18 years old. The "missing" 2 years represented a period during which traumatic events from childhood were repeated. Thus, the personal myth acted to repress a lifetime period.

A fixed and rigid personal myth may be characteristic of certain psychopathological disorders. However, for the nonpathological individual, Kris proposed that the personal myth was subject to fairly constant change and updating in the normal course of everyday experience. Moreover, there may be periods even for nontraumatized individuals when changes to the personal myth are rapid, far-reaching, and profound. One such period was identified by Erikson (1978) as the identity crisis of late adolescence when the self is in flux and new themes emerge and are discarded or elaborated. Kris argued that this was the period when the emerging individual attempted to answer the question "How did it all come about?" In Erikson's view, this period is characterized by themes relating to identity and role confusions and, later, to intimacy and isolation. The themes generated at this time, expressed as plans and goals (note that these need not be conscious), and the autobiographical knowledge to which they give rise may be critical in supporting the formation of generational identity.

The emergence of life themes in childhood has also been researched by Csikszentmihalyi and Beattie (1979). They investigated a group of individuals who had in common, extremely deprived childhoods. Some of this group became exceptionally successful in adult life, whereas others, although surviving their impoverished upbringing, did not achieve high-status professional occupations. Csikszentmihalyi and Beattie found that all the individuals they examined had what they termed *life themes*. Life themes were developed in response to existential problems facing the individuals in their childhood, such as extreme poverty, social injustice, and so on. The critical determining factor for later occupational success was the conceptualization of the problem and its solution. For instance, subjects who conceptualized their existential problem as one of poverty and its solution as ensuring a constant supply of money, tended not to attain high-status occupations. Indeed, one of their subjects who by thrift and careful investment had become a millionaire, nevertheless continued as a blue-collar worker in the factory where he had always worked. Other individuals who generated a more abstract conceptualization of the existential problems of childhood (e.g., poverty is the result of social injustice, therefore one must fight against social injustice) achieved professional occupations that provided the opportunity to implement, at least to some degree, solutions to their earlier universalist abstract conceptualization. From the point of view of the present discussion, all the individuals in the Csikszentmihalyi and Beattie (1979) study were able to provide highly detailed and vivid memories of critical moments in the evolution and attainment of their solutions to the life problems they had identified. Indeed, many memories were spontaneously produced and even corroborated by independent evidence the individuals (spontaneously) provided.

Life themes and personal myths are perhaps most strikingly evident in individuals who have suffered traumatic and stressful childhoods. Nonetheless, in the nontraumatized and not abnormally stressed individual, each lifetime period may present its own existential problems and, consequently, its own life themes specific to that period. Relevant to this is Cantor and Kihlstrom's (1985) notion of *life tasks*, which encompass lifetime period-specific problems to which an individual allocates problem-solving resources. According to these authors, life tasks are most clearly evident during a period of transition and they reported a study of first-year college students making the transition from high school to college student (Cantor, Brower, & Korn, 1984; cited in Cantor & Kihlstrom, 1985). The life tasks identified by the students centered around issues of identity, intimacy, achievement, and power, and were focused on the two broad themes of social and academic activities and how to prioritize and manage tasks within the two domains. Although in these abstract terms the life tasks appear general to all students, at the level of the individual, specific tasks were highly idiosyncratic and reflected personal projects. Thus, Cantor and Kihlstrom (1985, p. 25) commented that "one student considered living without family to involve learning to handle the stress of personal failure without 'dad's hugs,' " whereas another concentrated on the practical side of independence, that is, "managing money, doing laundry, eating well." It is also notable that Pillemer and his colleagues (Pillemer, Goldsmith, Panter, & White, 1988; Pillemer, Rinehart, & White, 1986) in studies of the recall of autobiographical memories from the first year at college found most memories to be recalled from the first term (perhaps the most intense phase of the transition period) and to be emotionally charged—as the plan-based theory of emotions predicts. Finally, the types of events recalled from the first year at university mirrored the life tasks identified by Cantor and Kihlstrom in their students.

The themes that appear to preoccupy first-year university students are, then, often associated with the attainment of highly specific "possible selves" (Markus & Nurius, 1986), such as the self as the good student, the competent individual living alone, the socially attractive person, and so forth. These themes are implemented, in memory, as dynamic plans with complex subgoal structures, which if achieved would effectively solve the existential problems of the period (e.g., how to overcome social isolation, how to achieve academic success). It is through this network of currently active themes of the self that knowledge of specific events comes to be encoded into the schemes and indices that form the structure of the autobiographical knowledge base. According to this account, autobiographical knowledge is a record of past selves in the sense that retained knowledge, and the particular organization of that knowledge, reflect the operation at encoding of the themes of a (past) active or working self. For example, themes associated with the "good student" possible self might facilitate and prioritize the encoding of events carrying goal-attainment knowledge for that self. After a retention interval (often of years or even decades) the individual may no longer recall the themes that characterized that period, although they retain access to the autobiographical knowledge structures created by the themes of the past "good student" self. It is these long-term memory knowledge structures of the self that constitute a major part of the "inventory of experience" and may underpin generational identity.

THE LOCATION OF GENERATIONS

Mannheim (1952) put forth an account of how generations were formed into social units. He first pointed out that biological or chronological criteria (e.g., that individuals were members of a generation by virtue of contemporaneous birthdates) cannot form an effective basis for defining generation identity. For instance, even though they were born at approximately the same time, the post-World War II generation of babies who became the youth generation of the 1960s were not the same generation in Britain as in China. Instead, argued Mannheim, generations have a social location that uniquely identifies them. The social location of a generation arise from shared experiences. The public events that impinge on a generation, shared cultural experiences, shared experiences of a type of event (e.g., going to a rock concert), common ways of responding to the world, common existential problems, and shared conceptual knowledge, all shape and locate particular generations. Mannheim (1952, p. 304) commented, "Mental data are of sociological importance not only because of their actual content, but also because they cause individuals sharing them to form one group—they have a socializing effect." Individuals who share a social-historical context and who take from experience knowledge of a similar type, form a social group: the *generation unit*. Members of a generation unit participate in what Mannheim termed the common destiny of the nexus of actual social and historical forces impinging on a specific generation.

From this perspective, it is clear that what members of a generation unit share are commonalties in autobiographical and semantic memory (see Mannheim, 1952, pp. 289–299, for a particularly insightful account of how memory might support generational identity). Obviously, however, no subgroup of a generation unit will share exactly the same experiences or identical conceptual knowledge. Rather, shared experiences will be tokens of particular types (cf. Rumelhart & Norman, 1983). To take an example from the 1960s youth culture, the event, a rock concert, is a *type* and the memories of individuals who attended different concerts are *tokens* of this type. Thus, what is shared in terms of autobiographical memories are types of experience of which the specific memories of individual rememberers are tokens. Conceptual knowledge too is shared by the members of a generation unit and the meanings of various concepts may be specific to a unit. Thus, the meanings of concepts such as party, drop out, freak, cool, counterculture, and so forth, were shared by the youth of the 1960s. Of course, and as Mannheim recognized, generational turnover is a continuous process and new generations overlap with the generations they immediately precede, they live in a world dominated by older generations, and also interact with the oldest generations of society. Consequently, conceptual knowledge must be very widely shared throughout all the generations of a society, otherwise there could be no communication between different generations. It would seem from this that the shared conceptual knowledge of a generation unit will typically be more in the form of an emphasis on or interpretation of particular aspects or domains of knowledge, rather than in the form of radically new concepts—which is not to deny that some new conceptual knowledge may be introduced by new generations.

Shared types of experience and an emphasis on, and unique interpretations of, certain domains of knowledge mediate the social location of a
generation. But even this powerful effect of memory cannot on its own
uniquely define a generation unit. What is required in addition, is what
Mannheim called a shared set of fundamental integrative attitudes. One way
in which to conceptualize these "attitudes" (and this may correspond only
in part to what Mannheim himself had in mind) is to recast them as shared
sets of plans and goals, almost as it were, as a shared self. The social-historical
existential problems faced by a generation unit and the conceptualization
of these problems by individual members of the unit lead to the construction
of plans and goals that are similar in type across individuals within the unit.
It is these common plans and goals that form the common destiny of a
generation unit. They also support the creation of different units within the
same generation. To return to the example of the youth of the mid- to
late-1960s, it was by no means the case that all individuals within this
generation participated in the hippie movement and radical student politics
of the age. Not everyone "turned on, tuned in, and dropped out," not
everyone trod the hippie trail, and even less sought an alternative lifestyle.
Other groups created quite different plans and goals arising from the
collective conceptualization of the existential problems confronting them at
their particular locus in the pattern of sociohistorical forces. For all groups,
however, the plans and goals, the themes of a unit, are established by late
adolescence (as Erikson, 1950, suggested) by which point the generation
unit as an identifiable social group has been formed.

From the present perspective, one of the most important points of
Mannheim's concept of generation unit is that it provides a mechanism for
the construction of collective plans and goals of a social group. Plans and
goals are critical in the formation of autobiographical memories and, thus,
an interactive (Mannheim would have said "dialectical") relation charac-
terizes the memories of individuals and the generation unit of which they
are part. As the unit emerges as a distinct social entity, experiences are
encoded into long-term memory at least partly in terms of the plans and
goals that define the generation unit. Thus, the plans and goals generated
as ways of solving certain sets of existential problems come to influence what
is retained in memory, whereas memory itself provides the knowledge base
that supports the pursuance of generation unit relevant goals.

THE LIFESPAN MEMORY RETRIEVAL CURVE

At this point it might be useful to briefly summarize the view of AM and
identity emerging from the foregoing discussion. Autobiographical memories are transitory mental representations constructed over multilayered

knowledge structures in long-term memory. Knowledge structures in the AM knowledge base were, themselves, constructed according to the themes (expressed as plans and goals) of previous selves and are accessible to the current version of the working self. Previous plans and goals are not, in general, explicitly represented in the autobiographical knowledge base. Rather, knowledge by its content and organization indirectly reflects the operation of older configurations of the goals and plans of the self. Of critical importance to generational identity are goals and plans that emerged during adolescence and early adulthood. Such goals and plans will be associated with the emergence of a stable and integrated self (Erikson, 1950) and because of this may play some enduring role in memory. Is there any evidence to support this conjecture?

One technique used by psychologists studying AM simply requires individuals to recall specific memories. Sometimes this is achieved using a free recall procedure in which the subject recalls as many memories as possible in a proscribed period of time (e.g., 30 minutes). Other procedures may require the retrieval of specific memories to cue words (i.e., words naming common activities, objects, or emotions). Once a set of memories have been recalled, the subject dates each memory and the memories are then plotted according to their age. The resulting plot is referred to as the lifespan AM retrieval curve (see Rubin, 1982, and Rubin, Wetzler, & Nebes, 1986, for detailed findings; also Conway, 1990a, and Conway & Rubin, 1993, for reviews). One possibility is that this curve will be a straight line starting at a high point corresponding to the most recent memory recalled and systematically declining to the oldest memory recalled. If this were the case, then it would show a forgetting function in which memories from recent periods of life were well remembered. But, as the age of the time period sampled increased, then fewer memories were recalled, demonstrating forgetting. And, indeed, this is what, at least approximately, happens when young college students are sampled in these types of experiments (cf. Rubin, 1982).

However, if the subjects sampled are over about 35 years of age, then a quite different AM retrieval curve is observed; Fig. 2.2 provides an idealized example. Figure 2.2 shows that the AM retrieval curve for adults over the age of 30 to 35 years has three components. The first component refers to the period when the rememberer was between zero to approximately 5 years of age and is known as the period of *childhood amnesia* (see Pillemer & White, 1989, for a review). Childhood amnesia is found in all adult rememberers and reflects the fact that most people can recall very few of the events they experienced when 5 years old or younger. The third component, labeled as *forgetting* in Fig. 2.2, covers the whole of the lifespan of 18- to 20-year-olds and is present in older adults back to the period when they would have been about 25 years of age. But it is the second

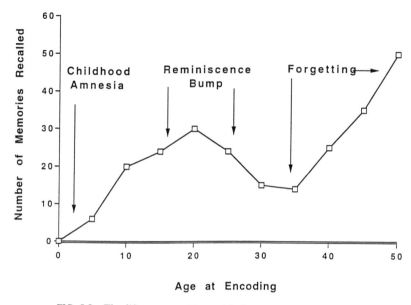

FIG. 2.2. The life-span autobiographical memory retrieval curve.

component, the *reminiscence bump*, which is of central interest here. Originally, observed by Franklin and Holding (1977), the reminiscence bump has since been reported in many studies using different experimental procedures, different patient and cross-national groups, and is even present in a procedure as unconstrained as free recall, as long as subjects are older than about 40 years of age (see Conway, 1990a, chap. 3, and Conway & Rubin, 1993, for reviews of these and related studies). Conway and Rubin (1993) considered a number of explanations of the reminiscence bump, including the differential encoding of events during the period 10 to 25 years of age, biases in memory sampling, additional rehearsal of memories from this period, and the potential special nature of events occurring at this point in life (e.g., many are first-time experiences; see Robinson, 1992). However, none of these explanations on their own can account for the full range of data. Instead, the data compel an account that draws on notions of the self and identity and in order to see this consider the findings from three further studies.

Fitzgerald (1988) contrasted the findings of two studies he performed. In both studies, individuals, with an average age of almost 70 years, recorded autobiographical memories. In one study, the standard word-cue technique was used with 40 words; in the other, the subjects were asked for three vivid memories. The AM retrieval curve for memories cued by words looks much like those from the similar procedures that produced Fig. 2.2. The plot of vivid memories was, however, quite different and showed only a reminiscence bump. Fitzgerald argued, therefore, that the reminiscence bump may be due in large part to the increased availability of vivid memories from the period 10 to 25 years, relative to other periods. But why should the vivid memories exist in greater frequency during this period? Fitzgerald dismissed the least interesting alternative, that this is just when important life events such as a first job or a marriage occur, because memories of such life events were found to make up only 14% of the memories in the reminiscence bump in Fitzgerald's study (cf. Fromholt & Larsen, 1992). Likewise, he found little support for a special period of cognitive abilities during adolescence and early adulthood that could account for stronger encoding. That is, although there are normal cognitive functions, such as rehearsal and imagery, that could account for why particular memories are given, there is no reason to expect that these mechanisms are especially effective in the period of the reminiscence bump. Instead, Fitzgerald focused on the notion of a "life narrative" (K. J. Gergen & M. M. Gergen, 1983) as a defining aspect of personality and identity. Vivid memories are an important part of this narrative and their increased frequency in the period 10 to 25 years reflects a period when identity emerges and stabilizes and that is, consequently, a critical period in the generation of a life narrative. The reminiscence bump, a collection of personally relevant vivid memories, is part of what remains in memory from this period.

Benson, Jarvi, Arai, Thiebar, Frye, and Goracke McDonald (1992) collected 10 vivid memories from groups of Japanese and rural midwestern American subjects. As expected, both groups showed marked reminiscence peaks. But, for the Japanese, the peak was in the 21- to 30-year-old decade of their lives; for the Americans, it was in the 11- to 20-year-old decade. These biases would seem to reflect sociohistorical differences between the two societies. In North America, the teenage period is highly valued and seen as a preparation for adulthood, which itself emerges at the end of the teen period. In Japan less value is placed on the teenage years, during which the individual is still considered a child. The full responsibility of adulthood is not taken on until the individual reaches the late 20s to early 30s. The shift in the reminiscence peak to span the decade of the 20s may reflect this later emergence of self and identity.

Finally, consider the work of Schuman and his colleagues (Schuman & Rieger, 1992; Schuman & Scott, 1989). In a large-scale study, a probability sample of 1,410 Americans over 18 years old were asked to list one or two especially important "national or world events or changes" from the last 50 years. Thus, as sociologists interested in the concept of generation, they asked for public rather than personal events. The five panels of Fig. 2.3 each present the data from one of the most-often-listed events. The percentage of the total responses to that category is plotted against the age of the person reporting that event at the time the event occurred. The ages are

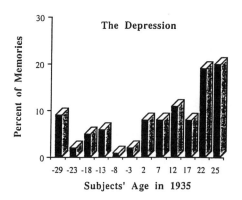

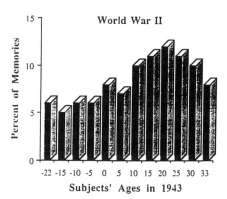

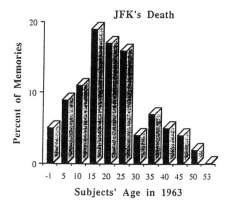

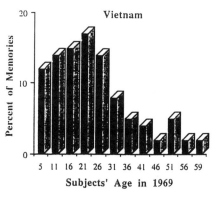

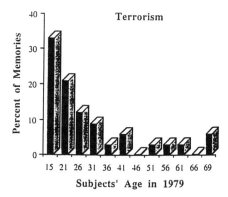

FIG. 2.3. Mentions of five important public events (from Conway & Rubin, 1993).

approximate because people are grouped into 5-year periods and because most of the events had long durations from which the midpoint was used (for other distributions, see Schuman & Scott, 1989). Negative ages simply mean the person reporting the event was not born at the time the event occurred. For all five events, the peak time of reporting occurred when the person was in their teens or 20s, that is, when the reminiscence bump occurs in AM. Thus, the important empirical observation is that people tend to report as important events and changes that happened in their late teens or early 20s.

The reminiscence bump in AM reflects a body of—perhaps vivid— memories that represent records of experiences that occurred during the transition from childhood to adulthood, one of life's major transitions. This set of memories relates to experiences that were of importance to the individual in the formation of a stable self and unique identity. At the same time, memories are also formed that relate to generation identity and there is a reminiscence bump in memory for public events too. Moreover, the exact location in time of the reminiscence peak may vary with societies and depend on a society's specification of when childhood ends and adulthood begins. Overall, these patterns of findings, now established over many different independently conducted research programs (Conway & Rubin, 1993), show how memory might support generational identity and maintain that identity across the lifespan. It is important to note that the reminiscence bump in AM is not usually observed in subjects much younger than about 35 years. In contrast, the reminiscence peak in memory for public events is present in subjects as young as 18 years of age, who are still in the period of identity formation. This suggests a potentially interesting difference in the time course of the formation of generational identity and the emergence of a life narrative in which the formation of generational identity precedes the establishment of a stable self. Perhaps, generational identity is one of the tasks to be fulfilled in the process of bringing about an enduring self. It is even possible that generational identity facilitates (or inhibits) later developments of the self.

FLASHBULB MEMORIES

Memory researchers have long been interested in highly vivid memories and how these arise. Often they arise in response to unique and surprising events involving the experience of emotions. Indeed, Brown and Kulik (1977) introduced the term *flashbulb memory* to convey the notion that certain types of vivid memories preserve knowledge of an event in an almost indiscriminate way, rather as a photograph preserves all the details of a scene. Flashbulb memories are unusual in that they retain minutiae not usually present in memories of everyday activities and differ further in that they also have what Brown and Kulik called a *primary*, or *live*, *quality*. One further striking feature is that flashbulb memories appear to endure for years and decades without noticeably degrading (see Conway, 1995, for a review of this area). Obviously, most flashbulb memories will be of events of high personal importance to a specific individual, such as the vivid memories sampled by Fitzgerald (1988), and so the actual events encoded in long-term memory will vary across individuals. There are, however, some events that may lead to the widespread formation of flashbulb memories in a social group as a whole. Brown and Kulik (1977) reasoned that events of national and international importance that were surprising and emotive might have this effect. In fact, their study took its impetus from the observation that 10 years after the assassination of JFK, many people still apparently retained highly detailed memories for their personal circumstances when they first heard the news of the president's murder. In order to appreciate the nature of flashbulb memories for the JFK news consider the following collection of memories:

> I was on my way home from the studios at Lime Grove and I had the wireless on and I heard this announcement, which was breaking into whatever program was on, that he'd [JFK] been shot and I remember as I heard those words I said aloud, I was quite alone in the car, I said aloud "Oh no, Oh, no" (Ludovick Kennedy, writer and broadcaster).

> I was with my ex-wife in a West End cinema when I became aware of something going on behind me and I turned round and I could see people in the back row of the balcony chatting busily to each other and even talking to the people in the row in front of them and I guessed that something pretty dreadful had happened—and you know the way today at football matches people create the "human wave" which moves across the stadium? Well in the same way the ripple came down the balcony and eventually I said to the man behind me "What's happened?" and he said "Kennedy's been assassinated" (Gerry Anderson, film producer).

> I was on the telephone with Miss Johnson, the Dean's secretary, about some departmental business. Suddenly, she broke in with: "Excuse me a moment: everyone is excited about something. What? Mr. Kennedy has been shot!" We hung up, I opened my door to hear further news as it came in, and then resumed my work on some forgotten business that "had to be finished" that day (R. Brown, 1977).

> I was seated in a sixth-grade music class, and over the intercom I was told that the president had been shot. At first, everyone just looked at each other. The class started yelling, and the music teacher tried to calm everyone down. About 10 minutes later I heard over the intercom that Kennedy had died and that everyone should return to their homeroom. I remember that when

I got to my homeroom my teacher was crying and everyone was standing in a state of shock. They told us to go home (J. Kulik, 1977).

The first pair of descriptions were reported in a television program marking the 30th anniversary of the assassination and the second was drawn from memories reported about 15 years after the incident. Note also Cohen's flashbulb memory for learning the news of the outbreak of World War II described earlier, which was over 50 years in age. In fact, one of the earliest flashbulb memories to be reported in the literature was of an event that took place some 33 years prior to its report:

My father and I were on the road to A—in the state of Maine to purchase the "fixings" needed for my graduation. When we were driving down a steep hill into the city we felt that something was wrong. Everybody looked so sad, and there was such terrible excitement that my father stopped his horse, and leaning from the carriage called: "What is it my friends? What has happened?" "Haven't you heard?" was the reply—"Lincoln has been assassinated." The lines fell from my father's limp hands, and with tears streaming from his eyes he sat as one bereft of motion. We were far from home, and much must be done, so he rallied after a time, and we finished our work as well as our heavy hearts would allow. (Colegrove, 1899)

The remarkable detail and durability of these memories for public events quite clearly sets them aside from most memories for most public events. However, the incidence of durable and detailed memories for one's personal circumstances when learning of public events must vary with the relevance of the actual events to particular social groups. Brown and Kulik (1977) directly examined this and in their study they recruited groups of Whites and African Americans who attempted to recall their personal circumstances when they first learned of various public events. Figure 2.4 shows the frequencies of flashbulb memories to learning the news of four different assassinations for the two groups. It can be seen from Fig. 2.3 that virtually all the African Americans and White Americans sampled in Brown and Kulik's study had flashbulb memories for how they learned the news of the assassination of JFK. In contrast, only the African Americans had high flashbulb memory rates to the remaining three news items. Brown and Kulik (1977) deliberately selected their target events so that they would vary in their relevance to the two groups and the resulting flashbulb memory rates confirm the variations in relevance. The important point for the present discussion is that different social groups may have flashbulb memories for different events and this surely supports group identity.

In later studies, similar cross-group differences were found. For example, Pillemer (1984) in flashbulb memory study of the attempted assassination of President Ronald Reagan found that only subjects who had a strong

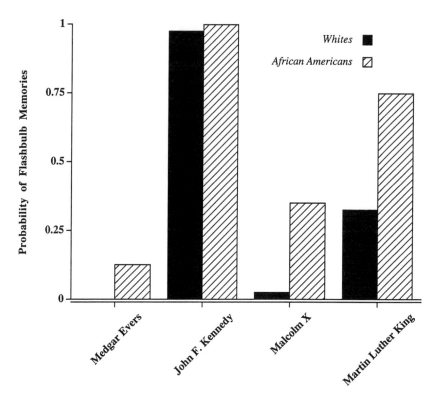

FIG. 2.4. Frequencies of flashbulb memories to four news events for two groups of subjects (after Brown & Kulik, 1977).

emotional reaction on learning the news developed detailed and durable memories. These subjects tended to be highly sympathetic to Reagan's political views and clearly were from an identifiable section of middle America. In a more direct cross-national study, Conway et al. (1994) found a very widespread incidence of flashbulb memories among U.K. residents for the resignation of the British Prime Minister Margaret Thatcher. Only a low rate was present in student samples from the United States and Denmark. More recent evidence (D. Wright, personal communication) has, however, not found a high rate of flashbulb memories for the Thatcher resignation in large-scale opportunity samples of U.K. nationals. These later groups have tended to contain subjects who were older than those sampled in the Conway et al. (1994) study and one possibility is that the resignation was only highly relevant to this younger group. This may be because this group had only ever known one prime minister during the period of the formation generation identity, Mrs. Thatcher, and her resignation was, consequently, a matter of major concern for younger but not older groups.

It seems possible that flashbulb memories may be more local to subgroups in society than even the foregoing research suggests. In a revealing television documentary,[1] a series of interviews with astronomers at the Anglo-Australian Observatory in Sydney asked them what they were doing when they first heard about the discovery of Supernova 1987a, on February 23, in the Large Magellanic Cloud. This was a novel discovery because it was the first Supernova viewable with the naked eye (if you were in the Southern Hemisphere). It was critical for astro- and particle physics because this was the chance to start looking for neutrinos. Comments by the astronomers indicated a high incidence of flashbulb memories for this event (e.g., "The news of its first appearance will never be forgotten," "running up and down the corridors of Imperial College knocking on people's doors saying they've discovered neutrinos," and most relevant, "everybody who was involved remembers what they were doing just like when Kennedy was assassinated. You remember what you were doing when you heard about it"). Undoubtedly, such shared flashbulb memories for events of significance to small subgroups in society must be common. A group supporting a sports team may have collective flashbulb memories for a particular success or disaster, the collapse of a financial institution may lead to flashbulb memories amongst workers in the money markets of the city, and so forth.

Why are such memories formed in the first place? There has been protracted debate concerning this question. Brown and Kulik originally proposed that in response to the surprise value of an experience and its personal consequentiality a special brain mechanism was triggered that made a durable record of all recent brain activity. In direct opposition, Neisser (1982) rejected the "special encoding" mechanism account and instead proposed that flashbulb memories arose through the process of rehearsal that spontaneously occurs as an individual repeatedly relates how they learned a significant item of news. Brown and Kulik (1977) suggested that flashbulb memories preserved events of "biological" significance, whereas Neisser argued that they functioned to integrate an individual's personal history with the history of their times. According to this latter view, flashbulb memories are like "benchmarks" where individuals line up their lives with the flow of public events. However, flashbulb memories serve many psychological and sociological functions and it seems that both these views are almost certainly too narrow (Conway, 1995). A different view is that flashbulb memories are records of moments when plans had to be revised. These might be personal plans (one's team is knocked out of the cup) and/or they might be societal plans (a sudden change of

---

[1] I am particularly grateful to Dan Wright of City University, who reported this program to me.

government). Plans, emotions, and the self are all critical influences on AM, and when they act in concert, perhaps in response to an external public event, then vivid memories are formed and these provide a record of initial and later responses to change. In the case of generational identity, public events that impinge on the newly formed shared plans of a social group will have a profound impact and will be stored in memory in a durable and detailed form. By this view, most flashbulb memories of public events should be available from when a rememberer was between about 15 to 25 years of age. In recent research in which Conway and Holmes (1996) sampled large groups of adults from 30 to 60 years old, it was found that freely recalled flashbulb memories associated with public events dated to the reminiscence period when the subjects would have been 15 to 25 years old. In contrast, flashbulb memories for private events mainly dated to events in the most recent decade of the remembers' lives. These recent findings, taken in conjunction with the work of Fitzgerald and of Schuman and his colleagues, strongly implicate the reminiscence period as a good source of vivid self-defining memories—a source of memories relating to the formation of generation identity.

CONCEPTUAL KNOWLEDGE

Earlier a distinction was drawn between autobiographical and semantic memory. AM consists of memory for experiences whereas semantic memory consists of conceptual knowledge. There have been no studies by memory researchers directly investigating differences in basic conceptual knowledge across, for example, different generations. There have, however, been occasional reports that at least hint at potentially intriguing differences. For example, Conway (1990b) conducted a series of AM retrieval experiments. In these experiments subjects retrieved specific memories as quickly as they could to cue words naming common objects and activities, such as jumper, money, hotel, chair, and so on. Each cue word was preceded by a prime that named an associated concept (e.g., chair might be preceded by the concept *furniture* or jumper by *clothing*). The aim of the study was try to speed AM retrieval by priming autobiographical knowledge and two types of prime were used. One type were semantic category superordinates (i.e., furniture or clothing), and the other type were goal-derived categories (Barsalou, 1985; e.g., birthday present or place to stay on holiday). It is known that semantic categories do not prime AM retrieval (Conway & Bekerian, 1987). Conway (1990b) found that goal-derived categories did speed memory retrieval, suggesting a close association between memories and this type of conceptual knowledge. However, in the course of preparing the stimuli for these experiments, Conway (1990b) encountered an inter-

esting problem. In order to create the appropriate stimuli pairings, production frequency norms were collected from a group of older subjects
(in the 30 to 40 years age range). Later these norms were used to generate
the stimuli for experiments in which undergraduates were to take part. In
a pilot study it was found that the subjects had no problems with the
semantic category pairs but quite often found the relations between the
goal-derived categories and their exemplars unexpected and unusual. Further investigations revealed that items that were good exemplars of goal-
derived categories for older subjects were not good exemplars for younger
subjects. Thus, hotel was a good example of a type of holiday accommo-
dation, and jumper was a good example of birthday present for older but
not for younger subjects. Many of undergraduate subjects had never stayed
in a hotel and it transpired that the most frequent birthday present in this
group was money.

Clearly, it is important that members of a society have similar conceptual
knowledge and the findings of Conway (1990a) indicate that both older
and younger subjects have the same concepts for so-called natural categories (Rosch, 1978), such as clothing, fruit, vehicles, sports, and so on. These
two groups differ, however, in the knowledge used to represent goal-derived
categories: categories that are more ad hoc and are very often featured in
everyday problem solving and planning. Thus, conceptual knowledge too
can be shaped by plans and goals and perhaps it is in this area of semantic
memory that differences between social groups, such as generation units,
will be most marked. A common characteristic of succeeding generations
has been the emergence of generational-specific ways of conceptualizing
the social world and this has often been reflected in generational-specific
uses of language. Reflect, for instance, on the characteristic language of
the beat generation, hippies, punks, and the dance culture of the 1980s.
Possibly, these linguistic styles are based on shared sets of goal-derived
categories that partition the social world for a generation unit in ways that
identify the existential problems confronting that generation. Semantic
memory may then also support generational identity.

Bugelski (1977) reported a particularly interesting finding relating to this
issue of language use, conceptual knowledge, and generational identity. In
Bugelski's very simple study, subjects noted the first few thoughts to come to
mind when they read a cue word. All the subjects were bilingual, and had
spoken Spanish as children and American English as adults. At the time of
the study, none of the subjects had spoken Spanish for at least 10 years and
many had not spoken Spanish since their childhood. Two lists of cue words
were employed, one in English and the other in Spanish. After recording
their thoughts, subjects then identified the time period in their life from
which the thoughts were taken. For English words, most thoughts (70%)
were from recent time periods and the fewest thoughts were from childhood

(13%). For Spanish words, 43% of thoughts were from recent periods as compared to 45% of thoughts from childhood. Indeed, Bugelski reported that many of his subjects were surprised by the apparently unexpected and spontaneous recall of forgotten events. One intriguing interpretation of these findings is that when it is possible to access the meanings of words that a person had at some earlier point in their life, then associated autobiographical memories from that period also become available. The conceptual knowledge, autobiographical memories, and characteristic language use of a generation unit may then remain available in memory for years and decades and so provide a continuing way in which a member of a generation unit differs from other groups in society.

Finally, consider a study by Sehulster (in press). In this study, a large group of subjects were asked to list their favorite films and they were also asked to list films that defined their era. It was suggested to subjects that we all have as it were a personal cultural era distinguished by songs, films, books, plays, and concerts that we regard as uniquely identifying our own era. The subjects listed the two types of films, *era films* and *favorite films*, and then indicated the age at which they saw them. Era films were virtually always seen when the subject was between 14 and 24 years of age. The mean age for favorite films fell outside this time and favorite films were viewed when subjects were, on average, in their late 20s. This was a simple study but a clear demonstration of the emergence of cultural identity in a period already seen as critical in the emergence of identity more generally. Undoubtedly, there will be many other knowledge domains that characterize one's era, from television shows to clothes, and these too will help determine identity. This, together with generation-specific conceptual knowledge, provides a knowledge base in long-term memory that can give continuity to generation identity.

CONCLUSIONS: GENERATION IDENTITY AND CHANGE

Findings from the study of AM give strong support to Mannheim's account of the basis of generation identity in human long-term memory. Similarly, there are good reasons for supposing that the long-term retention of conceptual knowledge is also influenced by the plans and goals that emerge from age 15 to 25 years. These sources of long-term knowledge continue to support generation identity across the life span. But does it therefore follow that an individual cannot change? Does it mean that once generational identity has been formed it cannot be changed? There is no research directly into these questions, but current views of the self tend to conceptualize self as a dynamic process highly sensitive to social context and in almost continuous flux. This contrasts with the notion of generation identity developed in the present chapter, which suggests that identity emerges during a unique critical period in late adolescence/early adulthood—a period that is not (perhaps cannot be) repeated later in life. As there is no research into changes in generational identity, this chapter closes with a provocative suggestion: Once formed, generational identity cannot change. Instead, individuals can take various positions to their generation identity, they can evolve new plans and goals that take them away from the imperatives established during the period of identity formation, but the original genera-tion-specific self remains as the self with which all later selves must be negotiated.

REFERENCES

Anderson, S. A., & Conway, M. A. (1993). Investigating the structure of autobiographical memories. *Journal of Experimental Psychology: Learning, Memory, and Cognition, 19,* 1178–1196.

Baddeley, A. D. (1986). *Working memory.* Oxford, England: Clarendon.

Barsalou, L. W. (1985). Ideals, central tendency, and frequency of instantiation. *Journal of Experimental Psychology: Learning, Memory and Cognition, 11,* 629–654.

Brown, R., & Kulik, J. (1977). Flashbulb memories. *Cognition, 5,* 73–99.

Benson, K. A., Jarvi, S. D., Arai, Y., Thielbar, P. R., Frye, K. J., & Goracke McDonald, B. (1992). Socio-historical context and autobiographical memories: Variations in the reminiscence phenomenon. In M. A. Conway, D. C. Rubin, H. Spinnler, & W. A. Wagenaar (Eds.), *Theoretical perspectives on autobiographical memory* (pp. 313–321). Dordrecht, The Netherlands: Kluwer.

Bugelski, B. R. (1977). Imagery and verbal behaviour. *Journal of Mental Imagery, 1,* 39–52.

Cantor, N., Brower, A., & Korn, H. (1984). *Cognitive basis of personality in a life transition.* Paper presented at the 23rd International Congress of Psychology, Acapulco, Mexico.

Cantor, N., & Kihlstrom, J. F. (1985). Social intelligence: The cognitive basis of personality. In P. Shaver (Ed.), *Self, situations, and social behavior: Review of personality and social psychology* (Vol. 6, pp. 15–34). Beverly Hills, CA: Sage.

Colegrove, F. W. (1899). Individual memories. *American Journal of Psychology, 10,* 228–255.

Conway, M. A. (1990a). *Autobiographical memory: An introduction.* Buckingham, England: Open University Press.

Conway, M. A. (1990b). Autobiographical memory and conceptual representation. *Journal of Experimental Psychology: Learning, Memory, and Cognition, 16*(5), 799–812.

Conway, M. A. (1992). A structural model of autobiographical memory. In M. A. Conway, D. C. Rubin, H. Spinnler, & W. A. Wagenaar (Eds.), *Theoretical perspectives on autobiographical memory* (pp. 167–194). Dordrecht, The Netherlands: Kluwer Academic.

Conway, M. A. (1995). *Flashbulb memories.* Hillsdale, NJ: Lawrence Erlbaum Associates.

Conway, M. A. (1996a). Autobiographical memories and autobiographical knowledge. In D. C. Rubin (Ed.), *Remembering our past: Studies in autobiographical memory* (pp. 67–93). Cambridge, England: Cambridge University Press.

Conway, M. A. (1996b). Autobiographical memories. In E. Bjork & R. Bjork (Eds.), *Handbook of perception and cognition: Vol. 10. Memory.* Orlando, FL: Academic Press.

Conway, M. A. (1996c). Failures of autobiographical remembering. In D. Herrmann, M. Johnson, C. McEvoy, C. Hertzog, & P. Hertel (Eds.), *Basic and applied memory: Theory in context.* Mahwah, NJ: Lawrence Erlbaum Associates.

Conway, M. A., Anderson, S. J., Larsen, S. F., Donnelly, C. M., McDaniel, M. A., McClelland, A. G. R., Rawles, R. E., & Logie, R. H. (1994). The formation of flashbulb memories. *Memory and Cognition, 22*, 326–343.

Conway, M. A., & Bekerian, D. A. (1987). Organization in autobiographical memory. *Memory and Cognition, 15*(2), 119–132.

Conway, M. A., Collins, A. F., Gathercole, S. E., & Anderson, S. J. (1996). Recollections of true and false autobiographical memories. *Journal of Experimental Psychology: General, 125*(1), 69–95.

Conway, M. A., & Holmes, A. (1996). *Flashbulb memories and generation identity: Differences between flashbulb memories of public and private events.*

Conway, M. A., & Rubin, D. C. (1993). The structure of autobiographical memory. In A. E. Collins, S. E. Gathercole, M. A. Conway, & P. E. M. Morris (Eds.), *Theories of memory* (pp. 103–137). Hillsdale, NJ: Lawrence Erlbaum Associates.

Csikszentmihalyi, M., & Beattie, O. V. (1979). Life themes: A theoretical and empirical exploration of their origins and effects. *Journal of Humanistic Psychology, 19*, 45–63.

Erikson, E. H. (1950). *Childhood and society.* New York: Norton.

Erikson, E. (1978). *Adulthood.* New York: Norton.

Fitzgerald, J. M. (1988). Vivid memories and the reminiscence phenomenon: The role of a self narrative. *Human Development, 31*, 261–273.

Franklin, H. C., & Holding, D. H. (1977). Personal memories at different ages. *Quarterly Journal of Experimental Psychology, 29*, 527–532.

Fromholt, P., & Larsen, S. F. (1992). Autobiographical memory and life-history narratives in aging and dementia (Alzheimer type). In M. A. Conway, D. C. Rubin, H. Spinnler, & W. A. Wagenaar (Eds.), *Theoretical perspectives on autobiographical memory* (pp. 413–426). Dordrecht, The Netherlands: Kluwer Academic.

Freud, S. (1914). Remembering, repeating, and working through. *Standard Edition* (Vol. 12, p. 145). London: Hogarth Press.

Gergen, K. J., & Gergen, M. M. (1983). Narratives of the self. In T. R. Sarbin & K. E. Scheibe (Eds.), *Studies in social identity* (pp. 254–273). New York: Praeger.

Higgins, E. T. (1987). Self-discrepancy: A theory relating self and affect. *Psychological Review, 94*, 319–340.

Kris, E. (1975). The personal myth: A problem in psychoanalytic technique. In *The selected papers of Ernst Kris* (pp. 129–143). New Haven, CT: Yale University Press. (Original work published 1956)

Mannheim, K. (1952). The problem of generations. In K. Mannheim (Ed.), *Essays on the sociology knowledge* (pp. 276–321). London: Routledge & Keegan Paul.

Markus, H., & Nurius, P. (1986). Possible selves. *American Psychologist, 41*, 954–969.

Neisser, U. (1982). Snapshots or benchmarks? In U. Neisser (Ed.), *Memory observed: Remembering in natural contexts* (pp. 43–48). San Francisco: Freeman.

Norman, D. A., & Shallice, T. (1980). *Attention to action: Willed and automatic control of behavior* (Tech. Rep. No. 99). University of California, San Diego.

Oatley, K. (1992). *Best laid schemes: The psychology of emotions.* Cambridge, England: Cambridge University Press.

Oatley, K., & Johnson-Laird, P. N. (1987). Towards a cognitive theory of emotions. *Cognition and Emotion, 1*, 29–50.

Pillemer, D. B. (1984). Flashbulb memories of the assassination attempt on President Reagan. *Cognition, 16*, 63–80.

Pillemer, D. B., Goldsmith, L. R., Panter, A. T., & White, S. H. (1988). Very long-term memories of the first year in college. *Journal of Experimental Psychology: Learning, Memory, and Cognition, 14*, 709–715.

Pillemer, D. B., Rinehart, E. D., & White, S. H. (1986). Memories of life transitions: The first year in college. *Human Learning, 5*, 109–123.

Pillemer, D. B., & White, S. H. (1989). Childhood events recalled by children and adults. *Advances in Child Development and Behaviour, 21*, 297–340.

Robinson, J. A. (1986). Autobiographical memory: A historical prologue. In D. C. Rubin (Ed.), *Autobiographical memory* (pp. 19–24). Cambridge, England: Cambridge University Press.

Robinson, J. A. (1992). First experience memories: Contexts and function in personal histories. In M. A. Conway, D. C. Rubin, H. Spinnler, & W. Wagenaar (Eds.), *Theoretical perspectives on autobiographical memory* (pp. 223–239). Dordrecht, The Netherlands: Kluwer Academic.

Rosch, E. (1978). Principles of categorization. In E. Rosch & B. B. Lloyd (Eds.), *Cognition and categorization* (pp. 25–49). Hillsdale, NJ: Lawrence Erlbaum Associates.

Rubin, D. C. (1982). On the retention function for autobiographical memory. *Journal of Verbal Learning and Verbal Behavior, 21*, 21–38.

Rubin, D. C., Wetzler, S. E., & Nebes, R. D. (1986). Autobiographical across the lifespan. In D. C. Rubin (Ed.), *Autobiographical memory* (pp. 202–221). Cambridge, England: Cambridge University Press.

Rumelhart, D. E., & Norman, D. A. (1983). *Representation in memory* (CHIP Tech. Rep. No. 116). San Diego: Center for Human Information Processing, University of California.

Salaman, E. (1970). *A collection of moments: A study of involuntary memories.* London: Longman.

Schacter, D. L., & Tulving, E. (Eds.). (1994). *Memory systems 1994.* Cambridge, MA: MIT Press.

Schuman, H., & Rieger, C. (1992). Collective memory and collective memories. In M. A. Conway, D. C. Rubin, H. Spinnler, & W. Wagenaar (Eds.), *Theoretical perspectives on autobiographical memory* (pp. 323–336). Dordrecht, The Netherlands: Kluwer Academic.

Schuman, H., & Scott, J. (1989). Generations and collective memories. *American Sociological Review, 54*, 359–381.

Sehulster, J. R. (1996). In my era: Evidence for the perception of a special period of the past. *Memory, 4*(2), 145–158.

Strauman, T. J. (1990). Self-guides and emotionally significant childhood memories: a study of retrieval efficiency and incidental negative emotional content. *Journal of Personality and Social Psychology, 59*, 869–880.

Tulving, E. (1972). Episodic and semantic memory. In E. Tulving & W. Donaldson (Eds.), *Organization of memory* (pp. 381–403). New York: Academic Press.

Tulving, E. (1983). *Elements of episodic memory.* New York: Oxford University Press.

Tulving, E. (1985). How many memory systems are there? *American Psychologist, 40*, 385–398.

Chapter 3

The Generational Basis
of Historical Knowledge

Howard Schuman
University of Michigan

Robert F. Belli
University of Michigan

Katherine Bischoping
York University, Toronto

The research discussed here tests more literally than Mannheim perhaps intended, the claim that "I only really possess those 'memories' that I have created directly for myself, only that 'knowledge' I have personally gained in real situations. This is the only sort of knowledge which really 'sticks' and it alone has real binding power" (1928/1952, p. 296). Moreover, an even stronger hypothesis can be drawn from his view that adolescence and early adulthood are a stage of life uniquely open to gaining knowledge about the larger world: "It is only then that life's problems begin to be located in a 'present' and are experienced as such. . . . The 'up-to-dateness' of youth therefore consists in their being closer to the 'present' problems . . . the older generation cling to the re-orientation that had been the drama of *their* youth" (1928/1952, pp. 300–301). Thus, knowledge of events should not only be acquired primarily from personally experienced situations, but should occur especially for events experienced during adolescence or early adulthood.

Schuman and Scott (1989)—stimulated by Mannheim's (1928/1952) ideas on personal experience and generational effects, and of Halbwachs (1950/1980) and others on collective memory—showed that attributions of importance to national and world events of the past half century tend to be a function of having experienced an event during adolescence or early adulthood.[1] However, their basic open-ended question to a cross-section of

---

[1] Similar results have been obtained by Scott and Zac (1993) using English data and by Schuman, Rieger, and Gaidys using Lithuanian data (1994). Interesting corroborative

Americans in 1985 called for respondents to mention any two "especially important national or world events or changes," and did not directly assess knowledge about the past. For example, a person could attribute special importance to World War II and the assassination of President Kennedy when asked to report any two especially important events from the past 50 years, yet that need not indicate a lack of knowledge about the Vietnam War or about other major events of the past half century.

The present study focuses on actual knowledge about the past, rather than on spontaneous mention of events that come immediately to mind in response to a general question about the past. It considers a set of 11 political, social, and cultural events spread over the past 60 years, with each event posed separately, so that respondents are not restricted to speaking about only one or two. In the theoretically most interesting cases, where the events occurred approximately midway in the life cycle of present older adults and therefore lead to predictions of nonlinear relations to cohort, substantial replications and extensions were carried out.

Although the main concern is with the generational basis of knowledge, other social identities are considered that might contribute to making facts from the past "stick," as well as the possible interaction of these identities with generational location. In addition, consideration is given to how generational experience can affect expectations about the recurrence in the future of an important type of political event from the past. At the conclusion of the empirical part of the chapter, reasons are discussed as to why events may (or may not) have differential impacts on cohorts, and there is speculation on the possible implications of the results for types of knowledge other than that of historical events.[2]

More specifically, the focus is on the following basic hypotheses about generational effects:

1. *Simple Linear Version.* People are least likely to have accurate knowledge of events that happened before their birth. As a correlate, they are also less likely to know about an event that occurred during their early childhood than do those who were already into adolescence or young adulthood when the event occurred. However, because there is often informal transmission of knowledge across generations—for example, chil-

---

evidence is reported by Pennebaker (1993), for example, that monuments tend to be built between 20 and 30 years after a war or other similar event, presumably by the generation that experienced the event at an earlier point during its own youth.

[2]"Cohort" and "generation" are used as approximately equivalent terms, but with different connotations. Cohort focuses on age ranges that are delineated with a fair degree of precision in terms of birthdate, but we do not restrict generation, as demographers might prefer, to "the temporal unit of kinship structure" (Ryder, 1965, p. 853). Generation refers more loosely and broadly to groupings in terms of birth years, but suggests also the shaping of beliefs by a historically significant period.

dren may hear or overhear the talk of their parents or grandparents—knowledge of past events should decline gradually rather than precipitously across cohorts.

2. *Complex Curvilinear Version*. Because adolescence and early adulthood provide a unique openness toward larger events, those who were past this stage when an event occurred should have somewhat less knowledge of it than those who were in their youth at the time. Although Mannheim (1928/1952) stated a specific age range (17–25) as crucial, it is unlikely that anything so precise can be applied literally today, especially a range generalized from casual observations in Europe in the 1920s. The range may also vary by type of event (e.g., simple dramatic events may have an impact at an earlier age than do more abstract events). If the basic curvilinear relation implied by this hypothesis is found, approximate age ranges for the maximum impact of events are best determined by empirical investigation.

3. *Other Social Attributes and Identities*. In addition to the primary age-related hypotheses, several specific social connections are explored that can modify general associations: (a) Education as an important source of nonpersonal learning about the past should have a direct effect on what is known, and may also interact with generational experience. The first part of this hypothesis is so obvious that education is treated as an essential control variable in all analyses, but its separate effects and its interactions with age are considered as well. (b) Knowledge of the past should also be a function of gender and race when they have personal meaning in relation to specific events. In particular, events concerning race are likely to be more meaningful and therefore better known by Blacks than by Whites, and events related to gender should show different effects for men and women. Furthermore, an event of continuing importance to one racial group (specifically, the name "Rosa Parks" for African Americans) should show weaker age effects than for a less involved racial group (Whites), because the latter should be more dependent on contemporaneous reports of the event for knowledge of it.

METHOD

Nine events from the past, represented by names of persons or in other ways, were first presented in 1991 to a probability sample of adults, age 18 and over, drawn from the three-county metropolitan Detroit area and interviewed face to face through the Detroit Area Study (referred to below as the DAS-91 sample). The most important results from a theoretical standpoint were then replicated in a larger national probability telephone sample carried out by the University of Michigan's Survey Research Center in the summer and fall of 1993, together with two new events added as further tests of the earlier findings; this 1993 national sample is referred to here as SRC-93.[3]

In both surveys, respondents were told midway in an interview:

> This next section concerns a few words and names from the past that come up now and then, but that many people have forgotten. Could you tell me which ones you have heard of at all, and, if you have, what they refer to in just a few words?

The 11 distinct events from the two surveys range from the "WPA," which dates from the 1930s, to "Christa McAuliffe," whose 1986 death in the Challenger explosion was the most recent event. Answers to all events were scored 2 if judged correct according to the coding criteria, 1 if judged partially correct, and 0 if the respondent said "don't know," or gave a completely incorrect answer. (Agreement between two coders on the scoring of 105 DAS-91 cases chosen at random ranged from 87% to 100% over the nine events, and for 223 SRC-93 cases from 80% to 91%.)

All 11 events are shown in Table 3.1, with the distribution of scores on each and examples of answers scored as correct (score of 2). Scores of 1 for partially correct were given to answers that were accurate but vague (e.g., connecting the Tet Offensive with Vietnam but with nothing more specific). Answers scored 0 as incorrect usually resulted from "Don't Know" responses rather than from erroneous statements, but errors that do occur will also be seen to be of interest from a generational standpoint.

The major analytic variable is age, which is treated as indicating cohort, though whether age has this meaning rather than one based on assumptions about the aging process itself will depend on the nature of the results. In order to present age effects graphically, most analysis has been done using 12 categories of age, as shown in Fig. 3.1 and most subsequent figures. The total age range is from 18 to 80; those 81 and over are omitted partly because they provide too few cases over too wide an age/cohort range (81 to 96 in the DAS data) and partly because even with education controlled interviewers rated the "understanding" of this subsample as appreciably lower than the rest of the sample. It seemed better to avoid

---

[3]The final DAS-91 sample size was 1,042 and the response rate was 78.1%. The SRC-93 sample was constructed from new RDD surveys of approximately 500 individuals each month from July through November, though most questions were asked in fewer than the 5 months, so the Ns vary from 1,010 to 2,382. Each monthly telephone survey uses an independent probability sample composed of a new RDD subsample of about 300 cases, with random selection within households, and a random subsample of about 200 individuals who had been interviewed 6 months earlier in a monthly survey (but not with these questions); the RDD component has an average response rate over the 5 months of 69.6%. The basic results are replicated between these two components, as well as between the DAS-91 and SRC-93 surveys, as shown later.

TABLE 3.1
Events From the Past: Distribution of Knowledge Scores

Event	Approx. Date	Knowledge Scores				N	Examples of Scores of 2
		0	1	2	100		
WPA (D)	1938	64%	7	29	100	1000	"FDR gave work to people in the 1930s"
Holocaust (D)	1945	23%	13	64	100	999	"Genocide on the Jews by the Germans"
Marshall Plan (D)	1947	79%	7	14	100	1000	"To help foreign countries after the war"
Joe McCarthy (D)	1954	64%	12	24	100	999	"1950s equivalent of the Salem witch trials"
Rosa Parks (D)	1955	21%	34	45	100	1000	"She wouldn't move to the back of the bus"
Tet Offensive (D)	1968	70%	15	15	100	1000	"Communists attacked us in Vietnam"
Tet Offensive (S)	1968	66%	16	18	100	1951	
Mylai, Village of (S)	1969	65%	17	19	100	1010	"The American army shot women and children; one fellow was court-martialed"
Woodstock (D)	1969	25%	14	61	100	1000	"That's the hippies' concert"
Woodstock (S)	1969	24%	15	61	100	1950	
Watergate (D)	1973	14%	37	49	100	1000	"When Nixon broke the rules"
John Dean (S)	1973	67%	21	12	100	1511	"Did a lot of testifying in Watergate hearings, blew the whistle on everyone"
Christa McAuliffe (D)	1986	49%	6	45	100	1000	"In the space shuttle disaster"

Note: Responses were scored 2 if judged correct, 1 if judged partly correct, and 0 if judged incorrect or the respondent said don't know (DK). Most zero responses resulted from DK answers. The letter *D* after an event indicates that the results are from DAS-91. The letter *S* indicates that the results are from SRC-93.

ambiguities in this regard.[4] Educational attainment is used throughout as a direct statistical control, and results were checked separately for interactions with gender and race.[5]

Our primary mode of analysis and presentation is through Multiple Classification Analysis (MCA), which organizes results from dummy variable regressions in the form of deviations from the grand mean (Andrews, Morgan, Sonquist, & Klem, 1973); the deviations are then converted into means by age categories, with adjustment to control for differences by education. In most cases, the three-category knowledge scoring (scores 0, 1, 2) is treated as a dependent variable, and graphs are shown for all important relations. Ordinary least squares (OLS) regression results are presented with each graph: first the unstandardized linear coefficient, with education controlled, then the coefficient for an added quadratic term, with significance levels in parentheses after each coefficient. A number of checks have been made to provide confidence that these approaches, which facilitate detailed inspection of the shape of relations, do not distort conclusions about statistical significance. For all analyses shown graphically, scores were also collapsed in alternative ways (2 vs. 1 & 0 combined; 2 & 1 combined vs. 0) and logistic regression (with and without quadratic terms) was used to replicate the OLS results. This provides a further test of both the coding distinctions and statistical approach. In the few instances where a conclusion would have been changed in substantive respects, they are noted in the text or footnotes. More generally, although coefficients and significance levels provide useful guides and checks, primary emphasis is put on patterns clear enough to be reviewed visually, rather than focusing on every effect that is significant for any part of a curve with these fairly large samples.[6]

---

[4]Even those in our 75- to 80-year-old category present some ambiguity, making it hard to be confident that cohort experience can be distinguished from present problems of functioning in some individuals. The final age categories vary slightly in size (5- or 6-year ranges) in order to preserve intuitively meaningful groupings by decade (e.g., 30s, 40s, 50s, 60s, 70s), yet also include those 18 and 19 who were in the original sample, as well as those age 80.

[5]Education is ordinarily used as a six-category control variable: 0–8, 9–11, 12, 13–15, 16, 17+ years of schooling, but when education–age interactions are examined graphically, education is reduced to four categories (8–11, 12, 13–15, 16+) and age to six categories (18–29, 30s, 40s, 50s, 60s, 70–80) in order to preserve cases. When race is employed as a separate variable, self-identification as African American or White is used and other ethnic groups are ignored, but for all other analyses no such exclusion is made. Interactive results for education, race, and gender will not be regularly noted, but will be reported when they affect substantive conclusions in important ways.

[6]For example, in Fig. 3.2, logistic regression shows a significant quadratic term for age for the Marshall Plan, although OLS regression does not. However, the logistic result is based on the change in the oldest (75–80) age category, because the coefficient does not approach significance when that category is omitted. The main conclusion about the generally monotonic relation of age to knowledge in this case is unchanged, leaving the nature of the effect for the oldest age group ambiguous and better explored with other items.

FINDINGS

Preliminary Results

Table 3.1 shows that at one extreme the Holocaust and Woodstock could be described adequately by more than 60% of the samples, whereas at the other extreme less than 15% of the respondents could provide an explanation scored as correct for the Marshall Plan or John Dean. (Detailed accounts were not required for a score of 2, and "pithy" summaries were accepted when they seemed to imply adequate knowledge of an event, e.g., "When Nixon broke the rules" for Watergate.) Differences of a few percentage points in knowledge of two events should not be treated as meaningful, because there is inevitably judgment involved in the level of completeness to require for a "correct" response to any particular event. However, more substantial differences, especially at the zero end of the scale, surely do reflect variations in knowledge across the populations sampled.[7]

Because of the assumed importance of education to knowledge, it is useful to compare its associations with those for age, as a way of getting a rough sense of the comparative strength of the two predictors. Because the associations for age are expected to be nonlinear in some cases, in Table 3.2 eta^2 is used as a simple measure of association, and six categories are employed for both variables. (Separate use of squared product-moment correlations with education, where the relation is essentially linear in all cases, shows them to differ only trivially from the eta^2's in Table 3.2.) Comparing columns 1 (age) and 2 (education) and focusing on the median values to deemphasize a large outlier for the Works Progress Administration (WPA), it can be seen that age typically accounts for about two thirds as much variation in knowledge of past events as does education.[8]

---

[7]For the two events included in both DAS-91 and SRC-93, the distributions in Table 3.1 are quite similar despite the fact that the populations, modes of administration, time points, and many other features of the two surveys were different. For Woodstock, the difference in marginal distributions between DAS-91 and SRC-93 does not approach significance. For the Tet Offensive, the difference is significant ($p < .05$) but small, and it does not approach significance when the comparison is controlled for race. African Americans constitute 20% of the DAS-91 sample, but only 9% of the SRC-93 sample, and their effect is to reduce the DAS-91 average age and education, both of which are correlated inversely with knowledge. Even without controlling for race, the relation of knowledge of the Tet Offensive to age is very similar in the DAS-91 and SRC-93 samples, so the present difference is not only small but does not extend to the analysis that is the main concern.

[8]Although primary interest is in separate events at particular points in time, a total scale was constructed by averaging the nine DAS-91 items. The mean of .93 ($sd = .5$) indicates that respondents averaged just slightly below a partially correct answer (score of 1). Only 2% of the sample received a perfect score of 2 on all nine events, and only 3% a failing score of 0 on all nine events. Because the nine knowledge item scores are all positively intercorrelated (mean $r = .30$), the reliability of the scale can be estimated as .79 (coefficient

TABLE 3.2
Eta Square for Events by Age, Education, Race, Gender

Event	Age*	Education**	Gender***	Race****
WPA (D)	.32	.04	.03	.02
Holocaust (D)	.04	.07	.00	.03
Marshall Plan (D)	.08	.12	.07	.04
Joe McCarthy (D)	.08	.11	.04	.05
Rosa Parks (D)	.01	.02	.00	.02
Tet offensive (D)	.06	.08	.13	.05
Tet offensive (S)	.06	.10	.12	.02
Mylai, Village of (S)	.14	.12	.04	.03
Woodstock (D)	.07	.15	.01	.12
Woodstock (S)	.06	.14	.02	.04
Watergate (D)	.04	.07	.01	.02
John Dean (S)	.09	.11	.01	.01
Christa McAuliffe (D)	.02	.08	.00	.07
Mean	.09	.09	.04	.04
Median	.07	.10	.02	.03

Note: The letter *D* indicates the results are from DAS-91, *S* from SRC-93.

*Based on six age categories: 18–29, 30–39, 40–49, 50–59, 60–69, 70–80. All associations significant at $p < .01$, except $p < .02$ for Rosa Parks.

**Based on six education categories: 0–8, 9–11, 12, 13–15, 16, 17+. All associations significant at $p < .01$, with direction positive in all cases.

***All associations significant at $p < .01$, except $p < .04$ for Woodstock in DAS-91, $p < .02$ for Watergate, and $p > .10$ (n.s.) for Holocaust, Rosa Parks, and Christa McAuliffe. See text for direction of associations.

****African Americans and Whites only. All associations significant at $p < .01$. See text for direction of associations.

The same kinds of associations were obtained for race and gender, as shown in Table 3.2. There are significant African American–White differences for each event, and they indicate greater knowledge among White respondents, except that knowledge of Rosa Parks is greater among African American respondents. Men had significantly higher correctness scores than women for six of the nine events, especially those dealing with military or foreign policy; however, the gender difference disappears for knowledge of Rosa Parks, Christa McAuliffe, and the Holocaust—broadly social rather than purely political events, of which two are about women. (All the race and gender differences remain statistically significant when education, age, and age squared are controlled using OLS regression, except that Watergate no

alpha), though its Guttmanlike nature makes this only approximate. The correlation of the overall scale with education is $r = .40$, indicating that education accounts for less than a fourth of the reliable variation in the scale. Thus, most of the variation remains to be explained by other variables.

longer shows a reliable gender difference.) Results by race and gender are discussed further when considering the knowledge items separately.

The Simple Linear Hypothesis of Generational Effects

The simplest form of the generational hypothesis is that knowledge of a past event decreases with cohort distance from the event. This hypothesis leads to prediction of an approximately linear relation of knowledge to age across the entire life span for events that occurred at the beginning of the total period we are dealing with (the 1930s through the 1980s), though perhaps with a plateau reached once there is a great deal of distance from the original event—because commemorations, school teaching, and other reminders may then provide occasional new sources of knowledge for some events.

The WPA, the earliest of the 11 events, should fit this prediction well. It was in existence and widely known between 1936 and the early 1940s, with the largest number of workers employed in 1938 (Howard, 1943, p. 534), the date used as a convenient marker for expected peak knowledge. Information should have been obtained by the estimated 8.5 million people who received support directly from the WPA, from their relatives and friends, and by those who heard about it at the time from radio or newspaper reports. Yet once ended, it was not something reenacted with fanfare on a 25th or other anniversary, nor the stuff of major film or television dramas. Thus, knowledge of the WPA should be greatest for those of the generation that participated in it, less for each later generation—gradually diminishing from the oldest to the youngest cohorts in this sample.

With education controlled, the trend shown in Fig. 3.1 fits this prediction quite well, with the peak at ages 70 to 74 in 1991, a cohort ranging from age 17 to 21 in 1938, and a nearly linear slope downward from the peak toward younger cohorts. Among the two youngest cohorts, a low lying plateau appears to have been reached, with most not knowing anything about the WPA but a tiny number having learned enough from some source to be scored correct (only 7 out of 193 respondents under age 30 received a score of 2).[9] At the oldest end there is an apparent drop in knowledge, which would fit nicely an assumption of the importance of adolescence—because the 75- to 80-year-old cohort was already moving beyond adolescence in 1938—but the small size of that subsample and other evidence to be presented makes such an interpretation uncertain at

---

[9]The significant positive quadratic coefficient shown in Fig. 3.1 is due to the leveling off among the youngest age categories: If the three youngest categories are omitted, the quadratic coefficient does not approach significance. In addition, when the 3-point scale is reduced to a dichotomy in either direction, the quadratic term in logistic regressions is no longer significant ($p > .10$).

Knowledge Score for WPA

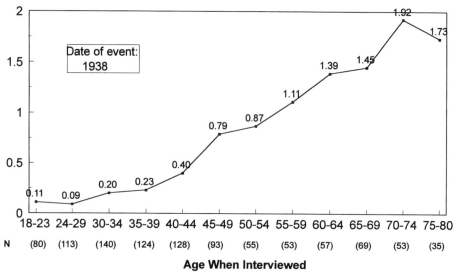

N   (80)   (113)   (140)   (124)   (128)   (93)   (55)   (53)   (57)   (69)   (53)   (35)

Age When Interviewed

Mean knowledge score: .65
Linear: b = .18 (.001); quadratic: b = .01 (.001)   Source: DAS-91

FIG. 3.1.   Knowledge of WPA by age, with education controlled.

best. It is better to treat Fig. 3.1 as essentially monotonic, and to look for important nonmonotonic relations on other items more suited to the theoretical issues posed by the end points of age.

For the WPA, cohort is unusual in being a much stronger predictor than education, as shown in Table 3.2. Thus, personal experience or transmission across the generations is considerably more important in this case than is formal learning. The personal nature of knowledge of the WPA, including its transmission, is revealed clearly in a number of responses, exemplified by the following two:

> Kept my dad working and food in my mouth when we were kids during the Depression. (Man, age 66)

> My grandfather worked on it. Provided work for people during the Depression, as I was told. (Man, age 47)

Altogether four explicit mentions were found of husbands employed by the WPA, 14 of fathers and 1 of a mother, and 2 of grandfathers. In this way, the WPA is unique among all our events in that knowledge of it is rooted in many individual lives.

Knowledge Score for WPA in Educational Categories

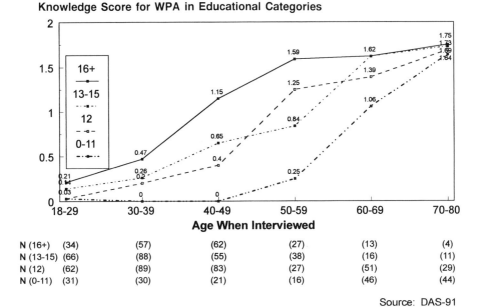

FIG. 3.2.   Knowledge of the WPA by age, within four educational categories.

There is also evidence in the MCA results of an interesting interaction ($p = .05$) between age and education in their effects on knowledge of the WPA. When the relation of age to knowledge of the WPA is examined graphically for different educational levels in Fig. 3.2, the most unusual group comprises those at the lowest educational level: They show little knowledge across the 18- to 59-year-old categories, then a sharp slope upward toward convergence with more educated persons at the oldest age levels. Thus, direct experience with the WPA is especially important at this educational level, with less evidence of remote transmission of knowledge across generations.[10]

Two other events asked about in DAS-91 go back almost as far as the WPA: "the Marshall Plan," first announced in 1947, and "Joe McCarthy," dating from the early and mid-1950s, with 1954 perhaps the high point in McCarthy's brief and fiery career. Neither is as well recognized today as the WPA, and the Marshall Plan has the lowest level of knowledge of all

---

[10]Interactions with gender and race were examined by repeating the age and education MCA separately for men and for women, and separately for African Americans and for Whites. The basic trend shown in Fig. 3.1 is replicated within each of these four categories with only minor differences. (Combinations of race and gender are not used because they yield very small samples for African American men and African American women when broken by age categories.)

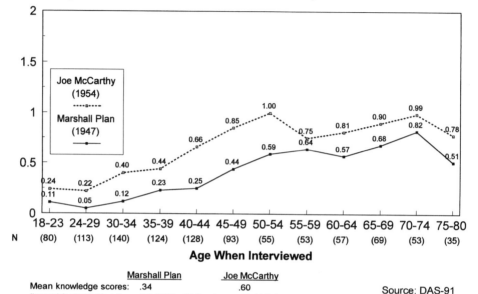

FIG. 3.3. Knowledge of Joe McCarthy and of Marshall Plan by age, with education controlled.

the terms presented. Figure 3.3 shows that the Marshall Plan peaks at ages 70 to 74, equivalent to ages 26 to 30 when the event first occurred, and when taken at face value this result suggests a slightly later point than was true for the WPA. This seems to be a plausible finding for such an abstract event, requiring more background in and attention to news reports than most other events individuals were asked about.[11]

The curve for Joe McCarthy presents more of a puzzle because it appears to be bimodal, with peaks at ages 50–54 (13–18 in 1954) and 70–74 (33–37 in 1954). Although either of these might possibly be explained if taken alone—the younger one more easily if adolescent experience is emphasized—the combination does not lend itself to any plausible interpretation. Moreover, the bimodality is located largely among men; women show a monotonic upward trend. Unless the bimodality for men can be replicated

---

[11]Age and education do not interact, because the lowest educational category does not converge with the others, as was the case for the WPA, no doubt because personal experience could not be a source of knowledge in this case. (The coefficient for men is significantly greater than for women, $p < .02$, and for Whites significantly greater than for African Americans, $p < .01$. However, the linear relations differ from zero [$p < .01$] for all four groups [men, women, African Americans, Whites] and here, as elsewhere, differences tangential to the main concerns have not been pursued.)

in some form, it seems better not to try to interpret it. Instead, the decline for ages younger than 50 should be emphasized, leaving the variations at older ages as probably a result of sampling error, as the numbers of cases in relevant age/cohort categories are not very large.

Not all events are anchored in a particular year or narrow range of years, as were the Marshall Plan and the WPA. The Holocaust was deliberately included among the nine words in DAS-91, and though it can be dated to the early 1940s, wide public knowledge first occurred only at the end of World War II when photographs of the Nazi death camps were published in the United States. Then, in later years, new cohorts of Americans learned in new ways about the Holocaust (including the use of the term *Holocaust* itself) through widely publicized books, films, and television dramas, which is exactly the opposite of what occurred with the WPA. Probably for this reason, the Holocaust is the best known of all the events used, with 64% of the DAS-91 sample scored as correct.

The basic trend, as shown in Fig. 3.4, is for a peak for the cohort ages 70 to 74, which was in its later 20s when reports and pictures from Auschwitz and other camps were first made public; then a high level of knowledge for those from 45 through 69, all of whom would have been young at points when later dramatic accounts of the Holocaust appeared; a still

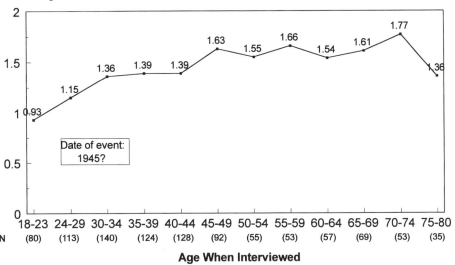

Knowledge Score for Holocaust

Mean knowledge score: 1.41
linear(p); quadratic(p): .05(.001); -.01(.001)   Source: DAS-91

FIG. 3.4. Knowledge of the Holocaust by age, with education controlled.

lower plateau for those in their 30s and early 40s; and finally continued decrease in knowledge among those now in their 20s—though that may have ended at least temporarily with a powerful new film (*Schindler's List*) having reached young audiences. None of these results is inconsistent with previous findings, nor with the theory behind the present study, because it is not the actual date of an event that is crucial, but the date or dates at which it becomes known to the general public. Thus, the Holocaust represents a limiting case where the experience of an event spans a wide range of cohorts, each of which can be considered to have been in its youth at the time the event became known.[12]

The Complex Generational Hypothesis:
Youth as a Critical Age Period

The simple linear prediction about knowledge of events from the 1930s, 1940s, and 1950s has been useful to test, even if the results are not altogether surprising. However, a less obvious implication of Mannheim's hypothesis is that people can fail to possess knowledge of events not only because they were born too late, but also because they were born too early. The generational assumption in this case is that people who are past a critical period of life—almost invariably pinpointed as adolescence and young adulthood—either lack the interest needed to register the event at all, or do not internalize it deeply enough for memory to endure once some time has passed. Thus, the more complex form of the generational hypothesis is the prediction of a concave relation of knowledge to the succession of birth cohorts, with its exact shape dependent on the date of the historical event and on the extent to which it is kept alive for the public by commemorations and other reminders.

The most efficient tests of this more complex hypothesis about cohort effects require events that occurred midway in the life span of the older persons who were interviewed. In such cases, the sample includes persons too young to have experienced an event as well as persons who were already well past their youth when the event occurred. Two events were chosen that fit this specification well: the Tet Offensive in Vietnam in 1968 and the Woodstock concert in upstate New York in 1969. The youngest people

---

[12]Age and education interact in the case of the Holocaust ($p < .05$), with the linear coefficient for age decreasing in size as education increases: .07 ($p < .001$) for those with 0 to 11 years of schooling, .06 ($p < .001$) for high school graduates, .05 ($p < .003$) for 13 to 15 years of education, .00 (n.s.) for college graduates. Thus, early actual experience has its clearest effect on the least educated, as was the case for the WPA, whereas the most educated learned about the Holocaust in ways independent of age. (None of the findings for the Holocaust is altered if the 23 respondents who identified themselves as Jewish to a later question on religion are excluded from analysis.)

in the samples were not even born at the time of the two events, whereas the oldest people—including those in their mid-50s and thus not just the very old—had already left their 20s at that point in time. In other respects, the two events are quite different from each other: Tet was an important turning point in the Vietnam War, but it is now seldom mentioned outside of books on that war; Woodstock was a public happening that came to symbolize much of the 1960s counterculture mentality, was subsequently incorporated into film, and was celebrated again on its 25th anniversary in 1994. The difference in lasting impact between the two events is shown clearly in the overall percentages of respondents in the national survey who could give a correct definition of each: 15% and 18% for Tet in the two surveys, 61% for Woodstock in both.

In DAS-91 both Tet and Woodstock showed clear evidence of the predicted curvilinear relations to age, but given the crucial theoretical importance of the curvilinear specification and the desirability of generalization across populations and modes of administration, the question was repeated for both words in 1993 using the larger SRC national telephone sample. Both sets of results are presented for both events in Figs. 3.5 and 3.6.

For the Tet Offensive, the predicted curvilinearity appears in almost perfect form: Using the national sample peak, maximum knowledge occurs for those ages 45 to 49, which places them in their early twenties in 1968 when the Tet Offensive occurred. The fall-off with present age appears in

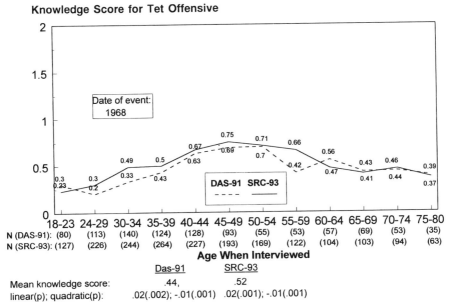

FIG. 3.5. Knowledge of the Tet Offensive by age, with education controlled.

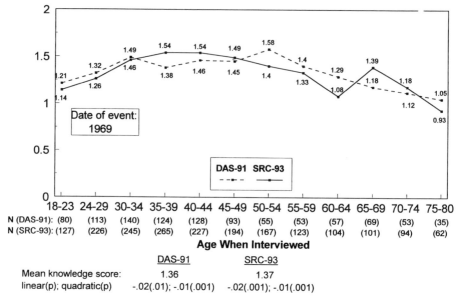

FIG. 3.6. Knowledge of Woodstock by age, with education controlled.

both directions, though not surprisingly, knowledge of Tet is a little greater among the oldest members of the sample who lived through it than among the youngest (and the overall positive linear trend is significant). However, the downward slope from the critical age period is clear on both sides of the peak.

For Woodstock, there is no single clear peak, but the basic curvilinearity seems evident as well. The knowledge peak for the larger national sample is a little younger for Woodstock than for Tet—roughly 35 to 44, which meant 11 to 22 in 1969 using both surveys for dating. But unlike Tet and all other events studied, ignorance is greater among the older cohorts than among the very young: This is the only case where the linear trend is negative. An interpretation of the difference from Tet is compelling: Woodstock was aimed at the young; it celebrated youth at the time and has been carried on primarily by the young, including many not even born in 1969. (The rise at ages 65 to 69 for SRC-93 is probably due to sampling error, because it does not occur at all in the DAS-91 sample.)

Thus, the more complex generational hypothesis receives substantial support from these data about two quite different events from the end of the 1960s, one a well-known cultural "happening" and the other an almost forgotten military and morale crisis. For these two events, it is evident that historical knowledge receives an important generational contribution from those in their youth at the time, though more sharply so for the event (Tet) that is less carried forward by the media and much less well known overall.[13] Moreover, generation provides not only a basis for knowledge, but also serves to shape ignorance. The wrong answers given to the Tet Offensive were examined and it was discovered that five of these referred to the Korean War, and that all five individuals (four men and one woman) were within the age range from 51 to 66 in 1991 (i.e., ages 13 to 25 during the 1950–1953 Korean conflict).[14]

One other event was included in DAS-91 from a later time point that might also be expected to show a curvilinear relation to age, but fails to do so: "Watergate," which is dated for convenience from 1973, though it extended over a somewhat longer period and is still being referred to today. It is also extremely well known, with the fewest respondents scored as having no knowledge at all, though it ranks lower in terms of perfect scores of 2 (see Table 3.1).[15]

Figure 3.7 shows that there is essentially a level degree of knowledge about Watergate among those beyond their 20s in 1991, with the only important variation occurring for the two youngest cohorts in the sample.[16] A plausible interpretation is to regard Watergate as too widely known to suffer a decrement of knowledge among older people as happened with Tet, but evidence to be presented later does not support this conclusion.

---

[13]Men show a significantly greater quadratic effect for Tet (but not for Woodstock) than women. This interaction with gender is discussed further later, because appreciation of its importance becomes clearer in the context of all the results.

[14]The cross-tabulation of substantively wrong answers by age categories is as follows:

	Korean War	Other Errors	
Ages 51–66	5	4	(Fisher's exact test:
Other ages	0	23	$p < .001$)

Most of the errors (18 of the 23) in the bottom right cell were by persons younger than age 51 (i.e., persons who would have had little or no knowledge of the Korean War). (This approach to "wrong answers" has been developed in a separate article by Belli, Schuman, & Jackson, in press.)

[15]For a score of 2 respondents were required to have mentioned Nixon and indicated something about alleged wrong doing, whereas 1 was scored if there was only vague mention of a "scandal" in connection with Nixon. This may have been too high a hurdle, but in any case the pattern shown in Fig. 3.5 is essentially unchanged if scores are dichotomized in both directions (2 vs. 0 & 1 combined, or 2 & 1 combined vs. 0) and use logistic regression. Nor do conclusions change when MCA's are run separately within race and gender categories, nor when other leads were explored in an effort to show an age curve for Watergate similar to that for Tet.

[16]When education is treated as an interactive variable, respondents with 16 or more years of education do show the hypothesized curvilinear relation. But in the absence of both replication and plausible interpretation, this cannot be given great weight.

Knowledge Score for Watergate

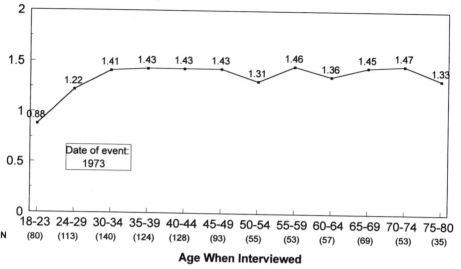

Mean knowledge score: 1.35
linear(p); quadratic(p): .03(.001); -.01(.001)   Source: DAS-91

FIG. 3.7. Knowledge of Watergate by age, with education controlled.

Two Extensions: The Village of Mylai and John Dean

The Tet Offensive provides a clear confirmation of assumptions about the importance of youth to historical knowledge, but results for Watergate do not conform to the same assumptions. It seemed useful to determine whether other events closely related to each of these replicated their respective patterns, or modified or disconfirmed them, because the goal is to generalize beyond any particular event. Late in the period of the 1993 surveys, two new events were added for this purpose.

As a comparison with Tet, "the village of Mylai" was chosen, which refers to a massacre of Vietnamese civilians by U.S. troops in 1969. It deals with the same war, just a year later, but the nature of the event is clearly different in all other details. Although the Tet Offensive was the far more important event strategically and historically—Karnow (1983) devoted 25 pages to the Tet Offensive and just four passing mentions to Mylai—Table 3.1 shows that Mylai is better known than Tet ($p < .001$, for a comparison of the univariate figures in Table 3.1). The sharper focus of Mylai and the later controversial trial of U.S. servicepersons may account for this difference, as suggested by 35 mentions of Lt. Calley, one of the main soldiers indicted for involvement in the massacre.

Knowledge Score for Mylai

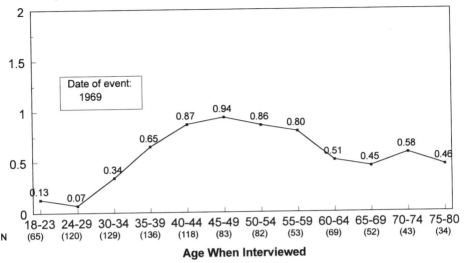

Mean knowledge score: 0.55
linear(p); quadratic(p): .05(.001); -.02(.001)

Source: SRC-93

FIG. 3.8. Knowledge of Village of Mylai by age, with education controlled.

As Fig. 3.8 shows, Mylai presents a curvilinear pattern strikingly similar to that for the Tet Offensive. The peak at ages 45–49 (21–25 in 1969) is exactly the same as occurred for Tet in the national sample. The overall finding shows that the pattern of knowledge for Tet was not a unique or idiosyncratic one from a theoretical standpoint, and thus provides further evidence for the importance of youth as a source of knowledge of the Vietnam War and presumably of other events of a similar nature.

As a comparison to Watergate, John Dean was chosen, with his main date of notoriety being 1973 when he testified before a Senate committee. If there is something about a major domestic political event like Watergate that makes it differ from military events like Tet, then Dean should replicate the shape of the results for Watergate. On the other hand, because it was expected and found that John Dean was much less well known today than Watergate, this might lead to a pattern more like that for the Tet Offensive and the village of Mylai.

Figure 3.9 for John Dean is clearly closer in appearance to the earlier findings for knowledge of Watergate than for Tet. As with Watergate, the youngest people in the sample show distinctively low knowledge, with "young" here extending upward toward age 39 (toward age 19 at the time of Dean's testimony). The twin peaks at ages 45–49 and 55–59 provide a

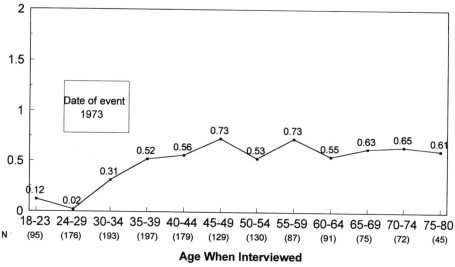

Knowledge Score for John Dean

Mean knowledge score: .46
linear(p); quadratic(p): .06(.001) -.01(.001)   Source: SRC-93

FIG. 3.9. Knowledge of John Dean by age, with education controlled.

hint of something distinctive, but in general the figure is basically similar to that for Watergate. And because Watergate as a total event is still generally familiar, whereas Dean is much less so, it seems unlikely that the overall knowledge of an event by the public is crucial for its relation to generation.[17] Reconciling the different results for Tet, Mylai, and Woodstock, on the one hand, and Watergate and John Dean, on the other, presents a challenge that is addressed later.

Watergate: Past and Future

Although knowledge of Watergate seems to be spread fairly evenly over all the cohorts that experienced it at the time, it seemed possible that the experience would have left a deeper impression on those who were passing through adolescence or early adulthood as the events of Watergate unfolded.

---

[17]There is a borderline interaction between gender and age for Dean ($p < .07$), which becomes more clearly significant ($p < .02$) when logistic regression is used with dichotomous coding. Men show the predicted curvilinear relation, whereas women show a more continuous monotonic increase with age. However, because a gender difference in this regard was not predicted, nor is easily interpreted, no great emphasis on it seems justified. Additionally, Watergate itself does not show such an interaction.

For such people, the incidents and revelations leading up to and through Watergate constituted their most salient knowledge of national politics—knowledge that could not be placed in the larger context brought by those who had lived through previous presidencies. Thus, it was hypothesized that this deeper form of knowledge would contribute to a greater sense of concern about the possibility of a similar occurrence in the future than it would for others who had themselves been older when Watergate took place.

To test this hypothesis, a new question was constructed, one not directly about knowledge but about expectations toward the future based on knowledge of the past:

> It is now 20 years since the Watergate crisis led to the resignation of President Nixon. Some people believe that the Watergate crisis *provided an important lesson for the future.* Others believe that the Watergate crisis may have been an important event in the past *but is not something to worry a lot about for the future.* Which of these two views is closer to your own?

It was predicted that those who had lived through the Watergate crisis during their adolescence and early adulthood would be more likely than others to regard Watergate as providing a continuing important lesson for the future (here coded as 2), rather than as a one-time occurrence not requiring much worry for the future (here coded as 1). The question was included in SRC-93 over 5 consecutive months.

Although the variation by age is not great, Fig. 3.10 presents a relation generally consistent with prediction. Those most worried about a future Watergatelike event were 35–44 in 1993, or more broadly 35–54, which translate into ages 15–24, or 15–34 in 1973, the year taken as the height of the Watergate crisis. Logistic regression of expectations about a future Watergate on age, education, and age squared shows the quadratic term to be highly significant ($p < .001$), and other analyses show the effect to be centered on the predicted age categories. The result points to a subtle generational effect of the Watergate experience on the way that personal knowledge influences expectations, even though no direct evidence was found of the experience on information about Watergate through the standard knowledge question and coding.[18]

Other Original Events

The original set of words from the past in DAS-91 included two other events not yet discussed, neither of which shows a simple generational influence, though each has a special characteristic that makes it unique

---

[18]We also compared responses to the Watergate expectations question for those knowing who John Dean was and those not knowing, with age and education controlled. The first group showed significantly ($p < .05$) more worry about a future Watergate than the second.

Future Expectation: Watergate

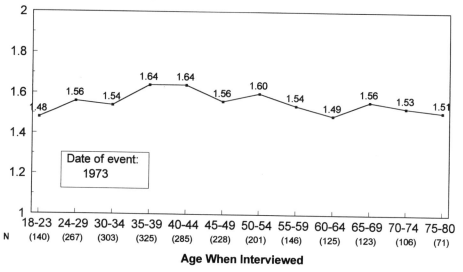

Mean score: 1.57
linear(p); quadratic(p): .00(n.s.); -.003(.01)

Source: DAS-91

FIG. 3.10. Expectations about a future Watergate by age, with education controlled.

theoretically. Assuming that generational effects on knowledge can be regarded as having been established in at least certain instances, examination of these two events can be helpful in further understanding the nature and limits of such influence, as well as in providing complete coverage of all the tests carried out in the two surveys.

The most recent event asked about was symbolized by the name Christa McAuliffe, the schoolteacher who died in the explosion of the space shuttle Challenger in 1986. A strong interpretation of the Mannheim hypothesis might lead to a prediction that the name Christa McAuliffe would be best known to those in their 20s at the time of the survey, with decreasing knowledge from that age point onward to old age.[19] However, Fig. 3.11 shows the youngest members of our sample as the least knowledgeable and a rather irregular pattern beyond age 29, with older people among

---

[19]Schuman and Scott (1989) provided 1985 data about spontaneous mentions of a then recent event (hostage taking) that would be consistent with such a conclusion. However, the number of mentions of hostage taking by young people in that report was very small, even though higher than for other age categories, whereas knowledge of Christa McAuliffe is much greater, so different proportions of the youth population are involved in the two different results.

Knowledge Score for Christa McAuliffe

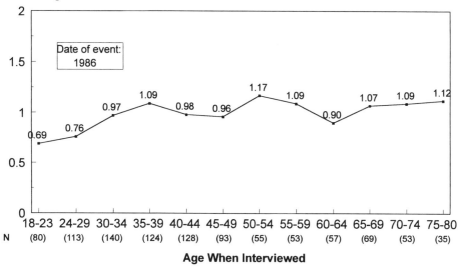

FIG. 3.11.   Knowledge of Christa McAuliffe by age, with education controlled.

the more knowledgeable. Evidently, a recent event does not necessarily produce the mirror image of an early event such as the WPA, though we should note that for 18- to 23-year-olds the level of knowledge of Christa McAuliffe is higher than their level of knowledge for most other events. There will be value in repeating this question in a decade or so to determine whether a different relation to cohort appears.[20]

The overall results for Christa McAuliffe for the total sample are not appreciably different within race and gender categories. However, gender does play a role as a main effect. As noted earlier, on a majority of the other words from the past, men are significantly more knowledgeable than women, with the largest differences involving military (Tet, Mylai) and political (Marshall Plan, Joe McCarthy) events. For Christa McAuliffe, and

---

[20]There is some added difficulty sampling from our youngest age category, because students living in college dormitories or at colleges outside the metropolitan region are not included in this DAS-91 area probability sample. One further complication for knowledge of Christa McAuliffe is a significant interaction between age and gender: For men there is no relation between knowledge and age, whereas for women there is a significant positive linear coefficient ($b = .05$, $p < .001$), with a sharp jump upward in knowledge for women 50 and older. Because this gender difference was neither predicted nor is easily interpretable, it has not been emphasized here.

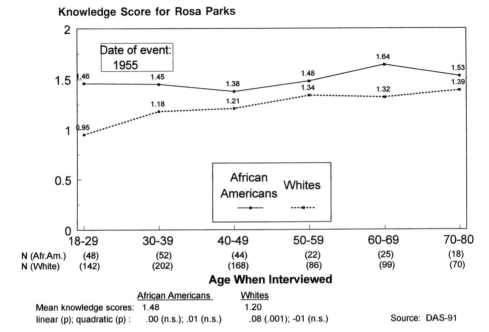

Knowledge Score for Rosa Parks

FIG. 3.12. Knowledge of Rosa Parks by age, with education controlled, separately for African Americans and Whites.

also for Rosa Parks, there is no difference by gender. An obvious interpretation is that when the subject is a woman, women are equally (though not more) knowledgeable than men. However, two other items (the Holocaust and Watergate) do not show greater male knowledge, which indicates that a more general explanation is needed.

It was expected and found that African Americans were more knowledgeable than Whites about the identity of Rosa Parks, though on all other items Whites score significantly higher than African Americans. For Rosa Parks, Fig. 3.12 shows the two racial subsamples separately (with six age categories to maximize sample size bases) because it was hypothesized that there would be a sharper positive age relation for Whites than for African Americans. For Whites, those born or reaching adolescence after the event should have lesser knowledge than those older, as is expected for other events, whereas for African Americans the continued teaching and remembrance of the civil rights struggle should keep the name Rosa Parks much more alive (as happened more generally with the Holocaust), and probably even more so in Detroit where Rosa Parks has continued to be somewhat active. The interaction shown in Fig. 3.12 is highly significant ($p < .001$), the linear trend for Whites equally so—though without a peak in the 1950s and early 1960s as would have been expected—and the relation for African

Americans showing little variation by age. (The findings are unchanged when logistic regression is used with other codings of the knowledge scores.) Thus, there is evidence in this case that generational effects will be less sharp when a symbol continues to be recreated for a particular group, whereas for the less involved group generational effects provide a more important source of knowledge, though in this case not with the precision anticipated.

DISCUSSION

This study yielded three important results that need to be integrated. The simplest is that events from 50 or 60 years back are ordinarily best known by those adults alive at the time and are decreasingly well known by later generations. The prototype is knowledge of the WPA, which is very high among those who were in their late teens in the late 1930s, still somewhat known by the children of this cohort, and almost unknown to young people today. It is useful to document the extent to which knowledge of an important social event is dependent on age, and, in this extreme case, very little dependent on education. Many people remember "as if yesterday" something important from our own youth—whether the WPA, the Cuban missile crisis, or even the dismantling of the Berlin Wall—and it is difficult to keep firmly in mind that these same events may mean little or nothing to first-year college students or others of the same age.

Of course, the extent to which age alone is crucial depends on the nature of an event and the degree to which it is recreated for new generations. Despite concerns that have sometimes been expressed about lack of knowledge of the Holocaust by Americans, it is one of the best known events studied, no doubt because it has been repeatedly recalled and recreated in many forms. Even for the youngest people in our sample, knowledge of the Holocaust is roughly at the same level as for Watergate and exceeded only slightly by knowledge of Woodstock. To be sure, the vividness or "force" of such vicarious knowledge is less certain, and some evidence is provided that concern about a similar future occurrence is less strong for those who were not in their own youth during the early 1970s when Watergate occurred. The extent to which dramatic recreations, such as films, can match or conceivably even exceed what Mannheim (1928/1952) called experience "personally gained in real situations" (p. 296) is a question that deserves further investigation.

A second important result is much less intuitively obvious: There is persuasive evidence that adolescence and early adulthood constitute a critical period during which events can have a significantly greater impact on knowledge than they do for people beyond this period, as well as for people not yet born. Two events from the Vietnam War (the Tet Offensive and the Mylai massacre) and one cultural event from the same period (Woodstock) show such an effect. In order to understand these effects, it is useful to consider three parts of the age curve separately.

For young people today, lack of knowledge of events like the Tet Offensive can be readily explained in the same way as for earlier events like the WPA. Most members of cohorts presently in their teens and twenties had either never heard of Tet or Mylai in the first place, or if they had, the words had passed by so quickly that they did not stick. Youth of today were simply not around when the events happened, though in the case of Woodstock a fair amount of transmission by media and word of mouth evidently occurred.

A somewhat similar type of explanation can be adapted to understand older adults' relatively low knowledge of events that occurred when they were past 30 or so years old. Many of these adults can be regarded as having been "not around" psychologically or socially for Tet or Woodstock, just as they may not be focusing on some events occurring today. To take an extreme example, if one has no interest in popular music, then even the names of major stars in a particular year may not be noted or recognized. So it is suspected that the relatively low knowledge of Woodstock by many persons past 30 when Woodstock occurred was due to a failure to acquire knowledge in the first place. In addition, even if the event was briefly noted at the time, lack of interest would have led to little thought or conversation about it, an absence of "rehearsal," which in turn makes for poor retention of information over the years (Baddeley, 1990). To draw on words that T. S. Eliot wrote in *The Four Quartets*, they "had the experience but missed the meaning."

But why did those in their teens and 20s during the late 1960s pay closer attention to and remember events like Vietnam and Woodstock? There are two empirically confounded explanations difficult to separate with our data: a particular openness of youth to new experiences, as proposed by Mannheim and others, and "first experiences" per se at whatever age they occur. Leaving that distinction for future research, it does appear that the period of youth provides most people with a variety of new experiences, which in turn make for lasting memories both personal and political (Rubin, Wetzler, & Nebes, 1986; Schuman & Scott, 1989). More specifically, adolescence represents for most people the first time that the larger political and social world becomes clearly perceived, and whatever "big" event occurs at that time may loom large and be likely to be remembered as of special importance.

That first experiences constitute an important factor in what individuals learn and remember has been shown in past social psychological studies. For example, Pillemer, Goldsmith, Panter, and White (1988) found that when Wellesley College alumnae were asked to report memories from their first college year, some 40% were from September of that year and of these more than a third were from the very first day at college. More generally, Robinson's review of this literature concludes that "memories of events clustered at the beginning of a novel and significant life period are maintained indefinitely in personal memory" (1992, p. 232).

Our later surveys included a small side investigation that demonstrates the great importance of adolescence and early adulthood in one sphere: preferences in music. Respondents were asked during 2 months in SRC-93 to "mention an event, a performer, or a style having to do with music over the past half century or so that you have especially liked," and this question was followed by: "How old were you when [that] first made an impression on you?" The findings are clear-cut. The median age of reported impression, irrespective of content, was 16 ($M = 19.2$), and although the age of impression increases slightly with the present age of the respondent (see Table 3.3), the more striking result is that all the median ages are quite young. Even those 75 to 80 years old in 1993 give a median age of 27 as their most impressionable point with regard to music. (For a similar study of musical tastes, see Smith, 1994.)

Furthermore, the content of the nominations is consistent with the self-reported impressionable ages. Those mentioning "the big bands" as the music they like best are now in their 60s; those mentioning the Beatles have a mean age of 40; and those mentioning "hard rock" and similar recent trends are currently age 30 on the average. More systematically, the correlation is $r = -.57$ ($p < .001$) between: (a) the mean ages in 1993 of the 376 respondents mentioning a particular performer, and (b) an independent estimate of the approximate year of the initial national fame of that same performer (e.g., 1941 for Frank Sinatra, 1955 for Elvis Presley, 1990 for Garth Brooks).[21] Music may be an extreme case where tastes are especially established during the period of youth and rehearsed frequently thereafter, and thus where cohort effects are readily discovered, but it seems likely that a life stage so powerful for musical preferences carries some of the same implications for other areas of life. Our results for the

---

[21]One hundred and nine mentioned performers could be tracked in this way. The primary source for dates was Clarke (1990), which lists nearly 3,000 performers and related entries. For each entry, we took as the initial date of public notice either a general statement to that effect or the first mention of a record being in the top 10 nationally in its genre or more generally. (Coding of these dates was done without knowledge of respondent ages.) This was a conservative approach, because for long-time performers (e.g., Frank Sinatra), someone quite young might have learned of them recently and this would have lowered the average present age of respondents for that performer. A scattergram shows some tendency for wider variation in dates of selected performers by younger respondents, but the heteroscedasticity is not marked. (Acknowledgment is due to Jan Palmer for her help in conceptualizing and coding the music responses.)

TABLE 3.3
Median Age of Music Impression by Present Age

Present Age	Median Age of Impression	N
18–23	14	(57)
24–29	13	(92)
30–34	15	(102)
35–39	16	(121)
40–44	15	(103)
45–49	17	(88)
50–54	16	(66)
55–59	17	(57)
60–64	16	(36)
65–69	16	(44)
70–74	19	(37)
75–80	27	(26)

Tet offensive and the village of Mylai, as well as for Woodstock, point toward such broader influences connected to cohort.

However, a third important result from the study is the failure to find distinctive generational effects for knowledge of Watergate and of John Dean, despite much analytic effort in that direction. These negative—and probably ineluctable—results indicate that a purely mechanical approach to cohort effects on knowledge is inadequate. Apparently not every event has a uniquely lasting effect on adolescents and young adults, for in the case of Watergate, people who were well past their youth in the early 1970s are as knowledgeable as those who were in their teens and 20s at the time. Nor can this be attributed to a kind of ceiling effect that prevents finer discrimination, or to continued recital or replaying of the Watergate events, for the same negative finding holds for knowledge of John Dean, now a forgotten figure for most Americans.

A clue to reconciling both the findings and the losings about cohort effects on knowledge lies in Fig. 3.13, which presents the earlier data on knowledge of the Tet offensive separately for men and women.[22] Two strong (and highly significant) differences are visible: First, men are much more knowledgeable about Tet and, second, the shape of the curve for men is much closer to the one hypothesized on the basis of generational assumptions. Both differences may be due to the greater interest of young men in military matters, but perhaps even more, to the fact that men in the peak ages shown in Fig. 3.13 were those most threatened by or attracted to personal involvement in the Vietnam War. Few women would have experienced Vietnam in quite the same highly personal way. For similar

---

[22]The larger SRC-93 sample is used here, but similar results appear in the DAS-91 data and also in the SRC-93 data on the village of Mylai.

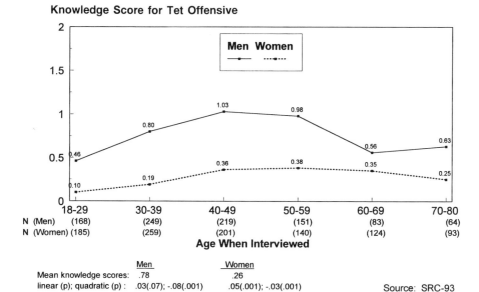

FIG. 3.13. Knowledge of the Tet Offensive by age, with education controlled, separately for men and women.

reasons, most older men beyond military age would have been less intensely concerned about Vietnam than men who were of or near draft age.

Furthermore, for those individuals who came to maturity during the Vietnam War, this was *the* war to attend to, whereas for most older folks it was probably dwarfed by the importance of World War II (or for a slightly later cohort by the Korean War). Watergate, on the other hand, was not preceded by a similar event, and so constituted a striking new experience for all adults alive at the time. In sum, it was the distinctive meaning that the Vietnam War had for men in their youth that was crucial and that made events from it especially memorable to them.[23]

If this explanation holds more generally, then the generational hypothesis about knowledge must be converted from one based entirely on assumptions about the life cycle to one that incorporates the Weberian principle (1956/1968) that subjective meaning is crucial to the connection between events and their effects. It is not just an automatic registering of events that occur during impressionable years, but the way events connect with the lives of real people. In some areas like music, or perhaps the arts

---

[23]Much the same reasoning with regard to age can be extended to Woodstock, but not with regard to gender. It is supportive, therefore, that for Woodstock there is not a significant difference in quadratic coefficients for men and women like that in Fig. 3.13, and the difference in mean knowledge scores is also much smaller for Woodstock than for Tet.

more generally, the connection is easily, almost inevitably made as these pursuits are discovered during adolescence; but with larger political and social happenings, the nature of the events themselves must create the connection of meaning. This research therefore neither confirms nor denies the curvilinear hypothesis about youth, but transforms it in a crucial respect.

Beyond the ideas and evidence presented here, there is the possibility of further generalization to the conditions that stimulate knowledge of other kinds. As elite interpretations of the more distant past change (e.g., of the impact of Christopher Columbus on Native Americans), cohorts growing up are likely to incorporate the new beliefs as part of their common sense assumptions about early American history. Furthermore, "first experiences" are likely to be a significant source not only of knowledge of history, but of personal knowledge and personal expectations more generally. Anecdotal evidence suggests that the first social science books students read, whether Emile Durkheim's *Suicide* or Peter Berger's *Invitation to Sociology*, make an impression seldom matched by later reading. The same should be equally true in other fields and other areas of knowledge as well. This speculation goes well beyond the data presented here, but it raises questions that deserve further exploration as an attempt is made to understand not only the generational basis of historical knowledge, but generational contributions to knowledge of all kinds.

ACKNOWLEDGMENTS

The research reported here benefited greatly from the ideas and commitment of Cheryl Rieger. Important help was also received from Charlotte Steeh, Director of the 1991 Detroit Area Study, and from the students who took part in that practicum. Acknowledgment is due also to the technical section staffs of the Survey Research Center. Support for the research came primarily from a grant from the National Institute of Aging (AG08951), with earlier support from the National Science Foundation (SES-8410078) and from the University of Michigan.

REFERENCES

Andrews, F. M., Morgan, J. N., Sonquist, J. A., & Klem, L. (1973). *Multiple classification analysis.* Ann Arbor, MI: Institute for Social Research.

Baddeley, A. (1990). *Human memory: Theory and practice.* Boston: Allyn & Bacon.

Belli, R. F., Schuman, H., & Jackson, B. (in press). Autobiographical misremembering: John Dean is not alone. *Applied Cognitive Psychology.*

Clarke, D. (1990). *The Penguin encyclopedia of popular music.* London: Penguin.

Halbwachs, M. (1980). *The collective memory.* New York: Harper. (Original work published 1950)

Howard, D. S. (1943). *The WPA and federal relief policy.* New York: Russell Sage Foundation.

Karnow, S. (1983). *Vietnam: A history.* New York: Viking.

Mannheim, K. (1952). The problem of generations. In *Essays on the sociology of knowledge* (pp. 276–322). London: Routledge & Kegan Paul. (Original work published 1928)

Pennebaker, J. W. (1993). On the creation and maintenance of collective memories. *Psicologia Politica, 6,* 35–52.

Pillemer, D. B., Goldsmith, L. R., Panter, A. T., & White, S. H. (1988). Very long-term memories of the first year of college. *Journal of Experimental Psychology: Learning, Memory, and Cognition, 14,* 709–715.

Robinson, J. A. (1992). Autobiographical memory. In M. Gruneberg & P. Morris (Eds.), *Aspects of memory: Vol. 1. The practical aspects* (pp. 223–251). London: Routledge & Kegan Paul.

Rubin, D. C., Wetzler, S. E., & Nebes, R. D. (1986). Autobiographical memory across the lifespan. In D. C. Rubin (Ed.), *Autobiographical memory* (pp. 202–221). Cambridge, England: Cambridge University Press.

Ryder, N. B. (1965). The cohort as a concept in the study of social change. *American Sociological Review, 30,* 843–861.

Schuman, H., & Scott, J. (1989). Generations and collective memories. *American Sociological Review, 54,* 359–381.

Schuman, H., Rieger, C., & Guidys, V. (1994). Generations and collective memories in Lithuania. In N. Schwartz & S. Sudman (Eds.), *Autobiographical memory and the validity of retrospective reports* (pp. 313–333). New York: Springer-Verlag.

Schwartz, B. (1991). Social change and collective memory: The democratization of George Washington. *American Sociological Review, 56,* 221–236.

Scott, J., & Zac, L. (1993). Collective memories in Britain and the United States. *Public Opinion Quarterly, 57,* 315–331.

Smith, T. W. (1994). Generational differences in musical preferences. *Popular Music and Society, 18,* 43–59.

Weber, M. (1968). *Economy and society.* Berkeley, CA: University of California Press. (Original English work published 1956)

Chapter 4

Art and Remembering Traumatic Collective Events: The Case of the Spanish Civil War

Juanjo Igartua
Dario Paez
University of the Basque Country, Spain

This chapter examines the processes by which societies, using works of art, remember traumatic political events. These works of art, especially popular narrative forms such as films and novels, will play an important role in maintaining, reconstructing, and assimilating collective traumatic events such as the Spanish Civil War (SCW). It briefly summarizes what some classical authors in the field of collective memory have stated about the processes involved in forgetting, maintaining, and reconstructing this memory. Later, the chapter discusses the "natural history" of forgetting, remembering, and reconstructing traumatic events. In order to do so, it focuses analysis first on Japan and its official history concerning World War II, and second on the war in Algeria and the French films on this issue, and finally on the SCW and the films and novels that have portrayed this event. In the specific case of Spain, a more detailed, systematic, and quantitative analysis on the Civil War is included. All these results allow the study to partially confirm the existence of memory cycles every 25 years. The chapter also investigates how the contents of these films have evolved over time. Finally, it empirically shows that exposure to entertainment films with a de-dramatization and relativity content will congruently affect the beliefs and attitudes toward the Civil War.

THE SOCIAL ACTIVITY OF RECONSTRUCTION:
FREUD AND BARTLETT

Classical authors in collective memory, such as Halbwachs (1925/1975, 1950) and Bartlett (1932/1990), insist on memory's institutional basis and on the social dynamics of remembering. Freud, on the other hand, is interested in the motivational nature of forgetting: Individuals repress that which is negative, or remember it in a distorted way. Nevertheless, as Erdelyi (1990) stated, the reconstructive processes posited by Bartlett (leveling, accentuation, assimilation, and conventionalization) are very similar to Freud's repression, displacement, and condensation mechanisms. These processes of forgetting, selecting, and reconstructing allow people to adapt the memory of traumatic events to their social frames of reference, to the dominant values and beliefs. On the other hand, when insisting on its normative nature and on the fact that it is based on present-day needs, Halbwachs implicitly coincided with Freud in the fact that collective memory is biased toward forgetting that which is negative, and toward having a positive image of the past. Both Freud and Bartlett insist that forgetting, the selective omission of events, is an example of the reconstructive labor of memory. This activity of remembering is performed by means of symbolic reconstructions of the past, both under the scientific banner of history and by means of narrative/dramatic artifacts.

Consider the reconstructive processes of memory studied by Bartlett. First of all, a story told by one person to another as if it were a memory is *simplified* and *condensed*. Details are reduced and simplified. This is the equivalent of *forgetting* or *repressing* some aspects of the event. Second, some details are *retained* and *remembered*. Certain aspects are stressed always with the idea of *assimilating* them to the frame or narrative schema of that memory. Third, memory is *elaborated*, and those details that are coherent with the general idea or position transmitted by the collective memory are emphasized. In other words, some details that go down well in the general frame of the story are included. This is collective memory's reconstructive or distorting activity. The important and basic process underlying all these aforementioned phases is conventionalization. Memory adapts itself to the conventions (usage, customs, values, stereotypes, etc.) of the group that constructs this memory. People start forgetting and including things, and these transformations allow that which is remembered to be coherent with the local stereotypes and values (Allport & Postman, 1952/1977; Bartlett, 1932/1990; Erdelyi, 1990).

Examples of these processes can be seen by studying the institutional mechanisms involved in remembering traumatic historical events. In the case of Japan, their history textbooks center World War II in the confrontation with the United States and its allies. These books accept that the starting point was the attack on Pearl Harbor (condensation and simplification). This allows these books to avoid mentioning the Japanese military aggressions in Asia, which began in 1931, or the atrocities that took place during these years (e.g., the abduction and raping of Chinese and Korean women, or the massacre of entire populations of innocent people). At the same time, they amplify the importance of those battles lost against the Allies (omission and assimilation). Japan is shown as a victim and the atomic attacks on Hiroshima and Nagasaki are presented as natural catastrophes, which allow the Japanese to exorcise any resentment felt against the "American friend" (conventionalization in a frame of "subordinated patriotism to the USA" so predominant nowadays in Japan). Only now, 50 years after the war is over, are people beginning to learn about these crimes, and in fact some Japanese leaders have publicly asked for forgiveness for the pain and sorrow beset on these Asian countries (Halff, 1991; Postel-Vinay, 1991). In Japan after the war, as in Germany at the end of the Nazi era, an important amnesty was handed out. In history textbooks the war era was declared taboo. If this is linked to what has been previously said, it becomes obvious how the reconstructive processes of collective memory are somewhat similar to Freud's repression and censorship phenomena.

Another way of viewing this situation would be to state that memory is orientated toward offering a normative view of the past that guides present-day behaviors: positive for the ingroup, negative for the outgroup. Memory allows one to defend the positive image of the group or collectively using social identity's defense mechanisms retrospectively.

Finally, Bartlett stressed that commemorations, rituals, and the group's needs and interests would be the affective and cognitive basis of social memory. This memory is developed starting from a collective affective activation in the schematic frame of rituals and social cycles (Bartlett, 1932/1990). Works of art are considered to be cultural artifacts, symbolic rituals of commemorations that allow social memory to have an external cognitive and affective frame.

THE SYMBOLIC RECONSTRUCTION OF THE PAST

Collective memory does not only exist in the individuals, but that in fact it is located in cultural artifacts. Analyzing the contents of cultural creations, as for example films, one may see how a social group symbolically reconstructs its past in order to confront traumatic events for which it is responsible (Paez & Basabe, 1993).

Using the example of the French film productions and the Algerian war, it can be seen that the external symbolic reconstruction of collective traumatic events has a number of phases. The Algerian war lasted from 1954 to 1962. For 8 years, this issue was taboo. Only politically and military censored films were allowed during these years on this topic. In this first phase above all there is *silence* (which was fought among others by critics such as Godard and his ambiguous satire *The Little Soldier*) and/or a *conventional version* of the issue that ignores the negative events. Following this era came a period of *amnesia,* or forgetfulness. Until 1972, a 10-year period, there were no direct references to the war, which officially did not exist or was not seen as a real war. A film such as *The Battle of Algiers,* which is in favor of the Algerian Front de Libération Nationale (FLN), was filmed in 1966 in Italy, but was censored in France until 1981. In 1972, an *individual memory* starts to emerge that stresses the subject's personal features and forgets the lost cause. In that year three films showed the most hidden aspects of the war and how normal people could turn into assassins. The French waited until 1986 to see more films produced on this issue. Nevertheless, in 1982, a conservative filmmaker, Schoendorffer, produced a film (*The Captain's Honor*) showing the impact of the war but in which tortures were just minor errors in a frame tending to highly evaluate French military honor. This film represented the final period: *idealized memory,* in which the social group's actions are positively evaluated. It was only 30 years after the war finished that Alain Tavernier produced a documentary on the Algerian war (*The War With No Name*), which focused on the soldiers' individual tragedies (Joassin, 1992). In the same vein, the monument built to commemorate the Vietnam War also stresses individual participation while it obviates the causes and sociopolitical reasons for the war. The memorial is a ritual symbol that expresses the contradictory collective memory of a "dirty" war dividing the country (Wagner-Pacifici & Schwartz, 1991).

Bertrand de Muñoz (1993) conducted a study on the quantitative and content production of novels referring to the SCW. It allows an illustration of the following evolution in the artistic expression of a traumatic event. There are six great periods. The first one lasts the 3 years of the Civil War (1936–1939). During this period, there are many dramatic novels and articles on the war from the standpoint of both sides: "During the fight there were some 50 titles, some better than others but all of them too close to the events to produce a great book" (p. 48). In a second period, the immediate postwar years, the novels portray a *conventional view* of the "winners," and a self-justification and praise on behalf of the side that "won." A third period would be the years from 1950 to 1960, which is a phase of amnesia with a scarce literary production: "The fifties and the beginning of the sixties, the years of objective realism and of a scarcer number of titles but evidently of a better quality" (p. 62). The fourth period is the dictatorship's last decade. Due to a less rigid censorship, some novels that start giving another version than that of the Franco regime start to emerge: "After the new 1966 Press Law novels will have another tone and argument quite different from the previous ones due to the concession of certain liberties and because of the three decades which separate the novels from what they are referring to" (p. 78). The fifth period comprises democracy's first years, it is the time to recover the critical memory toward the traumatic event. The Republican point of view strongly surfaces, and is shown as a counterpoint to the Franquist exaltations of the second period: "During the first stages of democracy in Spain there was a return to the features of the immediate post-war years with an eagerness to self-justify and praise their own side (this time the Republicans) which were very similar to those employed by the Franquists in their time" (p. 22). The sixth and final period begins in the 1980s. An idealized and distanced memory of the war appears. The dramatic nature of what is being told has been lost, and this is translated into a less affectively charged and a more ahistorical memory. Sometimes the war will only be a background in which to include a story or individual drama, not a collective one. As Bertrand de Muñoz (1993) stated, "The last period emerges at the beginning of the 1980's with novels in which in many cases the Spanish War is not shown as an addition of deeply felt events. The need to express one's point of view, to state what one feels about such cruel events has nearly disappeared. This fight of brothers against brothers is now just a remote memory, it is just a background in which eternal passions operate, it transcends history by way of mythification" (p. 14).

In general, although this must be taken with some caution, the semiotic instruments used on collective traumas first of all deny and later on give a conventional view of the situation. After this situation, and using a Freudian notion, they "forget." This is followed by a Durkheim phase of positive reconstruction of the past. In the case of unpopular events, which may divide the collectivity, the memory of the group members who took part in the event is put forward, and their individual tragedy is accepted. The sociopolitical cause of the trauma is forgotten.

It may seem likely that denial and "affective anesthesia" combined with nonsystematized intrusive memories and with assimilation and elaboration, acceptance of the traumatic past and stressing the positive aspects, may not only be a psychological process but also may be studied as artistic productions, at the level of collective symbolic artifacts (Horowitz, 1986; Pennebaker, 1993).

THE MEMORY CYCLE

Collective memories are maintained even as years and generations go by. Pennebaker (1993), after studying various examples, found that approximately every 20–30 years individuals and societies look back and reconstruct their past. The factors behind these 20- to 30-year memory cycles are the following:

1. The existence of the necessary psychological distance that remembering a collective or individual traumatic event requires. Time may soothe and lessen the pain that remembering a traumatic event produces.

2. The necessary accumulation of social resources in order to undergo the commemoration activities. These resources can usually be obtained during one's middle age. The events are commemorated when the generation that suffered them has the money and power to commemorate them.

3. The most important events in one's life take place when one is 12 or 25 years old. When these people grow older they may remember the events that happened during this period (chapter 1, this volume, by Pennebaker & Banasik).

A fourth explanation may be included that is apt in the commemoration of negative events:

4. The sociopolitical repression will cease to act after 20 or 30 years because those directly responsible for the repression, war, and so on, have either socially or physically disappeared.

This last explanation is even more important in dictatorship regimes. But remember that these four explanations are not mutually exclusive.

Now consider the evidence in favor of the 20- to 30-year memory cycle in the case of the films on the Spanish Civil War (1936–1939). Before beginning with this issue, note that until 1949 there was still guerrilla warfare going on in some parts of the countryside and the war did not really end until this last date.

Ripoll i Freixes (1992) studied those films in which the SCW is the main issue. His book presents some basic data with which to identify each film: the year it was produced, its nationality, and a synthesis of the screenplay. This information aids in answering two very important questions: What evolution or change has there been in the number of films on the SCW from 1940 to 1991? And, how has the image of the SCW evolved or changed in these films?

Ripoll i Freixes stated that a total of 66 Spanish and/or co-produced films (excluding short films, television series, and documentaries) on the topic of the Spanish Civil War were made during the period from 1940 to 1991. In order to evaluate the evolution in the number of films on the SCW, the total number of films produced during these years must be taken into account in order to obtain a percentage to allow further study on this evolution. On the basis of data supplied by Ripoll i Freixes (1992) and García Fernández (1992), the percentage of films on the SCW has been calculated in relation to the total number of films during the period from 1940 to 1991. Table 4.1 and Fig. 4.1 show this data.

As can be seen in Fig. 4.1, there are two periods in which the percentage of films on the SCW is at its peak. First of all during the period from 1940

TABLE 4.1
Total Number of Spanish and Co-produced Films: Global Data
and Data on the Films on the Spanish Civil War from 1940 to 1991

Period	Total Number of Films (1)	Number of Films on the SCW (2)	% of Films on the SCW out of the Total (3)
1940–1944	199	9 (13.6%)	4.52
1945–1949	198	2 (3.0%)	1.01
1950–1954	242	7 (10.6%)	2.89
1955–1959	345	5 (7.6%)	1.44
1960–1964	496	4 (6.1%)	0.80
1965–1969	671	7 (10.6%)	1.04
1970–1974	528	5 (7.6%)	0.95
1975–1979	533	8 (12.1%)	1.50
1980–1984	575	5 (7.6%)	0.87
1985–1989	316	11 (16.7%)	3.48
1990–1991	106	3 (4.5%)	2.83
TOTAL	4,209	66 (100%)	1.56

Note: Column 1 Source: García Fernández (1992); column 2 Source: Ripoll i Freixes (1992); column 3: On the basis of García Fernández (1992) and Ripoll i Freixes (1992).

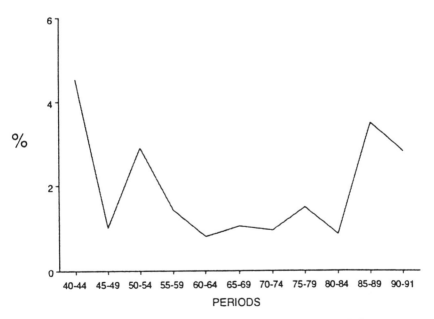

FIG. 4.1. Evolution in the percentage of films (nondocumentaries) produced between 1940 and 1991 on the topic of the SCW (Spanish productions and co-productions with other countries).

to 1944, a period corresponding with the postwar years. And second, there is an increase in the number of films from 1975 (Franco died and the beginning of the democratic process) onward. Moreover, there is a period of prolonged "amnesia" covering from 1950 to 1975 (a 25-year span).

A second type of analysis of a more qualitative nature shows how the image of the SCW has changed in these films. A coding frame was built and applied to each of the 66 films. The codes for analysis were the following: Is the repression/civil war justified or legitimized? (Yes/No); point of view (those who won or those who were defeated); affective tone (none, scarce, strong); view held of the Franco and his supporters (negative, ambivalent, or positive); view held of the defeated or Republicans (negative, ambivalent, or positive); do they stress the causes? (not at all, somewhat, a lot), do they stress the roles or characters portrayed in the film? (not at all, somewhat, a lot). The unit of analysis was the written synthesis of each film as mentioned by Ripoll i Freixes (1992). The content analysis was performed independently by two blind judges. In order to establish the reliability of this analysis, the percentage of agreement among judges was obtained as 69.5%. The next phase was to resolve together all possible discrepancies in the coding in order to recount frequencies and perform the subsequent analyses.

The first element analyzed was the evolution in these films of the justification of the repression/civil war. As time went on, there was a tendency toward delegitimizing the war. Justification is stronger in those films produced immediately after the end of the war, whereas delegitimization is stronger in those films produced just before and following Franco's death. These results are shown in Table 4.2.

In relation to the point of view adopted in these films, as years go by the Republican side gains importance and protagonism. The first films on the SCW tended to reflect the Franco and his supporters' (winners) point of view. It is only after the dictatorship has ended that the losers' point of view starts to appear in these films. The image of the winners and losers of the SCW evolves in different directions during the course of time. As years go by, the image of the Franco roles or characters is more negative, and on the other hand the Republican characters are more positive. Results are shown in Table 4.3.

In relation to the affective tone found in these films, this evolves significantly during the course of time. Those films produced closer to the end of the SCW refer to the war in a more dramatic way. As time passes, this dramatism is lower ($r = -.26$, $p = .03$) and there is more relevance attached to the sociopolitical causes of the repression ($r = -.26$, $p = .03$). As time passes, the affective distancing from the event allows the people to better analyze the context in which the war started. People want to know the causes behind what happened.

TABLE 4.2
Legitimation or Justification of the Repression/Civil War,
and the Films' Point of View on the SCW (Horizontal Percentages)

Periods	Justification of the SCW (% who answer "yes")	Point of View	
		Winners	Losers
1940–1944	88.9	100	0
1945–1949	50.0	50.0	50.0
1950–1954	85.7	71.4	28.6
1955–1959	80.0	100	0
1960–1964	50.0	100	0
1965–1969	71.4	71.4	28.6
1970–1974	20.0	80.0	20.0
1975–1979	37.5	12.5	87.5
1980–1984	60.0	20.0	80.0
1985–1989	27.3	27.3	72.7
1990–1991	0	0	100
TOTAL ($n = 66$)	54.5	57.6	42.4
Contrast statistic	$\chi^2(10) = 19.48$, $p = .03$ $r = -.45$, $p = .0001$	$\chi^2(10) = 33.19$, $p = .0002$ $r = .58$, $p = .0000$	

TABLE 4.3
View of the "Winning" and "Losing" Characters
in the Films on the SCW (Horizontal Percentages)

Periods	View of the "Winners"				View of the "Losers"			
	Negative (1)	Ambivalent (2)	Positive (3)	Mean	Negative (1)	Ambivalent (2)	Positive (3)	Mean
1940–1944	0	11.1	88.9	2.89	100	0	0	1.00
1945–1949	50.0	0	50.0	2.00	50.0	0	50.0	2.00
1950–1954	14.3	14.3	71.4	2.57	71.4	14.3	14.3	1.42
1955–1959	0	0	100	3.00	80.0	20.0	0	1.20
1960–1964	0	25.0	75.0	2.75	50.0	50.0	0	1.50
1965–1969	14.3	28.6	57.1	2.42	42.9	42.9	14.3	1.71
1970–1974	20.0	60.0	20.0	2.00	0	80.0	20.0	2.20
1975–1979	87.5	12.5	0	1.12	0	25.0	75.0	2.75
1980–1984	60.0	20.0	20.0	1.60	0	60.0	40.0	2.40
1985–1989	54.5	45.5	0	1.45	9.1	54.5	36.4	2.27
1990–1991	100	0	0	1.00	0	33.3	66.7	2.66
TOTAL ($n = 66$)	34.8	22.7	42.4	2.07	37.9	34.8	27.3	1.89
Contrast statistics	$\chi^2(20) = 51.43$, $p = .0001$ $r = -.67$, $p = .0000$				$\chi^2(20) = 50.17$, $p = .0002$ $r = .64$, $p = .0000$			

In summary, on the basis of the analysis of the films produced in Spain from 1940 to 1991 on the topic of the SCW, the image of the war shifts dramatically. In the immediate postwar years the films stress the winners' point of view. These films justify the war and there is a stronger affective tone or dramatism. Those that took part in the war on the Franco side are positively evaluated while the Republicans are negatively evaluated. This biased vision of the SCW evolves over time in the same way that the government's policy of "reconciliation and forgiveness" for both sides also grew stronger. The turning point in the image held of the SCW was 1975, Franco's death. The beginning of the democratic process implied the emergence of the "losers' " point of view. There was a delegitimization of the war. The Republican side started to appear as the main actor in these films. The Franco elements were seen as negative roles and the Republicans as positive. The causes of the conflict were stressed more than ever before.

CULTURAL ARTIFACTS, MEMORY PROCESSES, AND DEVELOPMENT OF BELIEFS AND ATTITUDES

Stressing the idea that memory is a collective process underscores the fact that semiotic objects (such as monuments, novels, television series, and films) help to mediate and are an external support for memory and forgetting. Vygotsky's sociohistorical theory (Paez & Adrián, 1993; Vygotsky, 1930/1979; Wertsch, 1985, 1988, 1991) is a theoretical approach stressing the importance of the semiotic instruments as "tools" with which to develop the higher psychological processes. An artistic creation (especially of the narrative type: novels and films) is a semiotic instrument aimed at affective and cognitive development (Vygotsky, 1925/1972). Miall (1989), a cognitive psychologist, also stressed the idea that art (in a broader sense) has as one of its functions that of inducing cognitive development. This author stated that the artistic or dramatic accounts allow individuals to redefine, modify, or question schemas (thought structures that refer to oneself and also to past affective experiences). The artistic semiotic instruments (among others, television series, and films) will not only "entertain" people, but will also develop the higher psychological processes (especially memory, emotions, and thought and evaluation structures such as beliefs and attitudes). From this perspective, and in this particular case, television series and films will be semiotic structures that impel or reinforce certain representations of the SCW.

In this research, it might be expected that the development or cultivation (Gerbner, Gross, Morgan, & Signorelli, 1980, 1990) of a certain notion on that event in the mass media (e.g., a positive image of the Republicans and the delegitimization of the SCW) would imply assimilating those ideas. Although this approach may seem very mechanistic, it does not overlook the fact that the impact would be mediated by a series of processes such as the level of cognitive production derived from these stimuli (which is at the same time related to the relevance or the subject's personal implication with the topic), the affective impact produced by the film or series, and the realism and credibility of the message (Flora & Maibach, 1990; Iyengar & Kinder, 1985; Oskamp, 1991; Perloff, 1985, 1993; Petty & Cacioppo, 1986; Potter, 1986). Moreover, variables such as previous and direct experience ("first hand") with the object or the issue to which the media refers (in this case the SCW) will mitigate the impact (Pratkanis & Aronson, 1994).

A research project was conducted (1994) to test the aforementioned ideas. Participants were 162 psychology students (74.1% women, 25.9% men with ages ranging from 20 to 46 years and a mean of 24.9 years). The participants had to fill in a questionnaire in their own classroom with the following scales and indexes. First of all, there was a scale measuring *clarity of the memory.* This scale was formed by 5 items with an internal consistency of .86. An example of these items is the following: Do you have clear images, vivid visual memories of the Spanish Civil War (answering format: 1 = not at all, to 5 = many)? Second, data on the *use or exposure of/to mass media* was obtained. Subjects were asked to state if they had or had not seen three television series based on the SCW and the postwar years. These series had been shown on television more than once during the 1980s and 1990s. The subjects were also asked if they had seen any of a list of 30 films produced from 1976 to 1994. In this list there were 18 films based on the SCW, and the remaining 12 were movies with great impact that had been box office successes (e.g., *Philadelphia*). These decoys were presented in order to make the aim of the study not so evident. Three exposures to the media indexes were created: total number of series the subjects had seen (range from 0 to 3, $M = .86$), total number of movies seen by the subjects (range 0 to 18, $M = 2.89$), and a global index obtained from adding up the number of movies and television series. Also included was a scale to evaluate the attitudes and beliefs on the SCW. A semantic differential made up of 5 pairs of items was used to evaluate the attitude toward the SCW. Examples of these items are the following: "the SCW a pleasant–unpleasant, close–far away, etc. event" (answering format = 1 to 7). In a first subscale on "general opinion about remembering the SCW," 10 items were included on if it was suitable or not to forget what had happened during the war, on the opinion held of each of the participants in the war, and on the emotions attached to remembering the war. Examples of these items are the following: "it is better to forget all that happened during the war and the postwar years," "when I think about or remember the civil war and postwar years I do so with sadness." A second subscale consisted of 7 items on the "beliefs on the causes of the SCW." Examples of items include: "The civil war started because the Franco military had no confidence in the Republic," "One of the main causes of the SCW was that the population had lost its confidence in the institutions, in the Republic." Finally, another 21-item subscale was included on the beliefs on the consequences of the war. Examples of these items are the following: "During the SCW deaths and shootings especially affected those who had lost," "In most families there were a great deal of personal losses and deaths caused by the SCW." In all the subscales, subjects had to answer using a Likert-type scale ranging from 1 = total disagreement to 7 = total agreement. A principal components factor analysis was conducted on each of these scales and subscales, extracting the following dimensions (due to space limits only a synthesis of these is presented in Table 4.4).

Remember that the people who took part in the study were university students and so did not have a "direct" but only a "mediated" experience with the SCW. This experience was obtained by what they had learned in school, by the generational transmission of facts, and by those facts presented by the mass media on the SCW. Both the television series and movies were produced from 1976 to 1991, and as in the qualitative study it is in this period when the SCW is seen through the eyes of the defeated side, stressing the causes of the war. On this basis, it can be hypothesized that more exposure to these productions would be associated with a stronger agreement with the attitude and belief dimensions on the SCW, which are congruent with the image shown in these movies and series. Due to its correlational nature, a caveat must be stated: If the posited association is found, it would be due to a "self-selection" process in which those subjects with a certain previous attitude toward the event may expose themselves to those movies or series that confirm their beliefs.

As a way of evaluating the role the mass media play in the processes of memory and cultivation of beliefs and attitudes toward the SCW, these processes are linked to the indexes of exposure to television series and movies on the SCW (these results are shown in Table 4.5). The first result is that there is a positive association between seeing series or movies on the SCW and the clarity of memory. Moreover, exposure to these cultural products is associated with stating that remembering the war produces negative self-reference emotions (sadness, guilt, shame, etc.). Having seen these cultural products is also linked to thinking that the conflict was a great collective disaster because it caused the country to split into two sides while also producing Spain's cultural, economic, and political isolation from the rest of the world. People also think this event has influenced the present-day political situation.

On the other hand, and referring only to the television series, those who have been exposed to more of these series tend to disagree with the idea that "it is better to forget what happened during the war and the postwar years." They also show less ambivalence toward those who took part in the war and have a more positive image of the Republicans who

TABLE 4.4
Dimensions of Beliefs and Attitudes Toward the SCW

Scale of Attitudes and Beliefs About the Spanish Civil War	Number of Items in Each Factor	Explained Variance	Mean in the Factor[a]
Attitude toward the SCW:			
A positive and nonimportant event	3	38.9%	1.49
A distant and incomprehensible event	2	27.8%	4.27
General opinions:			
It is better to forget what happened during the war and postwar years	2	22.1%	3.31
Ambivalence toward the participants and negative image of the Republicans	2	14.9%	3.69
Nostalgia and positive view of the past	3	13.4%	1.86
Negative self-reference emotions when remembering the war	3	12.0%	4.25
Beliefs about the causes:			
Franquist military had no confidence in the Republic. A climate of conflict	4	26.3%	4.18
The population had no confidence in the Republic	3	22.8%	3.14
Beliefs about the consequences:			
Collective disaster (death, misery)	4	17.9%	6.16
Social demobilization (staying away from politics) during the postwar years	5	11.3%	4.18
The Republicans were the main victims	4	9.9%	3.97
The country split up. Political, economic, and cultural isolation during the postwar years	3	6.4%	5.55
The past conflict has determined present-day politics	3	6.2%	5.25
Frustration, disillusion, and despair among the Republicans	1	5.7%	5.29
Climate of nonconfidence among the population during the postwar years	1	4.8%	5.56

[a]The items that formed a single factor were added up and the result of this sum (simple not weighted) was divided among the total number of items in that factor. If an item had factorial weights in more than one factor we included it in the one in which it had a stronger weight. In other words, a higher score in each of the dimensions reflects more agreement with this dimension. In the two attitude dimensions a low score is equivalent to evaluating the SCW, respectively, as a "negative and important," and "close and comprehensible" event.

are perceived as the main victims of the conflict. Moreover, having seen more movies on the SCW is related to believing that what started the war was the lack of confidence the Franco military had in the Republic. These subjects also believe that the population's social demobilization and staying away from politics was a consequence of the war, and among the "defeated" there was a feeling of great frustration, disillusion, and despair.

TABLE 4.5

Mass Media, Clarity of Memory, and Cultivation of
Attitudes and Beliefs on the SCW (Pearson Correlations)

Clarity of Memory, Attitudes, and Beliefs About the SCW	Having Been Exposed to the Mass Media		
	TV Series	Films	Global Index
Clarity of the memory about the SCW	.19**	.39***	.37***
Attitude toward the SCW:			
A positive and nonimportant event	−.09	−.05	−.07
A distant and incomprehensible event	−.07	−.03	−.05
General opinions:			
It is better to forget what happened during the war and postwar years	−.17*	−.07	−.11†
Ambivalence towards the participants and negative image of the Republicans	−.25**	−.03	−.09
Nostalgia and positive view of the past	−.07	−.03	−.05
Negative self-reference emotions when remembering the war	.11†	.20**	.19**
Beliefs about the causes:			
Franquist military had no confidence in the Republic. A climate of conflict	−.00	.14*	.11†
The population had no confidence in the Republic	−.01	−.08	−.06
Beliefs about the consequences:			
Collective disaster (death, misery)	.16*	.16*	.18**
Social demobilization (staying away from politics) during the postwar years	.02	.12†	.10†
The Republicans were the main victims	.19**	.04	.09
The country split up. Political, economic, and cultural isolation during the postwar years	.26***	.24***	.28***
The past conflict has determined present-day politics	.13*	.22**	.22**
Frustration, disillusion, and despair among the Republicans	.02	.12†	.10†
Climate of nonconfidence among the population during the postwar years	.07	.07	.08

Note: A higher score in each of the dimensions reflects more agreement with this dimension. In the two attitude dimensions a low score is equivalent to evaluating the SCW, respectively, as a "negative and important," and a "close and comprehensible" event.
†$p < .10$. *$p < .05$. **$p < .01$. ***$p < .001$.

Results show that it is plausible to conceive the mass media, especially those using a narrative format (films and series), as cultural artifacts that may exercise an influence in maintaining collective memory and contributing toward the cultivation and reinforcement of certain beliefs on events that have had a great affective impact on specific collectivities or social groups. For example, it is known that Oliver Stone's *JFK* played an important role in maintaining the idea of a coordinated plot in Kennedy's assassination. On the other hand, *Schindler's List* also had a great impact on public opinion, alerting it to the dangers of the Nazi revival and recovering the memory of the collective trauma produced by the Holocaust. In this case, the Spanish Civil War, seeing movies and series that are generally critical of the past helps to maintain the emotions felt toward the collective event. This is an element that Bartlett (1932/1990) considered as central in the persistence of collective memories. It also reinforces the beliefs on the view that the war was a collective disaster, on the impact the past has on the present and on the need to remember. Finally, it also gives us a positive image of the losers and is critical toward the past official history.

A final research project analyzed the impact of three movies based on events of the SCW had on the attitudes and beliefs toward this historical event. The previous study showed that there is a close association between having seen television series and movies on the SCW and the attitudes and beliefs toward this event. Nevertheless, one of the possible explanations for this effect could be that a self-selection process had taken place: People with certain beliefs would seek entertainment products that confirm their stance on that issue. In accordance with an experimental methodology, this idea may be dismissed due to the fact that subjects are randomly assigned to one condition or another (seeing one film or another, or being part of the control group). This guarantees the group's homogeneity from the very start.

In this new study, participants (psychology students with a mean age of 25 years) were randomly assigned to three experimental conditions (three different movies were used, and 26–30 subjects per group) and a fourth group remained as a control group (it did not see any film and was composed of 76 students). Movies were chosen on the basis of three criteria: being a recent production, having been a commercial success in Spain (which is an indirect sign of acceptance by the Spanish public), and on the basis of the image it showed of the Spanish Civil War. The movies were released in 1984 (the film entitled *Las Bicicletas son para el Verano*), in 1985 (*La Vaquilla*), and in 1990 (*Ay, Carmela*). The films were analyzed by nine judges who had already seen them in order to determine the image of the war, the position toward the actors or characters, and so forth, in each film. A coding system similar to the one used before in the qualitative documentary analysis of the movies was employed. The only difference was that it included a question on the "degree of perceived realism" of the events that take place in the film (using an intensity scale ranging from 1 = not at all, to 5 = a great deal). From the data obtained, it was obvious that there were differences among the three films.

The first film, *La Vaquilla*, did not justify the war (this is what 8 out of 9 judges thought) and it did not clearly state the point of view of either side in the war (4 judges thought it adopted the standpoint of the Franquists, 3 thought it was the Republicans' point of view, and 2 stated that it used arguments from both sides). There was an ambivalent image of the Franquists (7 out of 9 judges thought so) and of the Republicans (8 out of 9), and the image of the war was also ambivalent (5 out of 9 judges said so). On the other hand, the affective weight attributed to this movie, its perceived realism, and the fact of stressing the causes or sociohistorical context were low (in a 5-point scale the means were 2.44, 2.11, and 2.00, respectively). This movie delegitimizes the war but at the same time offers an ambiguous treatment of it, with little realism and without stressing the sociohistorical events that led to the war. It also offers an ambivalent image of both sides. The fact that La Vaquilla is a comedy may explain its low affective weight. This film is an example of a de-dramatized and individualistic form of remembering. There is not a positive homogeneous view of the Franco side, but there is a similarity between "winners and losers," both of them worked together in helping the national disaster take place.

The nine judges found only small differences between the other two films (Ay, Carmela and Las Bicicletas son para el Verano). Both delegitimize the war, which is perceived as something negative (8 out of 9 judges thought so of Ay, Carmela, and 7 out of 9 of Las Bicicletas son para el Verano). The movies adopt the Republicans' ("losers") point of view (9 out of 9 for Ay, Carmela, and 8 out of 9 for Las Bicicletas son para el Verano). There was a positive image of the Republicans (8 and 6 judges thought so for each of the films). The image held of the Franquists ("winners") was negative (8 and 7 judges agreed with this statement). Both movies were perceived as being realistic (mean scores were 3.88 and 4.00, respectively). They mentioned the sociohistorical factors leading to the war (3.22 and 3.88), and its affective weight or dramatism was high (4.55 and 4.33). In general terms, these two films share a similar approach to the SCW, although they are quite different types of films. Ay, Carmela is a comedy with a tragic end (the main female role is shot by a Franquist when she shouts out in favor of the Republic). On the other hand, Las Bicicletas son para el Verano is a drama with an "open" end (the film finishes at the end of the war but without such a dramatic scene as the one found in Ay, Carmela). The characters found in Las Bicicletas are a "normal" family with very down to earth and nonheroic situations (this is not the case of Ay, Carmela). Summarizing, La Vaquilla is in favor of a reconciliation between both sides and tends to foster forgetting and getting the past over with. Ay, Carmela and Las Bicicletas share a negative view of the SCW and a positive stance toward the "losers" (Republicans). This side is seen as the victim of the national disaster. Nevertheless, these last two movies differ in their dramatic weight and the "exceptional" versus "normal" nature of the characters in the film.

Two versions of the questionnaire were built, one for the experimental groups and another for the control group. The attitude and belief scale on the SCW was included in both due to the fact that this was the main dependent variable. The experimental groups' questionnaire had additional scales in order to measure the impact's mediating processes: the affective impact, identification with the characters, and degree of elaboration or reflection on the SCW while seeing the film. Watson's Positive Affect and Negative Affect Schedule (PANAS) scale (Watson, Clark, & Tellegen, 1988) was used to evaluate the impact on the subject's mood. It consists of two dimensions: positive affect and negative affect. The scale was completed before the film was shown and immediately after (internal consistency: for positive affect, .81 in the pretest, and .86 in the posttest; for negative affect, .76 in the pretest, and .91 in the posttest). Identification with the characters was evaluated by using a scale consisting of 17 items with an internal consistency of .93. The following are some examples of these items: "I have affectively implicated myself with the characters' feelings," "I have had the impression of really living what was being shown in the film." Response format ranged from 1 = not at all, to 5 = totally.

In order to evaluate the degree of elaboration or reflection on the SCW while seeing the film, a 5-item scale was used with an internal consistency of .77. An example of these items is the following: "I have thought about the Spanish Civil War." Responses ranged from 1 = not at all, to 5 = totally. These two last scales were presented immediately after seeing the films.

The following tables show that each film had a different impact on the attitudes and beliefs toward the SCW. This difference is especially visible when comparing the film that takes an "ambivalent and re-conciliation" stance (*La Vaquilla*) and the one that holds a positive but dramatic image of the "losers" (*Ay, Carmela*).

The data shown in Table 4.6 indicate that those individuals who saw the most ambivalent film (*La Vaquilla*) tend to reject a fatalist and dramatic vision of the SCW. These participants disagree with the idea that there was great social demobilization and a climate of distrust among the population as a consequence of the war. They also disagree with the idea that the main victims of the war were the Republicans. They also think that the Republicans did not suffer at the end of the war frustration, disillusion, and despair. There is more ambivalence toward those who took part in the war, and a more negative image of the "losers" (i.e., "there were neither good guys or bad guys"). These participants are also more skeptical of the idea that the war determined the present-day political situation, and also tend to reject the idea that the memories of the conflict produce in them self-reference negative emotions (such as sadness, guilt, or shame).

Those who saw the most dramatic film (*Ay, Carmela*) tend to express a more negative attitude toward the war and think that it was a close and understandable event. There is a more positive stance toward the "losers" and less ambivalence toward those who took part in the conflict. They also

TABLE 4.6
Differential Impact of Each Film on the Attitudes
and Beliefs on the SCW (Pearson Correlations)

Attitudes and Beliefs About the SCW	Film 1	Film 2	Film 3
Attitude toward the SCW:			
A positive and nonimportant event	−.03	−.11†	.00
A distant and incomprehensible event	.08	−.17*	.03
General opinions:			
It is better to forget what happened during the war and postwar years	−.06	−.02	.11†
Ambivalence toward the participants and negative image of the Republicans	.19**	−.16*	.05
Nostalgia and positive view of the past	−.06	.00	.01
Negative self-reference emotions when remembering the war	−.10†	.17*	.05
Beliefs about the causes:			
Franquist military had no confidence in the Republic. A climate of conflict	−.02	.13*	−.19**
The population had no confidence in the Republic	−.04	.01	−.06
Beliefs about the consequences:			
Collective disaster (death, misery)	−.04	.08	.07
Social demobilization (staying away from politics) during the postwar years	−.11†	.03†	−.03
The Republicans were the main victims	−.10†	0?	.05
The country split up. Political, economic, and cultural isolation during the postwar years	−.07	−.13*	−.04
The past conflict has determined present-day politics	−.23***	.18*	.01
Frustration, disillusion, and despair among the Republicans	−.11†	.06	.15*
Climate of nonconfidence among the population during the postwar years	−.15*	−.01	.16*

Note: Film 1: *La Vaquilla*; Film 2: *Ay, Carmela*; Film 3: *Las Bicicletas son para el Verano*. Each experimental condition was coded as either 1 (having seen the film) or 0 (not having seen it, which includes the rest of the experimental conditions including the control). This allowed us to evaluate each film's differential effect. In other words, a positive correlation means that those who saw the film had a higher than average mean, a stronger agreement with the belief dimensions (evaluating the SCW, respectively, as a "positive and insignificant" or "far away and incomprehensible" event).
†$p < .10$. *$p < .05$. **$p < .01$. ***$p < .001$.

share the idea that remembering the SCW or just thinking about it produces self-reference negative emotions. These subjects also express a higher agreement with the idea that it was the Franquist military lack of confidence in the Republic and the climate of political conflict that led to the war. Finally, they also agree with the idea that the conflict has determined the political situation nowadays, but they tend to reject the idea that this event led to a split in the country and to political, economic, and social isolation in the postwar years. Those who saw this film share a negative and catastrophic image of the Civil War.

The third film (*Las Bicicletas son para el Verano*), which offered a negative and dramatic vision of the SCW from a "normal" family's point of view, and without much dramatism, had less impact in the attitudes and beliefs on the conflict. Those subjects who saw this film agreed with the statement that "it is better to forget what happened during the war and postwar years," and reject the idea that it was the Franco military lack of confidence in the Republic that caused the war. They also believe that as a consequence of the war the Republicans were frustrated, disillusioned, and in despair. They think that after the war there was a climate of lack of confidence among the population. They had a negative vision of the war although they did not have a global explanation for the event and they favored forgetting this event.

In relation to the mediating processes, it was observed that a low impact of the films on attitudes and beliefs was associated with participants' low affective involvement with these films. On the other hand, a high affective induction (of a negative mood) and a stronger identification with the characters depicted in the films is linked to a stronger agreement with beliefs and attitudes congruent with the film's content. Moreover, in the most dramatic film (*Ay, Carmela*) there was a positive relation between negative mood and cognitive reflection ($r = .52$, $p < .001$, $N = 30$). In other words, an affective interest in the topic is linked to more cognitive reflection, and cognitive reflection is linked to a stronger impact on attitudes and beliefs (Igartua & Paez, 1995).

DISCUSSION AND CONCLUSIONS

In accordance with the idea of the existence of 20- to 30-year cycles in remembering events, 20 to 30 years after the end of the SCW (established in 1949, which is when the last actions of the rural guerrilla took place) there is an increase in the number of films produced on the topic of the SCW. This increase coincides with the biological and social disappearance of those responsible for the negative collective event. Although this "biological" fact is of utmost importance, it cannot be ruled out that those other factors mentioned by Pennebaker (1993) were not important in this specific situation. In relation to the content of the films on the SCW, as the years pass, there is a higher cognitive and affective distancing from the collective catastrophe, there is an increase in the ambivalent view of this event and more interest in understanding the real causes of why the event took place. With regard to the impact of having seen films and series that are critical toward the past, having been "exposed" to them helps maintain certain emotions toward the event. This is a central tenet in Bartlett's (1932/1990) idea of why collective memories are maintained. It also reinforces beliefs on the nature of the event having been a collective catastrophe, on the impact of the past on the present, and on the need to remember. Finally, there is positive view of the "losers" and a critical stance toward the official past.

The potential impact of popular works of art in influencing the collective memory of events was experimentally demonstrated among students who viewed one of three SCW-relevant movies. Those who saw the most ambivalent and de-dramatizing film shared a minimized vision of this event, they disagreed with the idea that due to the war there was isolation, greed, frustration, and lack of confidence among the population. They tended to disagree with the idea that the Republicans were the main victims, and were more ambivalent toward all those who took part in the conflict. Moreover, they disagreed with the "impact of the past on present days" (that the war has determined present-day politics), and remembering the war produced in them less negative emotions such as sadness, guilt, or shame. As an external semiotic mechanism, this type of work of art is effective in producing a de-dramatization and distancing from the event both cognitive and affectively.

The film depicting a more negative and critical view of the war from the point of view of a middle-class family and with a small amount of dramatic impact provoked in the subjects less change in their attitudes and beliefs toward the war. Moreover, although the subjects had a negative vision of the war, they did not agree with a sociopolitical explanation of the war and tried to forget this collective event. These results coincide with the opinion that a Spanish film critic has of *Las Bicicletas son para el Verano*: "One phrase finally defines the cinematographical nature of this biased and false version. The main actor, the head of the family, is the character who expresses it, when referring to the war he states: 'I think that in the end nobody will win.' This character . . . forgets and wants us also to forget that those who started the war, kept it going and finally won, and their allies, did win, and they won a lot" (Ripoll i Freixes, 1992, p. 158).

Finally, those experimental participants exposed to the film that offered a more dramatic vision of the war showed a more negative attitude toward the war and thought it was closer to them and could understand it better. This film produced a more positive attitude toward the "losers" and less ambivalence toward those who took part in the conflict. Remembering the SCW produced self-referent negative emotions. On the other hand, they stated more agreement with the sociopolitical causes of the war. Finally those subjects who saw this film (*Ay, Carmela*) were more inclined to believe that the past had shaped the present.

The results confirm the idea that having been exposed to films with a de-dramatized and relativizing content will congruently affect the beliefs and attitudes toward the SCW, and that exactly the opposite happens when exposed to a more dramatic film. Works of art act as "external containers" of emotions, beliefs, and attitudes toward the collective events of the past. But they also play an effective role in maintaining and reconstructing the historical past. Producing works of art or semiotic structures that commemorate the war stressing the individual participation while not paying much attention to the sociopolitical causes of the war, giving a neutral or ambivalent view of the event, will distance oneself from the collective event and foster forgetting instead of helping to express the contradictory collective memory of a war that split the country in two. Exactly the opposite will happen with semiotic structures that insist on the suffering and sociopolitical causes of the collective catastrophe. These semiotic structures will produce more emotional activity, more reflection, and a stronger identification with the characters. These processes are linked to a stronger agreement with critical and negative beliefs on the war. These different processes activated by the films are a sign of the struggle in search of "rendering some meaning to the past," which is a feature of the collective memory of traumatic collective events such as the SCW.

ACKNOWLEDGMENT

The writing of this chapter and some of the research reported herein was partially supported by grant PB 94-0475-CO2 from the Ministry of Education and Science, Spain.

REFERENCES

Allport, G., & Postman, L. (1952/1977). *Psicología del rumor* [Psychology of rumor]. Buenos Aires: Pléyade.
Bartlett, F. C. (1932/1990). *La memoria. Studio i psicologia sperimentale e sociale* [Memory: A study in experimental and social psychology]. Milano: Franco Angeli Editore.
Bertrand de Muñoz, M. (1993). Literatura de la guerra civil [Literature of the civil war]. *Anthropos, 148,* 6–24.
Erdelyi, M. H. (1990). Repression, reconstruction and defense: History and integration of the psychoanalytic and experimental frameworks. In J. L. Singer (Ed.), *Repression and dissociation* (pp. 1–31). Chicago: University of Chicago Press.
Flora, J. A., & Maibach, E. W. (1990). Cognitive responses to AIDS information: The effects of issue involvement and message appeal. *Communication Research, 17*(6), 759–774.
García Fernández, E. C. (1992). *El cine Español contemporáneo* [The contemporary Spanish movie]. Barcelona: CILEH.
Gerbner, G., Gross, L., Morgan, M., & Signorielli, N. (1980). The "mainstreaming" of America: Violence profile no. 11. *Journal of Communication, 30*(3), 10–29.

Gerbner, G., Gross, L., Morgan, M., & Signorielli, N. (1990). Trazando la corriente dominante: Contribuciones de la televisión a las orientaciones políticas [Current and leading trends: Contributions of television to political orientation]. *Revista de Psicología Social,* 5(1), 71–79.

Halbwachs, M. (1975). *Les cadres sociaux de la mémoire* [Social framework of memory]. Paris: Mouton. (Original work published 1925)

Halbwachs, M. (1950). *La mémoire collective* [Collective memory]. Paris: Presses Universitaires de France.

Halff, A. (1991). Reconstruire le passé: La mémoire retrouvée des crimes de Nankin [Reconstructing the past: The recovered memory of Nankin's crimes]. *Le Monde Diplomatique,* Aout, 27.

Horowitz, M. (1986). *Stress response syndrome.* Northvale, NJ: Aronson.

Igartua, J., & Paez, D. (1995). *El cambio de creencias y actitudes desde una perspectiva vigotskiana* [Change in beliefs and attitudes from a Vygotsky perspective]. Manuscript submitted for publication.

Iyengar, S., & Kinder, D. R. (1985). Psychological accounts of agenda-setting. In S. Kraus & R. M. Perloff (Eds.), *Mass media and political thought* (pp. 117–140). Beverly Hills, CA: Sage.

Joassin, A. (1992). Le cinéma et la guerre d'Algérie [Movies and the Algerian War]. *Avancées,* Novembre, 2, 20.

Miall, D. S. (1989). Beyond the scheme given: Affective comprehension of literary narratives. *Cognition and Emotion, 3,* 55–78.

Oskamp, S. (1991). *Attitudes and opinions.* Englewood Cliffs, NJ: Prentice-Hall.

Paez, D., & Adrián, J. A. (1993). *Arte, lenguaje y emoción: La función de la experiencia estética desde una perspectiva Vigotskiana* [Art, language, and emotion: The function of aesthetic experience from a Vygotsky perspective]. Madrid: Fundamentos.

Paez, D., & Basabe, N. (1993). Trauma colectivo y memoria colectiva: Freud, Halbwachs y la psicología política contemporánea [Collective trauma and collective memory: Freud, Halbwachs, and contemporary political psychology]. *Revista de Psicología Política, 6,* 7–34.

Pennebaker, J. W. (1993). Creación y mantenimiento de las memorias colectivas [The creation and maintenance of collective memories]. *Revista de Psicología Política, 6,* 35–52.

Perloff, R. M. (1985). Personal relevance and campaign information seeking: A cognitive response-based approach. In S. Kraus & R. M. Perloff (Eds.), *Mass media and political thought* (pp. 177–200). Beverly Hills, CA: Sage.

Perloff, R. M. (1993). *The dynamics of persuasion.* Hillsdale, NJ: Lawrence Erlbaum Associates.

Petty, R. E., & Cacioppo, J. T. (1986). *Communication and persuasion: Central and peripherical routes to attitude change.* New York: Springer-Verlag.

Postel-Vinay, K. (1991). Les japonais découvrent leur passé militariste. *Le Monde Diplomatique,* Novembre, 27.

Potter, W. J. (1986). Perceived reality and the cultivation hypothesis. *Journal of Broadcasting and Electronic Media, 30*(2), 159–174.

Pratkanis, A., & Aronson, E. (1994). *La era de la propaganda: Uso y abuso de la persuasión* [The era of propaganda: Use and abuse of persuasion]. Barcelona: Paidós.

Ripoll i Freixes, E. (1992). *100 Películas sobre la Guerra Civil Española* [100 movies about the Spanish Civil War]. Barcelona: CILEH.

Roda, R. (1989). *Medios de comunicación de masas: Su influencia en la sociedad y en la cultura contemporáneas* [Mass communication: Its influence on society and contemporary culture]. Madrid: Siglo XXI.

Vygotsky, L. S. (1972). *Psicología del arte* [Psychology of art]. Barcelona: Barral. (Original work published 1925)

Vygotsky, L. S. (1979). *El desarrollo de los procesos psicológicos superiores* [The development of higher psychological processes]. Barcelona: Crítica. (Original work published 1930)

Wagner-Pacifici, R., & Schwartz, B. (1991). The Vietnam veterans memorial: Commemorating a difficult past. *American Journal of Sociology, 97*, 376–420.

Watson, D., Clark, L. A., & Tellegen, A. (1988). Development and validation of brief measures of positive and negative affect: The PANAS scale. *Journal of Personality and Social Psychology, 54*(6), 1063–1070.

Wertsch, J. V. (1985). *Culture, communication and cognition: Vygotskian perspectives.* Cambridge, England: Cambridge University Press.

Wertsch, J. V. (1988). *Vygotsky y la formación social de la mente* [Vygotsky and the social formation of the mind]. Barcelona: Paidós.

Wertsch, J. V. (1991). *Voices of the mind: A sociocultural approach to mediated action.* London: Harvester Wheatsheaf.

Chapter 5

Commemorating

Nico H. Frijda
Amsterdam University

People commemorate emotionally significant events from their public past. In Holland, for instance, several commemorations have marked the 1953 flood that took 1,400 lives and a plane crash in Amsterdam that killed 500 people. The end of World War II is commemorated each year on May 4, the day the German troops surrendered. The 50th anniversary of the war's end was extensively celebrated in 1994 in France, and in 1995 in the Netherlands, in many towns and villages on the day the Allied troops entered there. Commemoration ceremonies were held in churches, at the foot of war monuments, at places where people had been shot or the executed buried. American and Canadian men of 70 years of age went to Europe and held reunions in the places where they had been as 20-year-old soldiers.

Commemorations of such public events like disasters and war are usually organized by governments, city boards, or citizen committees. Yet, participation is often massive. Individuals also hold private commemorations. They visit the graves of their relatives or friends, or, on their own, pass by a sign or a marker of an emotional memory, such as a plaque on a street corner indicating where someone had been shot. They watch television programs that review the past events or the public ceremonies.

These commemorations rest, to a large extent, on the emotions of those who suffered from the remembered events or who lost people in them. These emotions are still there, or wait for occasions to manifest themselves. Television programs broadcast people's expressions of grief during the public ceremonies and during the visits to the graves of those who died

50 years ago. Televised images of faces of people revisiting the place of one-time misery or disaster, such as a prison camp, are commonplace. One televised news program reported on the Paris concentration camp Drancy, and showed an ex-prisoner returned there for the first time, after 50 years; he stepped down from the taxi cab that brought him there, looked up at the camp's entrance, and let air escape from his pointed lips in the way people do on sudden pain (Trombley, 1995).

The memories are alive, even if the events were 50 years ago, and they need no commemorations to come to the fore. I have friends who describe how, up until the present day, they are suddenly caught off balance by seeing or reading something associated with the war, and sometimes it is only an indirect reference or an allusion to an event that befell someone else. Others describe the sudden and unexpected upsurge of diffuse emotion, of sadness, of tears, that disable the individual from finishing a story or continuing work, before even knowing why; but, after the fact, they find that it was an association to the events, or to some person's fate, that did it. Intrusive emotions such as these are common among survivors of disasters and other traumas (Horowitz, 1976). I know a woman, then 87 years old, who, having suffered a stroke, put a suitcase with a change of clothing in readiness "because at any moment they may come and get us." Many people, once every few months, wake up in perspiration from a dream of persecution or interrogation. Some of the emotions never go away. They come like thieves in the night, unexpectedly, because of some word or image. "Saturated by numbers, too dry for anyone, also for the poet who feels his throat be throttled, till forty, fifty years after the facts," as a poet expressed it (M. H. Frijda, 1995). Or as Primo Levi wrote in 1984:

> Since then, at an uncertain hour,
> That agony returns:
> And till my ghastly tale is told,
> This heart within him burns.
>
> Once more he sees his companions' faces
> Livid in the first faint light,
> Gray with cement dust,
> Nebulous in the mist,
> Tinged with death in their uneasy sleep.
> At night, under the heavy burden
> Of their dreams, their jaws move
> Chewing a nonexistent turnip.
> 'Stand back, leave me alone,
> Go away. I haven't dispossessed anyone,
> Haven't usurped anyone's bread.
> No one died in my place. No one.

Go back into your mist.
It is not my fault if I live and breathe,
Eat, drink, sleep and put on clothes.' ("The survivor," Levi, 1988)

And recollecting the traumatic events, or talking or writing about them, does not seem to be of real help. Levi, Kosinski, Bruno Bettelheim, and Améry all wrote extensively about their experiences from the imprisonment and persecution, and all four committed suicide years after the events.

Of course, persistence of emotions aroused by events of massive personal impact is not exceptional. There is something like a law of conservation of emotional momentum: The impact of major emotional events does not diminish with the course of time (N. H. Frijda, 1988). Time does not heal wounds; it only softens scars. This appears to be the rule and in the nature of response to psychological trauma. Persistent grief and emotional vulnerability after traumatic events are not illnesses needing cures. Some aspects of grief responses may require adjustment, as for instance an inability to experience grief, but persistence of grief as such, and of emotional vulnerability, is "healthy" and normal. It is not specific to the consequences of war, oppression, or disaster. Wortman and Silver (1989) described the "myths of coping with loss," on the basis of studying loss of a child. The wounds of incest, too, never heal. Dissociative experiences remain frequent (Ensink, 1992) and the woman who has experienced incest may continue to seek some sense in it for the rest of her life (Silver, Boon, & Stones, 1983).

Only recently has the insight been achieved that grief and other effects of major emotional events persist. Unlike 50 years ago, posttraumatic stress disorder is an accepted diagnosis, first of all because of the Vietnam War. But, in the years after 1945, most psychiatrists held to the dogma that psychological disturbance outlasting war experience for more than a few weeks had to be due to prewar dispositions to vulnerability. When developing the notion of "late injury" for emotional and relational disturbances in ex-concentration-camp inmates, Niederland (1980) encountered disbelief and strong opposition. "Stress may, it is true, cause psychological disturbance, but after termination or decrease of stress any health disturbance that resulted from it is rapidly gone, or weakens to such an extent that it does not represent a pathogenic factor" (p. 13). Note that such psychiatric thinking was not a purely academic matter. Before recognition of the late injury syndrome, the patient had to provide convincing proof that no psychic vulnerability existed before the war in order to obtain recognition of injury, and eligibility for financial support or compensation (Bergmann & Jucovy, 1982). Such things may not have disappeared entirely. Not long ago, a "comfort girl," a Korean woman forced by the Japanese occupants to serve as a military prostitute, was denied financial support because she could not prove that she had not done what she had done out of her own free will.

The major emotional events that I am referring to have usually lasted for a prolonged time: repeated bombardments, months of anxiety and uncertainty about one's fate and the fate of children and parents, loss of children and other kin, imprisonment under threat of life, torture. Their consequences often are permanent, and there is no reason to expect to be otherwise. A broken vessel never becomes whole. That would appear to be so in particular when the extremes of humiliation are involved that form part and parcel of many of the events concerned. Events in which one has been victim of arbitrariness and the destruction of self-determination and self-identity. Levi (1989) quoted the Austrian philosopher Améry: "Anyone who has been tortured, remains tortured. . . . Anyone who has suffered torture never again will be able to be at ease in the world, the abomination of the annihilation is never extinguished" (p. 25). Why should it be that the emotions remain? Because one cannot get rid of them? Because they have been avoided, or not adequately been "worked through" in subsequent years? I do not think so. This way of viewing them, although fairly current, is inadequate. Rather, it is because one has been confronted with events that cannot be undone, and experienced facts that have shattered basic convictions about life. It is because the confrontations have created unsolved problems and incorrigible expectancies. Those who experienced them know that there are things that humans do to humans, and that such things can happen to ourselves and to those we love. And we do not merely know this, but the expectancies are in our nerves and muscles. Certain things have happened and have been done, and thus can happen again and be done again. One moment you and they are there, and the next they have gone, wiped away, as dust. So it has been, and so it can be again.

Research in psychotherapy (e.g., Bandura, 1969) has shown that emotional expectancies are not made or unmade by information, but by living experience by ourselves or by others with whom we identify. And major harmful emotional events erode basic convictions that make life livable. One of these central convictions is a basic sense of invulnerability, such as makes it possible to face true dangers. It is that conviction that is destroyed when, in war or calamity, one sees one's kin and friends perish, as has been identified as the cause of "battle fatigue" in war pilots after prolonged courses of duty (Grinker & Spiegel, 1945). Another such conviction is the implicit "belief in a just world" (Lerner & Miller, 1978). That belief is often undermined in survivors of concentration camps and similar settings. Most likely, it is also weakened in their children, who may explicitly or implicitly have grasped what evil humans can perpetrate. Of course, one needs no survivor-parents to be faced with information on such evil. The media provide images virtually everyday. But knowing that it faced your parents, and that it might have faced you, brings it closer to home.

The loss of basic invulnerability and belief in a just world should not be underestimated when gauging the extent to which emotions underlying commemorations are alive. There not only is no end to the devastatingly dolorous memories, but there also is no end to the helpless and stupefied search for meaning: how the humiliations, the cruelties, the systematic destruction were ever possible. As already mentioned, useless search for meaning has been found in victims of incest, as well as in survivors of World War II and probably of any other war that sported systematic destruction. There is disbelief each time unexpected thoughts stumble across those events.

The recollections of war, destruction, and disaster are not to be painted in black colors only. For some, the war was their finest hour, or at least it contained such hours. Hardships, danger, and taking risks produced intense feelings that are rare in normal times. They required the investment of potentialities not often called on in peacetime activities and that one even may have been unaware of; it involved comradeship, personal closeness, and instances of personal self-sacrifice that fill many survivors with lifelong nostalgic memories or shining examples of what humans are also capable. For some, some of the events of war, oppression, and disaster belong to the few moments of life in which one coincided with oneself.

WHY COMMEMORATE SPECIFIC DAYS?

Thus, there distinctly exist emotional sources for commemorating. There are emotions on which commemorations can feed, or such emotions are easily awakened. Still, they do not explain that commemorations are in fact established and arranged. They do not explain that specific dates and occasions are chosen, that the celebrations are held at a specific day of the year, and at specific intervals of 1 year, or 5 or 10 or 100 years. They do not explain the fact that public ceremonies or celebrations are arranged, and people in whom the emotions are absent or pale participate in them. Many people take part who were not even born when the commemorated events took place. Each year in Amsterdam a 1941 strike protesting against the beginning of persecution of the Jews is commemorated. The people who attend these days are mostly under 30 years old, and their number has been increasing over the last 10 years. The population as a whole is often confronted with the relevant events. For months before the 50th anniversary of the end of World War II, Dutch newspapers and television presented articles and programs on the war and liberation, interviews with people recalling the events, detailed reports on what had happened on such and such a day in this or that place. Presumably, similar media activity occurred in other countries. Why? Evidently, there is a need to commemorate, or a need is satisfied by doing so. But, what is the need?

In fact, there is a paradox here. The war and its termination are vivid enough for some people, as just indicated. Why then should they seek a specific date to reexperience? And as regards the others: What do they seek in confronting what they did not experience? This chapter seeks some answers to these questions.

First, notice that commemorations are held for particular occasions: when the event concerned is exactly a year, 5 years, and so on, ago. One devotes attention to the event and its participants, and invests emotion in both of them on that particular day. Commemorations share this remarkable property with birthdays and funerals, marriages, and Christmas and New Year's Eve. All involve thinking and feeling about some person or persons, or some event, on a specific and publicly recognized day that bears a specific relation to the time of occurrence of the commemorated event, or to some moment in the life of the commemorated person. The occurrence of so many of such days suggests that people feel the desire to bring order into the amorphous flow of time, to structure it, and to mark their own position in the flow. It is not a very surprising desire. People have a strong urge for orientation in space, just as animals do. It is emotionally important to know where you are, what the objects around you are, what they might do to you, and what you might do to deal with them. Disruption of orientation is the most general basis for anxiety, and panic attacks are better explained by loss of sense of orientation and competence than by anticipation of particular threats (e.g., Mandler, 1984). As soon as the sense of time has emerged, next to the sense of space, the need for temporal orientation too will have emerged: the need to know about the past and the future, the need to create demarcation points in the continuity of time, to plan the moment of future events, to know about the cycle of the seasons and about the sequence of events that has led to one's present situation. There is, I think, a desire to own one's past and future, which stems from the general need for orientation.

This seems to be the core of the need to commemorate. It serves to define an individual's location in the temporal continuity. This has several levels: Some are more purely temporal, others more moral. Individuals seek to define their position with regard to the past from which they have sprung or that they have been part of. They seek to appropriate their past, to the extent that they are willing to own it. In particular, one seeks to define one's position with regard to the past one has been responsible for, or for which one is being held responsible, or that gives meaning to one's current activities. Much of that, it is true, goes well beyond temporal orientation only. Appropriation of the past, when it comes to the more moral levels, is part of the effort to define oneself, what is and is not part of oneself, what one wishes to make or retain as part of oneself, and what there is that one should blame on others, and possibly only retain as elements of one's fate. There are active choices here, that individuals and societies in fact are continuously engaged in making. It is a heavy burden to feel that one's fate is determined by the power of other people, and there is a need to perceive past events as results of one's doing, or that of one's ancestors. Equally strong is the need to make sense of one's fate, to understand it, and where possible to accept it or applaud it. One can negotiate with that burden or deal with that need by choosing what in one's past one appropriates, with the neglect of that which one either does not wish to appropriate or that one cannot blame on others. Commemorations indeed are highly selective along those lines. They tend to have blind spots for one's own war crimes or for the negligence that caused a severe disaster. Atypically, discussions in the foreign press, previous to the World War II commemoration, precipitated discussions in the Dutch press of the docile attitudes that made the toll among the Jews in Holland to be the heaviest in Western Europe (Ephimenico, 1995; Hilbrink, 1995).

Appropriating the past thus is an element in the construction of an individual's identity. It does so by the double way of their contribution to shaping or affirming the identity of one's group, and by accepting or redefining membership within that group. To the extent that it does, it shapes or activates the sense that this is the group to which one belongs, with those properties, this history, and this fate, with the potential it had and that it may still have and show in the future. Individual identity strongly derives from group identity, in particular when one is met by others as a member of one's group (Tajfel, 1981). Everything that colors the history of the group may color an individual's sense of identity, under those conditions. All this may be articulated by commemorations, or affirmed by them, or activated if it already was solidly there.

Construction of a person's identity as a member of a given group not only implies coherence with the past, but also with the other individuals sharing that past. The shared identity may extend over a large group or over the small group of the family. One may be a member of a nation or an ethnic group, and at the same or at other times may feel membership with one's family and derive part of one's identity from that: I am the daughter or son of such and such, and I carry the imprint of that belongingness.

Commemorating, thus, derives from the desire for orientation in time, for integrating oneself in one's past by appropriating that past, and by confirming one's identity by way of one's group identity. Public commemorations reinforce those various aspects quite explicitly, by the joint activity and joint emotions as such, the communication of emotions both in jointly listening to or looking at their public expression, and by freely manifesting one's own engagement in the issues at hand. Obviously, having and avowing a common past, and participating in a common tradition with all the social interactions of jointly recognizing the truth of affirmations about history and the valuing of the major actors in it, form for a group the strongest glue.

Commemorations, in general, have three major features that define their function. The first feature is the one just discussed, its performance at prescribed, socially shared moments of time. Of course, neither a particular time nor public and shared activities are required for commemorating lost people or past events. A person can go to the cemetery at any day, and lay down flowers, or go and stand before an ancestor's shrine, or sit down and reread the letters or open the photo album, reflecting on the person or the past. Almost everything a person seeks in commemorations can be done alone, and for the sake of one's individual temporal orientation and personal identity. But, even private commemorations are mostly performed on selected days. For example, wedding anniversaries after a partner has left or died, remembrance days of the death of a close one, birthdays of lost ones can stir and cause upset, sometimes even before realizing that it is the special date that does it, or that it was a glance at the calendar that set it off.

The second feature of commemorating is that something more than merely thinking of the event or person is done, something of a special, symbolic nature. One may stop to reflect, often quite literally so, and usually one does more, such as celebrating, organizing a meeting, a reading of some relevant text, or putting down flowers. One does it at the same time as others, and usually together with others. This applies equally to commemorations and to those other date-bound occasions for emotions and paying attention—the birthdays, funerals, and the like. Others are invited and drinks are served, at both the unhappy and the happy occasions. Commemorations of war and its termination are, of course, explicitly public and communal in many ways. Sometimes the streetlights come on and the traffic stops, as it was before World War II in Britain on November 11 at 11 o'clock, and still is in the Netherlands on May 4 at 8:00 p.m. Quite generally, people assemble in front of a statue or monument, listen to a speech by an official or a band playing the national hymn, and watch a wreath being placed. Of course, such things too can be done in private. Some people sit alone in their room on May 4 at 8:00 in the evening, but they still tend to look out of the window to the traffic coming to a stop, or watch the ceremonies on television. Or, all alone, they may bring flowers to a dear one who was killed, at that same communal moment. Even if private, these ceremonies occur in a communal context. One does something of the kind that others do, and at a moment that others do it, and one knows it.

This means that commemorations are rituals. Not only holding speeches, raising flags, and singing national hymns constitute rituals, but commemorating as such is a ritual. A ritual is an occasion that is defined by the social community or by tradition to perform some action that in general is also defined by the community or tradition, that in principle is performed publicly, and that is held to serve a moral or emotional goal. The community and the public may be restricted: They may be the family, the circle of friends, the tribe or the nation, or whichever the collection of individuals that exchanges habits or establishes norms. In the limiting case, it is a tradition set up individually.

Rituals in general serve to provide order, coherence, or stability (Staal, 1990). They exemplify orientation in time by constructing a constant through time. They do so by the fixed, recurrent moment of execution and by their prescribed or traditional form. In commemoration rituals, providing order and coherence also refer to the function of their content that is to create temporal anchorage through re-evoking past events and reinforcing group identity in that basis.

Commemoration rituals provide order and coherence in a manner that is of deep emotional significance. A commemoration constitutes the event as an objective fact of the world. It testifies that it is a true historical event with a social significance and emotional implication of objectively large magnitude. It thereby transforms the recall of the event into something other than the memory of an individual or set of individuals, and lifts it out above the level of thoughts and feelings that only exist within an individual, above that of subjective reactions to an event that every individual can see in their own way. Rituals are actions that say things, according to Leach (1971). What the ritual actions say—the laying of wreaths, the newspaper articles and TV shows, the speeches and ceremonies—is that the event was a true event, with a true emotional impact and true importance, or that the person commemorated could make an objective claim on respect and love. Rituals are messages extended to the annals of history, that is, to the communal representation of reality.

The fact that commemoration rituals address communal representations is again one of their major aspects. One of the core elements of a ritual is to establish as well as confirm an individual's coherence and bondedness with others. In commemoration rituals this has particular force, because it extends in two directions. The coherence and bondedness concern the commemorated individuals as well as the other people who loved them, one's fellows who also suffered from the commemorated events as well as those who also feel emotionally involved by kinship, friendship, or identification. Commemoration rituals, for a brief moment, dissolve the discontinuity between now and the past, between one individual and others, between those who are there and who are not there any more.

Discontinuity with the past is in some measure dissolved by the manner of focus on the past event or the persons concerned. Commemoration rituals, in this respect, fulfill to a large extent the same functions as funerals. At a funeral, the deceased is rendered present again. At many funerals, the deceased is addressed in the second-person singular, as if the person could hear it. One, moreover, describes how that person was, and what the person's qualities were. One devotes loving attention. One also affirms the affection that one held toward the person, and the bond that continues to exist. This does not preclude that, at the same time, one realizes and affirms that the person is gone forever. One says goodbye, takes one's leave with a formal last glance at the corpse, watches the interment or how the coffin slowly sinks toward the crematory oven, or, in other parts of the world, one sees the remains go up in flames. Sometimes those flames are arranged for precisely that purpose, months after the person actually died, as on Bali. Those features of funerals mark the transition of the person being with us toward not being with us anymore. They make it unmistakable that the deceased has not just departed for a voyage. They mark the individual's departure as final and irreversible, and they provide an image to which memory can later return and on which it can rest. Finally, at the funeral, one comes to accept the departure, or at least, the funeral has the function to assist in such acceptance by the images it provides. Only good things are said about the deceased, at least during the funeral. Commemoration rituals show most of these same features.

They not only share most of these features with funerals but also with other date-bound ceremonies. Consider birthdays. These, too, serve to affirm a bond, and to spend attention and affection by way of acts performed in public. One comes to visit, gives presents, and participates in the future of the person concerned by extending good wishes for the coming year of life. Or, take New Year's Eve: One often throws a party, even if only within the family. One looks back at the year that has gone by and lays out the good intentions for the coming one, and, again, one participates in the good fate of others by extending the wishes to them, which is symbolized in the kiss when the midnight bells sound.

All this shows that commemorations—like funerals, birthdays, and New Year's Eve—are transition rituals. They enact the transformation of the past into the present. In each public commemoration, one can recognize the three components that define transition rituals: the components of separation, transformation, and aggregation (Van Gennep, 1909). The separation component enacts that the object of the ritual leaves the role or position or mode of life, or that the previous life of the community will change. The transformation component performs the transition or evokes it symbolically. The aggregation component marks the entry into the new role, position, or mode of life, and affirms the new condition. In commemorations, separation is marked by presentations of life as it was before the event, the disaster, the termination of the war, or whatever is commemorated. In commemorations of the end of World War II, old and gray ex-soldiers or one-time members of the resistance forces walk in parade in their old uniforms. Paratroopers return to their drop zones and may get excited because the bridge they fought for has recently been replaced by a novel one (the incident concerns Normandy and was widely reported in the newspapers). Stories told, shown, and written revive the anxieties of the times or the adventures of searching for food and safety, the misery and fear, as well as the comradeship and the intimacy involved in sitting around a wood-splinter stove. The transformation component is represented on the one hand by the mourning, the band playing "The Last Post," and flags at the monument going half-mast, the visits to the graves, and on the other by the images of the liberation. The aggregation component consists of the holiday usually coupled to major commemorations, the fairs, dancing on the square as in France on July 14, and in Holland on May 5. It is also found in the writings and speeches emphasizing the lessons to be drawn from the past misery.

Presenting things as they were at the time, or the persons as we knew them, and the emotions evoked by them, the separation component has a complex role in commemorating. On the one hand, the presentations imply that it was so then, not now. On the other hand, they provide the memories, images, and emotions access to experiencing the bond that existed with the lost persons, and in some measure or in some way revive it. The presentations make the emotional bond come alive again or lead to experiencing it as still alive, the definitive absence of the persons notwithstanding. The experience of bonds with people that do not live anymore, the actualization of feelings toward them, be it affection or grief, is in fact one of the problems that commemorating poses, and one of the motivations for the explorations of this chapter. But understand it or not, commemorating contributes to the sense that the lost people are in some manner there, among us and with us, and that emotional bonds with them are still in force. It would seem that creating or reviving that sense is one of the major functions of commemorations.

Notice that the power of the presentation of how it was, and how the persons were, to evoke emotions and re-evoke bonds comes at least in part because in watching the presentations, and by performing the ritual acts, one in a sense participates in what happened then. It involves participation, in the same sense in which extending good wishes for the coming year, one tends to participate in building up that year, if only in the mind and in feeling. One imagines the future fate of the other in the latter example, and, with probably more force, one imagines the fate and feelings of the lost persons, and what they had to go through, in commemorations. Transition rituals generally owe some of their meaning and force to participation in the elementary sense in which the concept is used to understand religious experience (Éliade, 1957). It is a means both to integrate what has happened, and to decrease the distance to the lost individuals. That is, one adds the events to one's store of experience, and also appropriates something that belonged to the past and the remembered person. The memories and the knowledge of the past become more one's possessions.

Leach (1971) added: "Rituals are actions that say things; at the same time they are actions that do things." Commemorative actions, too, do things. They profess bondedness and loyalty with the commemorated individuals, and respect for who they were and for what they may have done, and they revive the bonds and loyalty and respectful relationship. What this means is discussed further later. Also, as pointed out earlier, they form or enhance solidarity with others for whom the events or persons have similar meaning, and they entrench the individual in the past and the group. Some of what commemorations seem to do may strike as superstitious, or as aspects of magical thinking. This applies in particular to a further aspect, namely, that commemorations may be experienced as a way to pacify the dead, to prevent them from coming back and haunting us. To fail to commemorate, to forget to put the flowers or recall the date often feels improper, as if the dead are neglected and one in that way has hurt them. Whether or not this implies magical thinking is discussed later, but note: The dead do actually haunt, in emotions and in dreams, as illustrated by Levi's poem quoted earlier.

UNFINISHED BUSINESS

There are conditions under which the need of ritual, the need to perform actions that do things, weighs with particular heaviness. For many, the past wars were of that nature: World War II, the Vietnam War, the civil wars in Africa, the Balkan war. Perhaps all wars contain that condition; perhaps disasters, too, have it. Incest often has it clearly, according to the fate of many victims and what they tell about it years later. Perhaps it is part of all evils "that man does to man" (Revault d'Allonnes, 1995). That is, for many of those who lived them the event is an unfinished business.

Earlier in this chapter I indicated that the emotions stemming from the past events are still alive and acute, however much time has passed. The emotions include those of panic, not of fearful memory. They include living grief, and not only sad recollection. They include stupefaction, disbelief, complete lack of grasp of what has happened, how it could have happened, and why it happened. This means that it is not the emotions that have not passed, but that the issues that precipitated the emotions are not over. They are still in operation, they still are current affairs.

What can that mean? First consider stupefaction. Perhaps every survivor of mass destruction—of the persecution of the Jews; of the retaliatory killing of all inhabitants of a village like Putten in Holland, Ouradour in France, or Lidice in the Czech Republic; of the Serbian massacres in Bosnia, and the killing frenzies in Rwanda—has experienced this: the naive disbelief and the amazement on how it has been or is being possible. The stupefied disbelief may come to the surface suddenly, when seeing a picture or reading some allusion. The question returns again and again: How on earth could it have happened? It just does not fit one's conceptions of life and the world, the convictions that should enable individuals to live their life coherently, and without which this is difficult. Absence of answers to these questions, absence of an outcome in the quest for sense and meaning, and disruption of the basic convictions make what happened to be unfinished business.

And then there is grief. No death of a loved person ever fully becomes a settled fact. The tentacles of love continue to search for their object, the empty place remains, in bed, in feeling, in expectations, as in an ion split away from its molecule. Of course, this is proper to love and not unique for the aftermath of social events like disaster, war, and oppression. However, the scale of the unfinishedness may find no parallel outside such events. Not only have attachment and love not been rounded off, but the expectations and sets toward one's social niche, in many cases one's whole social matrix, have been destroyed. The dead were lost by other people's acts, by their using their destructive liberty.

The deaths represent unfinished business for further, perhaps more subtle, reasons. The relationships to the lost ones often were not completed. Conflicts with fathers, mothers, and children have remained hanging, and render the loss opaque and troubled, and thought often cannot leave the broken off relationships alone (e.g., Bruggeman, 1994; Epstein, 1979). I had a good friend who until he died, for 20 or 30 years after the war had a recurrent dream about his parents in Poland saying to one another: Why doesn't Henri write us? There are further reasons why thoughts and dreams continue. There are interrupted expectations and fantasies on interactions and forms of life. There are attitudes and forms of readiness closely bound up with personal identity, such as the feelings that losing the emotions, and losing the longings for contact with lost life and lost lives would mean a last or ultimate surrender to the perpetrators of the evil that gave rise to the commemorated event.

Also, for many people, the loves and attachments that were cut off by the events had no natural termination point. Those left behind do not possess an image, or a memory, that can serve as such a termination point, to which the thoughts and feelings can return and find a moment of rest. Remember that the ritual function of funerals is to provide such a termination point. Many survivors of the wars did not bury their beloved. They do not know where their loved ones lie, and a large number of those who died do not lie at all but are blown away on the wind.

In the face of such events, the past is unfinished not only for those who suffered them, but also for many of their children, grandchildren, or friends. For them too, the stupefaction may exist. For them it may be linked to the unbridgeable gulf that separates them from their parents, whoever it concerns, to the unanswerable questions that most often are not asked: about how it was; about the tormenting uncertainty on how they would have behaved under the circumstances; whether they would have belonged to the good or the wrong side, the selfish or the helping; whether they would have usurped someone's bread. And, in fact, with regard to wars like World War II, Rwanda, or the Balkan, the past can represent unfinished business for those who allow the reality and moral issues of those events to reach them and become something of a reality.

All this is, of course, not unique for the events that people tend to commemorate. The past must have been as unfinished for the survivors of the massacres in France in the 14th century (e.g., Tuchman, 1978), or of those committed by the crusaders—for the French Catarrhs, for the Aztecs after the destruction, for the Armenians, for the survivors of the Gulag, and so on. In fact, the descendants of these groups may have commemorated or on occasion still do.

COMMEMORATING AS AN EMOTIONAL SITUATION

The major reason to want to commemorate is to make one's past one's own, and one of the most pressing aspects of the desire to appropriate one's past may well be to come to terms with its emotional significance.

It is fairly evident that most of those who participate in commemoration rituals are not emotionally engaged in the remembered event. Their reasons to participate are more formal. That is the usual case with rituals. Religious rituals, too, have real significance for only a few, and those that are emotionally engaged usually have to bring in that significance themselves (Humphrey & Laidlaw, 1994). That does not make rituals into empty formalities. Many of the others are caught by the emotional significance that the ritual and the commemorated event have for those engaged few. As with religious rituals, a minority carries the values that the ritual embodies, and the majority allows the minority to carry those values by at least agreeing with them, and by being willing to go along with them in the ritual.

Commemorations are not necessarily emotional events. They can merely be acts of recognizing a major point in history, as was the case with the 1989 commemoration of Columbus' voyage, for everybody but the Native Americans. But often they are emotional occasions, and many of the emotions are violent. Participants may cry, even if the event has rarely caused them to do so before. The emotions consist of sorrow or grief, of being upset by recollections, of being moved by the renewed emotional connection with the event or the lost people, or by the images of acts of help or heroism, of the moments of liberation or reuniting with those one was separated from or in uncertainty about. Or, there may be vivid and collective emotions of pride at a former victory or other achievement, or of enthusiasm for a dead leader or historical symbol.

Commemorations arouse the emotions by a confluence of several factors: the ritual presentations, the fact that others are present with whom one shares much of the experience and often talks with about the issue involved, and the very fact that the ritual forms a legitimate occasion for emotional display.

The emotions that commemorations arouse are often sought and desired. One goes to the public square or church, goes out on the street to take part in public enjoyment, or watches television. But the emotions often are not desired. One confronts the public ceremonies with distaste, or withdraws back home or out in the country. Usually, the emotions are mixed: They are both sought and disliked.

There are a number of reasons to dislike the emotions of commemoration, notably when public commemorations are officially organized. One did not ask for either the commemorations or the emotions. When confronted with them, one may stand exposed with one's emotions. There may be a conflict between the personal inclination to commemorate and the public ceremonies. Public ceremony may often be felt to serve the glory of the commemorators or a government more than the remembered persons, and the public noise may not make personal remembrance easier. There are things than can only be touched on with reticence, and words of heroism may seem hollow in cases where personal emotions have been involved. I know of at least one person from a resistance movement in an occupied country during World War II who wrote the evening before his execution to his family: "I have not fallen for a political ideal. I die and fought for myself." It does not lessen respect, because that respect concerns the lost person, and not the act or motives. And even without all that the emotions evoked by commemorations are unbidden ones, and so are the presentations and memories. Many of the emotions are difficult to manage, and in any case they hurt. There are things that are best left alone. What is the use of bringing them to the surface? Peace of mind is not to be gained that way; the misery cannot be undone; the lost ones cannot come back.

On the other hand, the emotional confrontations provided by commemorations are also sought, and there are good reasons for that. Major emotional events have emotional meanings that are often hard to come by. They have a potential for evoking emotions that may merely lurk in the background, or that is represented by stiffness of feeling or emptiness of recollection. The power to evoke emotions may be such that it is better to prevent them from coming. Yet, one would wish to vanquish the incapacity of feeling and defensive withdrawals. One may seek to circumvent the hesitations and reticence. One also seeks the emotions, and tries to establish contact with the thoughts and memories, and possibilities to finish the unfinished in this regard. Rituals play a role in dealing with emotional events that one has not been able to assimilate.

"Unassimilated emotional events" is an unpleasant and, what is more, inappropriate expression; and so is "unassimilated emotions," which is often used in this context. Both sound as if they refer to some sort of upset digestion. They mistakenly evoke the suggestion that something has been understood. But, of course, events exist about which one is unable to think in a balanced manner, or that cannot be remembered with some inner distance. Thinking about them causes upset, or associations dredge up feelings; for instance, a Jewish woman who survived an annihilation camp emerged from surgical anesthesia after an operation and was seized by a panic attack when she saw the tall chimney of the hospital's heating plant outside her window. Or, on the contrary, individuals may feel nothing when recalling the events, which feels eerie to them as well as to those close to them.

What is the cause? Why is it that some emotions do not pass by, or do not turn into emotionally balanced memories? Well, the answer is simple. War, persecution, disaster, and sexual humiliation involve events that just cannot be assimilated or integrated. Most people have not been made that way, and that is all for the better. Absence of integration is not a disturbance, if only because often it would represent a betrayal of family and friends and of one's own identity to be capable of remembering the events in a balanced manner.

Yet, people would wish they could assimilate the unassimilable, integrate what cannot be integrated. They would wish to be capable of more fully confronting their past and that of others, and appropriate it. There is unfinished business and the yearning to finish it. One would like to turn what has happened and what has befallen us into a part of our representation of the world and ourselves. Assimilating an emotion or emotional event means inserting how the world looks by and after the events into one's conceptions of the world and oneself and in the web of one's emotional ties and desires.

Rituals of commemoration, I propose, may offer at least some small possibility of doing something about past events being stuck in our throats, or at least for a moment to relieve the pressure. They can do so by calling up the images and memories of the events, by providing occasions for emergence of the feelings, at moments and in a context that it is acceptable and, owing to the public or formal nature of the ritual, in a way that allows the link to the world and to others to be retained. They sometimes allow a person to get around emotional defensiveness and to experience emotions in a somewhat more distant manner, that is, without unduly disturbing one's balance (Scheff, 1977). Ritual allows a person to experience emotions that are out of reach at other times, or that only come as thieves in the night. It is true, ritual too can leave a person off balance, thrown over, in full emotional turmoil. The emotions may increase the pressures rather than alleviate them. Rituals can do both things at the same time. What the relation between the two is, and what determines which one dominates, is not easy to say.

Rituals support coming to terms with one's emotions—insofar as they do that—not only because the emotions during ritual are socially respectable. During ritual, individuals are being accepted in their role as emotionally affected persons: that is, as a bereaved one, one who suffered, one who was unjustly treated, or whatever the focus. The ritual emphasizes the emotional significance of the commemorated event, and not so much the emotion. It invests the emotional significance with objectivity. As has already been alluded to, it makes clear that a sad or horrible state of the world is involved, and not so much an instance of sadness or horror. The commemoration is not about my feeling, my subjective state, my grief, because others, too, focus on that event or those events, and they, too, emphasize that something terrible has happened. The same applies to commemorations of happy events. They are about grandiose acts or about someone who is a hero or genius, not about my joy or admiration. This has an objectifying conse-quence for the individual. A commemoration ritual—any transition ritual—defines the person or persons involved as someone with a particular social role: that of a bereaved person, as a hurt and damaged person, as an unjustly persecuted one or as someone who has gone through much, or as someone with a shining stature in one's group. The ritual lifts people out of their subjectivity, places them in the new social role, and accepts them in that role. It is likely that the general weakness of ritual in Western society is harmful precisely for that reason: It leaves one alone with one's grief, and the grief is an essentially private affair.

It can indeed be expected that this makes the emotions more accessible and the notion of having the emotions more acceptable. One's emotions can merge into ritual manifestations and into the emotions of others. One stands out less and is less exposed, which may well be one of the main functions of mourning women in funerals in other cultures. In addition, rituals often provide a form, a model for emotional expression and thus save one the effort to find such form on one's own. Consider the models of stiffly swallowing one's tears or, on the contrary, of wailing loudly and passionately, being held by one's kin, of laying flowers and standing silently for a minute or so. Rituals of grief in other cultures may show this more clearly. Throwing oneself on the coffin, tearing one's clothes, pouring ashes on one's head, and wailing with outstretched arms come from molds offered by the ritual to give shape to one's emotions.

In ritual, even the emotion itself is experienced in a more objective way, toward which the individual has a certain distance (Scheff, 1977). The emotion becomes a story, or part of a story. It no more results from the pure confrontation with the emotionally significant event, it is an emotion that has been given form like emotions expressed in the theater and the arts, and it also feels that way. Rituals share the possibility of experiencing emotions in that manner with witnessing the emotions of others, in reality or in the theater. They also share it with publicly telling about one's emotions in a more or less formal context, outside an intimate relationship. It is not infrequent to hear someone reveal personal experiences during a public lecture that the speaker never told to the spouse or children; telling about the experiences within the intimate relationship would have been impossible to do or to manage. Commemorations, indeed, like other collective emotional situations, are a kind of emotion theater in which the individual is a player and the other participants are other players. The individual's emotions thus receive a more objective, less personal form by borrowing their format from the presentations, the context, and the acting in the communal play. This is, moreover, an aspect of the very participation in a commemoration. One slips into a role and in that way does not carry the full burden of going out of one's way to commemorate.

One uses that theater for one's emotional ends. Many of one's emotions can rest on the communal occasion as well as the communal form. They are free riders on the communal or ritualized manifestations. It always has been so. Consider Homer's comment, "So she spoke, Briseis, weeping, and the other women wept with her, because of Patroclos, but beyond that each for her own miserable fate" (*Iliad*, 19, 302). This, too, not only occurs in connection with unhappy emotions. Rituals allow one to come closer to the joys of those times, the friendships, shared dangers, risk taking of others on one's own behalf, the profound joys of liberation and the return of friends believed dead. Of course, it is precious to be able to experience or reexperience those joys, which at the time may have been lost in the miseries or overshadowed by the grief. It is next to impossible to dwell on these joys when there is not a public ritual context to model and legitimate them.

Finally, it may be that experiencing emotions fully may contribute to coming to terms with them. It is a common assumption in psychotherapy that it does, in Freud's hypothesis of grief work, as well as in those of desensitization and flooding. The assumptions may well be correct for the present context, if only because, making the emotions more accessible, commemorations may make the losses and horrors of the past more believable and allow some assimilation. The extent to which this is so, however, is far from clear. As already mentioned, among those who put in the most effort to confront the horrors of the past were several who in the end committed suicide.

THE PRESENCE OF ABSENTS

Commemoration rituals thus may contribute toward finishing the unfinished. However, other of their features may be more essential for achieving that end. Specifically, this applies to the central aspect of these rituals, attesting affection and showing respect.

It is a remarkable aspect of commemorations. As in funerals, flowers and wreaths are given to the dead, warm words are spoken, and signs of respect are made. Why? It seems peculiar, because the impulse to pay respect and to bring flowers is strong, although the dead cannot see or hear us and the flowers cannot give them pleasure. Is it defensive denial? Are they signs of magical thinking? Or is it that culture has taught us arbitrary conventions? The latter is an unlikely explanation, because the notion that the dead are gone forever is a solid element in Western cultural thought today, and, also, paying loyalty and respect to the dead would seem to be a nearly universal phenomenon. Then it is possible to consider these actions as efforts at renewed confrontation with the painful loss, in the way already discussed.

Neither of the aforementioned touches the core of what motivates the actions of showing affection and respect, and what one feels while doing so. Something would seem to be involved that is more actual, more psychologically real, more producing a real emotional yield. Showing respect and affection both maintain the emotional relationship with the lost persons.

The various forms of showing affection and respect are not merely ritual actions. They actually achieve constructing or maintaining a given relationship. They are the gestures of actual respect and love and care. The nature of these gestures is independent of whether the person to whom they are addressed experiences them or not. By performing them, one enters or establishes an emotional relationship of caring and respecting, in fact, one adopts a caring or respectful attitude. For respect this is perhaps clearest. Respect implies a relationship of submission; Respectful behavior is submission behavior, with the head bent. By executing the behavior, individuals recognize and accept the other's respectable qualities and respect-demanding position toward themselves. Giving presents, or giving flowers and wreaths fulfills a similar function. Presents or flowers are given not so much to give pleasure to a person, but to affirm or confirm the other person's respectable position, and at the same time one's own as the bearer of respect and, in the event, of gratitude, of owing something to the other. That is the major meaning of giving presents in social interaction, as has been shown by Mauss (1914/1957) and recently elaborated by Miller (1993). There is nothing magical in doing these things with regard to absent people, or even to explicitly dead ones. One adopts the respectful position and thereby puts the person to whom it is addressed in the corresponding position. A similar analysis can be given of manifestations of affection.

In other words, in the behaviors of commemoration, one calls up an inner attitude that adds to integrating the other person into one's emotional repertoire. One constructs the state of action readiness of which an emotional attitude consists (N. H. Frijda, 1986). Having an emotion is essential for being able to do so, because only through an emotion can the inner attitude or action readiness be more than mere representation or fantasy. Emotional changes are not effected by thinking and knowing, but by doing, by actually engaging oneself into the relationship with the person or thing that is the emotion's object; that much is evident from research in psychotherapy (e.g., Bandura, 1969; Turner, Calhoun, & Adams, 1992). Recognizing the other person, and accepting that person in whatever state includes a recognition of definitive absence, and perhaps some acceptance of that. They represent a little piece of a funeral.

The feeling of pacifying the dead, of preventing their haunting us should be understood in a similar manner. The ritual demonstrations of affection and respect implement the fact that love has not ended; and love implies taking care, and in part consists of the desire to make the other be well. Neglect is incompatible with those drives and feelings. Showing love and attentiveness, preventing neglect, are elements of taking care of someone. The desire of taking care may lead to action before one has recalled that it is no more of use, or notwithstanding having recalled it. Why should one deprive oneself of showing love and care, of reviving an element of the relationship, and particularly when ritual offers the movements?

Rituals make lost people present in additional ways, such as recalling the past events and describing their persons. The emotional profit can be understood along similar lines as described earlier. The sense that they have not altogether disappeared, that in some way they are present, is not primarily a matter of emotional denial, of illusionary wish fulfillment, or willing suspense of disbelief. Such explanations do not touch the core, because there is something real in the created sense of presence. The lost person is there for a moment, not so much as an image, but as the target of the inner attitude corresponding to one's relationship to the person. The inner attitude is that of being the person's friend, child or parent, teacher or pupil, or colleague. One can recreate such an inner attitude only by at the same time recreating an image of that person in a complementary role, as friend to oneself as a friend, as parent to oneself as a child, and so forth. Doing so has effects. The image consists of representing something of the other person's mode of being, that person's way of behaving toward you, and of viewing things. The effect is double. There is a presence that is not imaginary because it is not physical presence that is at stake. And one assimilates something of the person's mode of being and way of viewing things, and adds it to one's repertoire of experiencing things. The momentary identification adds to one's fund of modes of experiencing. One can of course neutralize these possibilities of extending the self by simultaneously realizing that the complementary person no longer exists and that this person's role in the relationship is a mere figment of imagination; but why do so and rob oneself of the enrichment, both in entering the relationship and in deriving the perspectives from that person's angle? The profit of entertaining the sense of relationship and presence in commemoration is similar to the profit of asking advice in front of an ancestor's shrine or of wondering how one's father or teacher would have approached a given problem.

In fact, commemorations may contribute to the acquisition of forms of seeing and experiencing over a broad spectrum. Consider the yearly commemoration of the strike during the war in Amsterdam. In a recent one, a young person walked with a board saying: "For your example." Or, as another young participant expressed it to me: "You make parents."

Public commemoration, of course, is a form of social sharing of emotions (Rimé et al., 1991). It is perhaps its most complete, most explicit form, in that emotions are shared mutually or collectively. That mutuality or collectiveness has itself emotional implications. It creates or strengthens feelings of bondedness or solidarity; it gives, if only for a moment, the feeling or illusion of commonality, and so comes close to one of the major motivations for social sharing of emotions. People share emotions in order to come to grips with them (Rimé, Mesquita, Philippot, & Boca, 1991), or because it alleviates anxiety (Schachter, 1959), or because it is in the nature of the emotion concerned (as with certain joys that make you embrace the bystanders). But the most basic reason is probably the desire to connect with others, the hankering for bondedness that is one of a human's most basic motivations (Baumeister & Leary, 1995). That motivation may be somewhat more readily apparent in collectivist than in individualist cultures (Hofstede, 1980), but nevertheless also is a dominant force in the latter. Consider most people's concern with social recognition, as well as the sudden emotions that may well up through signs or symbols of belonging, such as one's national anthem. Perhaps this is the decisive factor distinguishing whether one seeks or abhors public commemorations: Do they indeed provide some bondedness with others, or do they leave you alone with your personal emotions?

The desire for bondedness also goes in a different direction, namely, from those who were not witnesses to the remembered events to those who were. Our children, that is, the children of the survivors, often long to approach their parents, and painfully regret when that appears not possible. In fact, it often is not possible, or at least extremely hard. It is a common complaint among the children of extermination camp survivors, that the emotional life of their parents was and remains a closed book (Epstein, 1979). They have no part in their parents' experiences, and the latter hardly ever talk about it; if they do, it may be in the form of jokes or neutral reporting. The children remain outside what was a major period in the life of their parents and, moreover, one that colored their parents' relationship to them, in part by emotional inaccessibility, in part because the children often feel their miseries do not count in the face of what their parents have gone through. The silence of survivors of war and disaster toward their children is not only because it is difficult to talk about one's emotions. Emotions never can be explained to those who did not experience them; a person is bound to solitude except toward those to whom nothing needs to be told because they shared the experiences.

This silence toward the children, and this separation from them, can to some extent be alleviated in commemoration rituals. There is shared experience of emotional meanings that have obtained objective form through the ritual, the presentations, the objectification that is involved in the emotional manifestations in the ritual context.

COMMEMORATING THE PAST
AND LIVING THE PRESENT

The preceding suggests some background of the commemoration of public events. One wishes to be connected to one's history, one's group, and one's personal past. One wishes to be connected to lost individuals in one's past and to others who shared the history or with whom one would want to share it. One wishes to come to terms with emotional events that do not allow one's rest.

Is that the full story? It is not likely, in view of the fact that commemoration has its eyes to the past, whereas the present is filled with events that equal or surpass those that one commemorates. As I said, in 1995 the end of World War II was celebrated, but what is there to celebrate? Crimes to humanity have continued without interruption, and they will go on doing so.

However, commemoration is not only motivated by desires to link up with the past, or to come to terms with it. There exist motivations more distinctly relevant to the present. Which these are becomes clear on realizing that what is so often involved is unfinished business. The business touched on by many commemorations is unfinished not merely because one is unable to detach oneself from those who were lost. It is also because of the unresolvable question of how the events could come to pass in the first place. The business is really unfinished because it continues in precisely those aspects that make for the unresolvable questions. There is incessant cruelty, destruction on a grand scale not proportionate to the issues moving the destructors. There is incessant fear, incessant uncertainty about those one loves. There is continuous perpetration of humiliation and destruction of the identity of individuals, both at individual and collective levels. There is suppression of freedom of thought and there are the various forms of fascism, racism, and fundamentalism.

The intense need to give meaning to experienced misery, and to one's past generally, usually does not succeed in finding meaning in the past. But, it often does lead to seeing a tenor in the past with implications for the present and the future. Commemorations lead to reflecting on those implications. It is an aspect of the aggregation component of the transition ritual, it may give an urgency to the desire to come to grips with the past, it forms the sense of a commemoration that goes beyond simple orientation in time and strengthening group identity.

In itself, there is nothing beautiful or commendable in commemorating. There most certainly is in itself nothing attractive in finding a purpose of the past for the future. In 1989, the Serbs commemorated their defeat at the hands of the Turks in the Battle of the Blackbird Field, in 1389, and it formed the starting point for the Balkan wars of the 1990s (Glenny, 1992). It formed the occasion for rousing Serbian nationalism, under the theme that glorious fighting for the honor of the Serbian people was as possible now as it was 600 years ago. Flemish nationalists have yearly held the Yzer-pilgrimage, commemorating the 4-year defense of that region that cost thousands of lives in World War I; it has turned to little more than affirmations of nationalist animosity. For the Irish Protestants, the Battle of the Boyne that ensured their domination for some 300 years, has primarily been a recurrent occasion for affirming that dominance. The death of Rudolf Hess was commemorated by extreme rightist groups, as is Hitler's birthday, to glorify Nazi ideology.

It is well to remember that commemoration rituals influence emotions and emotion processing by exactly the same mechanisms as those that lead to collective manifestations of hatred. Mass aggression and blind enthusiasm for a leader are engendered by the arousal of group identity and collective focusing on certain emotional issues that in turn lead to emergent group norms. These norms may include that it is acceptable to show grief and that violence is abhorrent, but also that one's group is superior and the others devoid of human dignity, or that violence toward those others is acceptable and even recommendable (Rabbie & Lodewijkx, 1987; Turner & Kilian, 1972). Many commemorations are drenched in desires for vengeance, glorification of one's group, and calling glory what were outrages.

It all depends on the theme in the name of which a commemoration is held. In 1985, World War II was commemorated in (then) West Germany under the device formulated by its president: "It is not at issue to control the past. We know that that is impossible. The past cannot in retrospect be changed or undone. However, who closes the eyes for the past is blind for the future. Who does not want to be reminded of perpetrated inhumanity is vulnerable to its repetition" (Weizsäcker, 1985, p. 39).

What determines the commemoration device? I do not know. Power politics, propaganda, and access to the media may play vital roles. So may be the fact whether or not one's group is engaged in current controversy or oppression, real or imagined; so may be a group's morality, or that of its leaders and spokespersons, and the participating individuals. The main point here is that the functions of commemoration ritual at the level of the individuals' emotions and at that of the social reality are two very distinct issues.

ACKNOWLEDGMENT

This chapter is an adaptation of a speech, given on April 28, 1995, at the request of the Netherlands Organization for Scientific Research NWO, to recognize the 50th anniversary of the end of World War II and of the German occupation of the Netherlands.

REFERENCES

Bandura, A. (1969). *Principles of behavior modification.* New York: Holt, Rinehart & Winston.
Baumeister, R. F., & Leary, R. M. (1995). The need to belong: Desire for interpersonal attachment as a fundamental human motivation. *Psychological Bulletin, 118,* 497–529.
Bergmann, M. S., & Jucovy, M. E. (1982). *Generations of the Holocaust.* New York: Basic Books.
Bruggeman, J. (1994). The significance of absent objects in the analysis of transgenerational conflicts. *Zeitschrift für psychoanalytische Theorie und Praxis,* 9.
Éliade, M. (1957). *Le sacré et le profane* [The sacred and the profane]. Paris: Gallimard.
Ensink, B. (1992). *Confusing realities: A study on child sexual abuse and psychiatric symptoms.* Amsterdam: VU University Press.
Ephimenico, S. (1995). Le souvenir de l'holocaust en Hollande [Remembering the Holocaust in Holland]. *Le Monde,* March 10, 1995.
Epstein, H. (1979). *Children of the Holocaust.* New York: Putnam.
Frijda, M. H. (1995). *"Primo Levi,"* unpublished poem.
Frijda, N. H. (1986). *The emotions.* Cambridge, England: Cambridge University Press.
Frijda, N. H. (1988). The laws of emotion. *American Psychologist, 43,* 349–358.
Glenny, M. (1992). *The fall of Yugoslavia: The third Balkan war.* Harmondsworth, Middlesex: Penguin.
Grinker, R. R., & Spiegel, J. P. (1945). *Men under stress.* Philadelphia: Blakiston.
Hilbrink, C. (1995). *In het belang van het Nederlandse volk* [For the sake of the Dutch people]. Den Haag: SDU.
Hofstede, G. (1980). *Cultural consequences.* Beverly Hills, CA: Sage.
Horowitz, M. J. (1976). *Stress response syndromes.* New York: Aronson.
Humphrey, C., & Laidlaw, J. (1994). *The archetypal actions of ritual.* Oxford, England: Oxford University Press.
Leach, E. (1971). Ritual. In *International encyclopedia of the social sciences* (Vol. 13, pp. 521–526). London: Collier-Macmillan.
Lerner, M. J., & Miller, D. T. (1978). Just world research and the attribution process: Looking back and ahead. *Psychological Bulletin, 85,* 1030–1051.

Levi, P. (1988). At an uncertain hour. In *Collected poems* (R. Feldman and B. Swann, Trans.). London: Faber & Faber.

Levi, P. (1989). *The drowned and the saved* (R. Rosenthal, Trans.). New York: Vintage.

Mandler, G. (1984). *Mind and body: The psychology of emotion and stress.* New York: Norton.

Mauss, M. (1957). *The gift.* London: Routledge & Kegan Paul.

Miller, W. I. (1993). *Humiliation.* Ithaca, NY: Cornell University Press.

Niederland, G. W. (1980). *Folgen der Verfolgung: Das Überlebenssyndrom* [Consequences of persecution: The survival syndrome]. Seelenmord. Frankfurt: Suhrkamp.

Rabbie, J. M., & Lodwijkx, H. (1987). Individual and group aggression. *Current Research on Peace and Violence, 10,* 91–101.

Revault d'Allonnes, M. (1995). *Ce que l'homme fait à l'homme: Essai sur le mal politique* [What man does to man: Essay on political evil]. Paris: Editions du seuil.

Rimé, B., Mesquita, B., Philippot, P., & Boca, S. (1991). Beyond the emotional event: Six studies on the social sharing of emotion. *Cognition and Emotion, 5,* 435–465.

Schachter, S. (1959). *The psychology of affiliation.* Stanford, CA: Stanford University Press.

Scheff, T. (1977). The distancing of emotion in ritual. *Current Anthropology, 18,* 483–505.

Silver, R. L., Boon, C., & Stones, M. H. (1983). Searching for meaning in misfortune: making sense of incest. *Journal of Social Issues, 39,* 81–102.

Staal, F. (1990). *Rules without meaning: Ritual, mantras and the human sciences.* New York: Peter Lang.

Tajfel, H. (1981). *Human groups and social categories.* Cambridge, England: Cambridge University Press.

Trombley, S. (1995). *A concentration camp in Paris* [TV film].

Tuchman, B. W. (1978). *A distant mirror: The calamitous 14th century.* Harmondsworth, England: Penguin.

Turner, R. H., & Kilian, L. M. (1972). *Collective behavior.* Englewood Cliffs, NJ: Prentice-Hall.

Turner, S. A., Calhoun, K. S., & Adams, H. E. (Eds.). (1992). *Handbook of clinical behavior therapy.* New York: Wiley.

Van Gennep, A. (1909). *Les rites de passage* [The rites of passage]. Paris: Emil Nourry.

Weizsäcker, R. von (1985). Die Deutschen und ihre Identität [The Germans and their identity]. In *Von Deutschlandaus. Reden des Bundesprasidenten* (pp. 39–60). Berlin: Corso bei Siedler.

Wortman, C. B., & Silver, R. C. (1989). The myths of coping with loss. *Journal of Consulting and Clinical Psychology, 57,* 349–358.

Part II

SOCIAL AND EMOTIONAL PROCESSES OF COLLECTIVE MEMORIES

Chapter 6

How Individual Emotional Episodes Feed Collective Memory

Bernard Rimé
University of Louvain, Belgium

Véronique Christophe
University of Lille, France

Some years ago, the former prime minister of Belgium, Paul Vandenboey-nants, was kidnapped. One late afternoon after driving home from work, he was accosted by three men who were waiting for him in the garage. He was brutally attacked and taken away. A few days later, his kidnappers demanded a large ransom for his release. The news of the kidnapping shocked the entire country. Although retired from the government, Minister Vandenboeynants was still a very prominent figure in Belgium. A former president of the Christian-Democrat party, he had developed a public persona that appealed to the vast majority of Belgians. He was adept at using the media and was a spectacular communicator. In the late 1950s, he had been among the first politicians in the world to train with professional counselors to enhance his use of radio and television. He was also a powerful and influential businessperson famous for his battles with the Belgian Tax Administration both within and outside the courtroom. He was known to everyone in Belgium as "VDB"—the abbreviation of his name that he made famous in election campaigns.

His kidnappers had driven VDB to an isolated house out of the country, in northern France. There he was kept for a month. Most of the time he remained blindfolded and tied to a bed. He later reported that he felt his physical integrity and his life were under constant threat during his entire captivity. Secret negotiations were conducted between the kidnappers and the family. Although this was never made official, a part of the requested ransom was paid and eventually he was released. He was dropped by car in the middle of the night in a city nearby the Belgian border. There, VDB simply took a taxi and went back home. When this was known, the media rushed to his house. Yet, in the course of the following 2 or 3 days, he refused to speak publicly. Rumors circulated that in spite of his very strong personality, he was badly affected by the experience. However, a couple of days after his release, VDB scheduled a press conference.

At the appointed time, media from all over Europe gathered in a huge auditorium in Brussels. VDB entered, sat in front of the audience, and started telling in minute detail the story of his kidnapping and captivity. He spoke slowly, in control of himself, quite aware of the immense impact of his talk. Over the next 2 hours, an epic story unfolded. At every turning point of the story, the report made mention of how he felt and reacted emotionally. His narrative often referred to his private thoughts and mental ruminations while in the hands of his unpredictable captors. Naturally inclined to acting, the former prime minister used speech and voice modulation to elicit emotional effects in his audience. On the evening of his public appearance, all the TV channels devoted their news entirely to VDB's story. The narrative had been so well organized by the teller himself that several TV channels presented it with sections preceded with headlines simulating titles of book chapters. The same happened with newspapers on the day after. A novel had been made readily available by the victim to the media.

Vandenboeynants had reported with the talent of a novelist. The dramatic character of the story, the intriguing and mysterious aspects involved in the narrative, the emphatic tone of the teller, his continuous reference to his thoughts and emotions, and the striking sentences he used to express vivid elements of his situation all contributed to a remarkably powerful emotional experience for the listeners in the country and abroad. In the days and weeks that followed, the story was at the center of every conversation in Belgium. Most people had seen the broadcast narrative several times. A good number of Vandenboeynants' sentences and verbal expressions were known by heart by many. People on the streets would often repeat the prime minister's actual sentences, imitating his tone of voice and accent. A kind of immense national rehearsal of VDB's drama developed. The script and the related emotions were on everyone's mind.

Over time, VDB's story infiltrated the country's psyche in fascinating ways. After the initial telling and retelling of the drama, parts of it were soon reproduced in a funny manner and the story was repeated with a humorous tone. In the following weeks, several rock music bands across the country adopted Vandenboeynants' narrative as a theme for their songs. Rap groups simply added to their music loops of VDB's voice pronouncing some of the most famous sentences of his press conference. Amazingly, this type of music rapidly moved to the top of the national hit parade. The success was such that in nightclubs, VDB's rap started to be played every 10 records. All of the youth were dancing to the rhythm of the sentences telling this man's drama. Although the songs were intended to be humorous, they also conveyed key elements of the emotional script in an admiring and warm way. In some sense, VDB's emotional episode had become a legend.

VDB's story has been presented in detail because it provides a remarkable illustration of how individual experiences can be fed into collective memory. This chapter focuses on an important social psychological process that lies behind the VDB story and accounts for the transfer of private emotional experience to the wide community of which we are all a part. This process is called the *social sharing of emotions*. It rests on a single theoretical principle stating that every emotional experience tends to be socially shared. This principle is first documented by reviewing empirical evidence showing that when people experience an emotion, they later tell about it repetitively or share it socially with people around them (Rimé, 1989). Next, a further step is documented along the same line, which is called the *secondary social sharing process* (Christophe & Rimé, in press). This chapter argues that the net result of this double process is that the script of a private emotional episode is spread across the social group, feeding the collective mind with new social knowledge about emotions.

EVERY EMOTION TENDS TO BE SOCIALLY SHARED

The social sharing of emotion is a process that takes place in the course of hours, days, and possibly weeks and months following an emotional episode. It involves the evocation of the emotion in a socially shared language to some addressee by the person who experienced it (Rimé, 1989; Rimé, Mesquita, Philippot, & Boca, 1991a). It usually happens in the form of conversations in which individuals openly communicate about the emotional circumstances and their feelings and reactions. A good deal of empirical evidence supports the view that current life emotions, whether positive or negative, involve their social sharing in an overwhelming number of cases, occurring after positive as well as negative emotions.

This was first demonstrated in studies investigating participants' recall of emotional episodes of their recent past. Across various studies using some 1,384 emotional episodes, the observed proportion of cases in which participants reported having talked with people about the emotional episode varied from 90.0% to 96.3% (for a review, see Rimé, Philippot, Boca, & Mesquita, 1992). The figures did not vary with age or with sex. Neither the type of basic emotion (whether fear, anger, joy, sadness, or shame), nor the valence of the emotional experience (whether positive or negative) predicted the proportion of socially shared episodes. Furthermore, within the limits of investigated cultures (i.e., various Western European countries), no effect of culture was evidenced with respect to the global rate of socially shared episodes (Rimé et al., 1992; Vergara, 1993). Further data from these studies also revealed that socially sharing an emotion is initiated early after emotional events, and it is predominantly a repetitive process. Indeed, the respondents' modal response was that they talked first "on the same day" (50% to 59.2% of the cases, according to the study) and they talked about the episode "several times with several persons" (Rimé, Mesquita, et al., 1991; Rimé, Noël, & Philippot, 1991).

The short latency of initiation of the social sharing process after an emotion was confirmed across several diary studies in which participants had to report daily about the most emotional event of the day (Rimé, Philippot, Finkenauer, Legast, Moorkens, & Tornqvist, 1995). In two such studies involving 1,046 and 461 emotional episodes, respectively, the proportion of cases in which the social sharing was undertaken during the day the episode occurred amounted respectively to 67% and 58%, thus confirming the figures observed from recall studies. In a further diary investigation, participants reported everyday on the most emotional event of the preceding day. For a subsample of 354 emotional events, participants reported that they did socially share them in 74% of the cases. No significant variation related to type of primary emotion involved were found. In spite of the brevity of the period of observation involved in these diary studies (i.e., the hours immediately following the emotional episode), the social sharing was found as often repetitive, and in the majority of the cases, it occurred with several partners.

Follow-up studies in which participants were first contacted at exposure to some important emotion and then some weeks later further confirmed the generality of the social sharing process associated with emotion. In one such study, participants recently exposed to traffic, domestic, or work accidents were first contacted in an emergency clinic and later at a 6-week follow-up (Boca, Rimé, & Arcuri, 1992). At this follow-up, participants reported that they talked about their accident in 93% of the cases. Confirming the diary observations, they did so in the course of the first day in 60% of the cases. These data also evidenced the repetitive character of the social sharing, as it occurred more than twice in 83% of the cases, and was mentioned as having occurred about every day in no less than 35% of the participants. In another study conducted according to the follow-up method, the target emotional event was childbirth as experienced by young mothers (Rimé et al., 1995). Thirty-one women were followed-up during the 5 weeks after they left the maternity ward. The proportion of women who reported spontaneous social sharing about their delivery experience during the first week at home reached 97%. It was still 90% during the second week, and then evidenced a progressive decline during the next 3 weeks with 55%, 52%, and 32%, respectively. Comparable findings evidencing very high initial rates of social sharing of emotions immediately after they occurred and the progressive decline of these rates in the course of the weeks after were reported by Pennebaker and Harber (1993) from samples of individuals exposed to an earthquake, or to the U.S. residents responses to the initiation of the Persian Gulf War.

Laboratory research involving the experimental induction of emotion also confirmed that emotion usually involves the social sharing process (Bouts, Luminet, Manstead, & Rimé, 1995). In two experiments, students were exposed to either a low, a moderate, or a high emotional movie excerpt. After the movie, participants were left alone for 5 minutes with a friend who did not see the movie and their conversation was unobtrusively tape-recorded. These conversations showed that the high emotional movie elicited much more social sharing than the others. Moreover, individual differences in intensity of emotional reactions to the movies evidenced marked correlation's with the indices of extent of social sharing taken from the postmovie conversations. In other words, the more participants were emotionally aroused by the movies, the more they talked about it with their friend in the waiting room situation that followed. The latter finding is fully consistent with what was observed systematically from recall studies (Rimé, Mesquita, et al., 1991; Rimé et al., 1995), as well as from diary studies on the social sharing of emotion: The more an event was rated as emotionally intense or as involving important emotional disruption, the more frequent and the more extended its social sharing.

TARGETS OF SOCIAL SHARING

Overall, the general notion that emotional exposure elicits social sharing behaviors seems well supported. If this is the case, an important psychosocial counterpart is implied. That is, human beings are very frequently led to play the role of listener or recipient in the process of socially sharing an emotion initiated by some of their fellows. This opens a good number of further research questions about the social sharing of emotion. Thus, for instance, there should be investigation of the role of social sharing partner, the type of persons selected for this process, how such persons react and behave in a social sharing situation, the consequences their reactions have on the initiator of the process, the consequences that exposure to the social sharing of emotion has for the receivers, as well as the contribution of this type of social communication on the spreading of emotional information and scripts within a given social group.

The type of partner chosen for the social sharing of emotions is a question for which empirical data are now available. Rimé, Mesquita, et al. (1991) and

Rimé et al. (1992) observed that for all age groups, targets of social sharing are confined to the circle of intimates (i.e., parents, brothers, sisters, friends, or spouse/partner). People who are not part of this circle were only very rarely mentioned as having played the role of social sharing partners. Professionals (e.g., priests, physicians, teachers, psychologists) or unfamiliar or unknown persons are not likely to be selected for this role. However, within the circle of eligible intimates, gender and age differences compared to the chosen partner were observed. Among adolescents, family members (predominantly parents) were by far the most frequently mentioned partners for the social sharing of emotion for both males and females. The second most frequently mentioned social sharing partners were friends, who shared about one third of the emotional confidences. Among younger adults, a markedly different pattern occurred. In this age group, friends were mentioned about as often as was the case in adolescent data, but the role played by family members was dramatically lower, especially among males. As a counterpart, for both genders, spouses and/or partners emerged as important actors on the social sharing stage. Among older adults (age 40–60), the role played by family members in the social sharing of emotion was again markedly lower. Additionally, a considerable drop in the importance of friends was registered for males, but not for females. The most striking fact in this age group was the predominance of spouses and partners in the social sharing processes. This was especially true among men whose social sharing network virtually disintegrates at this age, leaving the spouse or partner as the exclusive sharing partner.

A particularly important question in this context is the one of the impact exposure to the narrative of the emotional experience of another person can have on the listener. There is a good deal of empirical evidence suggesting that such exposure may induce considerable emotional changes in the latter. Thus, Lazarus, Opton, Monikos, and Rankin (1965) showed that when individuals are listening to a distressed person, indices of their autonomic nervous system activity reveal increased arousal. Strack and Coyne (1983) had volunteers exposed to a 15-minute conversation with persons selected on the basis of the presence or absence of depressed mood. Mood measures administered following the conversations showed participants who were exposed to depressed persons to be more anxious, more depressed, and more hostile than those exposed to nondepressed ones. Similarly, Archer and Berg (1978) observed heightened anxiety to be manifested among individuals who listened to other people disclosing intimate aspects of themselves. Pennebaker, Barger, and Tiebout (1987) had videotaped volunteer Holocaust survivors talking about their traumatic past experiences. They assessed how deeply these persons disclosed their traumas by monitoring their skin conductance levels throughout the narrative. These video recordings were later used by Shortt and Pennebaker (1992), who displayed them to college students whose skin conductance was also monitored. The data evidenced negative correlations in skin conductance levels between speakers and listeners. Thus, the more the survivors revealed in-depth emotions, the more emotionally aroused were the listeners.

Thus, it should be concluded that exposure to the narrative of an emotion induces emotional responses in the exposed person. Yet, if this is the case, then a puzzling implication follows. If, as was concluded earlier, emotional exposure elicits social sharing behaviors, and if exposure to the social sharing of an emotion elicits in its turn an emotional state in the listening persons, then it should be predicted that these listeners would later be inclined to socially share with some third persons the narrative to which they were exposed. In other words, a process of *secondary social sharing* is expected to be developed by the listener once the latter leaves the situation in which the primary social sharing process occurred. Such a prediction does not exactly fit with what common sense expects. Indeed, socially sharing an emotional experience is often considered as an intimate matter presupposing confidentiality. In such matters, the implicit notion of confidentiality is generally enhanced by the fact that the addressee is an intimate person with whom one uses to share one's emotions. Thus, common sense would assume that secondary social sharing, or the fact that listeners would repeat to others what they were told would be the exception rather than the rule. Nevertheless, the rationale followed previously leads to the prediction to the contrary that once an emotion was socially shared, secrecy may well be the exception rather than the rule.

THE SECONDARY SOCIAL PROCESS: EMPIRICAL EVIDENCE

This prediction was tested by Christophe and Rimé (in press). The method used was a modified version of the *retrospective* method in which participants have to recall a recent emotional episode and answer questions about this episode. This method was used by, among others, Scherer, Wallbott, and Summerfield (1986) and Wallbott and Scherer (1994) to investigate emotional experience across cultures, and by Shaver, Schwartz, Kirson, and O'Connor (1987) to investigate prototypical knowledge of emotion. It was extended to the study of social sharing of emotion by Rimé, Mesquita, et al. (1991). In the modified version used for investigating the secondary social sharing process, 134 students were instructed to retrieve from their recent memories an episode in which someone had reported to them a personal experience involving an emotional state. Once such an episode was retrieved, participants had to briefly specify what happened to this person. They then answered questions on basic emotions felt while listening to the emotion narrative and extent of secondary social sharing. More specifically, they were asked if after their exposure to the social sharing situation, they themselves happened to tell to some other persons about the episode to which they had listened ("secondary social sharing"). Answers were collected on five successive items: (a) yes or no; (b) if yes, with what delay after the social sharing situation did they talk about the listened episode for the first time?; (c) how often did they talk about it?; (d) with how many persons did they talk about it?; (e) how often do they still talk about it now?

The puzzling prediction considered earlier was clearly confirmed. Contrary to what common sense would expect, socially shared emotional episodes are in no way kept confidential by receivers. In spite of the fact that they were intimates of the sharing person for 85% of them—the teller was a friend in 51.49% of the cases, a family member in 25.37%, the spouse or companion in 8.21%, and a nonintimate person in 14.93%—receivers who participated in this study did undertake secondary social sharing in a vast majority of the cases. Indeed, in 66.4% of the collected episodes, listeners acknowledged that they later talked about it to one or more persons. In spite of common sense illusions of confidentiality in this matter, listeners did so in a rather extensive manner, as secondary social sharing was reported by them as having occurred twice or more in 53% of all cases, and with two or more persons in 54% of cases. The number of times secondary social sharing occurred and the number of persons with whom it occurred varied as a function of the emotional intensity felt by the original listener in the initial social sharing situation.

The latter findings were particularly supportive of the general notion that the more an event is an emotion, the more it elicits social sharing. Yet, the test conducted was limited in one particular respect. It is possible that respondents rated as more emotionally intense precisely those episodes that they did happened to talk about more often. To overcome this limitation, a further investigation was conducted (Christophe & Rimé, in press). In this one, volunteers had to retrieve from memory a situation in which someone socially shared with them an emotional episode resembling those on a list of 20 events they were distributed. Three different versions of this list were prepared for the study. One was composed of events that ranked at the lower end of the list of life events developed by Holmes and Rahe (1967) (e.g., quarrel with a friend, death of a pet, unhappy love affair) and was intended to form a list of low emotional intensity events. A second list comprised 20 events ranking at the higher end of the Holmes and Rahe list (e.g., abortion, divorce, academic or professional failure) and represented a list of moderate emotional intensity events. A third list was made of 20 events taken out of those mentioned by Green (1990) as potential elicitors of posttraumatic stress disorder (e.g., sudden death of a close one, rape, exposure to disaster) and thus constituted a list of high-intensity emotional events. A between-subject design was created by randomly assigning each subject to one of those lists. Once participants had retrieved a situation in which someone had socially shared with them an emotional experience resembling those in the list they had received, they first had to describe briefly the emotional episode involved so that its correspondence with the list could later be checked by the investigators. Participants then completed the questionnaire covering the dependent measures. A total of 121 persons, 23 males and 98 females between ages 18 and 55 years ($M = 21.1$), completed the forms of the study, with 41 in the low-intensity, 42 in the moderate, and 38 in the high-intensity condition.

Regarding elicited emotions, the data confirmed that hearing another's emotional story is itself an emotional event. Indeed, as expected from previous studies, people reported having felt intense emotions while listening to the narrative of the emotional episode. On a 10-point scale assessing emotional impact, low-intensity episodes were rated as having less impact ($M = 6.29$) than moderate ($M = 7.83$) or high- ($M = 8.08$) intensity episodes. The last two ratings were not significantly different. A remarkable feature characterized results from the assessment of felt emotions while listening to social sharing. In all three conditions, participants rated the emotion of interest at nearly maximal level. People thus evidence a very marked availability to narratives of emotional episodes that occurred to others. Further examination of the profile of basic emotions revealed notable effects of the emotional intensity conditions. The more intense the listened-to episode, the more it elicited negative emotions like fear, sadness, or disgust. It may be that with more intense episodes, the general openness to receiving, as evidenced from ratings of interest, would be counteracted by the raising up of strong negative feelings. In this sense, the receiver of the social sharing may be trapped in a kind of approach–avoidance conflict. With very intense episodes, avoidance is likely to predominate, with the potential consequence that receiving the social sharing would be denied. Such a consequence was anecdotally documented by Pennebaker and Harber (1993). In the earthquake investigation mentioned at the beginning of the chapter, he noted that in the surveyed community, T-shirts appeared reading "Thank you for not sharing your earthquake experience."

Secondary social sharing was mentioned in 78.5% of the cases, and this figure was independent of conditions of intensity of the socially shared emotional episode. The latency of initiation of secondary social sharing did not vary across conditions either. In 40.5% of the cases, participants initiated secondary social sharing during the day of the social sharing situation. However, replicating the results of the previous study, the two measures of extent of social sharing—frequency of secondary social sharing and number of persons with whom secondary social sharing occurred— evidenced significant differences as a function of conditions of emotional

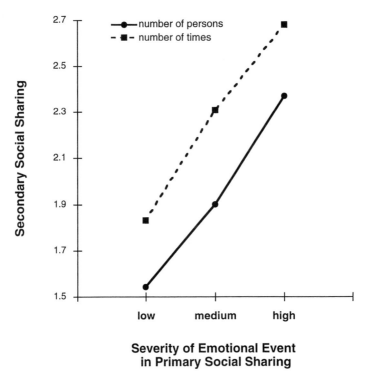

FIG. 6.1. Frequency of secondary social sharing and number of persons with whom secondary social sharing occurred as a function of severity of emotional event in primary social sharing. From Christophe and Rimé (in press). Copyright 1997 by Wiley. Reprinted with permission.

intensity of the shared episode. As shown in Fig. 6.1, respondents who reported about a high emotional intensity sharing manifested secondary social sharing more often than those who reported about either a moderate or a low-intensity sharing, these latter two groups failing to differ significantly. Finally, there was no difference between conditions for secondary social sharing still occurring at the time of the investigation. However, 47.9% of the respondents answered that they still happened to socially share the episode that was told to them. This happened at least once a day in 40.5% of the cases, and at least once a week in 25.6%.

POSITIVE VERSUS NEGATIVE EMOTIONAL EXPERIENCES

Thus, the two studies just described offered clear support for the prediction that exposure to the social sharing of an emotion would in turn elicit secondary social sharing. Secondary social sharing was recorded respectively in 66% (Study 1) and in 78% (Study 2) of the cases, with no significant difference between the two. Moreover, the findings of these two studies on secondary social sharing were closely consistent with earlier findings on primary social sharing. Indeed, both studies replicated that exposure to the sharing of more intense emotion elicits more repetitive social sharing, as well as social sharing targeted at a superior number of persons (Rimé, Mesquita, et al., 1991; Rimé et al., 1995). Also consistent with previous data (Rimé, Mesquita, et al.), secondary social sharing was found to be initiated on the day the episode was heard in 39% (Study 1) and 40% (Study 2) of the cases. Finally, with regard to perpetuation of social sharing (Rimé et al., 1995), 36% of respondents in Study 1 and 48% of those in Study 2 reported that they still happened to talk about the heard episode at the time of this investigation, which meant an average of several months after the original exposure.

However, in the first of the two studies just reviewed, most of the episodes referred to by participants were negatively valenced. In the second one, participants were assigned to retrieve and report about negatively valenced emotions. The question may thus be raised if secondary social sharing would occur with comparable frequency when positive emotional experiences are involved. The general principle that "every emotion tends to be socially shared" leads to the prediction that the valence should make no difference. Data collected on the primary social sharing of positively and negatively valenced clearly supported this prediction (e.g., Rimé, Mesquita, et al., 1991). Recently, Christophe and DiGiacomo (1995) tested the prediction for the secondary social sharing. Half of 88 persons were randomly assigned to a positive emotion condition in which they were asked to report on an episode in which someone had reported to them a positive emotional experience. The other half received instructions to refer to a negative emotional experience. The results from this study again confirmed that exposure to the social sharing of an emotion in turn elicits secondary social sharing, with 82.9% of the participants reporting some degree of secondary social sharing. In accordance with the prediction, no significant difference was observed between positive and negative emotional episodes for this figure. However, differences were found for a number of parameters of the secondary social sharing. Thus, for positive emotional episodes, secondary social sharing was initiated faster after leaving the original teller than was the case for negative emotional episodes. Also, positive emotional episodes elicited more repetition of secondary social sharing, and a superior number of target persons were involved. In sum, exposure to positive emotional episodes simply speeds up and enhances the secondary social sharing effect.

Earlier in this chapter, we stressed that people—especially intimates— are not expected to tell others about emotional events that had been confided to them. Yet, data from the reviewed studies show that this happens in a large majority of cases. If the implicit social norm is transgressed so widely, at least one should expect people to preserve the anonymity of the original source in the process of secondary social sharing. Christophe and Di Giacomo (1995) investigated this question in their study by asking people to rate on a 10-point scale (not at all–very much) the degree to which they revealed the identity of the person whose emotional experience they shared with some third persons. It was found that anonymity is not at all preserved. Respondents reported having revealed the identity of the source in 73% of investigated cases. A practical conclusion should follow from these findings. If one does not want an emotional experience widely exposed, one should not share it at all.

SOCIAL SHARING OF EMOTION AND SOCIAL KNOWLEDGE ABOUT EMOTION

Considerable attention has been given by scientists of various disciplines to the fact that people store a vast amount of information about emotional events, emotional feelings, and emotional responding (e.g., Russell, Fernandez-Dols, Manstead, & Wellenkamp, 1995). This information is shared in collective memory under the form of emotion prototypes (Shaver et al., 1987) or social schemata (Rimé, Philippot, & Cisamolo, 1990). Rimé (1995) suggested that the processes of primary and secondary social sharing were important potential contributors to the collective social knowledge about emotions.

Primary social sharing of emotion involves "repeated reproduction," wherein the same individuals report their memories of an episode on several different occasions. Secondary social sharing involves a different process, which Bartlett (1932) called *serial reproduction*, in which recalled information is transmitted through a chain of persons. Bartlett conducted a number of experiments in which folktales, prose, and pictorial materials were presented for serial reproduction. He observed that in such reproductions, the material was likely to be transformed into a caricature and its originally cognitively unclear aspects were likely to be modified into meaningful ones. Yet, Bartlett argued that memory is also affected by the people's store of relevant prior knowledge. In an ingenious study, he (Bartlett, 1932) asked volunteers to learn stories that produced a conflict between what was presented to them and the prior knowledge they possessed. He found that in participants' later reproductions of this material, they reconstructed the story rather than remembering it verbatim, and they did so in a manner consistent with their expectations. In this way, Bartlett provided evidence for the notion of schemata. Schemata free cognitive resources from the heavy analysis of all aspects of incoming information.

Consequently, cognitive resources may concentrate on the processing of more novel and unexpected aspects of the information.

Thus, in the secondary social sharing of emotion, people are likely to process the emotional information they are exposed to through the filter of their preexisting schemata of emotions. Information confirming these schemata will have a high probability of being neglected. In contrast, episodic elements failing to fit within prototypical frames of representation will be detected as salient, memorized, and later reproduced in serial repetitions. For episodes of weak emotional intensity, the process is likely to be of limited consequence for social knowledge of emotion, because the number of serial repetitions will generally remain low. For strong emotional episodes, however, there are reasons to expect that, due to the combination of the number of repeated reproduction and the related number of serial reproductions, community knowledge of emotion will be affected.

THE HUMAN BROADCASTER

The notion that emotional experiences are communicated and are feeding social knowledge of emotion was independently developed by Harber (K. D. Harber, personal communication, December 1995) under the concept of "the human broadcaster." Elaborating from former research conducted on how individuals face an emotional upheaval (Pennebaker & Harber, 1993), Harber proposed that the compulsion to communicate emotional experiences serves not only an intrapersonal need (for meaning, perspective, closure, etc.) but also an interpersonal need for news. Thus, the sender's urge to disclose supplies the receiver with useful knowledge. One of the predictions of this human broadcaster model is that a major event will "travel" farther than a minor event. A story travels when listeners are so disturbed that they, in turn, find disclosure outlets who may also find it necessary to tell others. Besides the story's intrinsic interest, there are two psychological features that determine how far a story travels: its emotional impact on the teller, and the narrative quality of the teller's disclosure.

A study recently conducted under naturalistic conditions by Harber and Cohen provided support for these predictions (K. D. Harber, personal communication, December 1995). This study, which is yet unpublished, investigated students who were required to visit a hospital morgue for one of their classes. Later, students were asked to supply the names of up to six people to whom they relayed their morgue experiences, and to then contact each of these people and determine how many people these primary contacts had themselves contacted. In addition, students contacted one of their contact's contacts, and found out how many disclosures these people made. Thus, a given student would tell how many of his friends he told, how many people each of his friends told, and how many people one friend of a friend told. The survey also included questions that measured students' emotional reactions, needs to communicate, rates of thinking, and some demographics. Results from the study showed that a story's travel is positively related to the student's pretrip ruminations, need to communicate to another, vividness of disclosure, and degree of emotional upset. A particularly interesting finding was that these factors correlate not only with how many people the student told, but how many people the student's friends' friends told. All in all, the results from this study conducted in naturalistic conditions were remarkably consistent with those of the previously described investigations.

CONCLUSIONS

The VDB case described at the beginning of this chapter can be considered a prototype of the social psychological process described and documented in this chapter. In this case, a person was affected by emotional circumstances and thus urged to socially share the experienced episode. The specific characteristics of the person and the particular intensity of the emotional episode resulted in social sharing conducted on an unusually large scale. Yet, empirical data reviewed in this chapter strongly suggested that any emotional experience would elicit, *mutatis mutandis*, a similar process. In the VDB case, the narrative of the emotional episode resulted in a strong emotional impact on the national audience. Data described in this chapter demonstrate that any exposure to the narrative of an emotional episode similarly results in a sizable emotional impact on the exposed person. The general rule that "any emotion tends to be socially shared" is playing its role here again. In the VDB case, large-scale social sharing resulted in a particularly large-scale secondary social sharing process. But data issued from questionnaire and naturalistic studies show that a similar process of secondary social sharing develops from any exposure to a social sharing situation, and the scale at which this process will develop and extend is a direct function of the intensity of the involved emotion. We argue that collective interests are served by secondary social sharing as it contributes to the spreading of emotional knowledge within a community. If emotional experiences need to be socially shared and if social sharing of emotion elicits secondary social sharing, extension and updating of the collective database with new individual emotional scenarios would be continuous. This process offers an ideal source for elaborating and refining socially shared emotion prototypes and emotion scripts.

REFERENCES

Archer, R. L., & Berg, J. H. (1978). Disclosure reciprocity and its limits: A reactance analysis. *Journal of Experimental Social Psychology, 14,* 527–540.

Bartlett, F. C. (1932). *Remembering: A study in experimental and social psychology.* Cambridge, England: Cambridge University Press.

Boca, S., Rimé, B., & Arcuri, L. (1992, January). *Uno studio longitudinale di eventi emotivamente traumatici* [A longitudinal study of traumatic events]. Paper presented at the *Incontro Annuale delle Emozioni*, University of Padova, Italy.

Bouts, P., Luminet, O., Manstead, S. R., & Rimé, B. (1995). *Social sharing of emotion: Experimental evidence.* Unpublished manuscript.

Christophe, V., & Di Giacomo, J. P. (1995). *Contenu du partage social secondaire suite à un épisode émotionnel négatif ou positif.* Manuscript in preparation.

Christophe, V., & Rimé, B. (in press). Exposure to the social sharing of emotion: Emotional impact, listener responses and the secondary social sharing. *European Journal of Social Psychology.*

Dakoff, G. A., & Taylor S. E. (1990). Victim's perceptions of social support: What is helpful from whom? *Journal of Personality and Social Psychology, 58,* 80–90.

Green, B. L. (1990). Defining trauma: Terminology and generic stressor dimensions. *Journal of Applied Social Psychology, 20,* 1632–1642.

Holmes, T. S., & Rahe, R. H. (1967). The social readjustment scale. *Journal of Psychosomatic Research, 11,* 103–111.

Lazarus, R. S., Opton, E. M., Monikos, M. S., & Rankin, N. O. (1965). The principle of short circuiting of threat: Further evidence. *Journal of Personality, 33,* 307–316.

Pennebaker, W. J., Barger, S. D., & Tiebout, J. (1989). Disclosure of traumas and health among holocaust survivors. *Psychosomatic Medicine, 55,* 577–589.

Pennebaker, J. W., & Harber, K. D. (1993). A social stage model of collective coping: The Loma Prieta earthquake and the Persian Gulf war. *Journal of Social Issues, 49,* 125–145.

Rimé, B. (1989). Le partage social des émotions [Social sharing of emotions]. In B. Rimé & K. Scherer (Eds.), *Textes de base en psychologie: Les émotions* (pp. 271–303). Lausanne: Delachaux et Niestlé.

Rimé, B. (1995). The social sharing of emotional experience as a source for the social knowledge of emotion. In J. A. Russell, J. M. Fernandez-Dols, A. S. R. Manstead, & J. C. Wellenkamp (Eds.), *Everyday conceptions of emotions: An introduction to the psychology, anthropology and linguistics of emotion* (pp. 475–489). Dordrecht, The Netherlands: Kluwer.

Rimé, B., Mesquita, B., Philippot, P., & Boca, S. (1991). Beyond the emotional event: Six studies on social sharing of emotion. *Cognition and Emotion, 5,* 435–465.

Rimé, B., Noël, M. P., & Philippot, P. (1991). Episode émotionnel, réminiscences mentales et réminiscences sociales [Emotional episodes, mental remembrances and social remembrances]. *Cahiers Internationaux de Psychologie Sociale, 11,* 93–104.

Rimé, B., Philippot, P., Boca, S., & Mesquita, B. (1992). Long-lasting cognitive and social consequences of emotion: Social sharing and rumination. In W. Stroebe & M. Hewstone (Eds.), *European Review of Social Psychology* (Vol. 3, pp. 225–258). Chichester, England: Wiley.

Rimé, B., Philippot, P., & Cisamolo, D. (1990). Social schemata of peripheral changes in emotion. *Journal of Personality and Social Psychology, 59,* 38–49.

Rimé, B., Philippot, P., Finkenauer, C., Legast, S., Moorkens, P., & Tornqvist, J. (1995). *Mental rumination and social sharing in current life emotion.* Paper submitted for publication.

Russell, J. A., Fernandez-Dols, J. M., Manstead, A. S. R., & Wellenkamp, J. C. (Eds.). (1995). *Everyday conceptions of emotions. An introduction to the psychology, anthropology and linguistics of emotion.* Dordrecht, The Netherlands: Kluwer.

Scherer, K. R., Wallbott, H. G., & Summerfield, A. B. (Eds.). (1986). *Experiencing emotion: A cross-cultural study.* Cambridge, England: Cambridge University Press.

Shaver, P., Schwartz, J., Kirson, D., & O'Connor, C. (1987). Emotion knowledge: Further exploration of a prototype approach. *Journal of Personality and Social Psychology, 52,* 1061–1086.

Shortt, J. W., & Pennebaker, J. W. (1992). Talking versus hearing about the Holocaust experiences. *Basic and Applied Social Psychology, 1,* 165–170.

Strack, S., & Coyne, J. C. (1983). Shared and private reaction to depression. *Journal of Personality and Social Psychology, 44,* 798–806.

Vergara, A. (1993). *Sexo e identidad de genero: Diferencias en el conomiento social de las emociones en el modo de compatirlas* [Sex and gender identity: Differences in social knowledge on emotions and in ways of sharing them]. Unpublished doctoral dissertation, Universidad del Pais Vasco, San Sebastian, Spain.

Wallbott, H. G., & Scherer, K. R. (1994). Evidence for universality and cultural variation of differential emotion response patterning. *Journal of Personality and Social Psychology, 66,* 310–328.

Chapter 7

Social Processes and Collective Memory: A Cross-Cultural Approach to Remembering Political Events

Dario Paez
Nekane Basabe
Jose Luis Gonzalez
University of the Basque Country, Spain

Social memory reflects the influence of social factors on individual memory. Collective memory, on the other hand, can be considered as distributed processes of memory or transactive memory (Wegner, 1988) with social functions. This chapter studies how individuals and groups assimilate and cope with past collective traumatic political events. Much of the research builds from Halbwachs' approach to social and collective memory. Specifically, the function of socially shared images of the past is to allow the group to foster social cohesion, to develop and defend social identification, and to justify current attitudes and needs. Halbwachs posited that past political events are remembered when they are commemorated and this commemoration serves each of these functions. However, traumatic political events are a problem in Halbwachs' theory. They are "silent memories," usually repressed, which voluntarily are forgotten and usually divide a society.

In synthesizing the research on how individuals and groups (in this case families) cope with past political traumas (Spanish and Latin American dictatorship periods), this chapter examines how social sharing, inhibition, remembering, and the attitude toward past and current society are related. It becomes evident that strong relations emerge between remembering negative political events, social sharing, and negative attitudes toward both past and current society. Interestingly, results do not support predictions based on neo-Freudian approaches to collective memory, between inhibition and rumination. Indeed, evidence is provided to suggest that the "conspiracy of silence," or the inhibition of talking about past traumatic events, plays an important social role in legitimizing a current society. In short, forgetting is one of the main processes found in collective memory.

SOCIAL MEMORY AND COLLECTIVE MEMORY

Some authors (Swidler & Arditi, 1994) confound collective memory with social memory. Collective memory asks how social groups remember, forget, or reappropiate the knowledge of the social past; or, as Jodelet (1991) stated, collective memory is the memory of society. Social memory can be conceived of as the influence that certain social factors have on the individual memory or the memory in society. Social psychologists within a collectivistic theoretical framework are interested in both these aspects of memory, but, particularly on the latter. Recent work on collective memory has developed in three directions. First, historians and sociologists describe how the social past has been constructed or reappropiated in order to serve current social attitudes and needs, especially when defining social identities and nations (Swidler & Arditi, 1994). As an example, the Israeli population reappropiated the events that took place in Massada, an isolated armed rebellion against the Romans that had been ignored in classical Jewish tradition, and started to experience this event as if it were a past precedent of the Tsahal, the Israeli army. This reappropiation of history is also a form of legitimizing the Israeli nation (Schwartz, Zeruzabel, & Barnett, 1986).

A second approach toward collective memory analyzes those factors that allow certain social events to be either retained or lost as part of the collective memory. Events are more likely to be remembered if they were commemorated, emotionally ladened and novel (as, e.g., political flashbulb memories; see chapter 8, this volume, by Gaskell & Wright), personally relevant, and if they took place during one's lifetime (see chapter 2, this volume, by Conway). Social events are remembered particularly if they happen during one's adolescence and early adulthood, a time that seems to be a formative period in one's social identity (Schuman & Scott, 1989). Finally, social events are more likely to form part of collective memories if they involve changes in the central aspects of social life. Connerton (1989) analyzed how even though the killing of French kings was not that strange in French history, the execution of Louis XVI during the French bourgeois revolution of 1793 had a very strong impact and is still remembered today. This is due to the fact that the other deaths did not alter the main aspects of French social life.

The third important line of research involves the analyses of those factors that lead negative and repressed, not commemorated or institutionally denied, events to be retained as an important aspect of the collective memory. Conflicts involving the reality and meaning of past political repression or collective political catastrophes in Latin America (i.e., Chile or Argentina) and Southern Europe (i.e., Spain and Portugal), are good examples of this third phenomenon (see chapter 13, by Marques, Paez, & Serra, on the Portuguese dictatorship and the colonial war).

An important question concerns how social groups remember, forget, or reappropiate certain knowledge from extreme negative past events. Or, in Pennebaker's terms, what are the dynamics explaining the fact that "silent events," such as denied mass executions, form part of the collective memories? Due to the fact that even basic data on these processes is scarce, this chapter focuses on some aspects of this topic.

TRAUMATIC COLLECTIVE EVENTS AND ASSIMILATION

Extremely stressful events, or those far from normal in everyday life, are perceived as being traumatic events with an affective impact on individuals and collectivities. Wars, political disasters, an economic crisis, periods of repression, and so on, are events that undergo a social process of assimilation and reconstruction. In the specific case of dictatorships, these impose a pervasive climate of fear, denial, or forced silence of the traumatic events (e.g., torture, collective violence). Repeated acts of violence generate a climate of diffused fear, which is linked to communication inhibition, individualism, and social isolation (De Rivera, 1992). For instance, both Spain (1939–1975) and Chile (1973–1989) suffered strong right wing dictatorships that led to, among other things, a large number of traumatic events taking place. In 1936, Spain had a population of over 30 million people, during the Civil War (1936–1939) nearly 1 million people died. After the war, 200,000 political prisoners were killed and between 700,000 and 1 million people were forced into exile. In Chile, out of a population of 10 million, 1.6 million people were forced to migrate or seek asylum, 50,000 people were detained as political prisoners, and 3,000 people were killed or "disappeared" (Jackson, 1965; Paez, Asún, & González, 1995; Thomas, 1962; also Lira, chapter 11, this volume).

Different theories have stated that after a period of silence and inhibition social dynamics usually involve the social awareness and articulation of the pain and suffering (Horowitz, 1986; Janoff-Bulman, 1992; Pennebaker, 1990). For instance, Horowitz (1986) stated that the involuntary activities of remembering (obsessive rumination) follow a series of phases (denial, avoidance combined with intrusion) that fulfill the role of both affectively and cognitively assimilating the event. But all these theories have one factor in common: They all focus on individual memory. This is the reason why Halbwachs' theory on collective memory is presented.

COLLECTIVE MEMORY AND TRAUMATIC EVENTS

Halbwachs (1950/1968) conceived of collective memories as those memories of a shared past that are retained by members of a group, class, or nation. The term refers to shared memories of societal-level events, especially extreme, intense events that have led to important institutional changes. Collective memory rests on events that have an impact on collectivities and have driven them to modify their institutions, beliefs, and values. Research conducted on vivid memories has confirmed that unexpected and emotionally laden events attract more attention and are better remembered than other more neutral events (Ibañez, 1992; Pennebaker, 1993; Ruiz-Vargas, 1993; Pennebaker & Banasik, chapter 1, this volume). Focusing on processes, collective memory will be the cross-generational oral transmission of events important for the group (Vansina, in Ross, 1991). The bases of collective memory are oral stories, rumors, gestures, or cultural styles, in addition to written stories and institutionalized cultural activities (Halbwachs, 1950/1968; Jodelet, 1991). Collective memories are widely shared images and knowledge of a past social event that has not been personally experienced, is collectively created and shared, and has social functions (Schuman & Scott, 1989).

Available empirical data confirms the reality of this phenomenon: asked about different traumatic events that had taken place during the last 40 years to themselves or to members of their primary groups, 66% of a sample of university students from Chile, Catalunya (Spain), and the Basque Country (also Spain) (mean age of the sample 22 years, range 18–35) answered that the most important traumatic event had happened to their grandparents' generation (8%), to their parents' generation (44%), or to the group in general (13%). Only 34% of the sample referred to themselves or to subjects belonging to their own generation.

Research conducted on memory as a collective phenomenon is based, even more than that of individual memory, on the socially distributed processes of remembering. Memory is something that takes place only inside individuals, but the distributed process of remembering has social functions and effects on a societal level. The collective memory of political catastrophes is a socially distributed memory. These events may not be publicly commemorated or preserved. In fact, they may even be institutionally repressed. But they are maintained as habits, oral traditions, monuments, and historical archives (Ibañez, 1992). For example, in the case of John F. Kennedy's assassination, although the official statements say otherwise, the public still accepts and believes that the president was the victim of a conspiracy (Basterra, 1993).

Different authors state that there are psychological processes that transcend a mere individual although they manifest themselves by means of these same individuals. These processes lean on individual activities and are actualized in them, but nevertheless they have their own autonomy and effectiveness. These phenomena are referred to as collective processes of memory (Garzón & Rodríguez, 1989; Wertsch, 1991). This perspective has recently been taken up by current social psychology. This approach states that cognition is not only an internal act but also an external and social one. Memory and thought are seen as a social interaction, and the focus of analysis is the social unit (Levine, Ressnick, & Higgins, 1993). Evidence shows that groups remember better than individuals and there are socially distributed memory systems in the dyads. These transactional memories are shared systems aimed at codifying, storing, and recovering information in which different members of the group are in charge of remembering specific areas or contents and not other contents (Wegner, quoted in Levine, Ressnick, & Higgins, 1993).

The meaning and articulation of the individual and collective levels of the processes must be studied, including the influence of macropsychological indexes on individual processes. In other words, the influence of social factors on individual memory should be studied. For instance, in a recent study, in individuals the level of social sharing of traumatic events is associated with more knowledge and more vivid memories of collective catastrophes such as the Spanish Civil War. These results are an example of the effects that interpersonal factors have on individual processes of memory.

Another procedure by which the collective processes involved in memory may be studied is by using aggregated data (i.e., average or means) for group units. There are statistical methods that allow checking the interdependence of responses (intraclass coefficient; Kenny, 1986). For example, we could use questions on social sharing (How often do you talk about violent acts related to the Spanish Civil War?), social inhibition (How often do you avoid talking about these events?), attitudes (Do you evaluate the Spanish Civil War negatively or positively?), knowledge (Do you have a clear image? Are you aware of the real causes which led to the Spanish Civil War?), and so on. There are tools to test the existence of interdependence within families (a significant positive intraclass correlation in these responses). Analyzing data on the family level for measures of social sharing, social inhibition, attitude, and knowledge about the Spanish Civil War allows the exploration of not just families, but broader social norms and social processes.

The group level of social sharing and social inhibition represents the collective processes of memory, and the group mean knowledge the content of the collective memory. Looking at the association between these measures is another way of contrasting the social processes involved in memory. Comparing the relations on an individual level (i.e., the correlation between individual scores on social sharing and attitude) with the relations on a group level (i.e., the correlation between a family's means or any other group unit on group social sharing and group attitude or norm) allows testing of both psychological and more social memory theories. Associations found on an individual level are not necessarily valid at the collective level, as has been shown by research comparing individual-level and aggregated data. Usually, attitudes have a moderate association with congruent memory on an individual level (i.e., a positive attitude toward an object is related with remembering better the available information on this object). An interesting example of the links between social memory and recall of facts related to the memory can be seen in the ways people in 12 European surveys think about and behave in response to health advertising. In one study, it was found that positive attitudes about the health advertisements were associated with poor memories of them. In fact, whereas attitudes toward a campaign progressively turn positive at the same time subjects remember their content less. Decrease in remembering appears to go along with a decrease in the social sharing of these issues. Because of saturation or because the campaign does not induce social discussion due to a dominant positive social climate toward their content, at the collective level the relations between attitudes and memory were exactly the opposite to those found on an individual level (Insua, Pizarro, & Paez, 1994). This example shows that collective level relations may be different from individual level relations, and at the same time confirm the central role of social sharing in collective remembering, one of Halbwachs' main ideas on social and collective memory.

Halbwachs' framework organizes the research on the social factors involved in individual memory and on the relations between the group level processes of memory. It should be noted that Halbwachs did not support the existence of a superordinate "group mind." Rather, he stressed the social nature of memory and, simultaneously, the importance of the social functions of distributed knowledge of the past on the individuals who form a group. Next, a brief overview of Halbwachs' theory is presented, including its possibilities and limitations in relation to traumatic collective events and "silent memories."

THE SOCIAL PROCESSES OF MEMORY

Halbwachs' classical work on collective memory stressed the social and constructive nature of memory. His approach suggested that social processes are essential to memory (Namer, 1987). According to Halbwachs, memory is social, first of all, because of its contents: People always remember a world in which other people also live. Memory of the past is always that of an intersubjective past, of a past time lived in relations with other people.

Pillemer, Rinehart, and White (1986, quoted in Conway, 1990) asked undergraduates to recall four distinct memories from their first year at college and senior students to recall memories from their second year. The vast majority of these memories mentioned interactions with other people. Memories featuring only the person who was remembering were comparatively rare. So, there is evidence to confirm Halbwachs' hypothesis on the dominant social content of memory. Second, memory is social because people often use socially given referential points, such as rituals, ceremonies, and social events to remember something. (Moreover, it is quite normal to use some referential time points to remember specific events or certain social ceremonies such as birthdays.) Different social groups use different spatial and temporal social reference points. Bartlett (1973) stressed the importance of schemata or cultural frameworks on the reconstructive recall of narrations, while already pointing out the social functions of schemata. Empirically, Robinson (1986) found that the academic term seemed to facilitate memory in a word-recall task and the pauses or finishing spots in a term are reliably marked by an increase in the number of recalled memories in cued autobiographical memory retrieval tasks. This research confirms that memory is determined by socially given landmarks.

Third, memory is social because people remember sharing memories and remembering together (Halbwachs, 1950/1968). Empirically, three different studies have shown that overt rehearsal (i.e., how often people talked about an event) is a good predictor of vividness of personally important events and/or flashbulb memories (Bohannon, 1988; Rubin & Kozin, 1984, both quoted in Conway, 1990). Actual high levels of emotional reactions when remembering personally important past events are associated with high levels of covert and overt rehearsal in the past, at least for pleasant events (Paez, Vergara, & Velasco, 1991). This evidence confirms Halbwachs' idea on the central role of social activity and social sharing in remembering. Confirming these ideas, knowledge about the Spanish Civil War was related to the level of socialization or social sharing (see Table 7.1). This association appeared both on an individual and group level (using family means as units of analysis). This last result is important because it is an example of what Halbwachs had in mind when thinking about collective memory.

Using groups as the unit of analysis allowed the study on a collective level of the relations between the memory of traumatic events and these processes of remembering. In this study, the degree of knowledge about the Spanish Civil War was measured using five items referring to the amount of information participants recalled. These measures assessed the degree to which participants had clear images and vivid visual memories, a clear memory of the actors and groups that took part in the war, and an image on the context or causes that led to the war. Answers ranged from 1 (*not at all*) to 5 (*very*

TABLE 7.1
Correlations Between Reevaluation, Rumination, Social Sharing,
Attitudes Toward the Spanish Civil War, Knowledge and
Information on the Spanish Civil War (SCW)

	Reappraisal	Rumination	Social Sharing	Attitude SCW	Knowledge SCW
Reappraisal	1.00	.09	.54**	.04	.44**
Rumination	.34***	1.00	.38**	.13	.09
Social sharing	.42***	.55***	1.00	−.24&	.45***
Attitude SCW	−.16*	−.02	−.09	1.00	−.32*
Knowledge SCW	.26***	.32***	.41***	−.20**	1.00

Note: A higher score implies more reevaluation, rumination, social sharing, evaluation of the SCW as something positive, and more knowledge about the SCW. The coefficients shown in the inferior triangular matrix belong to the individual scores. The superior matrix belongs to the collective scores. N individual = 189–195 subjects; N collective = 32 families.
$&p < .10.$ $*p < .05.$ $**p < .01.$ $***p < .001.$

much). Attitudes on the Spanish Civil War included two indexes on the pleasant versus unpleasant and positive versus negative nature of the war (responses ranging from 1 to 7). The indexes of the memory processes referring to different traumatic events included reevaluation measures (Have you voluntarily thought about this event in order to understand, assimilate, and explain it to yourself?), rumination (Have you thought about this event when you did not want to do so?), inhibition (Do you avoid talking or thinking about the event, and go on talking about another thing?), and social sharing (Do you usually talk about the event?). All these responses ranged from 1 (*not at all*) to 5 (*very much*).

As depicted in Table 7.1, on the individual level the knowledge about the Spanish Civil War is positively associated with the processes of reevaluation, rumination, and social sharing. Finally, the relations between inter- and intrapersonal processes, between social sharing and mental reevocation (rumination and reevaluation) were also confirmed. In other words, and as Halbwachs already stated, internal remembering is associated with the interpersonal repetition of a historical event (in this case the Spanish Civil War). Other studies have also shown that rumination and reevaluation of an autobiographical event, or an event that involves a person's extended identity, are correlated with the interpersonal communication of this event.

On a group or family level results show that collective memory (group mean on knowledge about the Spanish Civil War) is positively associated with stronger social sharing. More social sharing and greater knowledge are also associated with a more negative evaluation of the Spanish Civil War. These results are interesting because they confirm similar patterns comparing individual attitudes and interpersonal processes on social norms (group negative attitude), and social processes of memory and collective memory (group knowledge about the Spanish Civil War). As usual, when comparing individual and aggregated indexes (i.e., means of groups), the patterns of results were clearer on the collective than on the individual level (i.e., the family mean on social sharing is related to a negative social norm on the Spanish Civil War, but individual measures of attitude and social sharing are nonsignificantly related; Ostroff, 1993). One explanation for the superiority of the aggregated measures in relation to the individual measures is simply a methodological one: Aggregated measures are more reliable, because random error scores disappear at the mean level. However, some social psychologists (Kenny, 1986; Ostroff, 1993) have stated that the stronger association at the collective level is related to the emergent properties of group interaction. In other words, the aggregated variable represents the psychological construct on a higher level of analysis (i.e., memory on a distributed or collective level).

CONFRONTATION–INHIBITION, INTERNAL REHEARSAL, TRAUMATIC COLLECTIVE EVENTS, AND SOCIAL CLIMATE

According to Halbwachs, memory is social or intersubjective because it is based on language and on an external or internal linguistic communication with significant others (Halbwachs, 1950/1968). Memory is an account, a public rehearsal with important social functions—at least at a symbolic level. Different theoretical frameworks assert the idea that intra- and interpersonal cognitive processes play a central role in the construction and assimilation of stressful past events. Emotionally ladened events are conceived of as experiences that generate long-lasting cognitive intra- (rumination) and interpersonal (social sharing) processes. Social sharing is defined as the reevocation of the emotional event in a socially shared language and as a communication process or dialogue during which parts of the personal emotional experience are shared with social partners (at least at a symbolic level, as is the case when one writes a letter). A number of studies have shown that repetitive social sharing appears to be the modal response in the case of normal autobiographical events. No differences among emotions were found in the frequency of, or delay in, social sharing. Ruminative thoughts about autobiographical emotional events appear as a modal response (Paez, 1993; Rimé, Philippot, Boca, & Mesquita, 1992). Christianson and Loftus (1990) found similar results in traumatic memories. Frequency of social sharing and rumination has been shown to be stable across cultures and age groups (Rimé et al., 1992).

Rimé et al.'s (1992) approach suggests that social sharing does in fact play a functional role in the assimilation of an emotional experience. This perspective states that coping by means of sharing a past collective event is related to a more positive judgment of the current social climate. By confronting and talking about traumatic events, subjects are able to assimilate and elaborate their emotional experience, constructing more complex schemas and more subtle or moderate evaluations. According to this, the evaluation of a society will be more positive when there is a higher level of social sharing or communication than when there is not.

Other authors state that social sharing of upsetting autobiographical experiences could reactivate the emotional disruption rather than help assimilate it (Tait & Silver, 1989), and in this way, reinforce a negative evaluation of society. Tesser's theory of thought and the polarization of attitudes suggests that rehearsing and arguing about a relevant and conflict-laden event provokes a polarization of social attitudes (Fiske & Taylor, 1991; Tesser, 1978). If individuals share more of the collective past traumas, then there will be a polarization of attitudes because people can make the event fit more consistently into their social identity, thereby reinforcing a positive or negative attitude toward society. Following this line of argument, internal rehearsal about a collective event or rumination maintains the memory of a negative event and provokes a negative evaluation of the current emotional climate. In this context, rumination is defined as a form of conscious thinking, directed toward an event for an extended period of time. Rumination involves both automatic and controlled processes (Martin & Tesser, 1989). It can be conceived of as involuntary and obsessive thoughts or dreams associated with an event (Morrow & Nolen-Hoeksema, 1990; Norris, 1990). It is related to depression and intensifies negative affective reactions (Nolen-Hoeksema, 1991). As well, it appears to increase the likelihood of individuals recalling negative information and making negative inferences about events.

Rumination can be seen as a voluntary way to think about the event. A negative event can be viewed in a more positive way if the ruminating leads to understanding, explaining, and reappraising the event. Confirming this idea, Fairbank, Hasen, and Fitterling (1991), found that nondepressed and better adapted World War II veterans used more positive reappraisal to cope with traumatic war memories than veterans with Posttraumatic Stress Disorder. There were no differences in seeking social support or emotional expression. This suggests that reappraisal may be more adaptive than social sharing or emotional discharge. Of course, these results are valid for individual reality. A collective memory approach focuses on the relation existing between reappraisal, social sharing, attitude, and knowledge on an past group event that has not been personally experienced by the subject. But is there the same relations (i.e., a positive relation between reappraisal and attitude toward a traumatic event) at the collective level? This is the central issue in Halbwachs' approach to the functions and effects of distributed memory.

SOCIAL IDENTITY, ATTITUDES, AND THE SOCIAL FUNCTIONS OF MEMORIES

According to Halbwachs, memory is social because of its functions. Becoming a member of a social group means assuming and internalizing the common traditions and social representations shared by the group—in other words, sharing the group's collective memory (Ramos, 1989). Collective memory allows people to have a certain social identification, both on an individual and a societal level.

Halbwachs posited a global function and a group function of collective memory. The global function is the nostalgic function: Past society appears in part as a Golden Age, while also providing a stable and positive image on which to add new elements (see Bellelli & Amatulli, chapter 10, this volume). For example, in the past families were viewed as being more cohesive, and social life as less dangerous. Historical research has questioned the myth about the existence of a three-generation family in North America, in which elders lived together and were supported by the younger generations (Hareven, 1994). Chesnais' (1981) historical research also shows that each period is usually perceived as more dangerous than the recent past—even when social violence objectively declines. In a similar vein, in a survey on the nation's or the world's most important events remembered over the past 50 years, Schuman and Scott (1989) found that characterizations of World War II as a good and victorious war are more persistent in the Vietnam "dirty" War generation than in the members of the World War II generation itself. Schuman and Scott's interpretation of this result is in line with what Halbwachs mentioned as the nostalgic function of collective memory: This 1960s generation feels nostalgic about a social world they have not known directly, in contrast to their own youth's conflicted society of the late 1960s and 1970s (Schuman & Scott, 1989).

The second social function is related to group goals and needs. Memory is socially anchored on the actual needs and goals of groups. According to Halbwachs, collective memory is essentially a reconstruction of the past, which adapts the image of old facts to the beliefs and spiritual needs of the present (Halbwachs, 1950/1968; Middleton & Edwards, 1990; Schwartz, 1990). Ross (1991) reviewed different empirical research that clearly supports this approach at an individual level. The usual finding is that recall derived from past attitudes correlates more positively with current, rather than with past, real position or evaluative judgment. People exaggerate the consistency between their present (new) attitudes and their past opinions. Research on flashbulb memories has shown the influence that belonging to a group has on remembering. For example, many individuals (both White and African American) had flashbulb memories of John F. Kennedy's assassination, but only some of the White subjects, as compared to a higher percentage of African Americans, had flashbulb memories of the assassinations of Martin Luther King, Jr. and Malcolm X (Conway, 1990). Previously quoted research on the revival and reappropiation of Massada in Israel is an example of this reconstruction of the past in order to fulfill present societal needs.

According to Bartlett (1932/1973) as well as Halbwachs (1950/1968), group belonging and socially proscribed cognitive frameworks are essential to the processes of remembering. Informal groups and formal institutions have distinct effects on remembering. They organize systematic commemorations and forgetting in order to fulfill present needs and goals (Douglas, 1989). By the same token, current positive attitude toward, and evaluation of, a society should be related to forgetting negative collective events.

On the other hand, what happens when negative group events are important and affect their social identity? What are the processes and effects related to ambivalent or negative events, such as lost wars and mass murders committed by a nation? Because of the normative function of collective memory ("a lesson about the group"), it is assumed that remembering and social sharing about past collective traumatic events can have an impact not only on attitudes toward the past, but also toward current society. The studies have focused on the relation between sharing or confrontation, avoiding or voluntary forgetting, internal processes (rumination and reappraisal), attitudes, and social knowledge on political catastrophes. Are subjects more prone to confront or to avoid past group traumatic events? To what extent is voluntary forgetting or inhibition related to a negative event in comparison to a positive collective event? Does remembering negative past events have an impact not only on attitude toward the past historical fact, but also on current attitudes toward society? As usual, common sense suggests opposite answers to these topics. Research on posttraumatic stress offers some insights, but these studies are focused on individual responses to traumatic events that have been personally experienced. In order to give some kind of answer to this problem, a series of studies was conducted.

COPING WITH TRAUMATIC PAST EVENTS

In a transcultural comparative study using young student samples ($M = 22.6$ years) from four countries (Chile, Spain, the United States, and Great Britain), we examined several events that had taken place during a 40-year period. In the project, we analyzed confrontation and inhibition processes and their relation with the evaluation of their country's emotional climate. In this study, if any member of the subjects' family or acquaintances had suffered any of a series of traumatic events during the past 40 years, the participants were asked to indicate if they had talked (social sharing); avoided talking (inhibition); thought a lot about the event when they did not want to do so (rumination); or thought a lot about the event in order to understand, assimilate, and explain it to themselves (reevaluation). A list of the events can be seen in Table 7.2. All the responses ranged from 1 (*not at all*) to 5 (*very much* or *always*). The participants were asked to evaluate their country's emotional climate (1 = *very bad*, 5 = *very good*).

On the basis of the remembrance of traumatic events, we found that in Chile, and in the Basque Country and Catalunya (both Spanish samples), there were a higher number of remembered negative events. Moreover, in these three samples there was also a higher remembrance of events related with political persecution, violent acts, economic emigration, and coming back to the country after exile (see Table 7.2). We also studied the relationship between the evaluation of a country's social climate and remembering negative traumatic events. We found that, at least in both Spanish samples and in Chile, when there was a higher remembrance of traumatic events there was also a worse evaluation of the country. This confirms the existence of a relation between remembering extreme negative events that have affected one's own group and the evaluation of the affective climate. We performed a meta-analysis on the different countries (transforming r to z and weighting z scores by the number of subjects in each sample). From this analysis we obtained a correlation coefficient of $r = -.11$, $p < .05$, which confirms the relation between negative social climate and higher presence of negative traumatic events.

Confrontation or social sharing may help the cognitive and emotional assimilation of traumatic collective events. In fact, the results on how individuals in Chile, Catalunya, and the Basque Country cope with traumatic events that have happened to members of their group confirm the idea that people talk more than inhibit, and confront more than avoid the topic of tortures, political prison, and exile (see Table 7.3). The comparisons conducted on social sharing and inhibition scores show that there is more confrontation than inhibition of talking about the remembered events. People also think in order to reevaluate more than they "live" the rumination or the involuntary repetition of the event. The exception being that in Chile there were no differences between social sharing and reappraisal. In this country, there is more inter- and intrapersonal processing than in Spain. As depicted in Table 7.3, there is more social confrontation, reappraisal, and rumination in Chile, the country with the most recent traumatic collective past than in any other country. This confirms the idea

TABLE 7.2
Differences Between Countries in Traumatic Events

	Catalunya	Basque Country	Chile	USA	Great Britain	$\chi^2(gl)$ p
Victim of robbery, assault, or theft	91.1%	83.5%	90.6%	70.6%	34.6%	59.9 (4) $p < .001$
Victim of a violent act	28.3%	38.0%	25%	32.4%	7.7%	11.9 (4) $p < .02$
Having committed violent acts	47.2%	50.0%	34.4%	8.8%	23.1%	26.8 (4) $p < .001$
Being involved in suicides, homocides, or accidents	58.9%	63.9%	59.4%	50%	50%	3.5 (4) $p < .47$
Avoid or escape from homocides, accidents, or violent acts	44.4%	51.3%	46.9%	32.4%	46.2%	4.4 (4) $p < .34$
Suffer harm due to natural or human disasters	39.4%	51.9%	40.6%	32.4%	15.4%	15.7 (4) $p < .003$
Unemployment, being made redundant	77.2%	84.2%	62.5%	58.8%	34.6%	38.7 (4) $p < .001$
Achieve economic success	51.1%	47.5%	56.3%	58.8%	23.1%	10.0 (4) $p < .04$
Suffer economic, housing, or health problems	74.4%	71.5%	84.4%	55.9%	73.1%	9.7 (4) $p < .04$
Separations, divorce, adultery, or non-wanted pregnancy	76.1%	70.3%	82.8%	70.6%	42.3%	17.0 (4) $p < .002$
Suffer banishment, political exile, or jail	30%	44.9%	43.8%	11.8%	7.7%	27.7 (4) $p < .001$
Having emigrated due to economic problems	62.2%	57.6%	54.7%	5.9%	15.4%	52.6 (4) $p < .001$
Coming back from emigration, banishment, exile, or long absence	28.9%	34.2%	35.9%	8.8%	11.5%	14.0 (4) $p < .007$

TOTAL EVENTS (mean)	Catalunya	Basque Country	Chile	USA	Great Britain	F p
Total positive events	1.24	1.33	1.39	1.00	0.81	2.60 $p < .03$
Total negative events	5.85	6.16	5.78	3.97	3.03	18.49 $p < .001$

Note: Catalunya, $n = 180$. Basque Country, $n = 158$. Chile, $n = 64$. USA, $n = 34$. Great Britain, $n = 26$. $N = 462$.

that after a period of traumatic events and inhibition, a higher level of social sharing is expected. It was also found that when comparing response means to the variables on social sharing, inhibition, rumination, and re-evaluation for those participants who had answered that all the events had happened to them or to their "group," the same pattern of results already mentioned were obtained.

TABLE 7.3

Means for Subjects Remembering Political Prison
and Exile as One of Their Group's Traumatic Events

	Catalunya (n = 54)	Basque Country (n = 71)	Chile (n = 28)	USA & Britain (n = 6)
Social sharing	2.7[a]	2.1[ab]	3.1[b]	2.3
Inhibition	2.2	2.1	2.3	1.3
Reappraisal	2.2[ab]	1.7[ac]	3.2[bc]	2.5
Rumination	1.8[a]	1.4[ab]	2.1[b]	2.0

Note:

1) Due to the low number of subjects in the Anglo-Saxon sample this was not submitted to a t test.

2) Horizontal comparisons between countries: means sharing the same letter are significantly different ($p < .05$).

3) Vertical t tests:

Significant differences in Catalunya ($p < .05$):
  People talk more than ruminate, inhibit, or reevaluate.
  People reevaluate more than ruminate.
Significant differences in the Basque Country:
  People talk more than reevaluate or ruminate ($p < .05$).
  People reevaluate more than ruminate ($p < .01$).
  People inhibit more than reevaluate or ruminate ($p < .05$).
Significant differences in Chile ($p < .05$):
  People talk more than ruminate or inhibit.
  People reevaluate more than ruminate or avoid talking about the event.

These results suggest that after suffering a traumatic and inhibitory period, the social dynamics usually involve social sharing and confrontation. Indeed, after this period, there is a search for a way to express the emotional events at an individual and collective level.

INHIBITION–CONFRONTATION, RUMINATION, AND COLLECTIVE MEMORY

Because of the normative nature of collective memory aimed at defending social identity, a common response to a traumatic past event is silence and inhibition. Groups organize informal forgetting, reconstruction, and positive distortion of the past in order to defend group values and their own image. In the case of sociopolitical events, such as torture or comparable atrocities, people fail to talk openly about them because of the fear of repression or not knowing how others will respond to hearing about the events (Pennebaker, 1990). Social history studies suggest that forgetting and silence (people prefer not to talk or hear about concentration camp experiences) is a very common reaction (Wieviorka, 1992). The modal veteran's response to war experiences in the case of the Portuguese colonial war was silence or little talking (see Marques, Paez, & Serra, chapter 13, this volume). Halbwachs' framework does not propose clear mechanisms that allow for an explanation of how societies remember conflict-ridden collective events with negative aspects and conflicting meanings.

Freud also suggested ways to conceptualize collective memory, particularly with respect to traumatic events. Freud stressed that societal repression is directed toward forgetting traumatic collective events. Paradoxically, repression or social inhibition and censorship provokes the return of the repressed. On the basis of a neo-Freudian approach, social inhibition of public remembrance will be related to negative evaluation and higher involuntary, unpleasant internal rehearsal or rumination. Pennebaker (1993) stated that traumatic events tend to be inhibited, either because they are a painful reminder of the events, because they may reinforce the subject's or group's stigmatization (e.g., in rape cases), or because those affected by the trauma do not wish to disturb those close to them. Indeed, friends of traumatized individuals often cannot support memories of the events because the friends themselves are not able to find positive meanings to the upheavals. Currently, Pennebaker's (1993) research confirms that inhibiting the social sharing of traumatic group events impedes a cognitive assimilation process. Collective traumatic events that are not assimilated are more likely to remain in the subject's conscience as unwanted and ruminative thoughts. Suppression of these thoughts is associated with increased physiological arousal at an individual level, and with collective distress (Pennebaker, 1993; Wegner, Shortt, Blake, & Page, 1990). Inhibited traumatic events generate repetitive memories and collective distress, which can be expressed in both antisocial (increase in the number of aggressions, deaths by illness) and prosocial behaviors (increase in donations, etc.; Pennebaker, 1993; see also Pennebaker & Banasik, chapter 1, this volume). The results partially confirm the positive effects of confrontation, and the association between inhibition and rumination in some countries.

As depicted in Table 7.4, evidence has been found that social sharing and reappraisal are associated across three samples. Social sharing and inhibition show a negative relation only in the country with a more distant repressive past (Catalunya) and a lower level of conflict, suggesting that in the short term, and when there is a higher level of conflict, inhibition and confrontation are independent when faced with a traumatic collective event.

Inhibition and rumination are associated in the Spanish samples (a prediction derived from a Freudian approach). Contrary to what was expected, it is in those countries with a more distant traumatic past where both processes are linked. Similarly, a related study found that rumination was associated to inhibition in Belgium and the Basque Country, countries with a more distant traumatic past, but was not associated in Argentina

TABLE 7.4
Correlations Between Memory Processes for
Subjects Remembering Political Prison and Exile

	Catalunya (n = 54)	Basque Country (n = 71)	Chile (n = 28)
Social sharing with reappraisal	.43**	.64**	.30*
Inhibition with rumination	.26**	.47**	.01
Social sharing with inhibition	−.24**	.10	−.04
Social sharing with rumination	.33**	.50**	−.16
Reappraisal with rumination	.58**	.75**	.14
Inhibition with reappraisal	.20*	.41**	.04

*$p < .07$. **$p < .05$.

and Mexico (Paez, Ruiz, Gailly, Kornblit, Wiesenfeld, & Vidal, 1995). However, individuals who suffer direct traumatic events simultaneously show rumination and avoidance or inhibition, and both are related (Horowitz, 1986). These results indicate that, in the short term, inhibition is an effective strategy in coping with collective trauma, but not in the long term, as has been suggested by the existing literature on individual coping (Suls & Fletcher, 1985).

Internal involuntary (rumination) and voluntary (reappraisal) rehearsal are positively associated in general, but significantly only when the collective traumatic event was distant (Catalunya and the Basque Country). However, data from Mexico and Argentina, countries with a recent traumatic past, confirm that rumination and reappraisal are related: global $r(172) = 0, 17$, $p < .01$ (Paez et al., 1995). Voluntary thinking aimed toward understanding is, in general, associated with involuntary and repetitive thinking, and they are not opposing processes, at least in self-reported measures.

COMPARISON BETWEEN EXTREME NEGATIVE AND POSITIVE COLLECTIVE EVENTS

Bearing in mind the tendency to avoid remembering negative events, positive and negative events on the processes of remembering were also compared, studying the specific content of these events: violent acts; problems or economic success; and exile, emigration, or long absence. In each case, the answer given to the negative event was compared with the answer given to the positive event. The results of these analyses contradict Freudian ideas (nonconfrontation of negative events) and are congruent with the existing literature on the asymmetrical impact of positive and negative events (Lewicka, Czapinski, & Peeters, 1992).

As can be seen in Table 7.5, negative events are reevaluated and inhibited more than positive events. In the study, Spanish participants were

TABLE 7.5

Comparison Between Events in Processes of Social Sharing,
Inhibition, Rumination, and Reappraisal (means)

Events	Social Sharing	Inhibition	Rumination	Reappraisal
Negative Event: Suffer banishment, political exile, or jail	2.9	2.4[a]	1.8	2.7[b]
Positive Event: Coming back from emigration, banishment, exile, or long abscence	3.2	1.9[a]	1.8	2.4[b]

Note: $N = 50$ subjects with negative and positive events. Vertical comparisons: means sharing the same letter are significantly different ($a = p < .005$; $b = p < .07$).

asked if they talked or avoided talking about aggression, torture, or exile in reference to members of their families in the post–civil war years. Individuals were also asked if they knew that some member of their family had been tortured or suffered exile. As can be seen in Figs. 7.1 and 7.2, the results confirm the idea that remembering negative events mobilizes more coping. That is, participants whose family members have experienced negative events talk and inhibit more. Those who remember negative events share more than inhibit; other participants show no difference.

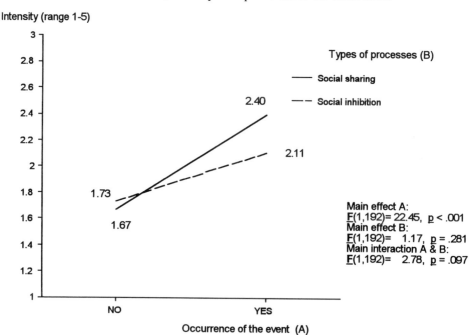

FIG. 7.1. Event: "Having been beaten up or victim of a violent act" (means).

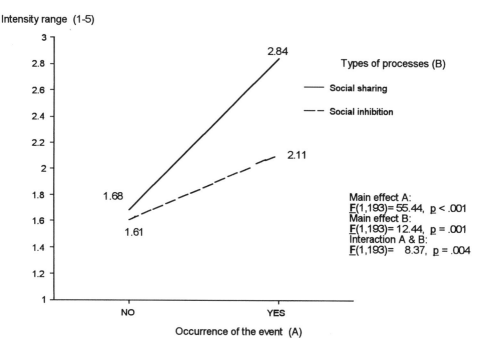

FIG. 7.2. Event: "Coming back from banishment, exile, or prison" (means).

COLLECTIVE MEMORY, SOCIAL CONTEXT, AND CONFLICT

Collective remembrance of past traumatic events is always built into struggles between differing social groups (victims and victimizers, those who support and those who are opposed to a repressive regime, etc.). The issue of whether to hold public trials and discuss past crimes is intimately related to the need to incorporate rather than punish surviving elements of the repressive regimes. Recency of repression effects the effectiveness of coping. Recent traumatic events are more emotionally ladened and provoke more conflict than more distant ones. In the case of the countries studied, Chile was still a dictatorship in 1989. Even now, public opinion in Chile is divided: Some people have a positive view of the dictatorship era, and want to "forget the past" and "not overreact to what happened." Another sector of the population has a very negative stance toward this period and wants the past to end, accept, and resolve all the crimes (see Lira, chapter 11, this volume). In Spain (in this case Catalunya and the Basque Country), the strongest repressive period took place from 1939 to 1955. It has been more than 18 years since the country evolved from a dictatorship to a democracy. Nowadays public opinion is divided between a negative image of the dictatorship years and a "collective forgetfulness." During the transition from a dictatorship to a democracy, not talking about the past was the predominant attitude, and so there is no conflict concerning remembering/forgetting traumatic collective events. Both in Catalunya and the Basque Country, public opinion is mainly nationalist, which is associated with a shared a negative image of the dictatorship. But, in the Basque Country, there is a more negative atmosphere toward the Spanish state and the Franquist past. In fact, the image of the past regime is more homogeneously negative in Spain than in Chile, and levels of social conflict about the past are higher in Chile than in Spain. Higher levels of social sharing and remembrance will provoke a more negative polarization in the judgments of the political atmosphere. This effect will be stronger when there is more recency and conflict.

Table 7.6 presents the correlations between the emotional climate and the different variables on social processing of memory. A positive emotional climate is associated with reevaluation in the country with a lower level of conflict with past traumatic collective events (Catalunya). On the other hand, evaluation of the social climate is negatively associated with social sharing and positively associated with inhibition in Chile.

Using a more reliable and valid measure of emotional climate, these results were confirmed in other Latin American countries. The country's emotional climate was factored into two dimensions: one referring to a positive climate (composed of positive emotions and general evaluations on the economic situation, confidence in the social institutions and the general affective climate), and a second one referring to a negative climate (composed of the following emotions: fear, sadness, and anger). In relation to the processing of violent acts, "having been a victim of tortures and war," and "having taken part in wars, fights, struggles, etc.," we find that confronting these events by talking to other people is related to a worse evaluation of the country. On the other hand, to avoid talking about these

TABLE 7.6

Correlations Between Evaluation of the Social Climate and Social Sharing, Inhibition, Rumination, and Reappraisal Processes (Only Subjects Who Remember Political Prison and Exile as a Traumatic Group Event)

	Catalunya (n = 54)	Basque Country (n = 71)	Chile (n = 28)
Social sharing	−.03	.12	−.30*
Inhibition	.02	.09	.26**
Rumination	.00	−.09	.10
Reappraisal	.21*	.04	.03

*p < .06. **p < .09.

events is related to a better evaluation of the social climate. The correlation coefficients between the country's climate (obtained by subtracting the positive climate from the negative climate) were $r = -.30$, $p < .001$, for social sharing; $r = .17$, $p < .01$, for inhibition; $r = -.09$, n.s., for rumination; and $r = -.29$, $p < .001$, for reappraisal. These results were found in a sample of 173 Latin American university students living in four countries with a recent past of traumatic events: Argentina, Peru, Mexico, and Venezuela (Paez et al., 1995).

In the long term, as is the case with research by Fairbank et al. (1991), reappraisal of past traumatic events is related to a more positive view of society. In the short term, reappraisal and social sharing are related to a polarized negative view of society. Similarly, inhibition acts as an effective coping strategy linked to a positive view of the current society. Rumination is not related to the evaluation of the social climate.

SOCIAL KNOWLEDGE, SOCIAL SHARING, AND ATTITUDES TOWARD PAST COLLECTIVE EVENTS AT AN INDIVIDUAL AND COLLECTIVE LEVEL

Results of research conducted on the Spanish Civil War, using a Basque sample of individuals and families, confirm previous findings and allow a more accurate description of the processes involved in social and collective memory. On a collective level, a negative attitude toward the historical event is related to social sharing, $r = -.24$, $p < .10$. A higher family mean on the topic of talking about the Civil War is related to a more negative social norm or group attitude toward this collective event.

Individual level measures do not show association probably because the sample had a large number of young people. Rumination does not show any influence on attitude either at an individual or collective level. Social sharing was associated with reappraisal and rumination (individual $r = .42$, $p < .001$ and $r = .55$, $p < .001$; collective $r = .54$, $p < .01$ and $r = .38$, $p < .01$, respectively). Individually and collectively, a negative attitude was related to more knowledge about the Spanish Civil War (respectively, $r = -.20$, $p < .001$ and $r = -.20$, $p < .12$). Reappraisal was related to more knowledge, both individual and collectively ($r = .26$, $p < .001$ and $r = .44$, $p < .05$). In order to contrast the specific influences, a multiple regression analysis was performed (Tables 7.7 and 7.8). In general, these results suggest that social sharing and remembering past negative events are associated with knowledge about the traumatic historical event. Specifically, remembering negative past events is related to a more negative attitude toward the Spanish Civil War in the context of a country where the attitude

TABLE 7.7
Multiple Regression Analysis of Attitudes Toward the Spanish Civil War

	D.V.: Attitude Towards the Spanish Civil War					
	Individual Level			*Collective Level*		
Independent Variables	*Beta*	*t*	*sig.*	*Beta*	*t*	*sig.*
Rumination	.09	.94	.32	.13	.57	.57
Social climate	−.08	−1.09	.27	.02	.09	.92
Total events	−.17	−2.00	.04	−.42	−2.05	.05
Inhibition	−.05	−.63	.52	.06	.26	.79
Reappraisal	−.14	−1.59	.11	.28	1.26	.21
Social sharing	−.00	−.02	.98	−.29	−1.15	.25
	MR = .25 *RS* = .06			*MR* = .55 *RS* = .29		

Note: Individual level = 189–195 subjects. Collective level = 32 families; 2–3 subjects from two or three different generations by family. A higher score implies more reevaluation, inhibition, rumination, social sharing, more traumatic events, negative climate in a country, evaluation of the SCW as something positive.

TABLE 7.8
Multiple Regression Analysis on Knowledge About the Spanish Civil War

	D.V.: Knowledge About the Spanish Civil War					
	Individual Level			*Collective Level*		
Independent Variables	*Beta*	*t*	*sig.*	*Beta*	*t*	*sig.*
Rumination	.12	1.44	.15	.07	.33	.74
Social climate	−.09	−1.46	.14	.07	.40	.69
Total events	.29	4.00	.00	.11	.53	.59
Inhibition	−.01	−.16	.86	−.22	−1.03	.31
Reappraisal	.04	.65	.51	.17	.76	.45
Social sharing	.19	2.27	.02	.30	1.20	.24
	RM = .51 *RS* = .26			*RM* = .54 *RS* = .29		

Note: Individual level = 189–195 subjects. Collective level = 32 families; 2–3 subjects from two or three different generations by family. A higher score implies more reevaluation, inhibition, social sharing, more traumatic events, negative climate in a country, and more knowledge about the SCW.

is predominantly negative toward the fascist period. In other words, the affective attitude on an individual level or the social norm on a collective level depend on gross remembrance, whereas knowledge depends on more complex processes such as social sharing. Results are similar at the individual and collective level, even if the fact of having lower statistical power at the collective level does not allow us to reach statistically significant results.

CONCLUSIONS

Oral history or the cross-generation oral transmission of collective events is an adequate definition of what Halbwachs considered collective memory. In this chapter we have studied the processes of remembering, rumination, and interpersonal communication associated with various traumatic events affecting the groups to which individuals belong. We studied events affecting the group even before the participants were actually born. In fact, most subjects selected an event that had happened to their grandparents, parents, or to their whole social group as the most important historical event.

According to Halbwachs, the image of the past is a social process because people remember sharing memories and remembering together. Halbwachs' perspective would state that the "internal" activities (rumination and reevaluation) and the interpersonal ones should be grouped together, and the latter would be the most important ones. Congruently with Halbwachs' (1950/1968) approach to social and collective memory, we found that internal memory has a positive relationship with external interpersonal repetition and the latter was more frequently found than the former.

On a collective level, comparing samples from Chile, Catalunya, and the Basque Country, we found that Chile, a country with a recent history of traumatic events and a higher level of social conflict with respect to collective remembrance, showed a higher level of social sharing, reappraisal, and rumination when compared to those other countries that had a lower level of social conflict and a more distant traumatic past. These results confirm those theories suggesting that after a period of trauma and sociopolitical repression, social dynamics usually imply social sharing and the public articulation of emotions, past pain, and suffering.

Confirming Halbwachs' idea on the central role of social activity and social sharing in remembering, we also found that knowledge about the Spanish Civil War was related to the degree of social sharing both on an individual and collective level. In other words, intrapsychic remembering processes are linked to social sharing and group knowledge is associated to group level communication of the past.

For Halbwachs, memory is also socially anchored to the actual needs and goals of the group. Collective memory is inextricably linked to social identity. Becoming a member of a social group means assuming and internalizing common traditions shared by the group. Collective memory is essentially a reconstruction of the past, which adapts the image of ancient facts to the needs of the present moment. Both repression and remembrance of traumatic events can influence one's current attitude toward society (Jodelet, 1991). Those informal chats on the topic of wars and disasters (i.e., "Sit down son, I've just remembered a story about when I was in . . .") are a source of representations transmitted toward the inside of groups. This "submerged informal history" is a source of collective memory that generates intragroup loyalties and intergroup hate (Uslar Pietri, 1992).

Because collective memories are normative, if there are a high number of traumatic memories within a group or country, then more members of the group or country will evaluate the country's emotional climate as negative. The research confirms the relation between frequency of perceived occurrence of traumatic events in groups that are close to the respondents and the respondents' negative evaluation of the emotional climate. Of course, this pattern can be seen as an effect of current attitude on the recollection of past group traumatic events. Memory distortions and reconstructions are a real phenomenon that cannot be denied. However, in the case of extreme negative events, undergoing a strong reconstruction is more difficult. The normative influence of the past is more important than the reconstructive influence of the present attitude toward the past.

Confrontation activities (which are thought to be more adaptive) were found more frequently than inhibitory behaviors both in an intrapsychic and interpersonal level. They were also associated with a negative evaluation of society in the case of a recent traumatic collective past. Social sharing and reappraisal were positively associated between them in general and were negatively associated with inhibition or interpersonal avoidance activities. Moreover, inhibition was associated with a better evaluation of the country in the Chilean and Latin American cases, suggesting that a positive image of the country is linked to social silence. This data supports the idea that a "conspiracy of silence" not only speaks louder than words, but also that it plays an effective ideological function: that of legitimizing the present situation. Results partially confirm Tesser's model of thought- induced attitude change: High social sharing was related to a more negative evaluation of the social climate in Latin America (Tesser, 1978). However, this was not due to thought induction (rumination or reappraisal) because in Chile there was no relation between social sharing, reappraisal, and rumination. In the case of a recent past of collective trauma, social sharing about past events provokes a group polarization in the attitude toward society, or at least a more negative attitude. In the long term (in those countries with less conflict about past collective traumas), reappraisal is related to a more positive view of society.

With respect to the differences between positive and negative events, the latter induce more coping mobilization than equivalent positive events, in particular inhibition and reappraisal. Negative collective events that are closer to participants (related to parents and members of the group) provoke more social memory processes: Those who have family members who experienced negative events talk and inhibit more on this topic than individuals who did not remember these negative collective events. Participants who remembered collective negative events share more than inhibit relative to other participants who show no differences.

Rumination is not related to a negative perception of the emotional climate. These results disconfirm the importance of involuntary reminiscences of past traumatic events on having a negative view of present-day society. Inhibition, avoidance, or voluntarily forgetting past traumatic events does not provoke rumination or a negative view of society in the short term, and in Chile and the other Latin American samples inhibition was related to a positive image of one's society.

In Spain, social sharing was related to more knowledge about the Spanish Civil War. More memories of negative past events were related to a negative evaluation of this historical event. This means that social sharing is specifically associated with a more complex and developed knowledge about the traumatic historical event, but it is not related to its affective evaluation. That is, it was remembering past negative events that showed a relation with a negative attitude toward the Spanish Civil War.

More relevant to the collective memory topic is that results of the group analysis (using family means as an index of collective processes) demonstrated that the participants' responses within families were intercorrelated and supported the influence of the collective processes of memory. Collectively, a negative attitude or social norm toward the historical event is related to high levels of social processing of the past (social sharing) and to a more developed collective memory (family mean knowledge about the Spanish Civil War). Reappraisal was related to more general knowledge about the Civil War. This implies that a social climate in which people socialize about a past traumatic event is related to a more emotional and polarized norm about this collective trauma and provokes a stronger re-evaluation or voluntary thinking about the event.

Even if the data is limited (because of the use of an introspective questionnaire or purposive samples), the results suggest that groups sharing their past collective traumas have a more emotional and complex memory about these events. We posit that the social function of sharing past traumatic events is to learn and have a clear image about the collective events ("those who do not remember their past are forced to repeat it"). Finally, results based on group means confirm the existence and interrelation of collective processes of memory. Although these are correlational data and it is quite difficult to distinguish cause from effect, they are an example of the social processes of memory or an interpersonal sharing of the past, and group knowledge does have an influence on the level of reflection.

ACKNOWLEDGMENTS

The writing of this chapter and some of the research reported herein was partially supported by grant PB 94-0475-CO2 from the Ministry of Education and Science, Spain.

REFERENCES

Bartlett, F. C. (1973). Los factores sociales del recuerdo [Social factors of memory]. In H. Proshansky & B. Seidenberg (Eds.), *Estudios básicos de psicología social.* Madrid: Tecnos. (Original work published 1932)

Basterra, F. G. (1993). John F. Kennedy, treinta años después [John F. Kennedy, thirty years later]. *Suplemento El Pais, 144,* 16–31.

Chesnais, J. C. (1981). *Histoire de la violence* [History of violence]. Paris: Laffont.

Christianson, S. A., & Loftus, E. (1990). Some characteristics of people's traumatic memories. *Bulletin of the Psychonomic Society, 28,* 195–198.

Connerton, P. (1989). *How societies remember.* Cambridge, England: Cambridge University Press.

Conway, M. (1990). *Autobiographical memory.* Milton Keynes: Open University Press.

De Rivera, J. (1992). Social structure and emotional dynamics. In K. T. Strongman (Ed.), *International review of studies on emotion* (Vol. 2, pp. 197–218). Chichester, England: Wiley.

Douglas, M. (1989). *Ainsi pensent les Institutions.* Florence: Usher.

Fairbank, J. A., Hasen, D. J., & Fitterling, J. M. (1991). Pattern of appraisal and coping across different stressor conditions among former prisoners of war with and without posttraumatic stress disorder. *Journal of Consulting and Clinical Psychology, 59,* 274–281.

Fiske, S. T., & Taylor, S. E. (1991). *Social cognition.* New York: McGraw-Hill.

Garzón, A., & Rodríguez, A. (1989). El individuo y los procesos colectivos [The individual and collective processes]. In A. Rodríguez & J. Seoane (Eds.), *Creencias, actitudes y valores: Tratado de psicología general 7.* Madrid: Alhambra.

Halbwachs, M. (1968). *La mémoire collective* [Collective memory]. Paris: Presses Universitaires de France. (Original work published 1950)

Hareven, T. K. (1994). Aging and generational relations: A historical and life course perspective. *Annual Review of Sociology, 20,* 437–462.

Horowitz, M. (1986). *Stress response syndrome.* Northvale, NJ: Aronson.

Ibañez, T. (1992). Some critical comments about the theory of social representations. *Ongoing Production on Social Representations, 1,* 21–26.

Insua, P., Pizarro, M., & Paez, D. (1994). Actitudes, representaciones y recuerdo de la información preventiva sobre el Sida: Procesos individuales y colectivos de la memoria [Attitudes, representations, and memory of preventive information about AIDS: Individual processes and collective memory]. In L. Valenciano & R. Usieto (Eds.), *Sida: Avances en el tratamiento Medico y Psicosocial.* Madrid: CESA.

Jackson, G. (1965). *La república Española y la Guerra Civil* [The Spanish Republic and the Civil War]. México: Grijalbo.

Janoff-Bulman, R. (1992). *Shattered assumptions: Towards a new psychology of trauma.* New York: The Free Press.

Jodelet, D. (1991). Representaciones Sociales: Un área en expansión [Social representations: An area of expansion]. In D. Páez, C. San Juan, I. Romo, & A. Vergara (Eds.), *Sida: Imagen y Prevención.* Madrid: Fundamentos.

Kenny, D. (1986). Methods for measuring dyads and groups. In W. Crano & M. Brewer (Eds.), *Principles and methods of social research.* Boston: Allyn & Bacon.

Levine, J. M., Ressnick, L. B., & Higgins, E. T. (1993). Social foundations of cognition. *Annual Review of Psychology, 44,* 585–612.

Lewicka, M., Czapinski, J., & Peeters, G. (1992). Positive–negative asymmetry or "When the Heart Needs a Reason." *European Journal of Social Psychology, 22,* 425–434.

Martin, L. L., & Tesser, A. (1989). Toward a motivational and structural theory of ruminative thought. In J. S. Uleman & J. A. Bargh (Eds.), *Unintended thought* (pp. 306–326). New York: Guilford.

Middleton, D., & Edwards, D. (1990). *Collective remembering.* London: Sage.

Morrow, J., & Nolen-Hoeksema, S. (1990). Effects of responses to depression on the remediation of depressive affect. *Journal of Personality and Social Psychology, 58*, 519–527.

Namer, G. (1987). *Mémoire et société* [Memory and society]. Paris: Editions des Méridiens.

Nolen-Hoeksema, S. (1991). Responses to depression and their effects on the duration of depressive episodes. *Journal Abnormal Psychology, 100*, 569–582.

Norris, F. H. (1990). Screening for traumatic stress: A scale for use in the general population. *Journal of Applied Social Psychology, 20*, 1701–1718.

Ostroff, C. (1993). Comparing correlations based on individual level and aggregated data. *Journal of Applied Psychology, 78*, 369–382.

Paez, D. (1993). *Salud, expresión y represión social de las emociones* [Health, expression, and social repression of emotions]. Valencia: Promolibro.

Paez, D., Asún, D., & González, J. L. (1995). Emotional climate, mood and collective behavior. In H. Riquelme (Ed.), *Era of twilight*. Bilbao-Hamburg: Horizonte-Department of Social Psychiatry, University of Hamburg.

Paez, D., Ruiz, J. I., Gailly, O., Kornblit, A. L., Wiesenfeld, E., & Vidal, M. C. (in press). Traumas colectivos y clima emocional: Una investigación transcultural [Collective traumas and emotional climate: A transcultural investigation]. *Revista de Psicología Política*.

Paez, D., Vergara, A., & Velasco, C. (1991). Represión, alexitimia y conocimiento social de las emociones [Repression, alexithymia, and the social knowledge of emotions]. *Boletín de Psicología, 31*, 7–39.

Pennebaker, J. M. (1990). *Opening up: The healing power of confiding in others*. New York: Morrow.

Pennebaker, J. M. (1993). Creación y mantenimiento de las memorias colectivas [The creation and maintenance of collective memories]. *Revista de Psicología Política, 6*, 35–51.

Pennebaker, J. M., Barger, S., & Tiebout, J. (1989). Disclosure of traumas and health among holocaust survivors. *Psychosomatic Medicine, 51*, 577–584.

Ramos, R. (1989). Maurice Halbwachs y la memoria colectiva [Maurice Halbwachs and collective memory]. *Revista de Occidente, 100*, 63–81.

Rimé, B., Philippot, P., Boca, S., & Mesquita, B. (1992). Long-lasting cognitive and social consequences of emotion: Social sharing and rumination. In W. Stroebe & M. Hewstone (Eds.), *European Review of Social Psychology, 3*, 225–258.

Robinson, J. (1986). Temporal reference systems and autobiographical memory. In D. Rubin (Ed.), *Autobiographical memory* (pp. 19–24). Cambridge, England: Cambridge University Press.

Ross, B. M. (1991). *Remembering the personal past*. New York: Oxford University Press.

Ruiz-Vargas, J. M. (1993). ¿Cómo recuerda usted la noticia del 23-F? Naturaleza y Mecanismos de los «recuerdos-destello». *Revista de Psicología Social, 8*(1), 17–32.

Schuman, H., & Scott, J. (1989). Generations and collective memory. *American Sociological Review, 54*, 359–381.

Suls, J., & Fletcher, B. (1985). The relative efficacy of avoidant and nonavoidant coping strategies: A meta-analysis. *Health Psychology, 4*, 249–288.

Swidler, A., & Arditi, J. (1994). The new sociology of knowledge. *Annual Review of Sociology, 20*, 305–329.

Tait, R., & Silver, R. C. (1989). Coming to terms with major negative life events. In J. S. Uleman & J. Bargh (Eds.), *Unintended thought* (pp. 351–382). New York: Guilford.

Tesser, A. (1978). Self-generated attitude change. In L. Berkowitz (Ed.), *Advances in experimental social psychology, 11*, 289–338.

Thomas, H. (1962). *La Guerra Civil Española* [The Spanish Civil War]. Paris: Ruedo Ibérico.

Ulsar Pietri, A. (1992). La historia sumergida [The submerged history]. *El Correo Español-El Pueblo Vasco*, October 23.

Wegner, D. M. (1988). Transactive memory: A contemporary analysis of the group mind. In B. Mullen & G. R. Goethals (Eds.), *Theories of group behavior* (pp. 185–208). New York: Springer-Verlag.

Wegner, D. M., Short, J. W., Blake, A. W., & Page, M. S. (1990). The suppression of exciting thoughts. *Journal of Personality and Social Psychology, 58,* 409–418.

Wertsch, J. V. (1991). *Voices of the mind: A sociocultural approach to mediated action.* London: Harvester Wheatsheaf.

Wierviorka, A. (1992). *Déportation et Génocide. Entre la mémoire et l'oubli* [Deportation and genocide: Between memory and forgetfulness]. Paris: Plon.

Chapter 8

Group Differences in Memory for a Political Event

George D. Gaskell
London School of Economics

Daniel B. Wright
University of Bristol, UK

John F. Kennedy was elected President of the United States in 1960. His youthful dynamism, his "association" with various celebrities, and his family ties produced a mythlike image of this leader of the free world. It is said this is the closest the United States came to monarchy since George Washington turned down the idea nearly 200 years ago. Kennedy presided over the Bay of Pigs invasion, the Cuban Missile Crisis, challenged the Mafia in the United States, and confronted Khrushchev in some of the most heated battles of the Cold War. On November 22, 1963, President Kennedy was shot and killed as he was driven through the streets of Dallas, Texas. The president's life and achievements, the manner of his untimely death, and what he might have achieved, touched the heart of the American public.

Several years later, Brown and Kulik (1977) used this event, and several other notable political events of the period, including Martin Luther King's assassination and the attempted assassination of Gerald Ford, as part of what is now considered to be a seminal contribution to the study of memory. Brewer (1992) commended the work saying that the paper is "innovative and opened up a new field of research" (p. 282) and "there were good reasons for researchers to be excited by the Brown and Kulik paper even though there were serious problems with both its theory and its data" (p. 284). Brown and Kulik asked a group of 80 people to recall what they were doing, who they were with, where they were, and when they first heard about these notable events. They found that people had remarkably good memories, particularly for John Kennedy's assassination. The recollections of these events appeared to be unlike "normal" memories. They had a " 'live' quality that is almost perceptual . . . like a photograph" and included idiosyncratic detail of little significance to the event itself. For example, one of the people they questioned recalled "I was carrying a carton of Viceroy cigarettes which I dropped" (p. 80). Furthermore, the clarity of these memories was apparently unaffected by the passage of time: They were "always there, unchanging as the slumbering Rhinegold" (p. 86).

For Brown and Kulik, these characteristics were so qualitatively different from memories for other events that they called them "flashbulb memories" to distinguish them from ordinary memories. They argued that these memories are the result of a neurological mechanism not used for memory of most events. They postulated that when a person encounters a surprising and consequential event, aspects of the immediate surroundings are imprinted in memory.

Inspired by this intriguing thesis, which corresponds with people's folk beliefs of memory (Brown, 1986), several cognitive researchers have explored the flashbulb phenomenon and investigated the validity of Brown and Kulik's claims. Researchers have used political events like Olof Palme's assassination in Sweden (Christianson, 1989) and the assassination attempt on Ronald Reagan (Pillemer, 1984), disasters (McCloskey, Wible, & Cohen, 1988; Wright, 1993), and autobiographical events (Rubin & Kozin, 1984). Other research has compared flashbulb memories with the recovery of repressed childhood memories (Loftus & Kaufman, 1992) and the recall of onerous initiation rites experienced in some cultures (Whitehouse, in press). Notwithstanding the amount of research, no flashbulb memory study has been able either to falsify or to demonstrate unequivocally the existence of the special mechanism that Brown and Kulik proposed. There are many conceptual and methodological problems associated with studying flashbulb memories that have hindered the progress of research (see Wright & Gaskell, 1995).

A problem with the flashbulb memory hypothesis is that although many people confidently report clear picturelike memories for certain events, these reports are not always accurate. Neisser (1982), for example, described his own vivid recollection of hearing about the attack on Pearl Harbor. Later, he discovered this memory to be wrong in some details. Several other examples exist where vividness of memory does not imply accuracy. It appears that, like memories for most events, flashbulb memories may be active reconstructions of the past. If this is the case, then flashbulb memories may be explained more parsimoniously with "normal" memory mechanisms.

In this chapter we do not discuss whether a special mechanism is necessary to explain these flashbulb memories. Instead, we focus on another aspect of Brown and Kulik's study that has been largely forgotten: the existence of group differences for memories of important political events. Brown and Kulik had built into their research a pseudo-experiment. Half of their sample was White and half was African American. They predicted that the African American respondents would have clearer memories for events of importance to the civil rights movement than would Whites. They argued that civil rights issues, such as the assassinations of Martin Luther King and Malcolm X, were of more importance for Blacks. As predicted, their Black respondents had clearer recollections of these events. Developing this aspect of Brown and Kulik's research, the study featured here investigated the relation between group membership and memory for a political event: Margaret Thatcher's resignation as prime minister of the United Kingdom. Before discussing the research, consider an outline of some of the ideas.

SOCIETAL THEORIES OF MEMORY

Memory as a phenomenon is an important topic in many different disciplines spanning the biological and social sciences as well as the humanities. This book is testament to the fact that memory research is not limited to psychology. That said, psychologists describe memory mostly from this perspective. The relevance of a particular literature in cognitive psychology has already been described to explain people's memories for major news events. Next consider the role of factors normally studied within social psychology.

The traditional paradigm within cognitive psychological studies of memory is to strip the memory processes of their meaningful social content. When Brown and Kulik asked people for their memories of major political events, they entered into a realm in which societal and cultural aspects cannot be divorced from the cognitive mechanisms. Their work prompted several other cognitive psychologists to study memory in its natural context. We discuss two interrelated ideas that are examples of the social dimensions of memory: the "value" of particular memory and how such memories fit into personal and social autobiographies. Implicit in this discussion is the notion of importance, with particular reference to the self-concept and social identity.

A Memory's Value

The reason why some memories are particularly vivid is that they play a significant function in the organization and structure of a person's identity. Selected memories become the props or pillars of a person's self-definition. In this sense, a flashbulb memory can be metaphorically thought of as a photograph that captures the flavor of an important event or phase in one's history. Like the photograph selected for a photo album, it does not exhaust the importance of the event or period in its totality, but it symbolizes, exemplifies, and evokes it. Because an event or phase of life can change in perceived importance, these *pillars* can also change: Some may erode over time, whereas others may be resurrected as a result of a revaluation of life periods. Extending the metaphor of the photo album, people often look at old photos in social situations for the pleasure of sharing memories with relatives or with old friends. With them, the event may be relived, its significance discussed, and related experiences recalled. Memories, in this sense, can be a shared property, the product of social reconstruction and part of the identity of a group. They map the significant events onto the history of a group.

The idea of a value for a memory was suggested by Abelson's article (1986), in which he presented the metaphor of possessions to explain a variety of empirical findings in research on beliefs and attitudes. The value of a belief is dependent on the importance or worth of that belief for the person. This notion is adapted into the idea that certain memories are more "valuable" to the person than are others (see Wright & Gaskell, 1992, for details).

Abelson (1986, his Table 4) listed several attributes that he claimed contribute to the value of a belief. To a greater or lesser extent, all of these coincide with various regularities of the recollections studied within flashbulb memory research. These include sharedness (with other people), uniqueness (compared with other people), extremity (compared with others), and centrality (to one's own self). A belief's value will result from a combination of these and does not necessarily require all these qualities for the belief to be a valued possession.

Consider the flashbulb memories Brown and Kulik collected about John Kennedy's assassination. Every American, it seems, shared a memory of this assassination. This sharedness had been reported in the popular magazine *Esquire*. As a massively collective memory, relived regularly in the media, it was a source of discussion for years. This shared element is what linguists describe as the "common ground" on which dialogue may be based. If you had no memory of the event, then you lacked a valuable possession for social discourse: You would in some ways seem an "outsider," almost un-American. In this case, sharedness is with almost every American. But sharedness need not involve the whole population, it might be among a community sharing a common environment, including local media or a small circle of close associates (friends, family, etc.). However, for major political events, the population of an entire nation is likely to share this common ground.

Now, if an individual's memory consisted of nothing more than the existing shared knowledge, then reciting this account to others would not advance the conversation. You, as an individual, would need to add something unique. For memories of major news events, this would be your own idiosyncratic circumstances in which you heard about the event. Brown and Kulik's results support this because all their 79 flashbulb recalls of John

Kennedy's assassination were "in some irrelevant detail, always unique." It would be these unique features, the personal perspectives, which could become a particularly valued part of the memory.

Extremity does not translate as well as the other attributes from attitude to memory research, but it could be supposed that this is a mixture of the interest of the memory content, emotions, and vividness: something akin to how good a story the recollection is. This could be a major source of bias, as recalls would be susceptible to both journalistic exaggerations and dramatic license.

The final attribute is *centrality*, or how the memory fits with other beliefs of the individual. This relates to the functions of these memories: how they help to structure the person's self-concept and locate them within chosen groups in society. Consider the following example from Ulric Neisser, a dedicated baseball fan (also known for numerous advances within cognitive psychology), giving "the quintessentially American" (Neisser, 1986) reply about what he was doing when he heard of the attack on Pearl Harbor. Evidently, he misremembered listening to a football game on the radio and reported listening to a baseball game (Thompson & Cowan, 1986).

> For many years I have remembered how I heard the news of the Japanese attack on Pearl Harbor, . . . I remember it well—listening to a baseball game on the radio. The game was interrupted by an announcement of the attack, and I rushed upstairs to tell my mother. This memory has been so clear for so long that I never confronted its *inherent absurdity* [italics added] until last year: no one broadcasts baseball games in December! (Neisser, 1982, p. 45)

Identifying an important national event with both a personal symbol and the national pastime helps to fit Neisser's recollection with the event's symbolic status. The recall of this event, and the bias that occurred, may have served to reinforce Neisser's social (American) and personal (baseball fan) identities. Personal history is "necessarily fragmented and idiosyncratic, but is also vivid and personally important in a way that the historian's larger view of events can seldom be" (Schuman & Converse, 1984, p. 38). It seems plausible that, for events of broader historical significance, people remember them through lenses of their private history. This increases the vividness of their account of the public event and gives a structure to their personal history (both of which are valuable in the Abelson sense).

Constructing a Personal and Social Identity

According to Neisser (1982), autobiographical information is remembered because the memory marks an intersection of personal and societal histories and becomes a *benchmark*, allowing the recipient to say "I was there" (Neisser, 1982, p. 48) at significant points in history. The function of these benchmarks is to structure autobiographical memory, which in turn defines the person's self/identity. They have what Fivush (1988, p. 277) described as "a self-defining function."

Tajfel's (1981) social identity theory, and its development in Turner's (1987) self-categorization theory, offers a preliminary framework for developing a functional analysis of social and personal memories in constructing an individual's autobiographical self. Social identity theory proposes that each individual strives for a positive self-concept. This self-concept is made up of a number of self-identifications or labels.

These identifications fall into one of two subsystems of the self-concept: the *personal identity*, made up of cognitions about the person's uniqueness and individuality; and the *social identity*, made up of the groups and social categories to which the person belongs. Belonging may be in terms of membership of a social category as in Tajfel's theory, but it may also be almost "imposed" on the individual through the sharing of a common culture, environment, and media. So for example, Yarmey and Bull's (1978) Canadian respondents also had vivid recollections of the U.S. president's death. Memories remain and/or become vivid recollections because they contribute positively to personal and social identity and thus serve to maintain or enhance self-esteem. A memory's value, therefore, can be viewed on three levels: Does it uniquely and positively locate the person as an individual? Does it identify the person as a member of a valued group? Is it part of the culture of a grouping for which the person shares a broader social affinity? This analysis maps Abelson's sharedness and uniqueness attributes onto their functional role of positive self-identification.

WHO REMEMBERS THATCHER'S RESIGNATION?

After 12 years as prime minister of Britain, during which she dominated British politics and made a considerable impact on international affairs, Margaret Thatcher resigned. Only the day before the "Iron Lady" characteristically pronounced "I fight, and I fight to win." Although her demise was not unexpected, the manner of it certainly took Britain by surprise and ended a political era.

Conway and colleagues (Conway et al., 1994) found that about 85% of a sample of British students had remarkable "flashbulblike" memories of what they were doing when they heard the news. Their recollections about a year after the event were detailed accounts and were consistent with their reports given only days after the resignation.

Thatcher's Generation

Margaret Thatcher was the longest serving prime minister since Winston Churchill. In her years in office from 1979 to 1991, the political landscape changed dramatically; few escaped the radical Thatcher policies. She rolled back the frontiers of the state, privatizing many public sector industries; she confronted the trade unions in a bitter war of attrition; she led the Falklands campaign against General Galtieri and the Argentineans; she enjoyed bashing the European Economic Commission and at home introduced a widely unpopular "poll tax." Hardly a month passed without some new mission to stamp the Thatcher vision on the unconverted.

Journalists and popular sociological commentators have coined the term the *Thatcher Generation* to describe the group whose formative years were dominated by her period as prime minister. Those born between 1965 and 1980 grew up in her political shadow. Whether Conservative supporters or supporters of one of the opposition parties, people's political views were either in accord or opposed to her ideology. There was no alternative.

Such a presumed impact on a generation is exactly what Schuman and Scott (1989) studied in their research on generations and collective memories. Schuman and Scott, building on Mannheim's ideas of generation formation, investigated the world events that American respondents described as especially important to them. The events that respondents mentioned tended to be from when they were between 15 and 25 years old. For older people it was World War II, middle-age people mentioned the Vietnam War, and for those who were in their late teens in 1963 it was the assassination of John Kennedy. According to Schuman and Scott, "for the majority . . . the memories refer back disproportionately to a time when the respondents were in their teens or early 20s, . . . adolescence and early adulthood is the primary period for generational imprinting in the sense of political memories" (p. 377). Would we find evidence of such a cohort effect with respect to recollections of the resignation of Margaret Thatcher?

More generally, this chapter investigates whether there are broader social class differences in memories of Thatcher's resignation. In the 1987 general election, the last that Thatcher won, a majority of those in the "higher" social categories voted Conservative (Thatcher's party), whereas those in the "lower" categories tended to vote for Labor (the main opposition party).

In British political science there is a vigorous debate about the relations between social class and political choice. In the 1970s, it was held that party identification derived from class identification (Butler & Stokes, 1974). In the 1980s, it has been argued that there has been a loosening of this association. For some political scientists, social class is no longer assumed to be a primary indicator of ideology; others have mapped new ways of segmenting the population to match social categories and ideological distinctiveness (Heath, Jowel, Curtice, Evans, Field, & Witherspoon, 1991; Weakliem & Heath, 1994). Regardless of the causal role of class on political ideology and voting preference, the fact remains that class is still highly associated with these measures. It therefore seems reasonable, though still not ideal, to use social class as a proxy measure for political identification and to ask whether memories for Thatcher's resignation vary by social class. The particular measures of social class in the research, based largely on the respondent's occupation, were dictated by the practice of the survey research companies who conducted the research. Although these measures of social class may not meet all the criteria of current sociological theory, they are adequate for present purposes.

The Thatcher Studies

Representative samples of the British public were asked about Margaret Thatcher's resignation. Three principle research questions are investigated: How clearly do people remember this event? Do some groups have clearer memories than others, in particular are there social class and generational effects? Are the responses stable across different contexts?

These studies were embedded in national "omnibus" surveys. Omnibus surveys include series of questions from several different clients and are an efficient method of asking a large number of respondents a few questions. Using surveys as opposed to the traditional means of investigating flashbulb memories via pen-and-paper questionnaires has several advantages and some disadvantages. More people can be asked the relevant questions. This increases the statistical power of analyses and the likelihood of detecting differences. The samples used are also much more representative of the general public and therefore realistic estimates of the population can be made as well as comparisons across different groups. Finally, by embedding these studies in surveys, it is possible to explore the psychological processes involved in the survey interview. This is important because much social and health policy, not to mention academic research, is based on survey results. Understanding both the cognitive and the social psychological processes involved in the survey interview can help to minimize the inherent biases (Gaskell, Wright, & O'Muircheartaigh, 1993). There are admittedly some disadvantages that come from using the survey format. Unlike laboratory-based studies or indepth qualitative interviews, respondents work under time pressures. Typically, four to six questions are asked each minute. As Krosnick (1991) described, this forces respondents to use a response strategy of low cognitive effort. Particularly for memory tasks, these constraints may adversely affect performance.

The three studies all used similar methodologies. Each was a face-to-face survey in people's homes and involved the respondent describing aspects of their memories for Thatcher's resignation (details in Wright, Gaskell, & O'Muircheartaigh, 1996). The first was embedded in the Office of Population Censuses and Surveys (OPCS) June 1992 omnibus survey and was designed in collaboration with Kavita Deepchand and Roger Thomas of the Joint Centre of Survey Methodology (JCSM). This took place about

1½ years after the resignation and involved 2,136 interviews. The second and third studies were conducted by the British Market Research Bureau International (BMRBI) during July/August 1992 and August 1993, respectively (approximately 1½ and 2½ years after the resignation). Here 4,289 and 511 respondents were asked the relevant questions.

The first study asked subjects to rate the *clarity* of their memories, how *important* they felt the resignation was, their *emotional reaction* to the event, and to try to *date the event*. Responses to the dating question are discussed elsewhere (Wright, Gaskell, & O'Muircheartaigh, in press). Here the first three questions, referred to as the *memory quality* (MQ) questions, are discussed. These are shown in Table 8.1. The response alternatives for all three studies were read to the respondents and presented to them on showcards.

The main question was whether the predicted differences among the social classes occurred. The measure OPCS use for social class goes from I for "professionals" to V for "unskilled." Figure 8.1 shows that the predictions were confirmed for each of the MQ questions. Statistical modeling confirms the visual inspection that not only did these characteristics all decline from Class I to Class V, but they did so in similar ways. This demonstrates large and predicted group differences in memory.

TABLE 8.1
Questions Used in Study 1

We would like to get an idea of how well people can remember events. I am going to ask you about two events in the past, to see how well you remember them. The two events are: Margaret Thatcher's resignation as Prime Minister, and the Hillsborough football disaster.

How clearly can you remember Margaret Thatcher's resignation as Prime Minister? Please choose one of the answers printed on this card.
  I can't really remember it
  I can remember it vaguely
  I can remember it fairly clearly
  I can remember it very clearly
  I can remember it vividly
At the time, how important an event did you think Margaret Thatcher's resignation as Prime Minister was? Please choose one of the answers on this card.
  Extremely important
  Very important
  Quite important
  Not very important
  Not important at all
For this next question, we are not interested in how good or bad you think the event was, just how strong your reaction to it was. In terms of your feelings, how strong was your reaction to Margaret Thatcher's resignation? Please choose one of the answers on this card.
  I didn't really have any feelings about it
  I didn't have any strong feelings about it
  I felt fairly strongly about it
  I felt very strongly about it

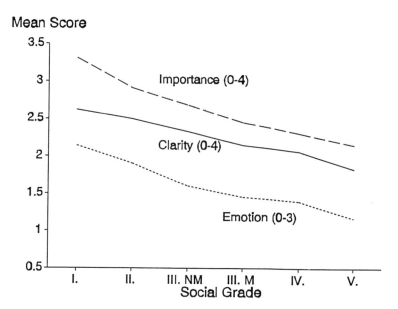

FIG. 8.1.   How the ratings of importance, clarity, and emotion with regard
to Thatcher's resignation varied by respondents' social grade (study 1).

This relation appears quite strong, but it is important to examine it more closely. It is possible that people of different classes rate the same memory quality (or level of importance or emotional reaction) with different responses. This is what Saris (1988) referred to as people having response functions between some true belief and their response.

Previous research observed these types of differences with regard to social class (Wright, Gaskell, & O'Muircheartaigh, 1994) and therefore this possibility was explored in the present study. People were also asked about their memories for another significant, but nonpolitical event, the Hillsborough football disaster. The relation between social class and the MQ characteristics for Hillsborough was different enough from Fig. 8.1 to persuade us that the relation between social grade and memories for Thatcher's resignation is not simply a methodological artifact.

Figure 8.2 plots the mean ratings for the memory quality questions across the age of the respondents. It can be seen that the resignation was considered to be important by most people. If Schuman and Scott's generational imprinting has occurred, then a marked peak would be expected from around the age of 23 to 33. Although these ratings vary significantly by age, there is no evidence for "Thatcher's generation" to show higher ratings than other age cohorts. If there is a peak, then it is for people in their 50s.

The second study tested whether the pattern observed in Fig. 8.1 was dependent on various aspects of the survey. In particular, often changing

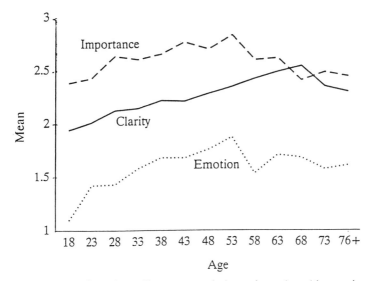

FIG. 8.2.   How the ratings of importance, clarity, and emotion with regard to Thatcher's resignation varied by respondents' age (study 1).

the order of survey questions affects the responses (see, e.g., Gaskell, Wright, & O'Muircheartaigh, 1995). The second study asked the three MQ questions in each of the six possible orders in which they could be asked. This manipulation was also designed to investigate the possibility of *priming* effects: That is, given the rapid pace of the survey interview, prior questions on the same topic may serve to activate memories that would otherwise remain dormant. Perhaps political issues are more salient to people in the higher social classes; given an appropriate priming question, the group differences would be smaller. The questions asked were essentially the same as those used in the first study. This study was embedded in the BMRBI omnibus survey. They use a slightly different way of measuring socioeconomic status, which ranges from *A* for professional to *E* for the unskilled.

Statistical analyses showed that although there were some differences in the responses depending on the question order, the relationship between the MQ responses and social class did not vary. In statistical terms, there were main effects but no interactions. This is important because survey researchers are seldom interested in the absolute values of responses but in comparing responses between groups. The lack of an interaction allows more confidence to be placed in the group differences observed.

The third study explored this relation using a different measure of memory. Respondents were asked to say if they could recall what they were doing when they heard about the resignation, who they were with, where they were, and how they heard about it. These personal circumstances are the putative "canonical" features of flashbulb memories. We also asked the

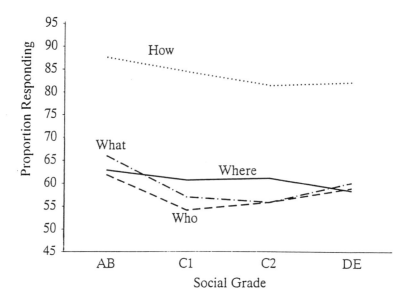

FIG. 8.3. The proportion of people in each social grade who said they could recall how they heard about Thatcher's resignation, what they were doing, where they were, and who they were with (study 3).

clarity question for comparison purposes with the earlier studies. Figure 8.3 shows the proportion of respondents who replied positively to each of the personal circumstance questions, plotted for the different social classes. For each, there is a statistically significant decline as one moves from Classes AB to DE. The decline is not as sharp as was found in the earlier studies. The responses to the clarity question show a similar pattern to that depicted in Fig. 8.1.

CONCLUSIONS

This research employed survey methodology to investigate aspects of flash-bulb memories for a political event. It is unusual in that this method allows the collection of data from national samples and the investigation of the relation between aspects of memory and group membership. Across three studies, there were consistent group differences in the memory quality of memories for Margaret Thatcher's resignation among the social classes in Britain. As predicted, the higher social classes, where Conservative supporters are in the majority, reported higher memory quality ratings. For them, the issue of Thatcher's downfall was a highly salient event that split the Conservative Party between those who felt that she had been around too long and those still committed to Thatcherism (A. Clark, 1993). Although there was clearly variation within these groups, the association between memory quality and social class was observed in all three separate studies. Further, no evidence was found for Thatcher's generation having better memories for the resignation as was predicted on the basis of Schuman and Scott's analysis.

As noted in the introduction, using surveys has limitations as well as advantages. Due to cost constraints, the number of questions asked was limited. It would have been very useful to have included questions on voting behavior and interest/involvement in politics. With these, the analyses could have been considerably more refined. The assumption that social class is a proxy for group membership is admittedly crude. Notwithstanding these limitations, the results are consistent and statistically reliable.

A final methodological issue is the reliance on only a single political event. It is difficult to generalize from a study of the "Iron Lady" to all major events. As H. H. Clark (1973) noted, whereas there is valuable information that can be drawn from the so-called method of single cases, caution on generality is necessary. The diversity of political events and the heterogeneity of the population are such that the resulting memories are likely to reflect this variability as regards to sociodemographic characteristics. It is trite to say that further research is needed, but in such research there is a requirement to explore more political events and to explore in more detail, using both qualitative and quantitative methods, the social affinities or group memberships of the respondents. This may help to further understanding of the ways in which memory operates in a social context.

REFERENCES

Abelson, R. P. (1986). Beliefs are like possessions. *Journal of the Theory of Social Behaviour, 16,* 223–250.
Brewer, W. F. (1992). The theoretical and empirical status of the flashbulb memory hypothesis. In E. Winograd & U. Neisser (Eds.), *Affect and accuracy in recall: Studies of "flashbulb" memories* (pp. 274–305). Cambridge, England: Cambridge University Press.
Brown, R. (1986). *Social psychology* (2nd ed.). London: The Free Press.
Brown, R., & Kulik, J. (1977). Flashbulb memories. *Cognition, 5,* 73–99.
Butler, D., & Stokes, D. (1974). *Political change in Britain.* London: Macmillan.
Christianson, S.-Å. (1989). Flashbulb memories: Special, but not so special. *Memory and Cognition, 17,* 435–443.
Clark, A. (1993). *Diaries.* London: Phoenix.
Clark, H. H. (1973). The language-as-fixed-effect fallacy: A critique of language statistics in psychological research. *Journal of Verbal Learning and Verbal Behavior, 12,* 335–359.
Conway, M. A., Anderson, S. J., Larsen, S. F., Donnelly, C. M., McDaniel, M. A., McClelland, A. G. R., Rawles, R. E., & Logie, R. H. (1994). The formation of flashbulb memories. *Memory and Cognition, 22,* 326–343.

Fivush, R. (1988). The functions of event memory: Some comments on Nelson and Barsalou. In U. Neisser & E. Winograd (Eds.), *Remembering reconsidered: Ecological and traditional approaches to the study of memory* (pp. 277–282). New York: Cambridge University Press.

Gaskell, G. D., Wright, D. B., & O'Muircheartaigh, C. A. (1993). The reliability of surveys. *The Psychologist, 6,* 500–503.

Gaskell, G. D., Wright, D. B., & O'Muircheartaigh, C. A. (1995). Context effects in the measurement of attitudes: A comparison of the consistency and framing explanations. *British Journal of Social Psychology, 34,* 353–362.

Heath, A., Jowel, R., Curtice, J., Evans, G., Field, J., & Witherspoon, S. (1991). *Understanding political change: The British voter.* Oxford: Pergamon.

Krosnick, J. A. (1991). Response strategies for coping with the cognitive demands of attitude measures in surveys. *Applied Cognitive Psychology, 5,* 213–236.

Loftus, E. F., & Kaufmann, L. (1992). Why do traumatic experiences sometimes produce good memory (flashbulbs) and sometimes no memory (repression)? In E. Winograd & U. Neisser (Eds.), *Affect and accuracy in recall: Studies of "flashbulb" memories* (pp. 212–223). Cambridge, England: Cambridge University Press.

McCloskey, M., Wible, C., & Cohen, N. (1988). Is there a special flashbulb-memory mechanism? *Journal of Experimental Psychology: General, 117,* 171–181.

Neisser, U. (1982). Snapshots or benchmarks? In U. Neisser (Ed.), *Memory observed: Remembering in natural contexts* (pp. 43–48). San Francisco: Freeman.

Neisser, U. (1986). Remembering Pearl Harbor: Reply to Thompson and Cowan. *Cognition, 23,* 285–286.

Pillemer, D. B. (1984). Flashbulb memories of the assassination attempt on President Reagan. *Cognition, 16,* 63–80.

Rubin, D. C., & Kozin, M. (1984). Vivid memories. *Cognition, 16,* 81–95.

Saris, W. E. (1988). *Variation in response functions: A source of measurement error in attitude research.* Amsterdam: Sociometric Research Foundation.

Schuman, H., & Converse, P. (1984). The intersection of personal and natural history. In T. B. Jabine, M. L. Straf, J. M. Tanur, & R. Tourangeau (Eds.), *Cognitive aspects of survey methodology: building a bridge between disciplines* (pp. 38–43). Washington, DC: National Academy Press.

Schuman, H., & Scott, J. (1989). Generations and collective memories. *American Sociological Review, 54,* 351–381.

Tajfel, H. (1981). *Human groups and social categories.* Cambridge, England: Cambridge University Press.

Turner, J. C. (1987). *Rediscovering the social group.* Oxford, England: Blackwell.

Thompson, C. P., & Cowan, T. (1986). Flashbulb memories: A nicer interpretation of a Neisser recollection. *Cognition, 22,* 199–200.

Whitehouse, H. (in press). Fears and flashbulbs, speeches and scripts: Cognition, emotion, and politics in Melanesian religion. In R. H. Barnes, H. Morphy, & M. Banks (Eds.), *Fear and the control of emotion.*

Weakliem, D. L., & Heath, A. F. (1994). Rational choice and class voting. *Rationality and Society, 6,* 243–270.

Wright, D. B. (1993). Recall of the Hillsborough disaster over time: Systematic biases of "flashbulb" memories. *Applied Cognitive Psychology, 7,* 129–138.

Wright, D. B., & Gaskell, G. D. (1992). The construction and function of vivid memories. In M. A. Conway, D. C. Rubin, H. Spinnler, & W. A. Wagenaar (Eds.), *Theoretical perspectives on autobiographical memory* (pp. 275–293). Dordrecht, The Netherlands: Kluwer Academic.

Wright, D. B., & Gaskell, G. D. (1995). Flashbulb memories: Conceptual and methodological issues. *Memory, 3,* 67–80.

Wright, D. B., Gaskell, G. D., & O'Muircheartaigh, C. A. (1994). How much is "Quite a bit"? Mapping between numerical values and vague quantifiers. *Applied Cognitive Psychology, 8,* 479–496.

Wright, D. B., Gaskell, G. D., & O'Muircheartaigh, C. A. (1996). *Flashbulb memory assumptions: Using national surveys to explore cognitive phenomena.* Manuscript submitted for publication.

Wright, D. B., Gaskell, G. D., & O'Muircheartaigh, C. A. (in press). Temporal estimation of major news events: Re-examining the accessibility principle. *Applied Cognitive Psychology.*

Yarmey, A. D., & Bull, M. P., III. (1978). Where were you when President Kennedy was assassinated? *Bulletin of the Psychonomic Society, 11,* 133–135.

Chapter 9

When Individual Memories Are Socially Shaped: Flashbulb Memories of Sociopolitical Events

Catrin Finkenauer
Lydia Gisle
Olivier Luminet
University of Louvain, Belgium

Until the late 1970s, memory was viewed as an essentially individual possession. A significant turning point in this way of thinking was advanced by Neisser (1978), who argued that memory, as it occurs in everyday life, was powerfully influenced by social factors. Indeed, social processes have now been demonstrated to affect encoding, retrieval, and the maintenance of memories. Memory, then, may best be considered a social rather than an individual faculty (Bartlett, 1932; see Edwards & Middelton, 1986).

A particularly intriguing phenomenon in this context is that of *flashbulb* (FB) memories (Brown & Kulik, 1977). FB memories are distinctly vivid, precise, concrete, long-lasting memories of the personal circumstances surrounding people's discovery of shocking events, such as assassinations of public figures. That is, people remember with almost perceptual clarity details of the context in which they first heard about the news, such as what they were doing, with whom, and where they were. Even though FB memories are not as accurate or permanent as the photographic metaphor suggests (Neisser & Harsch, 1993), their forgetting curve is far less affected by time than is the case for other types of memories investigated in basic memory research (e.g., Bohannon & Symons, 1992).

To explain FB memories' superiority in recall, it is assumed that certain characteristics of the discovery situation lead to strong associations between the actual news and the surrounding details of the context in which the person learns about the news. In the debate as to whether memory is a social or individual faculty, FB memories represent an interesting case. On the one hand, FB memories are individual because they consist of people's memory for their personal discovery context. On the other hand, they are social memories in two respects. First, they involve a collectively shared memory for the actual news itself. Second, it is generally proposed that interpersonal rehearsal plays an important role in maintaining and consolidating FB memories. This opens the possibility that individual memories become social through interpersonal communication (Christophe & Rimé, in press) and collective remembering (Middelton & Edwards, 1990).

The purpose of this present chapter is to investigate the question of how FB memories surrounding a national upheaval are created and maintained. It first reviews previous research on FB memories. It then describes recent developments in theories of emotions and presents a theoretical model of FB memories that relies on emotion theory. Subsequently, it presents a study examining FB memories for the unexpected death of the Belgian king Baudouin in which these assumptions have been tested. The chapter concludes by discussing the implications of the suggestions and findings for theories on FB memories.

EARLY EVIDENCE FOR FB MEMORIES

Although the term *flashbulb memory* was coined and popularized by Brown and Kulik (1977), the phenomenon had already been observed nearly 100 years earlier by Colgrove (1899). He had asked people where they were when they heard that President Lincoln, who had guided the country through the Civil War, was shot. He observed that 72% of the people were able to give a vivid description of their experiences 34 years after the event.

Colgrove's findings matched those reported by Brown and Kulik about people's memories of nine different, noteworthy, and unexpected events (mostly assassinations) and one single self-selected personally relevant event. The shooting of John F. Kennedy, November 22, 1963—13 years before—represented their most prominent example of the selected historic events. The assassination of the charismatic and popular president in Dallas, Texas, created an extraordinarily powerful and widely shared FB memory. Ninety-nine percent of the participants recalled with almost perceptual clarity where they were, how they learned about the assassination, what they were doing at the time, how other people reacted on hearing the news, their own emotional reaction, and what they did immediately after hearing the news. Also, idiosyncratic details of the individual's reception context were always named. Not surprisingly, Kennedy's assassination was not the only event that created such memories. Other deaths, assassinations, or assassination attempts of public figures also led to FB memories, but to a lesser degree: President Kennedy's brother Robert F. Kennedy (56%), President Gerald Ford (49%), and the Spanish General Francisco Franco (38%). Furthermore, African American participants showed significantly more FB memories for leaders who were active in the civil rights movement in the United States—Malcolm X and Martin Luther King—suggesting that events holding more consequences and importance for the individual lead to more FB memories. Finally, almost all subjects retrieved a personal memory of FB-like quality, indicating that events do not have to be of national importance to elicit such memories.

To explain their findings, Brown and Kulik proposed a theoretical model of FB formation and maintenance. Their model parallels the neurophysiological Now-Print! theory (Livingston, 1967). To initialize FB memory formation, the original event has to be new and unexpected and elicit surprise. If an event is routine and common, it is not attended to and hence does not lead to surprise. In other words, the event's novelty determines the level of surprise. Given a sufficient level of surprise, the event is then evaluated in terms of personal consequences or importance that are equated, in their perspective, with emotional arousal. Both surprise and consequentiality are considered necessary for FB formation. Yet, the degree of consequentiality alone is hypothesized to determine the degree of elaboration of the FB memory: the greater the perceived consequences, the more detailed the resulting FB memory.

Additionally, Brown and Kulik proposed that overt and covert rehearsal lead to further elaboration of FB memories. Overt rehearsal takes place during conversations in which the event is talked about, whereas covert rehearsal takes place when the person thinks about it. Higher consequentiality is assumed to evoke more frequent overt and covert rehearsal of that which is all or part of the FB memory, which ultimately leads to greater FB memory elaboration. Overt rehearsal is thus considered more than a simple reproduction of the brain events constituting the memory. It is a constructive social process that is promptly produced when an audience exists that cares about the story.

In sum, the role of overt rehearsal in FB memory is twofold. First, it improves the FB memory by consolidating existing memory traces. Second, it is a constructive process that takes place in a social context. By telling and retelling the story about the news and how it was learned, people gradually construct a story that matches the social demands of the interpersonal situation. In this sense, social factors in the form of overt rehearsal are likely to operate on the FB memory and its contents.

BASIC ELEMENTS OF FB MEMORIES: CONSEQUENTIALITY, EMOTIONALITY, AND REHEARSAL

Based on Brown and Kulik's theoretical propositions, a variety of researchers investigated different factors involved in FB memory formation and maintenance. Christianson (1989), for example, asked Swedish participants to recall the circumstances in which they heard of the assassination of the Swedish prime minister Olof Palme in February 1986. A large majority of the participants evidenced exactly the same detailed FB memories at a recall session 1 year after the first part of the study had taken place. They reported very high values of surprise and consequentiality on learning about the assassination. Moreover, participants reporting high levels of emotional arousal evidenced a better recall of the context in which they learned of the assassination than participants who reported low levels of emotional arousal. The significance of emotionality for FB memory formation was further confirmed in a variety of studies in which high levels of emotional arousal were repeatedly associated with better recall of the reception context (Bohannon, 1988; Pillemer, 1984).

The processes described in FB memory research—forming memories for salient events and vividly remembering them at later times—are common in memory as it occurs in everyday life. The same principles probably apply to most of our vivid and well-preserved memories, though their significance is usually personal rather than political. However, presidential assassinations increase the probability of overt rehearsal in a way that personal events never could. The role that overt rehearsal plays in the creation and maintenance of FB memories is thus most pronounced for FB memories of historic events.

Surprisingly, the relation between rehearsal in the form of conversations or media exposure and FB memories has not received consistent support in the literature. For example, few participants in Pillemer's (1984) study reported that they had rehearsed their FB memory of the assassination attempt on Ronald Reagan on March 30, 1981. Yet, participants did not regard the event as highly consequential, probably because they quickly heard that Reagan was not severely injured. Consequentiality is, however, associated with subsequent rehearsal. Thus, low consequentiality in this study may explain why rehearsal was unrelated to FB memories. Indeed, when investigating FB memories for the explosion of the space shuttle Challenger, Bohannon (1988; Bohannon & Symons, 1992) found that rehearsal of the Challenger disaster played a major role in maintaining FB memories. The shuttle turned into a fireball less than 2 minutes after lift-off on January 28, 1986, in full view of the watching crowd. The disaster killed the entire crew. It received great attention because the crew included Christa McAuliffe, a schoolteacher chosen to be the first civilian on a shuttle crew. The media was flooded with stories about Challenger in the first weeks following the accident. Subjects who recounted this event many times and followed the media also showed a better recall over time. As regards the role of rehearsal in FB memories, this study suggests that strong emotions cause people to repeat their story about the discovery of the news more often and seek out more information about the event by talking

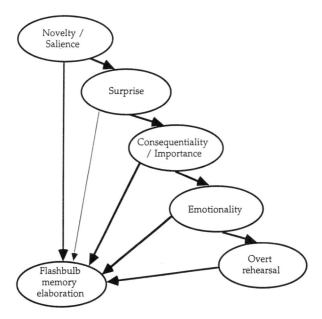

FIG. 9.1. Flashbulb memory formation and maintenance derived from Brown and Kulik (1977) and subsequent research. Brown and Kulik (1977) did not propose the thin line. We added this link because subsequent research based on Brown and Kulik's model provided evidence that surprise has a direct impact on FB memories (Christianson, 1989; Rubin & Kozin, 1984).

to others or following the media. Overt rehearsal thus probably affects FB memories through practice of existing memory traces and through reconstruction of the event by means of own and other's social narratives.

The original model did not assume that surprise influences FB memory formation directly. Yet, Brown and Kulik (1977) considered that "whenever attention is sustained at some high level, beyond some critical time, a FB is created" (p. 96). Hence, an event has to be new and unexpected to raise attention. Increased attention is associated with an orienting response and cortical arousal (Schmidt, 1991), and thus leads to surprise. If the orientation response is maintained because the stimulus material holds significance for the individual, it may be more thoroughly processed thereby leading to a FB memory. It thus seems reasonable to assume that not only the level of emotional arousal but also the level of surprise influences the elaboration of FB memories (see Fig. 9.1).

To summarize, research provides evidence in favor of Brown and Kulik's model. Consequentiality, emotionality, and rehearsal lead directly to a better recall of FB memories. The findings also indicate that high levels of surprise lead to a better recall of the reception context.

A COMPREHENSIVE MODEL OF FB MEMORY
FORMATION AND MAINTENANCE

A shortcoming of the earlier studies on FB memory is that they lacked firm theoretical bases. Given the absence of underlying theory, most researchers assessed only some of the proposed variables and ignored others. A first attempt to empirically examine a comprehensive model of FB memory formation was made by Conway and his colleagues (1994). Following Brown and Kulik (1977), they predicted that high emotionality and consequentiality determine FB memory formation, and rehearsal is a determinant for FB memory maintenance. Extending Brown and Kulik's model, Conway and his colleagues suggested that FB memories represent not only specific features of the reception context, but also conceptual and abstract knowledge about the original event. Hence, they proposed that the recipient's prior knowledge of issues related to the original event is of central importance to FB memory formation. Prior knowledge facilitates the organization and assimilation of the information, thereby leading to more elaborate and consistent FB memories.

In order to test their predictions, Conway and his colleagues conducted a large test–retest study of FB memories. Their target event was the resignation of the British prime minister Margaret Thatcher. Mrs. Thatcher had been prime minister for 11 years. She presided over major changes in the British society and led the country through the Falkland war. She was known as the "Iron Lady" for her opposition to the Soviet Union during the cold war. Even though the political context favored her resignation, it was unexpected: The day before, Mrs. Thatcher had announced that she would continue her fight. Two weeks and 11 months after Thatcher's resignation, a large group of participants completed a FB memory questionnaire. At both data collection phases, they described their memory for the reception context. Two sets of questions assessed the hypothesized determinants of FB memories: variables that influence the encoding of FB memories (i.e., emotionality, personal importance the event held for the individual, and prior knowledge of UK politics) and variables that influence the maintenance of FB memories (i.e., rehearsal of the original event).

Based on research evidencing FB memory consistency, Conway et al. (1994) operationalized FB memories as those memories that were highly consistent from one data collection phase to the other. They considered as non-FB memories those memories that were vulnerable to forgetting over time, much like typical autobiographical memories. As predicted, participants who had FB memories reported higher levels of surprise and emotional intensity, rated the event as more important, rehearsed the event more often in the form of thoughts or conversations, and followed the media more frequently than participants who had no FB memory.

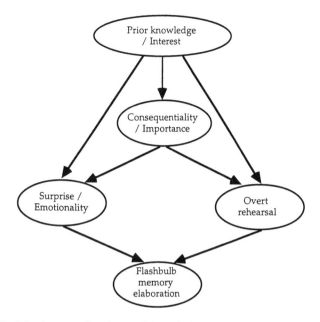

FIG. 9.2. A comprehensive model of flashbulb memory formation and maintenance (Conway et al., 1994).

Also, confirming their hypothesis, participants with FB memories had more prior knowledge of Thatcher's government and interest in politics than those without (see also Conway, chapter 2, this volume).

Applying structural equation models, Conway and his colleagues sought to identify the interrelations among the factors involved in the formation and maintenance of FB memories. In their model (see Fig. 9.2), prior knowledge was central to the formation of FB memories because it determined the personal importance of the event, the emotional reaction to it, and the frequency of subsequent rehearsal. In fact, prior knowledge about the issue facilitated the assimilation of new information to existing semantic structures in memory. Therefore, it was considered common to the formation of all memories.

Their model further emphasizes the critical role of personal importance for the formation of FB memories in that it triggers an emotional reaction to the original event. In other words, when an event is highly important and is then associated with high emotionality, FB memories are formed. If importance does not reach a sufficient level, no relation with emotionality occurs and FB memories are not formed. Because many participants reported not having rehearsed the news, they proposed that rehearsal does not play a critical role in FB memory formation or maintenance. In the case of FB memories, it simply contributes to sustaining their contents.

This conclusion, however, is surprising because the data show that rehearsal mediates the relation between importance and FB memories, just as the emotional reaction does.

This model represents a first attempt to develop a theory of FB memory formation and maintenance. Despite the substantial role emotions play in the Conway et al. (1994) model, a better understanding of FB memories suggests a more specific analysis of the emotions and appraisal processes. Although the role of emotions in memory is undisputed (e.g., Christianson & Loftus, 1991; Heuer & Reisberg, 1990; Wagenaar & Groeneweg, 1990), models that integrate autobiographical memory and emotion theories are rare. As discussed later, recent developments in emotion theories offer theoretical concepts that are quite relevant to FB memory research.

CONTEMPORARY THEORIES ON EMOTIONS
AND FB MEMORIES

Emotions are multifaceted syndromes rather than unidimensional responses (e.g., Averill, 1982). They consist of dynamically interacting responses sets (e.g., behavioral, expressive, cognitive, and/or social) and no single response is a necessary or sufficient condition for the entire syndrome. Contemporary theories view emotions as largely adaptive responses to the perceived demands of a person's environment. Emotions function to prepare the individual to cope with the environment (Frijda, Kuipers, & ter Schure, 1989). Additionally, emotions serve to communicate the person's emotional state to others in the social environment (Smith & Lazarus, 1990).

Scherer (1984) proposed that the environment is continuously evaluated on various dimensions relevant for the individual. These so-called *stimulus evaluation checks* are automatically performed by mechanisms that constantly scan the individual's environment. These appraisals nearly instantaneously provide different outcomes that lead to different emotional states. The emotional states, in turn, provoke physiological reactions that prepare the individual for an interaction with the environment (Frijda, 1986). One fundamental evaluation check is that of novelty (e.g., Smith & Ellsworth, 1985). It causes the individual to attend to or divert attention away from a respectively novel or common event. The appraisal of change or novelty in the environment thus leads to an orientation reaction and is involved in the emotion of surprise (e.g., Frijda, Kuipers, & ter Schure, 1989). Another important appraisal is that of personal importance (Lazarus & Smith, 1988; Scherer, 1984). This appraisal is a process of relating one's goals and beliefs to environmental realities. It leads to a more specific emotional arousal that can consist of one distinct emotion or, as is often the case in real-life events, complex emotional states.

The purpose of the entire appraisal process is to determine what the situation implies for the individuals' well-being in light of their personal wants, needs, beliefs, abilities, goals, and expectations. Therefore, it is commonly assumed that appraisals are influenced by antecedent person characteristics, such as beliefs about oneself and the world, personal goals and needs, prior experiences and expectations, internalized emotional schemata acquired during life-time, or general knowledge, such as attitudes and self-concepts (e.g., Smith, 1993). Thus, the cognitive appraisal of an emotional situation necessarily involves situational and conceptual knowledge stored in a person's memory.

A final issue concerning contemporary views on emotions should be considered. For a long time, researchers regarded emotions as short-lived and intrapersonal phenomena. More recent developments, however, provide extensive evidence showing that emotions involve long-term social processes. Rimé and his colleagues (for a review see Rimé, Philippot, Boca, & Mesquita, 1992) found that most people talk about their emotional experiences with others. This phenomenon, called *social sharing of emotion* occurs for about 90% of emotional episodes, is initiated quite early after the emotional event, is repetitive, and involves several successive addressees (e.g., Rimé, Mesquita, Philippot, & Boca, 1991; Rimé, Philippot, Finkenauer, Legast, Moorkens, & Tornqvist, 1996). The studies also reveal that more intense emotional experiences elicit more frequent social sharing than less intense ones. Overall, it seems that social sharing of emotion is an integral part of emotional episodes.

We consider that emotion theories offer important propositions for the development of causal models of FB memory formation and maintenance. From the aforementioned approaches to emotions, it becomes evident that it is imperative to integrate emotion theory and research on FB memories. Also, research needs to differentiate between different emotional responses, such as cognitive appraisal, immediate subjective feeling state, and social sharing of emotions. The following section suggests a theory on FB memories that takes into account different initial emotional responses (i.e., appraisal and emotional reaction) to the news and long-term interpersonal emotional reactions to the news (i.e., overt rehearsal). Thus, it considers that both the immediate emotional responses and their social aftermath are necessary for the formation and maintenance of FB memories.

INVESTIGATING THE ROLE OF EMOTIONS IN FB MEMORIES: THE DEATH OF THE BELGIAN KING

Virtually all significant traumatic experiences are associated with emotions. As can be seen in Fig. 9.3, emotions affect FB memories in two major ways. A first influence is direct. Emotional appraisal leads to emotional arousal,

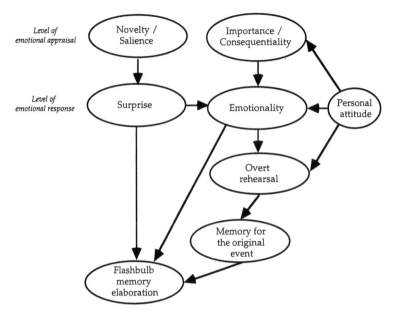

FIG. 9.3. An emotional-integrative model of flashbulb memory formation
and maintenance (Finkenauer, Luminet, Gisle, El-Ahmadi, van der Linden,
& Philippot, 1996).

which, in turn, notifies the brain to encode all of the associated events
directly and indirectly related. In other words, a new and significant event
causes the person to react with surprise and emotional arousal. These
emotional responses lead to the encoding of surrounding details—relevant
and irrelevant—and thereby to the creation of a FB memory. A second
influence is indirect. The degree of emotional arousal causes the person
to engage in overt rehearsal of what happened. Overt rehearsal causes the
original event as well as the reception context to be reevaluated and reconstructed on a personal (through conversations) as well as a societal
level (through media). This frequent reevaluation will be incorporated
with the original memory and finally represents the detailed and specific
reconstruction called FB memory.

    To test our model we investigated people's FB memories for the death
of the Belgian king Baudouin, which was announced Sunday, July 31, 1993,
at about 2:30 a.m. He died of a heart attack, at the age of 62, in his vacation
residence in Spain at about 9:30 p.m., the day before. The news was unexpected for almost everybody and had an enormous impact on the Belgian
population. Baudouin had been king for 42 years and was considered by
many as the father of the nation. He had a strong unifying influence on
a nation that is deeply divided by linguistic and cultural conflicts between

the Flemish and the Walloon population. The media was flooded with stories about the king's death. Television and radio channels replaced their programs with broadcasts on the royal family. The Monday following his death, the French-speaking papers covered the event on about 60% of their pages. Six months after the king's death, 55% of the Belgian people interviewed for a survey indicated it was the event that had marked them most during 1993 (Lits, 1993).

From a theoretical perspective, the king's death is immediately appraised by people as highly novel. The outcome of this appraisal elicits surprise. Surprise then contributes directly to the formation of FB memories. Almost simultaneously, a second appraisal process evaluates the importance and the consequences that the original event holds for the individual. The level of appraised importance, then, along with the effects of novelty (or surprise) determines the intensity of the emotional reaction. Ultimately, emotionality has a direct influence on FB memory.

Beyond direct effects, emotional arousal affects FB memories indirectly through its social aftermath. Greater emotionality leads to more subsequent rehearsal, because the more people are upset, the more they engage in social sharing of emotions and the more they follow the media. It is important to note that these overt rehearsal processes not only concern the reception context, but also the original event. Overt rehearsal thereby leads directly to an improved recall for the details of the original event. In turn, the memory of the original event strengthens the memory for associated matters, thereby assisting in the encoding, maintenance, and retrieval of FB memories. Finally, the personal attitude (i.e., the variable that in our research reflects Conway et al.'s prior knowledge and interest) toward the issue affects the importance attributed to the event, the emotional reaction, and subsequent overt rehearsal.

The study on reactions to the king's death involved a large group of French-speaking Belgians ($N = 399$) of various age groups and background (Finkenauer, Luminet, Gisle, El-Ahmadi, Van der Linden, & Philippot, 1996). Seven to 8 months after the death, participants recalled the circumstances in which they first heard the news, and answered questions concerning their discovery of the news—such as time, ongoing activity, informant, and where they were (FB memory elaboration). Comparable to Bohannon's study (1988), they were also asked to remember specific details about the original event. A review of the literature on FB memories and on emotions led to the consideration of scales that directly assessed personal consequentiality and importance; novelty; surprise; emotional arousal (i.e., emotionality); overt rehearsal (i.e., frequency of talking about the event and following the media); and personal attitude, which in this study was assessed through the degree to which the person reported having a favorable attitude toward the royal family in general. Even though this

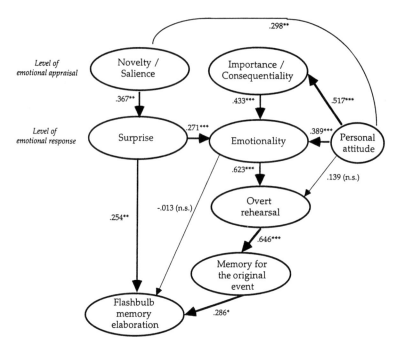

FIG. 9.4. Standardized model parameters derived from the emotional-integrative model of flashbulb memories (Finkenauer et al., 1996). Numbers represent standardized parameter estimate comparable to beta weights in regression analyses. *p < .05; **p < .01; ***p < .001.

latter variable is not equivalent to Conway et al.'s prior knowledge about politics, it was believed that both these variables reflect the same theoretical construct of antecedent person characteristics. That is, it was expected that personal attitude would evidence the same mediating qualities as prior knowledge in Conway et al.'s model.

The structural equation approach (SAS CALIS procedure; Hartman, 1990) tested the theory. On the whole, the model provided adequate statistical fit (for more detailed information, see Finkenauer et al., 1996). More importantly, Fig. 9.4 indicates that all proposed causal paths are significant, except for the Emotionality–FB memory path and the Personal attitude–Rehearsal path.

Thus, in the data set, emotionality did not determine FB memory directly and prior personal attitude did not determine the amount of rehearsal. However, the indirect influence that emotionality had on FB memories is particularly strong: the greater the level of emotionality, the more one talked about the King's death and followed the media. This led to a better recall of the original event, which in turn consolidated the FB memory.

TOWARD AN EMOTIONAL-INTEGRATIVE THEORY
OF FB MEMORY FORMATION AND MAINTENANCE

The purpose of the study was to develop a theory on FB memory formation and maintenance. Even though previous researchers generally agree on the determinants of FB memories (i.e., emotionality, surprise, rehearsal, personal importance, and novelty), they show major differences in the assumed mechanisms underlying the development and lasting qualities of FB memory. The structural modeling approach allowed the examination of the causal relations between the various factors assumed to influence FB memory formation and maintenance. The data provide strong support for a theory that reconciles previous models of FB memory formation and maintenance with theories on emotions. They also suggest that previous models may be simplistic accounts of relations between the characteristics of the original event and FB memories.

The Relation Between Cognitive Appraisal
and Emotional Responses

To instigate the creation of FB memories, an event has to be unexpected and uncommon, thereby eliciting surprise (Brown & Kulik, 1977; Scherer, 1984). If an event is routine and common or expected, it is not attended to and hence does not lead to surprise. Consequently, no FB memory is formed. Novelty thus plays an important role in the formation of FB memories in that it triggers the surprise necessary to provoke encoding and further emotional processing (see Fig. 9.4 for more details). The literature on emotions suggests that different appraisals lead to different emotional feeling states and that surprise precedes a more specific emotional response (Smith & Ellsworth, 1985). The initial reaction of undifferentiated surprise thus leads to an emotional reaction. The emotional reaction, on the other hand, results directly from the cognitive appraisal of personal importance (Brown & Kulik, 1977; Scherer, 1984).

The Role of Surprise and Emotional Reaction
in FB Memories

Given the differences between surprise and emotionality, it was expected that both subjective responses would make differential contributions to FB formation. However, only surprise is significantly associated with FB memory. The magnitude of the encoding process is determined by the effect of surprise (Christianson, 1989), confirming that an increased orienting response leads to enhanced recall (Schmidt, 1991). The lack of direct association between emotionality and FB memory might be due to the time elapsed between the moment the original event occurred and the assessment of FB memories. In fact, it has been shown that people talk about emotional situations within a short delay after the emotional event takes place (Rimé et al., 1991, 1992, 1996). Regarding these findings, it is possible that the impact of the social aftermath of the emotional reactions overshadows the immediate impact of emotions on FB memories. The former may become increasingly important over time. Future studies need to include two data collection phases (i.e., one immediately after the original event takes place and one after several months) to determine the respective impact of the immediate and long-term emotional reaction and its social aftermath on FB memories.

Emotional Reaction and Rehearsal in FB Memories

Paralleling the findings on social sharing of emotions (Rimé et al., 1991, 1992), emotional reactions and subsequent overt rehearsal are closely related: The more an event is emotionally arousing, the more it is socially shared with others, and the more people follow the media. In light of this evidence, appraisal of importance and subsequent emotional reaction contribute less directly to FB memories, but more indirectly through increased rehearsal of the original event. Hence, emotionality and overt rehearsal play an important role in FB formation and maintenance, because high emotionality leads to more rehearsal (see Fig. 9.4).

Relevance of Memory for the Original Event

Overt rehearsal processes are related directly to the memory of the original event. Rehearsal thus plays a role in the reconstruction and creation of shared memories. This becomes especially obvious with regard to the media (Middelton & Edwards, 1990). The media continuously distributed information about the king's life and his active role in the Belgian politics for his 42-year reign. Also, people engaged in repetitive conversations about the death (more than half of the participants reported having talked about the event more than six times). The reception context, however, probably constitutes only part of what is talked about. Another part of people's conversations concerns the news event itself, thereby establishing a collective memory for the original event rather than consolidating the individual FB memory. Taken together, these rehearsal processes probably contribute to make an individual memory a shared one. The data reveal that, on an individual level, overt rehearsal leads directly to an improved recall for the details of the original event. In turn, the memory of the original event strengthens the FB memory. Indeed, the original event is irremediably related to the memory of the context and personal feelings the individuals experienced when they heard the news. Rehearsal, thus, consolidates the memory for the original event, which is linked to the memory of the reception context. Rehearsal thereby has an indirect, but important, impact on FB memories.

A more general remark concerning memory for the original event and FB memories is warranted. The data do not allow us to disentangle which factors facilitate and enhance the encoding of the two types of information, that is, the original event and the idiosyncratic reception context. Future laboratory studies should aim to examine systematically the role of emotional appraisal, emotional response, and social rehearsal on the encoding, maintenance, and retrieval of the original event and the reception context, respectively.

**Impact of Knowledge Structures on Components
of the Emotional Reaction**

Emotional processes draw on knowledge structures stored in the individual's memory. Knowledge structures contain not only general semantic knowledge about the issue, but also personal attitudes and beliefs. Like Conway et al.'s (1994) proposition concerning prior knowledge or interest about politics, the personal attitude toward the royal family (the measure of prior knowledge used here) affected the importance attributed to the event and the emotional reaction. Contrary to their findings, though, the personal attitude toward the royal family did not relate to subsequent rehearsal. Rehearsal took place in an overwhelming fashion (discussed earlier). Independent of their personal attitudes, it seems that individuals could hardly avoid participating in the rehearsal process. It is possible that less emotional national events give people the possibility to deliberately choose whether or not they want to rehearse. In this case, it is likely that the person's attitude and involvement in the issue determines subsequent rehearsal.

CONCLUSIONS

Two major conclusions can be drawn from these findings. First, they show that combining emotion theory with theories on FB memory formation and maintenance is fruitful. A combination of the two approaches is a useful way of enhancing the knowledge about memory as it occurs in everyday life.

Second, the results underline the importance of social factors in memory formation and maintenance. Previous models considered social factors (i.e., overt rehearsal) as mere by-products of the characteristics of the original events. Social mechanisms in the data set were an important determinant of FB memories. They result from the emotionality with which people react to the announcement of an unexpected political event that holds importance for them. People engage in social sharing of emotions and follow the media. In this sense, overt rehearsal is more than a simple reproduction of the brain events constituting the memory. It is a social process that affects FB memories. It improves the individual FB memory by consolidating existing memory traces. In other words, by talking about the event and being exposed to the media, the memory for the reception context is improved. However, recall, in form of overt rehearsal, is almost always (re)constructive, because it takes place in a social context. Overt rehearsal thereby affects the FB memory and its contents. Also, it contributes to creating a collective memory for what happened, that is the political event as such. The data thereby suggest FB memories should be considered a special case of memory, that is, as an individual and a social faculty.

REFERENCES

Averill, J. R. (1982). *Anger and aggression: An essay on emotion.* New York: Springer-Verlag.

Bartlett, F. C. (1932). *Remembering.* Cambridge, England: Cambridge University Press.

Bohannon, J. N. (1988). Flashbulb memories for the Space Shuttle disaster: A tale of two theories. *Cognition, 29,* 179–196.

Bohannon, J. N., & Symons, L. V. (1992). Flashbulb memories: Confidence, consistency, and quantity. In E. Winograd & U. Neisser (Eds.), *Affect and accuracy in recall: Studies of "flashbulb" memories* (pp. 65–91). Cambridge, England: Cambridge University Press.

Brown, R., & Kulik, J. (1977). Flashbulb memories. *Cognition, 5,* 73–99.

Christianson, S.-Å. (1989). Flashbulb memories: Special, but not so special. *Memory and Cognition, 17,* 433–443.

Christianson, S.-Å., & Loftus, E. F. (1991). Remembering emotional events: The fate of detailed information. *Cognition and Emotion, 5,* 81–108.

Christophe, V., & Rimé, B. (in press). Emotional and social responses to the social sharing of emotion. *European Journal of Social Psychology.*

Colgrove, F. W. (1899). Individual memories. *American Journal of Psychology, 10,* 228–255.

Conway, M. A., Anderson, S. J., Larsen, S. F., Donnelly, C. M., McDaniel, M. A., McClelland, A. G. R., Rawles, R. E., & Logie, R. H. (1994). The formation of flashbulb memories. *Memory and Cognition, 22,* 326–343.

Edwards, D., & Middelton, D. (1986). Conversation with Bartlett. *Quarterly Newsletter of the Laboratory of Comparative Human Cognition, 8,* 79–82.

Finkenauer, C., Luminet, O., Gisle, L., El-Ahmadi, A., Van der Linden, M., & Philippot, P. (1996). *Flashbulb memories and the underlying mechanisms of their formation: Toward an emotional-integrative model.* Manuscript submitted for publication.

Frijda, N. H. (1986). *The emotions.* Cambridge, England: Cambridge University Press.

Frijda, N. H., Kuipers, P., & ter Schure, E. (1989). Relations among emotion, appraisal, and emotional action readiness. *Journal of Personality and Social Psychology, 57,* 212–228.

Hartman, W. M. (1990). *The CALIS procedure: Extended user's guide* (SAS Tech. Rep. No. P-200). Cary, NC: SAS Institute.

Heuer, F., & Reisberg, D. (1990). Vivid memories of emotional events: The accuracy of remembered minutiae. *Memory and Cognition, 18*, 496–506.

Lazarus, R. S., & Smith, C. A. (1988). Knowledge and appraisal in the cognition–emotion relationship. *Cognition and Emotion, 2*, 281–300.

Lits, M. (1993). *Le Roi est mort . . . Emotion et médias* [The King is dead . . . Emotion and medias]. Bruxelles: Editions Vie Ouvriére.

Livingston, R. (1967). Reinforcement. In G. Quarton, T. Melenchunk, & F. Schmitt (Eds.), *The neurosciences: A study program.* New York: Rockfeller University Press.

Middelton, D., & Edwards, D. (Eds.). (1990). *Collective remembering.* London: Sage.

Neisser, U., & Harsch, N. (1993). Phantom flashbulbs: False recollections of hearing the news about Challenger. In E. Winograd & U. Neisser (Eds.), *Affect and accuracy in recall: Studies of flashbulb memories* (pp. 9–31). Cambridge, England: Cambridge University Press.

Neisser, U. (1978). Memory: What are the important questions? In M. M. Gruneberg, P. E. Morris, & R. N. Sykes (Eds.), *Practical aspects of memory* (pp. 3–24). London: Academic Press.

Pillemer, D. B. (1984). Flashbulb memories of the assassination attempt on President Reagan. *Cognition, 16*, 63–80.

Rimé, B., Mesquita, B., Philippot, P., & Boca, S. (1991). Beyond the emotional event: Six studies on the social sharing of emotion. *Cognition and Emotion, 5*, 435–465.

Rimé, B., Philippot, P., Boca, S., & Mesquita, B. (1992). Long-lasting cognitive and social consequences of emotion: Social sharing and rumination. In W. Stroebe & M. Hewstone (Eds.), *European review of social psychology* (Vol. 1, pp. 225–258). Chichester, England: Wiley.

Rimé, B., Philippot, P., Finkenauer, C., Legast, S., Moorkens, P., & Tornqvist, J. (1996). *Mental rumination and social sharing in current life emotion.* Manuscript submitted for publication, University of Louvain at Louvain-la-Neuve.

Scherer, K. (1984). Emotion as a multicomponent process: A model and some cross-cultural data. *Review of Personality and Social Psychology, 5*, 37–63.

Schmidt, S. R. (1991). Can we have a distinctive theory of memory? *Memory and Cognition, 19*, 523–542.

Smith, C. A. (1993). Evaluations of what's at stake and what I can do. In B. C. Long & S. E. Kahn (Eds.), *Women, work and coping: A multidisciplinary approach to workplace stress* (pp. 238–265). Montreal: Mc Gill-Queen's Press.

Smith, C. A., & Ellsworth P. C. (1985). Patterns of cognitive appraisal in emotion. *Journal of Personality and Social Psychology, 48*, 813–838.

Smith, C. A., & Lazarus, R. S. (1990). Emotion and adaptation. In L. A. Pervin (Ed.), *Handbook of personality: Theory and research* (pp. 609–637). New York: Guilford.

Wagenaar, W. A., & Groeneweg, J. (1990). The memory of concentration camp survivors. *Applied Cognitive Psychology, 4*, 77–87.

Chapter 10

Nostalgia, Immigration, and Collective Memory

Guglielmo Bellelli
Mirella A. C. Amatulli
University of Bari, Italy

Kleiner (1977) defined nostalgia as "the desire to come back to an idealized past" (p. 11), wherein individuals attain their freedom from conflict. Although the term employed to designate it is quite recent, nostalgia is a diffuse feeling, which has been extensively described in both mythology and literature. After presenting a brief review of some of the main sociological and psychological studies on this topic, our aim is to consider nostalgia related to migratory phenomena, to which it is strictly linked,[1] and to demonstrate how it is also linked to what Halbwachs (1950) defined as *collective memory*. Collective memory is more than a mere collection of factual shared memories: In fact, its collective nature derives from the sharing of the meaning and interpretations generations give to recalled specific events[2] more than from the mere sharing of them. Finally, we show how nostalgia has been analyzed more frequently at an individual and intrapersonal level, and how its social functions have been neglected.

---

[1] In this respect, Alleon and Morvan (1989) coined the expression "myth of Ulysses," comparing it with the myth of Oedipus.

[2] Jodelet (1994) observed that, in migrations, the identification with the receiving society is rarely complete. It may also be an important instrument to exploit and spread one's own identity, protecting it from assimilation, as well as for sharing the memory of the group into which it is integrating.

NOSTALGIA: ITS ORIGINS AND DEVELOPMENT

Studies on nostalgia show the evolution of the concept from a medical term to part of the literary and everyday domain. The word *nostalgia* was coined in 1688 by Johannes Hofer, a young medical student who read a dissertation entitled *Dissertatio medica de nostalgia* at the University of Basel. The word, of Greek origin, comes from the combination of two other words: *nostos* (return) and *algos* (grief), which together mean sadness emerging from the desire to go back home.

At first the word had a specific medical connotation because it indicated a real illness, having sometimes mortal effects as several historical documents show; it was a sort of psychosomatic condition affecting mainly Swiss soldiers who were away from home. These young soldiers were not able to adapt to foreign customs and behaviors and could not forget their parents and all their close relations. Therefore, they usually felt the "imperious need" (Pinel, 1821) to go back home and see their native villages. If they were not allowed to do so they started suffering insomnia, anxiety, lack of appetite, sometimes associated with high temperatures, which remained if their desire to go back home was not fulfilled.

Sometimes the sad recollection of the past is determined by simply listening to songs and melodies. Rousseau (1763/1992) referred to a famous folk mountain melody, the so-called "ranz-des-vaches," which shepherds played with their horns. This melody immediately evoked in Swiss soldiers enlisted in France and Belgium memories of the past, generating such an intense nostalgic state that those who played, sang, or simply whistled it were punished.

In the 19th century, many clinical studies examined nostalgia, trying to define the symptoms, causes, and treatment of this illness. In 1821 in the *Encyclopédie Méthodique,* Tarde, a military doctor, and Pinel published a very important article stating that nostalgia is not exclusively experienced by soldiers, but by all those who are away from home. In the course of time, as Starobinski (1966/1992) showed in his profile of nostalgia, the word *nostalgia* loses its medical connotation to designate a passion or a feeling. According to Prete (1992), the term appeared for the first time in the Italian lexicon in 1863, and more exactly in the "Vocabolario della Crusca," whereas the first Italian literary appearance dates back to a letter by Leopardi, written on October 17, 1825.

In the 20th century, nostalgia became the topic of musicians, painters, writers, and poets such as Carducci, Ungaretti, Hugo, Baudelaire, and Proust, among others. Nostalgia soon acquired various and contrasting forms: Sometimes it is a nostalgia caused by the absence of familiar things— native language, village, and relatives—sometimes it is caused by the absence of the past, which has already ended. This dualism is also literary:

In fact, in his *Anthropology*, Kant maintained that the person who feels nostalgia desires to go back to his childhood more than to his native village, which is a kind of Holy Land or enchanted island. Thus, it seems that the recalling, which is typical of nostalgia, may be oriented not only spatially, but also toward a particular time, to which one cannot return (e.g., "Ulysses will once again see his native Ithaca"). In other words, although going back to our native space is physically and logically possible, going back to our past is impossible and inconceivable.[3]

MIGRATION AND NOSTALGIA

Sociological inquiries consider nostalgia a symptom of a difficult and more or less conflicting adaptation of immigrants to the social and cultural environment of the receiving country.[4] One of the most famous researchers on the topic of emigration in the United States, Handlin (1951), described the drama of transplantation, the disruptive effects of the "shock of aliena- tion" the emigrants suffer, and their hopeless awareness that they would never be part of American society. Ruesch assumed that the cultural change produces stress, exhaustion, tension, and undermines the immigrants' physical and mental health, increasing their death rate (Ruesch, Jacobson, & Loeb, 1948, quoted in Frigessi, Castelnuovo, & Risso, 1982).

Most empirical studies refer mainly to immigrant workers with low quali- fications (manual, temporary, and unemployed workers)[5] and less fre- quently to higher classes, such as foreign professionals or university stu- dents.[6] In Holmes and Rahe's (1965) stressful events scale, the migratory experience occupies the 24th position and is frequently indicated as a relevant risk factor for physical and mental health. More often represented as an individual response to migratory stress, nostalgia has been investigated by psychiatrists,[7] who considered it as an affective reaction to separation (see, e.g., Tseng et al., 1993; Baier & Welch, 1992), linked in its pathological forms to depression and melancholia (Taylor, 1986; Martini & Volterra, 1989) or neurasthenia (Micouin, 1989).

---

[3]Prete (1992) edited an anthology of classical and modern studies on nostalgia.

[4]Studies on the integration of immigrants are too numerous to be quoted exhaustively. The following studies referred to are more recent and more centered on nostalgia.

[5]For example Nicassio, Pate, and Kirby, 1984, on Indo-Chinese and Vietnamese in the United States, or Neto and Mullet, 1982, on Portuguese immigrants in France.

[6]Hojat and Herman, 1985, on Iranian and Philippine doctors who immigrated to the United States; Miller and Harwell, 1983, or Cox, 1988, on university students.

[7]See Odegaard (1932) and Malzberg and Lee's (1956) classical analyses. Frigessi, Castelnuovo, and Risso (1982) stressed the relation between nostalgia in a psychiatric sense and psychiatry itself.

NOSTALGIA AND PSYCHOANALYSIS

Psychoanalysts have also studied (Mancini, 1993) nostalgia, exploring its internal aspects more than its social origins.[8] Kaplan (1987) distinguished a normal nostalgia from a pathological one: The former is a universal affect giving way to an intense mental state, an intense and unsuppressible mood linked to particular recollections of the past, whereas pathological nostalgia is characterized by a refusal to accept that the past is over and therefore irreversible.

Sohn (1983) distinguished between a real nostalgia and a false one. The real nostalgia has "by definition a nearly clinical quality, being similar to a depressive situation"; the false one, represented as "a nearly pleasant psychic state," "which can be easily obtained through artifacts or elements of the psychological domain, which can be recollected in an extremely easy manner" (Mancini, 1993, p. 93) is a mere defense from the first one, and its aim is that of relieving suffering. Thus psychoanalysts,[9] as psychiatrists, have considered nostalgia as an individual pathology, linked to narcissistic themes (Andreoli, 1989; Sands, 1985), to the compulsion to repeat, to the death instinct (Sohn, 1983; Osorio, 1988), and more often to transfer analysis.[10] With regard to this, when dealing with the nostalgic recollection of the past in a therapeutic context, Sohn (1983) emphasized the emerging solitude and points out that therapists feel estranged when faced with it. In some way, they feel countertransferally distant from the relation with the patient.

A COGNITIVE PERSPECTIVE ON NOSTALGIA

Fisher (1990) considered nostalgia as an unsuppressible activity of thought rumination associated to one's own home or native village. This activity interferes more or less strongly with the involvement in actual experience and often may be accompanied by psychosomatic symptoms.[11] Fisher in-

---

[8]Starting from the analysis of the internal and external motivations of migration, L. Grinberg and R. Grinberg (1984) suggested a distinction into four phases: from the initial succession of sadness for what has been lost and fear for the changes the new environment imposes, to the final phase which consists in the integration and rediscovery of the pleasure of thinking and desiring and the ability of planning the future. Nostalgia belongs to the third phase, which is a type of withdrawal into the past, mixed with a first embodiment of elements from the new culture.

[9]Who generally use, without making any difference, the terms nostalgia and homesickness.

[10]In the references we have included the most recent studies of the last 10 years. There is also some Jungian contributions on the archetypic experience of nostalgia (Araujo & Ruiz, 1983; Peters, 1985).

[11]In 1688, Hofer suggested quite a similar representation (see Frigessi et al., 1982, pp. 12–13).

dicated four different modalities in the study of nostalgia.[12] The first one links nostalgia to separation and loss and their effects (Bowlby, 1969, 1973, 1980). The second modality is linked to Mandler's (1975) interruption theory, according to which nostalgia would be the consequence of the interruption of old familiar routines. The third one recalls the control theme (Fisher, 1986): Transition from the familiar environment to a new extraneous environment would give way to a temporary loss of control and the need to face new demands. The last hypothesis is based on the changing of roles (Oatley, 1988; Wapner, Kaplan, & Ciottone, 1981).

The need to overcome the conflict between old and new roles would cause an increase in self-attention and thus a smaller number of resources available for everyday life: "It might be expected that the self-focused attention could dominate resources and reduce capability available for daily life" (Fisher, 1990, p. 96). Fisher's analysis, which is also based on various empirical studies mainly carried out with students making the transition to university (Fisher, Elder, & Peacock, 1990; Fisher, Frazer, & Murray, 1984, 1986; Fisher & Hood, 1987, 1988; Fisher, Murray, & Frazer, 1985) is centered on the competition between the native environment and the new environment with respect to attentional resources.

The new environment is in fact seen as being able to attenuate nostalgia as it provides stimuli that attracts the individuals' attention and distracts them from recalling one's native environment.[13] It may also reinforce nostalgia or transform it into escapism, its extreme form, when it generates or leads to an increase in job strain. However, Fisher also considered nostalgia as an individual reaction, substantially maladaptive, even if not necessarily pathological, linked to psychosocial determinants, which she tried to analyse.

NOSTALGIA AND THE PSYCHOLOGY OF EMOTION

Nostalgia has often been neglected by those psychologists studying emotions, who have been more frequently interested in basic emotions: "The only references in literature ... appear in the studies on the affective lexicon,where the systematic interest in placing this host of affective terms into a semantic space is prevailing" (Bellelli & Saldarelli, 1990, p. 1).

Frijda (1986) quoted nostalgia as a typical "nonbasic" emotion, and as such deprived of the specific modes of action readiness, physiological ac-

---

[12]The author prefers to use the term *homesickness*.

[13]The author points out the similarities existing between nostalgia and depression and also traces the main difference: Depressive subjects reveal more rapid RT in the retrieval of negative memories, whereas nostalgic subjects are even more rapid in the retrieval of positive memory, provided that it is associated to one's own home or native country.

TABLE 10.1
Three Different Perspectives on Nostalgia

Frijda (1986)	Johnson-Laird & Oatley (1989)	Ortony, Clore, & Collins (1988)
Emotion defined primarily by its object	Complex emotion (basic mode: happiness)	Valenced reaction to the consequences of events (unpleasant)
Cannot be specified by action tendency or activation mode	Experienced as a result of a high-level self-evaluation	Focusing on consequences for the self
Does not have characteristic facial expression	Self-evaluation about your own state	Prospect irrelevant
Activation states merely on the mental plane	Referred to a past event	Well-being (distress) emotion
Nostalgia is awareness that something past, while desired, cannot be regained, except by maintaining proximity in thought	Complex emotion: to feel mildly sad as a result of remembering one's happiness in a past situation	Unpleasant reaction to consequences for the self of a past event (event of loss)

Note. This table reports a synthesis of some observations carried out on nostalgia by Frijda (1986), Johnson-Laird and Oatley (1989), and Ortony, Clore, and Collins (1988).

tivation, and expression, which can be therefore primarily defined according to its own object. He defined nostalgia as the awareness of something past and desired that cannot be acquired but through memory. The components of nostalgia, therefore, are desire—that is, the absence of the object—and the presence of the same object through memory: Either component can prevail at a given moment.

In Johnson-Laird and Oatley's model (1989), nostalgia belongs to the group of "complex emotions," that is, those emotions that, differently from basic emotions, owe their origin and specificity to a propositional content, reflecting a higher-level cognitive appraisal. Like all other complex emotions, nostalgia can be traced back to a fundamental mode—in this case, happiness—and is originated by the evaluation of a past event related to one's individuality. In the authors' definition, nostalgia is "to feel mildly sad as a result of remembering one's happiness in a past situation," which singularly and paradoxically defines it as a happiness-related emotion that brings about a mild unhappiness.

In Ortony, Clore, and Collins' model (1989), authors who do not agree with the distinction between basic and nonbasic emotions, nostalgia is included in the group of emotions (meant as "valenced reactions") that refer to "prospects irrelevant" events (having no influence on the individual's future goals and actions), which the authors also defined as "well-being emotions": Nostalgia belongs to the negative (that is, nondesirable) sub-group of these emotions, which they called "distress emotions," and is oriented toward a past event. When the past event can be considered as the "loss" of something loved, nostalgia is also a "loss emotion." In other words, it belongs to the subgroup of emotions that also includes sadness, mourning, and so on. In Ortony, Clore, and Collins' model, nostalgia retains a certain ambiguity,which is accentuated by the rigid classification proposed by the authors themselves (Bellelli & Saldarelli, 1990, pp. 2–3).

A SOCIOCONSTRUCTIONIST ANALYSIS OF NOSTALGIA

In sociological and constructionist studies on emotions, there seems to be a small number of references to nostalgia. Kemper (1987) studied nostalgia together with guilt, shame, pride, gratefulness, and love, and considered it a secondary emotion that is culturally changeable, and therefore different from the four basic emotions (fear, anger, depression, and satisfaction). These are physiologically based and thus universally and cross-culturally valid. Besides, they appear first in the individual's evolutionary develop-ment and have relevant effects on social relationships. Secondary emotions are acquired through the agents of socialization that define and label emotions, while individuals experience autonomic reactions of primary emotions.

Davis (1979) considered nostalgia as an answer to the need of main-taining continuity in one's own life:

> (1) The nostalgic evocation of some past state of affairs always occurs in the context of present fears, discontents, anxieties, or uncertainties even though they may not be in the forefront of awareness and (2) it is these emotions and cognitive states that pose the threat of identity discontinuity . . . that nostalgia seeks marshalling our psychological resources for continuity, to abort or, at very least, deflect. (pp. 34–35)

Davis' work is important because it individuates a function of nostalgia linked to social change. It represents the possibility of maintaining the stability of one's own world amidst external uncertainties and conflict. However, this hypothesis remains linked to the individual sphere.

TWO TYPES OF NOSTALGIA

The event appraised in nostalgia is not simple but dual: On the one hand, the past event recalled is generally pleasant for the individual and brings

TABLE 10.2
The Two Profiles of Nostalgia

Features	Desire (Homesickness)	Memory (Nostalgia)
Quality	negative	positive
Length	longer	more rapid
Physiological activity	intense	weak
Expression	marked	not marked
Search for control	yes, strong	no

Note. From Bellelli (1991).

about a positive affective state. On the other hand, the individual might evaluate the event in terms of loss of something that has been recalled but is actually absent. In such a case, the deriving negative state can generate other "negative" emotions, such as sadness or anger (e.g., when the loss cannot be modified or escapes the individual's control; Bellelli & Saldarelli, 1990, p. 3).

Bellelli and Saldarelli (1990) identified two different profiles of nostalgia, which greatly differed as to emotional quality, intensity, length, physiological activation, and expressive reactions. These two profiles, which individuals both labeled nostalgia, were elicited by two different situational scripts: the absence–desire of one's own home and close relations, and the proximity–memory of events or emotionally relevant moments of one's own past life (not necessarily linked to a spatial displacement).

These two different profiles of nostalgia (for more details, see Table 10.2) also emerged in another experiment (Bellelli, 1991), whose independent variables were, as in the previous research, the situational scripts of desire and memory and emotion labeling (presence vs. absence of label). The dependent variables were different from the abovementioned research using this time the subjective experience and the emotional behavior.

Amatulli (1990) replicated this experiment and studied some cross-cultural differences between Italian and English participants. She found that both English and Italians maintain the distinction between these two types of nostalgia, though a few differences between the two groups emerged. She also observed that English participants seemed to make a distinction between homesickness and nostalgia. *Homesickness* is more frequently used to indicate what is called *nostalgia–desire*, whereas *nostalgia* seems to denote what is called *nostalgia–memory*.

Though speculatively this chapter suggests that nostalgia–desire, which is considered typical of immigrants, has a specific function: maintaining basic scopes and values, threatened by the need to confront and integrate oneself in the social environment of the receiving country. Nostalgia–memory, which is considered typical of old people, has instead the function of reconstructing identity and the self's cohesion when faced with the flowing of events, which is often incoherent. It also has the function of confirming and idealizing the social order, though projected into the past.

In this connection, Mininni and Amatulli (1991) compared a large number of texts (immigrants' letters, interviews with old people and soldiers' letters) and identified different rhetorics[14] of nostalgia:

> Emigrants claim to contend with their allocation in a physically and socially different space by safeguarding their identity in the utterance time. Old people's nostalgia is the—rather joyful—pretension of recovering their Self-belonging to another time as if it was always identical in their reference space. Nostalgia derives its dysphoric dimension from appraising these claims as impossible and this feeling becomes more and more acute in the soldiers' social condition. (p. 162)

Already considered as a typical literary emotion, according to Mininni (1995), nostalgia is "an epochal feeling as it pervades every life experience in our contemporary society, which is marked by a progressive aging and large migrations" (p. 314). More than an individual answer, nostalgia appears strictly linked to a social order. Immigrants or old people are not mere individuals who experience nostalgia: Indeed, they may be seen as emblematic figures of a deeper change in society and in everyday social relationships.

CONCLUSIONS

More than an individual answer, nostalgia appears strictly linked to a social order. In this way, it comes back to Halbwachs, who considered nostalgia as an affective memory; this allows people to escape from the constraints of society and represent past society as an attractive place. This link between the present and the past exploits social continuity and society appears at the same time as a constrained and desired value (Namer, 1987). In their research on collective memories of various generations, Schuman and Scott (1989) showed how people of different ages, though sharing the superficial memory of various events, may differ as to the meaning they attribute to them. Thus, they individuated two different kinds of collective memory: the recalling of events not personally experienced and have been collectively elaborated by one's own generation and the recalling of a past that

---

[14]"The linguistic expression of a given emotion is not limited to its identifying lexeme, but passes through the whole range of levels which organize human language into a semiotic system, from prosody to syntax, from the utterance grammar to text rhetorics" (Mininni, 1991, p. 157).

has not been directly experienced though its meaning has been shared. This second type of collective memory appears to be quite similar to Durkheim's (1901) notion of collective representations.

Nostalgia does not simply feed on these memories, it is continuously made up by them: The reference to the personal sphere, like the recalling of private events associated with the main public events (those that Brown and Kulik (1977) called flashbulb memories), represent the possibility of access to the collective story and at the same time the reconstitution of the coherence of the self through a social belonging (see Neisser, 1982).

REFERENCES

Alleon, A. M., & Morvan, O. (1989). Entre Ulysse et Penelope: De l'exil au retour [Between Ulysses and Penelope: From exile to return]. *Bulletin de Psychologie, 42*, 328–333.

Amatulli, M. (1990). *Memoria e desiderio: La mente nel cuore della lingua.* Unpublished dissertation, University of Bari.

Andreoli, A. (1989). Le moi et son objet narcissique [The ego and its narcissistic object]. *Revue Française de Psychanalyse, 53*, 151–196.

Araujo, A., & Ruiz, Z. D. (1983). A propos des premiers rapports des refugiés politiques latino-américains avec l'institution [About initial relationships of Latin-American political refugees with the institution]. *Information Psychiatrique, 59*(1), 35–38.

Baier, M., & Welch, M. (1992). An analysis of the concept of homesickness. *Archives of Psychiatric Nursing, 6*, 54–60.

Bellelli, G., & Saldarelli, R. (1990, June). *The representation of affective states: First observation on nostalgia.* Paper presented at the General Meeting of the European Association of Experimental Social Psychology, Budapest.

Bellelli, G. (1991). Une émotion ambigue: La nostalgie [An ambiguous emotion: Nostalgia]. *Cahiers Internationaux de Psychologie Sociale, 11*, 59–76.

Bowlby, J. (1969). *Attachment and loss: Vol. 1. Attachment.* New York: Basic Books.

Bowlby, J. (1973). *Attachment and loss: Vol. 2. Separation, anxiety and anger.* New York: Basic Books.

Bowlby, J. (1980). *Attachment and loss: Vol. 3. Loss, sadness and depression.* New York: Basic Books.

Brown, R., & Kulik, J. (1977). Flashbulb memories. *Cognition, 5*, 73–99.

Cox, J. L. (1988). The overseas student: Expatriate, sojourner or settler? *Acta Psychiatrica Scandinavica, 78*(344, suppl.), 179–184.

Davis, F. (1979). *Yearning for yesterday: A sociology of nostalgia.* New York: The Free Press.

Durkheim, E. (1901). *The rules of sociological method.* Glencoe, IL: The Free Press.

Fisher, S. (1986). *Stress and strategy.* Hillsdale, NJ: Lawrence Erlbaum Associates.

Fisher, S. (1990). *Homesickness, cognition and health.* Hillsdale, NJ: Lawrence Erlbaum Associates.

Fisher, S., Elder, L., Peacock, G. (1990). Homesickness in a school in the Australian bush. *Children's Environments Quarterly, 7*, 15–22.

Fisher, S., Frazer, N., & Murray, K. (1984). The transition from home to boarding school: A diary-style analysis of the problem and worries of boarding school pupils. *Journal of Environmental Psychology, 4*, 211–221.

Fisher, S., Frazer, N., & Murray, K. (1986). Homesickness and health in boarding school children. *Journal of Environmental Psychology, 6*, 35–37.

Fisher, S., Murray, K., & Frazer, N. (1985). Homesickness and health in first-year students. *Journal of Environmental Psychology, 5,* 181–195.

Fisher, S., & Hood, B. (1987). The stress of the transition to university: A longitudinal study of psychological disturbance, absent-mindedness and vulnerability to homesickness. *British Journal of Psychology, 78,* 425–441.

Fisher, S., & Hood, B. (1988). Vulnerability factors in the transition to university: Self-reported mobility history and sex differences as factors in psychological disturbance. *British Journal of Psychology, 79,* 309–320.

Frigessi, Castelnuovo, D., & Risso, M. (1982). *A mezza parete: Emigrazione, nostalgia, malattia mentale* [At midway: Emigration, nostalgia, mental illness]. Torino: Einaudi.

Grinberg, L., & Grinberg, R. (1984). A psychoanalytic study of migration: Its normal and pathological aspects. *Journal of the American Psychoanalytic Association, 32,* 13–38.

Halbwachs, M. (1950). *La mémoire collective* [The collective memory]. Paris: PUF (New York: Harper & Row, 1951).

Handlin, O. (1951). *The uprooted.* Boston: Little Brown.

Holmes, T. H., & Rahe, R. H. (1965). The social readjustment rating scale. *Journal of Psychosomatic Research, 11,* 213–218.

Hojat, M., & Herman, M. W. (1985). Adjustement and psychosocial problems of Iranian and Filipino psysicians in the U.S. *Journal of Clinical Psychology, 41,* 130–136.

Jodelet, D. (1994). Memorie che si evolvono [Memories which evolve]. In AAVV, 1994 *Memoria e integrazione.*

Johnson-Laird, P. N., & Oatley, K. (1989). The language of emotions: An analysis of semantic field. *Cognition and Emotion, 3,* 81–123.

Kaplan, H. A. (1987). The psychopathology of nostalgia. *Psychoanalytic Review, 74,* 465–486.

Kemper, T. (1987). How many emotions are there? Wedding the social and autonomic components. *American Journal of Sociology, 93,* 263–289.

Kleiner, J. (1977). On nostalgia. In C. W. Socarides (Ed.), *The world of emotions.* New York: International University Press.

Malzberg, B., & Lee, E. S. (1956). *Migration and mental disease. A study of first admissions to hospitals for mental disease, New York, 1939–41.* New York: Social Science Research Council.

Mancini, A. (Ed.). (1993). *Solitudine e nostalgia* [Loneliness and nostalgia]. Torino: Boringhieri.

Mandler, G. (1975). *Mind and emotion.* New York: Wiley.

Martini, G., & Volterra, V. (1989). La depressione, tappa fondamentale del viaggio nella psicosi. *Psichiatria generale e dell'Età Evolutiva, 27,* 57–74.

Micouin, G. (1989). De la nostalgie à la neurasthénie: Une rupture epistemologique [From nostalgia to neurasthenia: An epistemologic gap]. *Bulletin de Psychologie, 42,* 322–327.

Miller, D. F., & Harwell, D. J. (1983). International students at an American University: Health problems and status. *Journal of School Health, 53,* 45–49.

Mininni, G. (1995). "Già qui?"—"Sentivo la nostalgia." Per un approccio diatestuale ad un'emozione metastabile. In G. Bellelli (Ed.), *Sapere e Sentire: Emozioni, conoscenza e vita quotidiana.* Napoli: Liguori.

Mininni, G., & Amatulli (1991, May). *Nostalgia: A diatextual analysis of a metastable emotion.* Paper presented at the Small Group Meeting on Emotion Knowledge: Social, cognitive, linguistic aspects, Bari.

Namer, G. (1987). *Mémoire et société* [Memory and society]. Paris: Méridiens Klinsieck.

Neisser, U. (1982). "Snapshots or benchmarks?" In U. Neisser (Ed.), *Memory observed: Remembering in natural contexts* (pp. 43–46). San Francisco: Freeman.

Neto, F., & Mullet, E. (1982). Résultat d'une enquête sur les conditions de vie des migrants Portugais [Results from an inquiry on living conditions of Portuguese immigrants]. *Orientation Scolaire et Professionelle, 11*(4), 355–368.

Nicassio, P. M., & Pate, J. K. (1984). An analysis of problems of resettlement of the Indochinese refugees in the United States. *Social Psychiatry, 19,* 135–141.

Oatley, K. (1988). Life events, social cognition and depression. In S. Fisher & J. Reason (Eds.), *Handbook of life stress, cognition and health* (pp. 543–557). Chichester, England: Wiley.

Odegaard, O. (1932). *Emigration and insanity: A study on mental disease among Norwegian-born population in Minnesota.* Copenhagen: Lewin & Munskgaard.

Ortony, A., Clore, G. L., & Collins, A. (1988). *The cognitive structure of emotions.* Cambridge, England: Cambridge University Press.

Osorio, L. C. (1988). Recentes avancos na teoria e na pratica psicanaliticas [Recent advances in psychoanalytic theory and practice]. *Revista Brasileira de Psicanalise, 22,* 119–144.

Peters, R. M. (1985). Reflections on the origin and aim of nostalgia. *Journal of Analytical Psychology, 30,* 135–148.

Pinel, P. (1821). Natura, cause, rimedi [Nature, cause, remedy]. In A. Prete (Ed.), *Nostalgia: Storia di un sentimento* (pp. 69–77). Milan: Cortina.

Prete, A. (Ed.). (1992). *Nostalgia: Storia di un sentimento* [Nostalgia: History of a feeling]. Milan: Cortina.

Ruesch, J., Jacobson, A., & Loeb, M. B. (1948). Acculturation and illness. *Psychological Monographs, 62,* 5.

Rousseau, J. J. (1992). Il suono natio [The dream nation]. In A. Prete (Ed.), *Nostalgia: Storia di un sentimento* (pp. 67–68). Milan: Cortina. (Original work published 1763)

Sands, S. (1985). Narcissism as a defence against object loss: Stendhal and Proust. *Psychoanalytic Review, 72,* 105–127.

Schuman, H., & Scott, J. (1989). Generations and collective memories. *American Sociological Review, 54,* 359–381.

Sohn, L. (1983). Nostalgia. *International Journal of Psycho-Analysis, 64,* 203–211.

Starobinski, J. (1992). Il concetto di nostalgia [The concept of nostalgia]. In A. Prete (Ed.), *Nostalgia. Storia di un sentimento* (pp. 85–117). Milan: Cortina. (Original work published 1966)

Taylor, R. E. (1986). Homesickness, melancholy, and blind rehabilitation. *Journal of Visual Impairment and Blindness, 80,* 800–802.

Tseng, W., Cheng, T., Chen, Y., Hwang, P., et al. (1993). Psychiatric complications of family reunion after four decades of separation. *American Journal of Psychiatry, 150,* 614–619.

Wapner, S., Kaplan, B., & Ciottone, R. (1981). Self-world relationships in critical environmental transitions: Childhood and beyond. In L. S. Liben, A. H. Patterson, & N. Newcombe (Eds.), *Spatial representations and behaviour across the life span.* New York: Academic Press.

Part III

THE CONSTRUCTION, DISTORTION, AND FORGETTING OF COLLECTIVE EXPERIENCES

Chapter 11

Remembering: Passing Back Through the Heart[1]

Elizabeth Lira
Latin American Institute of Mental Health and Human Rights, Chile

This chapter examines remembering and forgetting 21 years after the 1973 military coup and 4 years after the transition to civilian government in Chile. The Chilean dictatorship, which ruled over the country from 1973 to 1990, was accused of human rights abuses throughout this period. One of the first measures of the transition government regarding human rights abuses was the creation of a national commission. The Report of the Chilean National Commission on Truth and Reconciliation (1993) confirmed the responsibility of state agents or people in its service in these crimes. Some victims identified by the truth commission were sentenced to death (59) by wartime court martials (Consejos de Guerra). Other people (101) were shot while supposedly trying to escape imprisonment (*ley de fuga*). Other situations (93) that ended in death, justified under the "state of war" or "state of siege," were also included.

The majority, at least 815, were killed by torture. As depicted in Tables 11.1 and 11.2, more than 1,000 of the people were kidnapped and disappeared during this period. Mainly between 1973 and 1975,[2] people were placed in detention and confinement for several months or years without charges. The attitude adopted by the judiciary caused an important aggravation of the process of systematic violations of human rights (America's Watch Report, 1991).

---

[1]The title has been taken from Eduardo Galeano (1992), "To remember. From the Latin *recordis*, to pass back through the heart," from *The Book of Embraces*.

[2]For more information see Tables 11.1 and 11.2.

224

LIRA

TABLE 11.1
Individuals Affected by the Dictatorship in Chile (1973–1988):
Vicaría de la Solidaridad* Annual Reports

Repressive Situations	Period	Total
Kidnappings and disappearances	1973–1987	734
Deaths by execution	1973–1987	2,220
Massive detentions without a formal denouncement	1983–1988	8,863
Massive registered detentions	1983–1988	24,431
Individuals' detention	1976–1988	12,065
Individuals' threat	1977–1988	3,946
Ilegitimates pressures' denouncement	1978–1988	1,243
Internal exile	1980–1987	1,257

Note: This figure corresponds exclusively to the cases registered by the Vicaría.
*Vicaría de la Solidaridad (Vicariage of Solidarity) was created by the archbishop of Santiago, Chile, of the Catholic church to provide legal, social, medical, and psychological services to those people affected by human rights violations.

TABLE 11.2
Statistical Information of People Killed—
National Commission of Truth and Reconciliation

Victims of human rights violations	2,115
Victims of political violence	164
TOTAL VICTIMS	2,279
Cases without sufficient information	641
TOTAL CASES	2,920

Note: After the report, more than 1,500 new cases were formally denounced to the Corporación Nacional de Reparación.

Violations of human rights cannot be viewed exclusively from the perspective of isolated individual abuses. Their implications are far more extensive, because they describe not only a system's response to conflict, but a general ambiance of political threat, both of which lead to an atmosphere of chronic fear (Lira, 1988). Persecution of those who have been identified as "enemies" of the ruling power in the country included political leaders, priests or religious women, trade union leaders, members of leftist parties and human rights activists, as well as the general population.

Fear, confusion, and general distress were some of the subjective consequences presented by the affected people. Feelings of helplessness, defenselessness, and impotence were engendered, not only in those affected, but especially in those who were unable to discern what really might happen to them. For these, the sense of constant threat became an unbearable feeling—an unending torture itself, whether or not this threat materialized.

In the political context of transitions to democracy, it is said that it is necessary to maintain historical memory or social memory as a collective process remembering what occurred during the dictatorship. It is also said that it is necessary to forget and forgive the human rights violations in the name of social peace.

Memory is understood as the ability to remember events and experiences from the past. Memory is also the ability to conserve and remember past states of consciousness and everything associated with them. Memory is also described as the psychic functions that permit individuals to represent the past as past. Social memory can be understood, in this context, as the memory of subjective processes associated with historical events that have traumatically affected everyday life. Social memory implies giving meaning to those events. In this sense, social memory entails not only objective remembering, but subjective meaning conferred on the past.

Memory is not identical to history and does not imply a critical perspective. Memory is reconstruction of past emotions, feelings, and perceptions. It is related to social history and to private experiences. New experiences may allow new meanings and valuations of the past. When this occurs, it differentiates these memories from other experiences that are not psychologically redefined.

Memory makes possible retrospective perception and makes necessary reflection on how the past is present in Chileans' daily lives. This past has been called "an open wound." For many women and men, indelibly marked by the dictatorship, this wound will not scar. These people include relatives of disappeared, the widows and orphans, and the tortured. For them, the impunity of their victimizers and the political proposition coming from different sectors of the society to forget the past makes healing and true reconciliation impossible.

This open wound affects not only the victims and their families but all Chilean society. It is part of a historical dilemma confronted by Chile from its foundations in the 16th century and continuing in the social and political conflict of the 19th and 20th centuries. This social and political conflict intensified in the early 1970s. Once again, Chile faced basic issues:

> For the present generation of Chileans, as for their ancestors, this basic dilemma persists: how to make Chile a land of liberty while maintaining political order; how to achieve economic progress without exploiting the working classes; how to maintain social order and create social justice without imposing the terrible "weight of the night" on the Chilean people. This is the historical legacy and current challenge of Chile. (Loveman, 1988, p. 7)

OUR MEMORY

The military dictatorship revealed the authoritarian foundation of social relations and institutional structures in Chilean society. It was as if the dictatorship were the chemical catalyst within a darkroom revealing a series of photographs that had previously been blank sheets of paper. The anti-democratic features in Chilean society were deeply rooted in the country's socialization practices of family relations, schools, labor organization, business, university life, and the country's political institutions.[3]

From this perspective, the military government's ideological discourse and its authority stigmatized various groups as "enemies of the Patria" and, with this, pretended to justify political repression and human rights violations. Because of censorship and manipulation of the mass media, this discourse went virtually unchallenged in public. Under these circumstances, the meaning of "Patria" was altered. It no longer referred to a shared identity rooted in common socialization, education, and political traditions and beliefs. The so-called subversives, extremists, and leftists were defined as non-Chileans, antipatriots, and traitors, not only excludables but subject to extermination. It was as if antagonistic versions of reality had demonized social relations engendering terror and death, then fear and silence.

Public silence accompanied private horror and suffering. Public "normality" brought clean streets, manicured plazas, imposing skyscrapers, and public monuments. Throughout the country, the cities' walls were freshly painted, erasing the murals and political slogans, and attempting to erase all political memory. Political repression occurred simultaneously with profound economic, technological, and institutional transformations. These transformations, called "modernizations" by the military government, were welcomed by many Chileans, even as political threat and repression created a nation of enemies.

THE DILEMMA OF MEMORY
IN THE CHILEAN TRANSITION

In South America, only in Paraguay did military government endure longer than in Chile. The effort to replace the dictatorship and return to civilian government faced both subjective and objective impediments. Torture, kidnapping, disappearances, and other forms of political repression can be understood as traumatic experiences for the victims. They can result in an individual trauma that implies the breakdown of the psychic structure. This occurred in a context where there was also a partial breakdown of

---

[3]Touraine (1967) focused on the authoritarianism in the political socialization of Chilean people. The study in which the working class was used in a sample of 920 cases covering 68 national industries showed that almost 100% of the interviewed affirmed that "the most important thing that a child must be taught is to obey his or her parents." In the same research, it was observed that the interviewee's concept of family relationships was crossed by a strong notion of "property"—in the sense defined in the Roman law (Nazar, 1972).

the social structure, the so-called regimes of exception. In other words, legal and political structures, which supposedly guarantee human life and rights to all the members in a given society, can become threatening and devastating for most of them during the "state of exception" period.

From a psychological perspective, this chapter has spoken of the social damage to the individuals as a result of trauma produced by the violations of human rights.[4] The concept of *trauma* has been the basis for understanding the subjective impact and the consequences of human rights violations. *Extreme traumatization* as a specific concept denoted the political meaning of this type of trauma (Lira, Becker, & Castillo, 1990), which is closely related to Bettelheim's theory (Bettelheim, 1979). This idea emphasizes the radical disruption in the goals and ideals (the "lie project") that individuals have established during their lives with continuing destructive impact on their identities, and families and social relations.

The boundaries between fantasy and reality, under such threatening conditions, were changed when reality proved to be worse than the worst fantasy imaginable. Therefore, it became difficult later to discriminate between the inner and the outer world. The symbolizing process was distorted. Through this process, the outer world—the body, the feelings, and the words—took on new meanings associated with the situation of persecution and torture.

Dissociation is a central coping mechanism for survival within constantly threatening living conditions and especially under torture. Dissociation shaped the subsequent reactions described as the main features of trauma. By dissociating, individuals establish a partial disintegration of their egos to avoid overwhelming anxiety that would lead to total disintegration (Weinstein & Lira, 1987).

The first therapeutic goal, when those victims requested therapy during the dictatorship, was catharsis through the reconstitution of the traumatic experience, its emotional elaboration, its connection to the existential and contextual meaning of the subject's life and its relationship to his or her vital experience (Cienfuegos & Monelli, 1983; Lira & Weinstein, 1984). Many of the symptoms observed did not reflect psychopathology per se. Rather, people's behaviors, thoughts, and emotional patterns were concrete expressions of political violence that had marked and destroyed individual bodies, lives, and social interactions (Lira, 1988).

Calling oneself a survivor implies recognizing that there was the risk of death—a closeness of death, a time of dying that left the taste of death with those who survived. Interestingly, many of those who did not share this experience believe that if the terror that affected the survivors is forgotten,

---

[4]It has been considered that all the people arrested during the first 3 years were physically and psychologically tortured. For this reason, it is estimated that more than 200,000 people could be tortured in the whole period.

then Chile's unacknowledged collective terror could also be forgotten. Despite wishful thinking, the present is heavily influenced by a traumatic past.

At the beginning of the transition, different positions facing the past quickly emerged. When the truth commission's report was known, these positions were explained from different political sectors. Pinochet and his supporters underlined their historical role in Chile. Their view claimed that he was the hero who had saved the Patria from totalitarian communism, reestablished law and order, provided the constitutional foundations of a modern democracy, and permitted a peaceful legal transition from authoritarian rule to elected government (Loveman, 1990). Their words and actions proclaimed that theirs was the true past. They described the past as an unending battle against subversives. Those few who had died, Chileans were reminded, were the enemy of the Patria. The vision of the victims and human rights institutions were the opposite. They had suffered political repression in the past. They demanded justice and public acknowledgment of human rights violations to the Chilean society.

Concerning these conflicting visions, which rigidly remain in the society, it is important to add information coming from public opinion polls (August–September 1990) regarding human rights issues. In GEMINIS Poll,[5] 85% of a Santiago population sample answered that only a part of the human rights abuses perpetrated during the military dictatorship is known. The same percentage approved the creation of the truth commission. Related to the past abuses, 31.5% agreed that it was necessary to investigate and then give the pardon to the responsible parties. The majority, 59.2%, said that more investigation was necessary and then those who were responsible should be punished. Only 7.9% accepted the need to investigate without punishing anyone. At that moment, it reflected the Chilean society's basic ethical concern with human rights issues.

In the CERC poll (the sample was taken considering the whole population of the country),[6] only 2% of the Chilean people feared divisions and confrontations if the past of human rights abuses were openly spoken. Although this perception was not predominant, over time it became the main argument facing human rights past abuses, underlining the risks of political violence associated the demands of justice and truth.

Confronted by the threat of uncontrollable emotions and political violence, Chileans feared conflicts, overvalued the consensus, and avoided the risk of political instability. They censured their words and deed, fearing a return to the horror, by allowing the past to govern and pacify the present. Nevertheless, there are permanent signals from society that the open wounds will not heal.

---

[5]Private Office.

[6]Centro de Estudios de la realidad contemporánea (Center of Studies of the Contemporary Reality).

These threats and traumatic experiences that originated in political repression require later social acknowledgment of the political origin of this suffering. Without social validation, traumas become private suffering, and cannot be addressed. The Report of the National Commission of Truth and Reconciliation built a bridge between private suffering and social policies.[7] As the report noted, "During all these years, these testimonies, this pain, have rarely been little listened to." The experience of offering testimony to official representatives who, for the first time, neither scoffed nor harassed the relatives for having brought it forward who listened, were moved and showed respect for the pain being exposed. This experience in itself, as relatives said publicly and privately, has been a step toward healing. When publicly receiving the report, President Aylwin acknowledged the state's responsibility for political repression and responsibility for social reparation.

WOMEN AND MEMORY

The Uruguayan writer Eduardo Galeano (1992) wrote: "To remember. From the Latin *recordis*: Passing back through the heart" (p. 11). This implies a "working through" process differentiating the private experience from the social ones.

In this chapter, I reflect on the social impact of violations of human rights, of this "open wound," and the place of memory and suppression of memory for women who were the objects of political repression. It is not possible to discuss this without relating it to the network of human rights organizations created to confront political persecution. These human rights organizations attended the immediate urgent medical and psychological needs of victims. They maintained a network of solidarity, publicly denounced human rights violations, and attempted legal defense. Their work and the efforts to document the violations provided the raw material for the Retting Commission Report.

Other examples of the social impact of rights violations have emerged in the creation of social memories through poetry, essays, novels, clandes-

---

[7]The National Commission for Truth and Reconciliation was established on April 25, 1990. The commission issued the final report on February 9, 1991, also known as the Rettig Report. Important elements in the recommendations of this report are pensions and economic compensations to the relatives of the slain due to the human rights violations. It is also recommended to establish aid programs for health care and programs to reintegrate survivors and their families in society. The National Corporation for Reparation and Reconciliation was established on January 31, 1992, to carry out the recommendations made in the Rettig Report.

tine writings, videos, films, plays, "art actions,"[8] paintings, photographs, murals, and tapestries (*arpilleras*). These cultural and artistic contributions to memory accumulated questions and responses. They became a living memory, a cultural documentation of dictatorship.

Two examples of this cultural documentation make clear the role of women and their suffering and resistance during the dictatorship. The first, the *arpilleras*, became worldwide symbols of the suffering of Chileans under the dictatorship. The second, a play (now a film *Death and the Maiden* by Ariel Dorfman),[9] raises questions of the proper political and private response to the dictatorship in the early years after transition.

THE ARPILLERAS

The making of colorful tapestries is a traditional Chilean art. During the dictatorship, the *arpilleras* became an expression of individual and collective memory. The first *arpilleristas*, which were organized in workshops, were women looking for their children and husbands who had been detained by the military regime. Later, other *arpillera* workshops were organized by women in Santiago and other regions.

The *arpilleras* provided income and were also a psychological resource. They began as a politicized grief support group (Ritterman, 1991). The *arpilleristas* invented strategies to challenge the fear by depicting political repression. They developed a new form of struggle against authoritarianism. *Arpilleras* were a form of political resistance during the dictatorship, telling the "story of a divided Chile in graphic and visible form. They contain figures immersed in the daily life of a dislocated society. Certain themes recur, such as disappearance, hunger, torture, and the wounded family—a metaphor for a divided country" (Agosin, 1994, p. 12).

Arpilleras revealed the daily suffering of poor people and the impact of human rights violations during the military dictatorship. In this sense, they were "memories" of those times. People around the world were genuinely moved by the dignity of this peaceful form of political protest by women whose family lives and economic situations had been tragically violated. With the transition to a civilian government, new *arpilleras* appeared calling for truth, justice, and punishment of the victimizers. During this transitional period, these expectations were not met. The political *arpilleras* virtually disappeared, and others became tourist handicrafts rather than expressions of political sentiment.

---

[8]Art Actions (*acciones de arte*) is the name of a certain type of "intervention" in public space developed in the streets, plazas, buildings, or museums drawing attention to the political violence and its effects on human beings and social life.

[9]*Death and the Maiden* is a film directed by Roman Polanski, with Sigourney Weaver, Ben Kingsley, and Stuart Wilson, based on Ariel Dorfman's play (1994).

Modern Chile could absorb nonpolitical *arpillera*. With the continuing need for income, the women displayed the environment, vegetable stands, and the countryside themes for their tapestries. Suppressing patchwork memory left the political *arpillera* as stored away collectors' items just as political leaders wished memories of dictatorship could be stored.

DEATH AND THE MAIDEN

The human body is the bearer of individual memory. It has registered the gesture, the word, the "mother" tongue, the glance, and the trust. It has responded with its ability to smile, to cry, and to enjoy. It has experienced support or helplessness; and it has suffered fright, mistrust, overprotection, and rigidity. It has recorded both the hints of primary attachments and the social bonds built from the family, the school, the "others," with both the present and the missing persons. These relationships have imprinted this body with shocks, mistreatment, suspicions, cruelty, or, through smiles with tenderness, warmth, and caress.

Ariel Dorfman's play *Death and the Maiden* presents the traumatic memory of a tortured woman. For women, torture has a special meaning almost inevitably linked to sexual violence and humiliation. There are three characters in Dorfman's play. Pauline is the protagonist. The two other characters are Gerardo, her husband, and a medical doctor, who could be her torturer. The play takes place at night.

Pauline was tortured for "reasons of state" and raped numerous times by her torturer. But Pauline has not forgotten; in fact, she remembers traumatically. She wants to exorcise the past to recover the present, with vengeance replacing the justice that seems impossible to obtain. Pauline could also be a woman raped and abused for private reasons at the whim of the dominator. She is surrounded by ghosts; she could be a woman abused during war or the Holocaust, an Indian, a poor woman from any shantytown, a refugee, a Jew, an African American, a Guatemalan, a Salvadoran, or a Chilean. This woman's memory, inscribed in her body, in her basic reactions, in her eroticism, has been altered by torture.

Unspeakable emotions and experiences have invaded her internal world and stamped themselves on her social relations. They have pervaded her affective senses with what is impossible to put in words. In this woman, repeated rape as part of a "treatment" afforded to "subversives" has imprinted an emotional memory that is as current as the day it occurred. However, it is not only a private matter. The meaning it has for her has been defined, in part, politically. It was done by a functionary of the government, ostensibly in the exercise of his duties, in the name of the state he served, and the nation that made her its enemy.

Pauline confronts a person she supposes to be her torturer, cajoling her husband to assist her in exacting confession and vengeance. All the time the supposed torturer claims that Pauline has confused him with someone else, though he reconstructs the past as if she were a witness to it. The tale of the doctor is a substitute for the public confession Pauline requires, but also makes clear the impunity that permeates and defines the transition from the military to civilian government in Chile. The impunity reinforces the authoritarian past, a past that the transition and its reforms cannot modify. Ariel Dorfman (1991), referring to his play, commented:

> When we leave tyranny behind, what do we do with the consequences of the tyranny that remain in the country and in the psyche and in the sex and in the body of the people themselves? How do we deal with the past? This has been a century of savagery. Horrible things have been done in the name of the common good, of the state, of the nation. The horrors have been a central experience of the century. Millions of the victims of the century have been women, but resistance in Latin American countries has been mainly developed by women. Their memories will not let the past be forgotten.[10] (p. 2)

CONCLUSIONS

The first steps in the political transition period in most Latin American countries has consisted of initiating discussions about truth, justice, social reparation, reconciliation, impunity, memory, and suppressing memory (olvido). In beginning to face the past abuses, "truth" has had to be converted from what had been an officially sanctioned version to a version that victims could recognize.

A high priority of transition has been a reestablishment or building of a fair political order (Zalaquett, 1990) that provides an ethical, political, and subjective framework to deal with these problems in the long term. When torture and other repressive situations can be placed in their social and political context, societies can face the aftereffects not only as private matters, but as a concern for public policy that compensates and rehabilitates victims and seeks to prevent future similar outcomes.

---

[10]The Agrupación de Familiares de Detenidos Desaparecidos in Chile and other survivor groups were mainly organized by women. In Argentina, resistance movements started with the Mothers of Plaza de Mayo (Madres de la Plaza de Mayo) and the grandmothers' organization (Organización de Abuelas). In El Salvador, the Mother's Committee Oscar Arnulfo Romero existed from 1977. (COMADRES) The Group of Mutual Support (Grupo de Apoyo Mutuo) in Guatemala was started in 1984 by relatives of disappeared people.

Breaking the silence at the social level implies less "sanitized" truth. The most important material for the reconstruction of truth was the memory of the survivors. Although truth is insufficient, it is an essential aspect of the social and political process implying a public acknowledgment of the victims' suffering. If this process does not take place, societies are doomed to repeat the past; and the victims are doomed to private heartaches.

The traumatic nature of human rights violations generated distressing emotions and meanings not only for the victims. This perhaps explains the efforts in many sectors of Chilean society to silence all discussion, arguing that its persistence may bring calls for vengeance, violence, and confrontation. But society cannot decree loss of memory, even if it will not support its validation. Those who need to remember will find a way, even if it is distorted, to sustain it.

From the beginning there has been enormous resistance to full disclosure of human rights violations in Chile. Psychological interventions on both clinical and research levels have included ethical and professional perspectives closely linked to political assumptions. Alleviating the human suffering and stopping human rights violations were the main objectives during the dictatorship. Thus, denunciation was a start for social memory. When the transition started, the former attitude of advocacy and ethical commitment tended to undermine a general sense of scientific or professional detachment. It was believed that it was necessary to integrate in a more explicit way the connections between psychology and politics, between private stories, testimonies, and history.

Concerned with the consequences of political violence and torture, ethical, social, and political questions were raised about the future, trying to better understand what happens simultaneously to individuals and society. In this sense, reflecting on the political context changed the psychological perspective and the approach to therapy. From a psychological perspective, some situations are known that falsify memory under particular conditions: traumas, abnormal conditions of consciousness, repression, and blockages. Certainly frequent reevocation keeps memories fresh and alive. A memory evoked too often and expressed (e.g., as a story) tends to become rigid, stereotyped, and crystallized, which will take the place of the original memory.

The memories of extreme experiences of injuries suffered or inflicted can be themselves traumatic. Recalling is painful or at least disturbing. A person who has been wounded tends to block out the memory so as not to renew the pain; the person who has inflicted the wound pushes the memory deep down to alleviate the feeling of guilt (Levi, 1989). Memory or its suppression is a great dilemma for Chilean society today. There are countless individuals who died or disappeared that never rest in peace. However, some people still have the strong desire turn the page and forget while others elect to continue living. This is not an abstract dilemma. It is experienced by the Chilean people as well Argentines, Uruguayans, and Salvadorians in their daily lives. Like all historic dilemmas, there is no simple consensus as to how it should be resolved.

Openly acknowledging the past and recognizing their "private" truth can be extremely threatening to the victimizers and to political stability. Many have argued that examining the past only leads to retraumatization and the reopening of old wounds and scars. The deep desire to simply forget, though legitimate in certain ways, also becomes an impossible proposal. To be able to forget, it is necessary to remember.

From experience, it is necessary to recognize and differentiate historical events and diverse interpretations of them. It is necessary to differentiate the fantasies and emotions associated with the past, especially the idealizations, the desires, and hopes tied up with the losses, frustrations, and suffering. These emotions are not only individual. They influence collective attitudes toward politics and the commitment, or lack thereof, with the fate of Chilean society presently. In this process, literature and other forms of art represent one approach to integrating what we were, what we are, and what we wish to be or not to be.

The Dorfman play illuminates the connection between art and therapy, metaphor and pain, society and silence, as did the arpilleras. The victims need to have their experience validated by society, by those outside themselves, to make their private horror part of history, and part of what others recognize as true, valid, and shared. A social memory has to be constructed to openly confirm what happened to them as individuals, which must go beyond the individual remembrances.

Through art and other public reminders of the past, individuals are allowed to recognize individual and collective history through the fear, impotence, exhaustion, sadness, and anguish that resurface. Individual suffering can be recognized and validated. People can obtain more information about what happened. However, this also requires understanding the relation between suffering and the political context that induced it. It must be understood that the present is not "a return to democracy" as imagined, but rather the creation of a different "democracy" that has incorporated institutional and ideological aspects of the military regime. It must be emphasized that the elaboration of the past in psychological, cultural, and ethical terms cannot be separated at least for now. Because the present political order continues to operate in an atmosphere of lingering threat and fear while not punishing most of the victimizers, successful therapy must confront (i.e., force us to recognize) the present effects on patients of the new political system as well as the trauma of the past. This confrontation at the social level, which is collective memory, is also essential to prevent repetition of the horror.

ACKNOWLEDGMENT

I wish to thank Brian Loveman for his collaboration in discussing this text and offering suggestions for revisions.

REFERENCES

Agosin, M. (1994). Patchwork of memory (Journal–Chile). *NACLA Report on Americas, 27*(6, May–June).

America's Watch Report. (1991). *Human rights and the "politics of agreements." Chile during President Aylwin's first year.* New York.

Bettelheim, B. (1979). *Surviving and other essays.* New York: Knopf.

Cienfuegos, A. J., & Monelli, C. (1983). The testimony of political repression as a therapeutic instrument. *American Journal of Orthopsychiatry, 53,* 43–51.

Dorfman, A. (1991). *Death and the maiden.* New York: Penguin.

Dorfman, A. (1993). Comments on the play *Death and the Maiden.* Unpublished manuscript.

Galeano, E. (1992). *The book of embraces* (C. Belfrage, trans.). New York and London: Norton.

Levi, P. (1989). *The drowned and the saved.* New York: Vintage International Random House.

Lira, E. (1988). Consecuencias psicosociales de la represión política en Chile [Psychosocial consequences of political repression in Chile]. *Revista de Psicología de El Salvador, 28,* 143–159.

Lira, E., Becker, D., & Castillo, M. (1990). Psychotherapy with victims of political repression in Chile. A therapeutic and political challenge. In *Health services of the treatment of torture and trauma survivors.* Washington, DC: American Association for the Advancement of Sciences.

Lira, E., & Weinstein, E. (Eds.). (1984). *Psicoterapia y represión política* [Psychotherapy and political repression]. México: Siglo XXI Editores.

Loveman, B. (1988). *Chile: The legacy of Hispanic capitalism.* New York: Oxford University Press.

Loveman, B. (1990). Democracy on a tether. *Hemisphere, 2*(2).

Nazar, V. (1972). El autoritarismo en la clase obrera [The authoritarianism in the working class]. *Revista del CEREN* (Centro de Estudiios de la realidad nacional). No. 13, Santiago, Chile.

Report of the Chilean National Commission on Truth and Reconciliation. (1993). South Bend, IN: University of Notre Dame Law School.

Ritterman, M. (1991). *Hope under siege.* Norwood, NJ: Ablex.

Weinstein, E., & Lira, E. (1987). *Trauma, duelo y reparación* [Trauma, grief and reparation]. Santiago, Chile: FASIC Editorial Interamericana.

Zalaquett, J. (1990). Confronting human rights violations committed by former governments: Principles applicable and political constraints. *Persona y Sociedad, 6*(2–3).

Chapter 12

The Construction of Remembering and Forgetfulness: Memories and Histories of the Spanish Civil War

Lupicinio Íñiguez
The Autonomous University of Barcelona

Jose Valencia
University of the Basque Country, Spain

Félix Vázquez
The Autonomous University of Barcelona

Despite the permanent memory of the Spanish Civil War in the social imaginaire, its investigation, leaving historical studies aside, has not been the object of noteworthy study in social science. This abandonment is in direct contrast to its stubborn presence in the mass media. With the celebration of the 50th anniversary of the end of the Civil War coinciding with the centenary of General Franco's birth, it seems that the attention of the media has somewhat awakened in the past decade. However, if we examine what underlies current accounts, it is clear that there is an almost complete reliance on the *presentist conception* of history, that is, a reading of the past through categories of the present. Obviously, a presentist conception imposes a certain order onto events; in doing so, it gives legitimacy to a certain narrative conception. Events placed early in that narrative, we argue in this chapter (e.g., the assassination of a key figure), are turned into causes of succeeding events. The narrative turns descriptions into a fixed chain of cause and effect leading up to the present. It has a power not only within the collection of events it chooses to make a sequence of, but imposes a "regimen of truth" on all other candidates: They are admitted into legitimate debate only if they fit the narrative's criteria.

In fact, Spain has seen few processes that have generated so many interpretations and debates as the Civil War. It is a framework of feelings and intense experiences, full of polemical and controversial issues. These are not only limited to a *historiographical viewpoint* and/or a *political dimension*, but are also open to a *dimension of ethics* and *experience*. It is a conflict that not only transcends identification with one of the warring bands, but also forms part of the most private side of personal experience.

Depending on the implicit or explicit ideological leanings of historical studies of the Civil War, the results of the conflict are shown as obeying a careful plan designed to one end. Frequent omissions include the many different ups and downs, the unforeseeable accidents, the conditioned decisions, and the situational confusion. The whole process is converted into the perfectly linked, modulated progress of a predetermined plan that always shows the when, who, how, and what, and could not possibly have been changed by any event, all integrated in a sequence of events that appear as the fruit of infallible political calculations. In other words, investigations of what happened at the beginning and in the middle of some social event are always undertaken with full knowledge of how it all ended. Moreover, the conception of what is happening held by participants (of all kinds) while events are ongoing affects the process as it develops. It is therefore of the greatest importance to be aware of the versions at issue—for participants and later commentators—in order to account as completely as possible for the social events under discussion.

And so it is very interesting to study the construction of remembering around the Civil War. It is not a simple process of evoking and recovering elements fixed in a historical moment but rather a remembering that produces narratives legitimizing, maintaining, ordering, and conditioning social life. In other words, remembering brings about *normative* and *prescriptive* effects.

Before going further, we should make clear what conception of remembering we are going to use. Remembering is understood to be knowledge of the past, not in the sense of the coincidence of memories with a fixed reality, but rather as a semantic ordering of events. Remembering is a generative, nonmechanical reconstruction; it is the proposal of a narrative in a dialectic of argument (Middleton & Edwards, 1990), and it is the negotiation of antithetical postures marked by a sense of the past.

THE CONSTRUCTION OF REMEMBERING
AND FORGETFULNESS

Order of Events and Discursive Unity

One general feature of dominant discourses on traumatic conflicts in the past is the use of argumentative repertories and rhetorical strategies favoring the sketching and definition of a *presentist past* to the detriment of social memory. They are also characterized by the legitimizing guarantee of a certain *social order*.

Remembering plays a determining role in this type of account and interpretations. As remembering and witnesses of the past increase and/or established order is questioned, or even if the remembering process becomes blurred with time, people are faced with a conversion of remembering into history, in such a way that the past takes on an objective aspect and becomes the reference for and confirmation of the natural superiority of the present.

This conversion of remembering into history obviously brings about a loss of confidence in people as it can question their ability and competence to produce discourses around the past; it also simultaneously makes them give in to the evidence (Pennebaker, 1990) of factual materialization ordered in accordance with the results of the present. In this way, the distance between the weight of the organized sequencing of facts and the bringing together of the discourse in one whole single unit is made all the more obvious with the fragility of remembering, "which, contrary to historiography, reveals a clear taste for disorder and jumble; imitation and authenticity jostle here, all that is serious with what is futile, what is authentic with everything delirious or all that is prepared" (Brossat, Combe, Potel, & Szurek, 1990, p. 40). Therefore, in the face of history, which directs its discourse at the present and future by attempting to assure the perfect continuity in the future of the order it legitimizes, remembering defends a process of differentiation with respect to the present; according to Sebastiani (1991), the act of remembering is, in this sense, a potentially subversive act.

Thompson (1978) suggested that all history is eventually dependent on its social purpose, being created even where it is nonexistent. In this way, as Thompson assured that there will be no question that the social purpose of history demands an understanding of the past that relates it directly or indirectly with the present.

Nevertheless, it is not possible to clarify or interpret a social phenomenon without explaining how it was constituted. Ibáñez (1989) stated that the social phenomena "themselves" have memory, to the extent that they "contain" the frameworks of the social relations that instituted them and not only because they are relative to a specific historical period or because time has caused them to change. In fact, it might be said that "as happens with the future, the past is not 'already written' either, given that its characteristics are brought up to date by specific later developments which, by definition, do not exhaust all the possibilities. It is no longer that the future partially depends on the past, but rather that the past acquires some of its features in accordance with the future which is effectively produced" (Ibáñez, 1989, p. 111).

The recognition of this aspect is important insofar as it questions the objectivity of psychosocial wisdom by placing it in society and not in the presumably stable discoveries to which standard historiography has us accustomed. Through this knowledge, it is possible to consider the relevance of remembering, a relevance that is kept in check by the double character of process and product that any past event or process possesses. In a dialectic exchange, this double character propitiates rereadings and reinterpretations of social practice, which at all times does not only favor the semantic and generative reorganization of the past, but also gives rise to the possibility of questioning the current social order. This is why it is imperative that the constituted social order must furnish remembering with logical consistence, that is, that subsequent facts must only be accessible through the reexamination of the occurrence of certain precedents. In other words, stories must be proscribed and history constructed in such a way that not only those who were present at the sociohistorical moment of the event may have news of what really happened, but that a specific discourse may assure its future continuity.

However, the character given to a discourse does not proceed exclusively from the checking of the actual occurrence of the events themselves, but from the type of discourse in which they are reported (Calvo González, 1993; Lozano, 1987; White, 1987). In fact, events appear as real because they are reminded and could be in one point of a chronological sequence, and not because they had really happened. It is not enough with a chronological account to consider them as historic. The possibility of being accounted in different ways means that, simultaneously, they could be taken as keys of reality or potentially false. For that reason, to be consider as historic, a fact must be susceptible to, at least, two accounts of its existence (White, 1987, p. 34).

To a great extent, the importance of discourse is that different events construct it, but at the same time, that discourse enables the constitution of the events that give it sense (Ricoeur, 1985). The "narrative phrases," as one of the different ways to describe the action (Lozano, 1987), gain special relevance in the conversion of remembering into history. These types of construction are characteristic, and differentiate discourse from historical knowledge; they refer to at least two events separated in time, though they only describe the first of them (Danto, 1965).

Narrative phrases constitute one of the possible descriptions of an action but always depend on ulterior events unknown to the agents but that, on the other hand, are "known" to the historian. The structure of the narrative phrase enables the description of events to be modified in accordance with what is known about ulterior events. As Simionescu and Padiou (1990) assured, when referring to the construction of the history of Romania in the National Museum in Bucharest, "whoever controls the present does not only have the power to shape the future but also to remake the past" (p. 227).

However, why is it that the past is so important that there may be this greed for it? What is in play with the remembering of traumatic processes?

As was pointed out at the beginning of this section, among the particular features of dominant discourses, the defense of presentist remembering and the legitimacy of a certain social order stand out. It is through this presentist remembering and the defense of a particular political system that the transition and conversion of remembering into history becomes possible.

After the Spanish Civil War, the totalitarian system based its legitimacy on the result of the conflict by operating on remembering in the way discussed earlier. People are no longer dealing with the updating of shared events and the stabilizing of the chronological, ordered sequence of events, which, from the first expression opened by the discourse, show their consummation, and in which witness is only borne to the "truth" of what happened, the clinical asepsis of the facts.

The Ends and the Means: The Establishment
of the Link Between Present and Past

The conversion of remembering into history and the inclusion of formulated, fixed ends in a narrative order must have an effect on society. As Castoriadis (1975) noted, "For all necessary, finished theology, everything is ruled from the end, postulated and determined from the beginning of the process by means of the postulation and determination of the means which will make it appear to have been done" (p. 19). This is what is suggested by the dominant discourse circulating on the social circuit relating the Civil War, its effects, and democracy as the final outcome.

These considerations are certainly not trivial. Consider the current political state in Spain, a system of parliamentary democracy. The a priori recognition of democracy as a desirable aim irrevocably sanctions the validity of certain meanings that were annulled in the process known as "political transition," some meanings being legitimized to the detriment of others. As Berger and Luckmann (1967) suggested, legitimization is not prescriptive just for persons actions, it also informs on the nature of things.

The discourse on the transition has a marked diacritical nature. That is to say, like any discourse, it has latent values that can only be understood in opposition to other values, even though they might not be made explicit. When a discourse asserts some description of a state of affairs, it expects to be understood as backing or endorsing it, or, at a deeper level perhaps, endorsing the set of values that description represents. To assert, for example, that "democracy is the power of the people" is to contrast that value-laden definition implicitly against other rivals. This is what is meant by the diacritical feature of discourse. Here, what is in opposition are sets of values deployed in the defense of democratic order. The most revealing expression may be recognized today in the daily discourses and practices that are more or less closely linked to state policy; appreciate in these, usually in embryonic form, the effects of the confrontation of the Civil War.

The diacritical nature of these discourses enables analysts to identify how they work in the development of the political system. The introduction of successive stages in time allows the discourse to claim that the system is "progressive," and suggests very strongly (to adherents of the discourse, at least) that the system reaches its end through gradual—and wholly normal and predictable—evolution. This strategy of succession allows the present to be linked to the past and history to be ordered, as it includes all occurrences in society within the framework of one coherent unit full of meaning. This strategy of narrating a predictable succession is, of course, motivated and informed by the diacritical force of the discourse: that is to say, it is no mere "cleaning up" of a messy story, but a manifestation of the values that the discourse holds dear and a way of imposing them on the unwary reader. As Taylor (1984) suggested, what is implicit in the discourse is explicit in current practice, and acts in the future as a referential framework for individual action.

It is equally relevant to examine the predominant discourse on history given in different political processes, where the object to be explained is made to seem the protagonist; however, this protagonism acts as a legitimizing element and shows that the process is verified. In fact, history is not presented as a framework but rather, from a narrative distance, a *hegemonic discourse* is drawn up on history that is basically *self-referring*. Here, the legitimacy of one specific political model appears as a synonym of social legitimization. Obviously, this self-referring construction of history and its legitimization act as guarantors of historical continuity through the framework of social discourses, and produce social effects that impose a system of images, reminders, and forgettings (Páez, Insúa, & Vergara, 1992) on the remembering of the period, acting in such a way as to facilitate the governability favored by a "legitimized present" in which norms and democracy stand out as common sense.

Democracy as "common sense" (Íñiguez & Vázquez, 1992) implies that groups and collectives have knowledge that works in terms of evidence and consensus. Here is the diacritical nature of democracy. In fact, in this way individuals establish how things happen and must happen, which enables both the explanation of why things have happened and the determination of their appearance.

It is useful to make a parallel analysis of all of the conceptual terminology, because on many occasions, it goes beyond mere description and becomes the epicenter of discourses and propitiator of practices. For example, consider the concept of *consensus*, which was used generously during the years of the Spanish transition (del Águila & Montoro, 1984) and even after the transition as a discursive bridge between the Spanish Civil War and the current political system (Íñiguez & Vázquez, 1995). It has, in this way, been the source of other concepts, and more importantly, it has weighed heavily on practices, evolution, exchanges, and the styles of both public and anonymous actors. It was therefore one of the main keys to the "management" of the transition and, of course, the negotiation or, more exactly, the *pact on the past*: "It is a point [the past] which, in short, tends to be made obvious in political discourse. The concealing is based on a previously, implicitly, agreed terrain to confront new problems from different angles" (del Águila & Montoro, 1984, p. 253). In other words, it is a pact on what has to be remembered and what should be forgotten, which includes the Civil War, postwar oppression, and the ostracism to which any discourse directly or indirectly striking any aspect related to the conflict is subjected.

THE SPANISH CIVIL WAR BETWEEN REMEMBERING AND HISTORY

How "Ordinary People" Remember History

Next we develop some of the most relevant results of one of the empirical studies made around the social construction of the remembering of the Spanish Civil War.

A conceptual distinction should be established between remembering and history. *Remembering* refers to different nominal narratives of the events that occurred between 1936 and 1939. *History* corresponds to the process of conversion of these narratives into the reified, institutionalized history of the period.

This difference is similar to the one developed by Connerton (1989), who made an explicit distinction between *social memory* and *historical reconstruction*. One of the specific bases that distinguishes the two concepts is that historical reconstruction is basically what professionals of history do when they search for and identify traces of past events. This effect is closely related to the authority they gleam from an activity characterized as being scientific. We have tried to go further by identifying another, maybe more fundamental, base: the ideological and political effects.

Connerton also suggested that historical reconstruction is independent from social memory in the sense that even what has been forgotten may be rediscovered by history, but he admitted at the same time that any historical reconstruction may be strengthened by the social memory of groups, as is, for instance, the case of oral history. Once again, this chapter goes further on this point and gives credit to the added value in terms of the understanding of social and political action, of social memory.

With these parameters, the design of the empirical investigation is synthesized in two useful analyses: The first consists of the apprehension of *narratives* through recourse to oral history or another technique that brings out the experiences of the protagonists in the process. The second consists of the apprehension of *remembering*, with the use of two kinds of analytical tools: those that give access to discourses circulating socially, and those that enable the remembering of the population to be identified.

Obviously, these views are neither incompatible nor exclusive. This chapter deals with the second, the analysis of the concept that "ordinary people" currently have of this historical process.

Rewriting Remembering:
The Spanish Civil War of Young Students

This section presents one of the empirical approaches to the narratives on the definition of the Spanish Civil War circulating among a very specific population, the students of the Autonomous University of Barcelona. Some of the aspects commented on in previous sections are illustrated. To this end, a study was designed with the purpose of initiating a useful analytical mechanism to gain access to the processes of remembering and reminding of the Spanish Civil War. There were two basic aims in the analysis developed here: to identify the elements or bases through which different discourses on the Spanish Civil War are driven as they circulate on the social circuit, and to identify the characteristic elements and establish the different positions from where the aforesaid discourses are made.

A survey method was used in the study. A questionnaire was administrated consisting of four open-ended questions. Although the main argument directing the survey was the analysis of the Spanish Civil War, only the first question dealt with the subject directly: "How would you explain what the Spanish Civil War was to a person who did not know?"

The survey was carried out in a totally anonymous manner. The only personal information requested was age, sex, and the faculty where the person studied. The survey was made on a sample of 313 third-year psychology students in the Universitat Autònoma de Barcelona.

Procedure of Analysis

The results were obtained by the statistical and lexicometric package SPAD_T (Bécue, 1991), which enables automatic content analysis of textual information. The operations are part of the conglomerate of techniques known as "Automatic Analysis of Texts and Discourses," which designates a group of systematic methods through which it is possible to *describe, synthesize,* and *classify* textual information independently of its features or source. The main aim of most of these methods is to produce an exhaustive description and/or systematic ordering of the body of a text that is both descriptive and statistical.

The method used was specially inspired in data analysis, as conceived by the French school of statistics (Benzecri, 1973) and is based on the use of statistical procedures, such as factor analysis of correspondence and hierarchical classification of statistical subjects, which allow different indexes to be calculated to obtain a synthesis and categorization of text variability. This type of analysis facilitates the treatment of a large amount of text data, which would otherwise be difficult to deal with (Lebart & Salem, 1988).

In order to be able to apply these analyses to text information, it is necessary to create different types of contingency tables depending on the information being handled and on the analyses being applied ("Replies × Lexical Forms," "Lexical Forms × Texts," etc.). It is possible to apply the factor analysis of simple correspondence to these tables, as well as the automatic classification methods.

The factor analysis describes large tables of data by projecting them on a space of n dimensions, which retains a large amount of the original information. The classification synthesizes data by grouping from different homogeneous classes into individual groups from the information available. These analyses may be complemented by lexicometrical methods, such as alphabetical glossaries, the concordances between lexical forms or the selection of replies and characteristic lexical forms that make up the body of the analysis.

Description of Results

Four groups of information were obtained through statistical analysis using the SPAD_T package: a general, lexicometrical description of the components shaping the corpus under study; information on the conceptions of the Spanish Civil War; information classifying responses of individuals according to most characteristic replies; and a third set of information allowing the categorization of different lexical forms.

Lexicometrical Analysis. The total number of replies was 313. The total number of words collected was 16,190, of which 2,461 were different. For analysis, words appearing 20 times or more were selected in order to enable the statistical calculations. The final corpus of the analysis was made up of 14,006 words.

Conceptions of the Spanish Civil War. The organization of the information available on the conceptions of the Civil War were analyzed by means of a contingency table of "Individuals × Words" ($n = 313$ individuals and $p =$

87 words). The initial table was submitted to an Analysis of Simple Correspondence, which provided 6 factors. However, interpretation could only be made of the first four, which, as a group, explain 15.64% of the variance. The interpretation of each was carried out from the absolute and relative contributions of each word to each factor. The following four polarities were identified:

Polarity 1: Causes vs. Effects. The first factor (Own value: 0.2719, explained percentage of variance: 4.05%) shows the polarity between the identifiable causes of the Civil War and the effects it had.

Polarity 2: Agency vs. Victimization. The second factor (Own value: 0.2158, explained percentage of variance: 3.22%) distinguishes between the identification of responsibility and protagonism, and the effects that the protagonism of the conflict has on people.

Polarity 3: Reconstruction vs. Objectivization. The third factor (Own value: 0.1972, explained percentage of variance: 2.94%) shows the polarity between the elements rebuilding imagination of the conflict against the elements that specify and place it in history.

Polarity 4: Identification vs. Experience. The fourth factor (Own value: 0.1860, explained percentage of variation: 2.77%) distinguishes between subjects victimized in the imagination of the war and the elements that identify, store, describe, and shape the real experience of the event.

Classification of Responses. To enable identification and definition of the different kinds of reply, as well as the "possible" ascription of these replies to categories of responses of individuals, the study undertook their classification. This classification gave the identification of six groups that is not blind or mechanical, but is informed by the theoretical framework initially established: that is to say, a classification sensitive to the diacritical force of the discourses represented in the informants' replies.

This classification gave the identification of six groups whose description was made by using the replies and the characteristic lexical forms in each as a criterion. Note that these groupings are not meant to represent the once-and-for-all beliefs of individual informants; rather, they are a gathering together of the discourses that are present in their responses. Consider the following groupings and their descriptions:

Group 1: Chroniclers. A group of people characterized by their direct, first mention of the chronological moment of the development of the conflict. They relate a series of events that frequently do not coincide with the succession of facts registered by history. They give simultaneous explanations accompanying the story of what happened in time.

The Civil War began in Africa, among the army which was then fighting to maintain the lands which theoretically belonged to Spain. General Franco, together with other members of the high command of the army, came to Spain in order to gain power. They reached Madrid, deployed troops and invaded the Government. General Franco proclaimed himself Head of the Spanish State but the East of Spain rose up against this proclamation (Aragon, Valencia, Navarre ... the "Reds") and they declared war on Franco's troops. The war lasted three years (1936–1939) and ended with the victory of Franco (the "Nationals"). The Nationals had right wing policies and governed as a dictatorship for about 40 years.

Group 2: Objectivists. This group puts emphasis on the takeover of government and generally makes precise reference to the dates of the conflict. They occasionally point to the Franquist dictatorship as the cause of the Civil War and give some information about the participation of other countries in the conflict, generally lauding one of the contending sides.

It was an armed conflict which began on the 18th July 1936 and ended in each area of Spain when the victorious army went in (normally in 1939). The causes were political; the rebellion of a series of generals (among them the one who would become Head of State, "Caudillo" Franco) against the II Spanish Republic. It seems that this uprising was caused by the remembering of the chaotic I Republic and also because the government in power since 1931 had not solved the problems of the international economic situation caused by the "crash" in 1929. The rebels, or nationals, crossed the strait with their troops (of the Moroccan army) and from the beginning gained the support of most of the West of Spain. They received help from other fascist governments of the time (Germany and Italy) and received the passive support of the remaining western democracies. On the other hand, the Republican Government, despite having one of the most advanced constitutions of the time, only received help from the USSR. Finally a fascist dictatorship was imposed for 40 years.

Group 3: Antagonists. People who offer an explanation for the Civil War in terms of confrontation and substantial opposition between groups for ideological reasons. They make some descriptions of the consequences of the conflict.

The Spanish Civil War was a conflict between two groups which had very different ideologies. Some were right wing monarchists and the others left wing republicans. Unfortunately for the country, the monarchists and fascists won pushing the population into a long period of dictatorship and repression. There were more reds in the north of Spain than in the center and the south.

Group 4: Deideologizers. The discourse of this group basically emphasizes the affective derivations of the conflict. Their interventions on the reasons for the Civil War seem to lack any kind of ideological argument.

I would say that it was a huge negative event which marked the existence of those who had the misfortune of living through it and that even today there is still 'waste' (same as influences) from what happened then between people and above all, on a general level in Spanish society. If we could measure how absolutely negative it was, we would truly understand that it must not happen again (as it is repeated in other places) either here in Spain or in any place.

Group 5: Polarizers. A group of people who recognize, generally without naming, two groups in contention (but a contention empty of any political substance) and a group of causes, also empty of ideology but with heavy affective connotations, which allude to a series of reasons that, in their opinion, explain the conflict.

The truth is that not even I can explain the Spanish Civil War. Like in all wars, it was a conflict of interests; on one hand, a dictator, General Franco, with all the army backing him; on the other all those who opposed another dictatorship. Apart from this, I suppose there were other factors, such as economic, social etc. But the truth is that I don't really know what happened. The thing is the two sides went to war. Many people died on both sides (all Spanish citizens). The Franco partisans were much better trained, they were the army, and they ended up winning and imposing a dictatorship (that few people wanted) which did not come to an end until 30 years later.

Group 6: Philohistorians. A group that makes a description based on the chronological succession of identifiable historiographical elements. On occasions the statements and explanations are of a certain ideological nature, though most usually the expressions are objective.

The Spanish Civil War occurred at the beginning of the 20th Century when, following a political crisis, two very different ideological groups were formed in Spain. The first group defended democracy at all costs and the others believed that the best thing for the country to work well was the forming of a Republic. The War lasted three years (from 1936 to 1939) and during this period there was an atmosphere of tension in the whole country as a direct consequence of the situation of fighting between people of the same country that maybe before had been colleagues, neighbors . . . and who at this time were killing each other for the sake of ideological questions. The war affected everyone, from very small children to adults who were forced to intervene. The victory of the Republicans was compensated, for this group, by the figure of the dictator Franco, although after him appeared what we would call democracy, as seen through the monarchy in the figure of King Juan Carlos.

Classification of Words. Thematic analysis of the replies, carried out by classifying the lexical forms, has also demonstrated the convenience of extracting the following six configured categories of the various options of the Spanish Civil War:

Category 1: Chronological. This category of answers explicitly recognizes the confrontation (*Civil War, Spanish, conflict, regime*), emphasizes the time aspect (*three, were, years, lasted*), chronologically identifies the limits of the conflict (*1936, 1939, 1936–1939*), and refers to the participants (*Band, nationals, right winders, politicians, Franco, republicans*).

Category 2: Conflictual. These replies are characterized by their spontaneous reference recognizing the existence of contending elements (*bands, side, two, other, others*), their mention and ideological identification (*reds, fascists*), and the explicitness of their connections (*fight, confrontation*).

Category 3: Characterizing. These bring together all the concepts that usually shape the discourse referring to the origin (*coup d'état, army, Franco, Republic, military*) and development of the Civil War (*when, all, politics, people, Spanish, situation, government, moment*).

Category 4: Affective. This category includes all the terms and concepts that allude to an emotional translation of the conflict, such as, for instance, *brothers.*

Category 5: Polarizing. The participants in this category allude to the specific fact of the war (*war, country, period, politicians*) and to the confrontation between two opposing positions (*different, they, people, his/her, groups, their, all*).

Category 6: History making. This is a category of words that recognizes the existence of ideas in conflict (*ideas, ideologies, same*), translated into personal confrontation (*people, policies*).

CONCLUSIONS

With our question we identified the main narratives on the Spanish Civil War to reveal the discourse, or discourses, given in society about the event. We obtained a configuration of bases offering an approximation of great heuristic power, to describe and understand them. In this way, the continual "causes vs. effects," "agency vs. victimization," "reconstruction vs. objectivization," "identification vs. experience," configure narratives that can be classified as chronological, conflictual, characterizing, affective, polarizing, and history making.

These different narratives, which show the most coherence with respect to the hypotheses of Halbwachs (1950), concern different social groups. Aside from the interest that the identification of these groups that maintain different positions might have (their sociological and demographic characteristics, etc.), it is true that they could easily be recognized and clear differences could be shown. Later studies should eventually lead to a detailed description of the correspondences between narratives and social groups or categories.

This would, therefore, be a useful work, as it is through their belonging to a social group that individuals participate in the building of remembering. We agree with Connerton (1989) who stated that the idea of an individual memory completely separate from social memory is a meaningless abstraction. Nevertheless, the most important implication of this statement is that the different social groups, categories, and collectives, each with its own past, will surely have different social memories that shape and are shaped by their own intersubjectivity. Every memory, as personal as it may be—even of events that are private and strictly personal and have not been shared with anyone—exists through its relation with what has been shared with others: language, idiom, events, and everything that shapes the society of which individuals are a part.

In our initial discussion, we also sought the connection with ideology and political action. Remembering has something to do with both. We have maintained that the fundamental relationship is related to legitimization, and more specifically with the legitimization of the democratic order. Therefore, one of the consequences of the gradual conversion of social memory into history is the considering of the democratic order as the context that reduces the conflict, the fight, that the war represents. Another consequence is undoubtedly the presentation of a social context of continuity in time that favors identity as a collective unit, and restates progressiveness. As a result, unity between collectives and the political system is firmly asserted. This unity is guaranteed by the objectivization of certain enemies from the past, which must be fought in order to maintain the system—an aspect that falls back once again on legitimacy.

ACKNOWLEDGMENTS

Previous versions of this chapter were presented at the 19th Annual Scientific Meeting of the International Society of Political Psychology, Washington, DC (USA) and XXV Congreso de la Sociedad Interamericana de

Psicología, Julio 1995, San José (Puerto Rico). The authors are grateful to Miquel Domènech (Universitat Autònoma de Barcelona, Spain) and Bernardo Jiménez (Universidad de Guadalajara, México) for their help. We would like to thank Charles Antaki (Lancaster University, UK) for commentary on the arguments in the chapter and for helping us through our difficulties with English.

REFERENCES

Aguila, R. del, & Montoro, R. (1984). *El discurso político de la transición española* [The political discourse of the Spanish transition]. Madrid: CIS/siglo XXI.

Bécue, M. (1991). *Análisis de datos textuales. Métodos estadísticos y algoritmos* [Content analysis: Statistical methods and algorithms]. Paris: CISIA.

Benzecri, J. P. (1973). *L'Analyse des correspondences* [Analysis of correspondence]. Paris: Dunod.

Berger, P., & Luckmann, T. (1967). *The social construction of reality.* London: Allen Lane.

Brossat, A., Combe, S., Potel, J-Y., & Szurek, J-Ch. (1990). *En el Este, la memoria recuperada* [In the east, recovered memory]. Valencia: Edicions Alfons El Magnànim.

Calvo González, J. (1993). *El discurso de los hechos* [The discourse of actions]. Madrid: Tecnos.

Castoriadis, C. (1975). *La institución imaginaria de la sociedad: Vol. 2. El imaginario social y la institución* [The imaginary institution of society]. Barcelona: Tusquets.

Connerton, P. (1989). *How societies remember.* Cambridge, England: Cambridge University Press.

Danto, A. C. (1965). *Analytical philosophy of history.* Cambridge, England: Cambridge University Press.

Halbwachs, M. (1950). *La mémoire collective* [The collective memory]. Paris: PUF.

Ibáñez, T. (1989). La Psicología Social Como dispositivo deconstruccionista [Social psychology as deconstructionist device]. In T. Ibáñez (Coor.), *El conocimiento de la realidad social.* Barcelona: Sendai.

Íñiguez, L., & Vázquez, F. (1992). *La democracia ya no es democracia sino sentido común. Notas críticas y alguna constatación práctica (Inédito)* [Democracy is no longer democracy but common feeling. Critical notes (unedited)].

Íñiguez, L., & Vázquez, F. (1995). Legitimidad del sistema democrático. Análisis de un discurso auto-referencial [Legitimacy of democratic systems: Analysis of a self-referential discourse]. In O. D'Adamo, V. García, & M. Montero (Eds.), *Psicología de la acción política.* Buenos Aires: Ediciones Paidós.

Lebart, L., & Salem, A. (1988). *Analyse statistique des données textuelles* [Statistical analysis of textual passages]. Paris: Dunod.

Lozano, J. (1987). *El discurso histórico* [The historical discourse]. Madrid: Alianza Editorial.

Middleton, D., & Edwards, D. (Ed.). (1990). *Collective remembering.* London: Sage.

Páez, D., Insúa, P., & Vergara, A. (1992). Halbwachs y la memoria colectiva: La imagen histórica de Europa como un problema psicológico social [Halbwachs and collective memory: The historical image of Europe as a social psychological problem]. *Interacción Social, 2,* 109–125.

Pennebaker, J. (1990). *Opening up.* New York: Morrow.

Ricoeur, P. (1985). *Temps et récit: 3. Le temps raconté* [Time and narrative. 3]. París: Éditions du Seuil.

Sebastiani, Ch. (1991). In Jedlowski & M. Rampazi, *Il senso del passato: Per una sociologia della memoria* (pp. 43–49). Milán: FrancoAngeli.

Simionescu, P., & Padiou, H. (1990). Rumanía. Cómo narraba la Historia el Museo Nacional de Bucarest [Rumania: How the history of the Bucharest National Museum was told]. In A. Brossat, S. Combe, J-Y. Potel, & J-Ch. Szurek (Eds.), *En el Este, la memoria recuperada.* Valencia: Edicions Alfons El Magnànim.

Taylor, Ch. (1984). Philosophy and its history. In R. Rorty, J. B. Schneewind, & Q. Skinner (Eds.), *Philosophy in history* (pp. 17–30). Cambridge, England: Cambridge University Press.

Thompson, P. (1978). *The voice of the past.* Oxford, England: Oxford University Press.

White, H. (1987). *The content of the form: Narrative discourse and historical representation.* Baltimore: Johns Hopkins University Press.

Chapter 13

Social Sharing, Emotional Climate, and the Transgenerational Transmission of Memories: The Portuguese Colonial War

Jose Marques
University of Porto, Portugal

Dario Paez
University of the Basque Country, Spain

Alexandra F. Serra
University of Porto, Portugal

Epidemiological research has shown that between 25% and 40% of the people who were either victims or initiators of massacres, combat, or wars, as well as those who were victims of other forms of extreme violence, endure symptomatic states such as Posttraumatic Stress Disorder (PTSD). This percentage increases to 60% in rape victims (Davidson & Foa, 1991; Echeburúa, 1992; Janoff-Bulman, 1992; Modell & Haggerty, 1991). The more these traumatic events display characteristics of collective violence and repression, and the more intense they are, the more they tend to generate psychological disorders (Davidson & Foa, 1991; Janoff-Bulman, 1992). The psychological concomitants of traumatic events comprise several dimensions: psychophysiological hyperreactivity (Davidson & Foa, 1991; Janoff-Bulman, 1992), intrusive thoughts and memories (Horowitz, 1986; Steinglass & Gerrity, 1990), cognitive and behavioral avoidance symptoms, as well as problems to seize, grasp, and express inner emotions and establish intimate relationships (Davidson & Baum, 1986). In addition, traumatic events drastically alter the view of oneself, of the world, and of other people (Janoff-Bulman, 1992), resulting in a lack of the positive cognitive biases that characterize normal situations and positive mood (Janoff-Bulman, 1992; Taylor & Brown, 1988).

Apparently, traumatic events have but a relative impact on individuals. In the months and years following the experience of a traumatic event, about 50% show signs of important psychological disorders, and of these only about one third go through a phasic process of shock–disturbance– bereavement–recovery. A small percentage of people may present a state of chronic bereavement (18%) or delayed bereavement (3%; Wortman & Silver, 1989). So, an important number of individuals who have in some way taken part in a collective catastrophe adapt without having to process lasting negative emotions. Still, a large number of people do suffer from intrusive memories and affective disorders, alternating with cognitive, be- havioral, and affective avoidance. Although social support is known to reduce the impact of traumatic events (Davidson & Baum, 1986; Janoff- Bulman, 1992), individuals cannot easily find such support when they attempt to overcome the impact of these events (Pennebaker, 1990).

Because there are a large number of individuals who remember trau- matic events vividly and privately, one may wonder how these massive traumatic events are processed in social memory. One way to deal with these events is institutional and informal forgetting and repression. A sec- ond way is the transgenerational transmission of information about the traumatic event. Another, is the collective reconstruction of the past.

INSTITUTIONAL RESPONSES TO TRAUMATIC EVENTS: FORGETTING AND REPRESSION

In countries where collective political catastrophes have taken place—in- cluding Germany, Italy, France, Spain, Argentina, Chile, and Uruguay, just to mention a few—the institutional response has been to forget and to neutralize what happened (Becker & Lira, 1989). An illustration is the French case:

> Once the IV Republic was stabilized . . . extreme meticulousness was quickly replaced by a desire to erase wounds, hide the degree of national involvement in a twin repressive regime: Vichy and Berlin. Enhance the myth of the liberation fight against the occupying forces, an event which has gone down in history under the name of the Resistance. All this implied that in a short term span there were a lower number of sentences, and a marked tendency towards amnesty. The main goal seemed to be to soften charges of "collabo- ration with the enemy," in other words, treason. This climate of permissive forgetfulness was intellectually stirred in the 1960s when the North American historian Robert O. Paxton wrote a book on the Vichy years. Field-Marshall's Petain regime allied itself with Hitler much more deeply and enthusiastically than the Nazis had demanded. Petain (whose death sentence was commuted by De Gaulle for life imprisonment), played a major part, not only in re- pressing the Resistance but also in doing so with the Jews. The myth of Petain's "inside shield" whilst De Gaulle had the "outside sword" was blown to pieces. Vichy's was a racist and autonomous national project and not a mere vassal of the occupying forces. (El País, 1994, p. 14)

The aforementioned example expresses a general phenomenon in post-war Europe: forgetting and repressing the event as an important way of dealing with collective traumatic events in social memory. Furthermore, it shows that forgetting may function as the basic process allowing the subsequent reconstruction of the past. The creation of the myth of the general population's active resistance to the detriment of evidence of the active and passive support of the Nazi and fascist regimes illustrates this fact.

According to Pennebaker (1993), silenced events are shared events that lead to an important change, and so people avoid talking about them. This avoidance may be imposed by a repressive government or an authoritarian institution. It may also result from its perception by most of the population as a shameful event about which it is better not to talk. That is, institutional forgetfulness is not specific to dictatorial forms of government or drastic political changes. Voluntary forgetfulness also predominates in pacific transitions from repressive dictatorships to more or less tutored democracies without a sharp break with the past. It is common to witness how different forms of amnesty emerge, which leave the repressors alone and the repressive institutions as they are. In Spain, for instance, after the transition from Francisco Franco's dictatorship to the present monarchic democracy, "an implicit agreement reached during the transition repressed any reference to the Franquist era (and to anti-Franquism). Reasons of political prudence recommended that it should be this way. But possibly it is not good to indefinitely prolong this caution: as psychoanalysts state, that which is repressed comes back if we do not face it" (Unzueta, 1994, p. 18). This is a good example of the belief in the return of the repressed past, which is an idea clearly based on a Freudian approach.

Concerning the institutional repression of traumatic memories, Freud argued that collectivities confront common crimes by covering the location of the crime with discrete monuments which allow us to forget them. This may take the form of modernization and embellishment. In the same vein, Pennebaker and Banasik (chapter 1 in this book) discuss how collectivities that have been stigmatized following the occurrence of political crimes—as is the case of the city of Dallas, Texas—tend to modernize their buildings instead of commemorating tragedy sites with monuments.

Silenced events may be the most important events in the development of collective memories. Moreover, when people try to avoid thinking about undesirable thoughts, they usually cannot do so. For example, in Spanish-speaking South American countries, the decision to forget the atrocities and tortures perpetrated by the army has been officially sanctioned by law, as was the case of the Argentinean "Punto Final" law. This is a very important political decision, which shows that forgetting is not opposed to memory but in fact is a "form" of memory (Brossart, Combe, Potel, & Szurek, 1992, pp.

25–26). Accordingly, it is also unusual for collectivities to commemorate negative events. Historical episodes considered to be negative, painful, humiliating, and so on, usually are not remembered by a collectivity or institution. Brossart (1992) mentioned several examples. In France, the "bloody week" of 1871, the 1940 surrender, and Dien Bien Phu are not commemorated. In Germany, May 8th is a normal labor day. As Robert Frank once said: "What is sadly memorable is commemorated with difficulty" (Brossart, 1992, p. 60). In Portugal, May 28, 1926—the beginning of the dictatorial regime—is just another normal calendar day. Similarly, the occupation of the former Portuguese colonies of Goa, Damao, and Dio by the Indian Union army, on December 19, 1961, is not remembered.

Informal Silence and Forgetting

Not only is institutional forgetting frequent, the voluntary informal silencing of negative events occurs quite often as well. In the case of traumatic events, there are elements that suggest that a collective dynamic of silence and forgetting takes place both among those defeated and those who have won. For example, only 30% of those who survived the Holocaust had shared their experiences in the United States (Faúndez, Hering, & Balogi, 1990; Padilla & Comas-Díaz, 1986; Pennebaker, 1990; Sichrowsky, 1987). Research conducted in the field of social history is a reminder of the problems that emerge when trying to actively remember a negative past, and of the predominance of an attitude aimed toward forgetting.

Thompson (1988) mentioned some examples. In the words of Quinto Osano, a metallurgic worker at the Fiat car company who survived the Mauthausen concentration camp, "We do want it to be told, but in our inside we want to forget; deep inside, in our thoughts and our hearts. It is instinctive: try to forget although we make other people remember it. It is a contradiction, but that's the way it is." Similarly, in the city of Torino, the stronghold of the Italian labor movement, the humiliating period of the fascist domination under Mussolini has seldom been mentioned in the workers' spontaneous life stories; a self-censorship, a silence that Luisa Passerini describes as a deep "scar, a violent suppression of the many years which human lives are a testimony of a deep scar in everyday experience" (Thompson, 1988, p. 164).

An ex-concentration camp prisoner and writer, Jorge Semprún, described the difficulty of remembering and forgetting his experience in Buchenwald: "During a long time I did not want to write about this experience. I knew that forgetting was the only way of not committing suicide. And I forgot. I had an amnesia cure but from the day I wrote the first book on my experience of solitude entitled *The Long Trip* all has come back again. My cure has worked only in some ways" (Alameda, 1994, p. 76). In brief, societies confront traumatic events by repressing the event and/or displacing its meaning. Nevertheless, due to its traumatic nature and to the lack of a cognitive effort aimed at assimilating them, repressed events reappear and reemerge: That which is repressed crops up again.

Institutional Forgetting and Its Consequences for War Veterans

Freud developed his hypotheses on the compulsion of repetition, precisely by having to confront many Austrian veterans' repetitive war thoughts and dreams. Traumatic events that are assimilated with difficulties cannot be remembered because they are extremely painful, driving people to try to forget them. But, simultaneously, and due to their impact, they emerge again and again, putting people in a situation in which they cannot remember and they cannot forget (Horowitz, 1986). Without known exception, research on the traumatic effects of war (e.g., Freud's studies on war neuroses after World War I, or research on PTSD during the last few decades) supports this fact. Indeed, most research considers involuntary memories of traumatic events held by people who have lived through a lost war as mere psychological symptoms, to the detriment of the social dynamics from which they emerge and in which they evolve.

While trying to forget the war, society rarely gives the veterans significant social support. Veterans are thus deprived of institutional support or professional help that could allow them to view their experience in a positive way (Modell & Haggerty, 1991; Pennebaker, 1990). Consequently, and paradoxically, this silence and lack of assimilation of the negative events will increase the number of informal memories on what veterans are trying to forget. This is a clear case of silent collective memory (Pennebaker, 1993). In support of the damaging effects of such collective silence, namely, in the United States, several studies have shown the existence of higher rates of PTSD among the Vietnam veterans than among veterans from other wars or nonveterans. For instance, in a 1987 study, Modell and Haggerty (1991) found that 30% of the Vietnam veterans suffered from PTSD at some time of their lives, and 15% were still suffering from it when the study was conducted. These percentages were 6 times higher than those found in veterans from other wars, and 12 times higher than those found in people of the same age who did not go to war.

Institutional forgetting is, no doubt, a frequent response to collective traumatic events. Collective silence and dismissing the role of society as a whole ends up by reinforcing the strength of both individual and collective level informal memories. As a result, what appears on the surface to be institutional forgetting and silence actually corresponds to hidden rumination and suffering. But forgetting and silence are neither the only processes, nor necessarily the most important ones used to deal with traumatic events. Probably reconstructing the past is more adaptive. Indeed, groups and collectivities may apply themselves to more creative strategies to cope with these kind of events. In many cases, one can observe an active effort of reinterpretation, so that what was initially soiled, felt as a tragic disaster, or as a frustrating event, progressively becomes spotless and easy to deal with. One important question to ask is, how do groups and individuals remember and informally reconstruct past traumatic events? In fact, this is the main theme both of this book and the present chapter.

THE SOCIAL ACTIVITY OF SHARING
AND RECONSTRUCTING THE PAST:
FREUD, HALBWACHS, AND BARTLETT

As discussed elsewhere in this book (Paez, Basabe, & Gonzales, chapter 7), Halbwachs (1950/1968) and Bartlett (1932/1973) stressed the institutional basis of remembering and its links to social activity. Freud, on the other hand, stressed the motivated nature of forgetting: Individuals repress that which is negative, or, if they remember it, they do so in a distorted way.

Nevertheless, as put forth by Erdelyi (1990), the reconstructive processes of memory posited by Bartlett (leveling, accentuation, assimilation, and conventionalization) are very similar to those proposed by Freud (repression, displacement, condensation, and rationalization). Table 13.1 compares both these theories of memory processes.

These processes of forgetting, distorting, and reconstructing allow individuals to parallel the memory of traumatic events with the social frames of reference built around the dominant values and beliefs (conventionalization). One interesting aspect of this comparison is that it allows people to put together a motivational (or "hot") explanation of the reconstruction process, aimed at defending social identity, with a cognitive (or "cold") explanation of the same process, due to the effort of understanding the social world on the basis of social memory frameworks or "schemas." With respect to Halbwach's work, it is also interesting to note the implicit agreement between this author's and Freud's and Bartlett's views. On insisting on the normative nature of a collectivity's memory and on its basis on the collectivity's current attitudes and needs, Halbwachs implicitly assumed that collective memory is biased toward forgetting that which is negative while it is also aimed toward constructing a positive image of the past and of the collectivity.

The following example, extracted from the oral history of the labor movement in Italy, sets a nice illustration of how the conventionalization and justification functions of collective memory in a social mobilization emerge in individuals' discourses:

TABLE 13.1
Theories of Memory Processes

General Process	Bartlett	Freud
Forgetting and retention	Leveling, forgetfulness, omission of some details and retention of others	Repression, forgetfulness of unpleasant facts and feelings
Recall and simple distortion	Numerical and qualitative accentuation, moving from the periphery toward the central aspects	Condensation, unifying separate into a whole meaning
Recall and reconstruction	Assimilation, addition of detail and distortion in view of the expectations, theme, prejudice, attitudes, and values	Displacement, changing the meaning
Explanatory process	Conventionalization, adapting to the culture	Rationalization justification of negative facts and feelings in a positive light

Nearly half of the metallurgic workers whom Portelli interviewed when re-calling the history of the postwar strikes, located the death of a worker at the hands of the police in 1953 instead of 1949. They also located it during the three days of barricades and street fights which followed the gunning of 2,700 men from the steel works, instead of in the context of a peaceful strike in which it really happened. In fact nobody died during those three days. But ... the events are not the most interesting part of this story. The death of Luigi Trastulli would not mean that much for the historians if it were remembered "correctly." After all, the death of a worker by the police in the postwar years in Italy was not so strange. . . . What makes it interesting is the way in which the people's memory works. (Thompson, 1988, p. 157)

This quotation clearly shows how events are condensed and reorganized in search of internal coherence (conventionalization and justification), and, at the same time, of providing a heroic vision of the workers' move-ment. This vision would be a prescriptive lesson of the past, therefore fulfilling a normative function.

Another example of conventionalization of the past may be found in Portugal. After the 1974 revolution in Portugal, the former dictatorship's secret police was disbanded, and many of its agents and officers were sent to jail for their responsibility in crimes like torture, unfounded imprison-ment, or physical elimination of political dissidents. But, by the beginning of the 1990s, the Portuguese government endowed some ex-agents of this police, who acted as informants in the ex-colonies, with a medal for "hon-orable services to the country." In other words, there is an assimilation between the past activities of a secret police under the old regime and the current activity of other organisms that serve the present regime, under the common denomination of "loyal services to the country." The second study was specifically aimed to illustrate a similar process of repression and reconstruction of the past in the case of the Portuguese colonial war, and also the transgenerational transmission of information.

The Portuguese War in Africa

The war in which Portugal was involved against the liberation movements of its former colonies in Africa shows many similarities with the Vietnam War (cf. Guerra, 1994). The African war started in Angola in 1961 and swiftly spread to Mozambique and Guinea-Bissao. By that time, about 1,500 soldiers were based in Angola, and a few battalions were present in the remaining colonies. When the war ended in 1974, there had officially been 280,000 troops involved in combat in the three colonies. As in the United States, many were the internal attempts against the continuation of this war. Some of these attempts were led by officials close to the regime. Others by student movements or political parties who maintained their solidarity with the colonial liberation movements, and by sectors of the Catholic church. However, the Portuguese form of government was not a democratic one, and these attempts faced institutional repressive actions, namely from the state police (DGS). According to official statistics, the war caused 8,831 casualties among Portuguese soldiers, and about 30,000 were wounded. From the latter, about 4,000 were permanently disabled (Guerra, 1994). Among the members of the Portuguese association of disabled war veterans (ADFA) there are nearly 14,000 people who suffer psychic and physical illness. The estimation of prevalence of PTSD among all the veterans who participated in that war ranges between 30,000 and 140,000, according to different sources (Albuquerque, 1992; Guerra, 1994). In epidemiological terms, these estimations would indicate that, in Portugal, PTSD would be from 1.5 to 7.0 times higher than the percentage found in North America, across the entire population.

Stressors associated with the death of fellow soldiers and the actual fighting and wounds inflicted in combat are among the most important features found in any war. Other emotional stressors common to participants in the Portuguese and Vietnam Wars were civilian abuse, tough survival conditions, and atrocities that are frequent in guerrilla warfare. However, Portuguese soldiers had to stay for 2 years in the combat zone (Albuquerque, 1992) with occasional short-term leave, whereas North American soldiers stayed less than 1 year in the Vietnamese combat front and had leaves that took them away from the combat zone. Nevertheless, Portuguese soldiers had the advantage of being called into ranks and leaving for the combat zone always with the same unit, and so they could count on the social and psychological support of people they got to know

TABLE 13.2
A Comparison Between the Portuguese
Colonial War and the Vietnam War

	Portuguese Colonial War	Vietnam War
Length of the war	13 years (1961–1974)	11 years (1964–1975)
Total number of troops	800,000	2.8 million
Troops in combat	280,000	1 million
Casualties (per 1,000 soldiers)	.29	.54
Chronic psychological problems	30,000–140,000	500,000

Note. From Albuquerque (1992) and Guerra (1994).

fairly well. This is something that did not always happen in Vietnam. Table 13.2 is a comparison between the Portuguese colonial wars and Vietnam.

Another important factor is that PTSD has not been officially recognized in Portugal as a incapacity produced by the colonial war, and so most patients receive little economic compensation or specific medical or social help (Albuquerque, 1992). Even the medical community does not pay much attention to this disorder, showing a great lack of understanding in its diagnosis. There are two possible reasons to explain this situation: (a) The nature of the psychopathology (especially the patient's avoidance of any stimulus or reference to the war) may induce the physician not to establish the link between past and present symptoms and the war experiences, and (b) The predominant political climate in Portugal tries to forget some of the unpleasant consequences of the colonial wars (Albuquerque, 1992).

The remainder of this chapter concentrates on two studies conducted in 1993–1994 in Portugal. In these studies, male and female youths ranging from 14 to 18 years of age answered questionnaires on issues related to the Portuguese participation in the colonial war. These pupils did not live through the war days (which ended in 1974), and present-day school manuals generally include little information on the Portuguese colonial war. Although there are several official accounts of the Portuguese colonial war (e.g., Resenha Histórico-Militar, Portuguese Army Headquarters) and several commemorative events have taken place induced by relatively small groups and institutions. In 1994, with the 20th anniversary of the end of this war, more widespread actions and social discourses emerged in the Portuguese media. The data were collected just before the emergence of these commemorative actions. Hence, it was possible to check for the transgenerational informal transmission of information, and its impact on the emotional and explanatory levels. The study also attempted to analyze the pupils' perceptions of those veterans and the war in general.

In one study (herein referred to as Study 1), a sample of 82 high school pupils of both sexes was asked to report on their memories about members of their families being involved in general traumatic events (e.g., "During the 40 last years were you or any member of your family victims of an accident, theft, muggings, etc.?"). Also included were two questions of a political nature (e.g., "During the last 40 years, were you or any member of your family involved as victims (or actors) in a violent event, like torture or war?"). Overall, 21% of all the subjects reported that close acquaintances were both victims and actors, 12% reported that these acquaintances were victims but not actors, and 18% reported that acquaintances were actors but not victims of political violence. These results may illustrate the effects of the former dictatorship and colonial war in Portugal. Participants were asked to report on their rumination, reevaluation, inhibition, and social sharing relative to this topic, independent of their direct personal involvement in the event. The answers were provided in response scales ranging from "never" (1) to "very often" (8). Results supported the neo-Freudian idea that repression induces reevocation. There were positive correlations between avoidance or inhibition of social sharing and rumination about collective traumatic events ($r = .31$, $p < .05$ and $r = .29$, $p < .05$, respectively, for victims and actors of war-related and political violence). Notice that, as shown by Paez, Basabe, and Gonzales (chapter 7, this volume), social sharing is equally related both to rumination and to inhibition. Results of the Portuguese study again supported the relation between, on the one hand, social sharing and rumination ($r = .28$, $p < .05$, $r = .16$, $p < .10$, respectively, for victims and for actors) and, on the other, between social sharing and reevaluation. Further, in line with Paez et al., the latter correlation was stronger than the former ($r = .49$, $p < .05$ and $r = .61$, $p < .05$, respectively, for victims and actors). In brief, the results indicate that there is a relation between inhibition or repression, and repetitive thoughts. However, social sharing is not the opposite of inhibition, and it can reinforce rumination and reappraisal.

This study also observed that a negative perception of the political and social climate (e.g., "In your opinion, the social climate of the country is ... fearful, hostile, sad"; 1 = low, 8 = high) was positively associated with social sharing and reevaluating an indirect experience of violent events, either as a victim or an actor. In other words, according to the data, the more the subjects talk about a member of their family or an acquaintance having been a victim ($r = .27$, $p < .05$) of violence, or an actor ($r = .19$, $p < .10$) in this kind of violence, the more negatively they evaluate their country's political climate. Due to the fact that from 1975 onward Portugal was not directly involved in a war, and torture was eradicated from the political system, it is worth remembering that these responses were given in regard to social memories held by the youth who answered the questionnaire. This fact shows that the transgenerational transmission of traumatic past events reinforces a negative view of the contemporary social system, while showing the impact of the past over the appraisal of the present.

The second study (herein referred to as Study 2) attempted to tap more directly the image held of the Portuguese colonial war and of the veterans in 98 Portuguese pupils. All subjects reported to be acquainted with at least one veteran. Half of the participants considered this veteran to be a close relationship. Also, 67% of the subjects reported that their acquaintance was alive. Twelve percent of these personal acquaintances suffer permanent physical problems and 37% suffered from temporary physical problems. With respect to mental health, 12% of the subjects reported that their acquaintance presented chronic psychological problems and 51% reported temporary psychological problems. Subjects also indicated that in 27% of the cases the veteran suffered family problems. In more than 50% of the cases, the war experience, as stated by their acquaintances, was considered from "negative" to "very negative." In 38% of the cases, this experience was judged as "neither positive or negative."

Briefly, these preliminary results reveal that Portuguese youths know about a collective traumatic event that is certainly akin to the former dictatorship and the colonial war. But data in Study 2, regarding the perception of colonial war veterans, suggests that silence about the war was the modal response. Indeed, 67% of subjects reported that their personal acquaintance talked very little about the war in the family milieu, and 62% reported that these acquaintances did not speak about the war, in general. The data obtained in Study 1 also suggests that members of the subjects' primary groups who were victims of war- and of political-related violence, share more than other individuals who do not have close relationships in these conditions (means are 4.85 and 3.96, respectively; $t(76) = 1.79, p < .05$, one-tailed). These results are congruent with other results (see Paez et al., chapter 7, this volume), and, at least in the case of victims, support the idea that closeness to traumatic collective events increases coping mobilization. The results also suggest that sharing experiences on the Portuguese colonial war is directly related with a negative impact in the subjects' social environment. Confrontation and social sharing about traumatic events is supposed to fill an adaptive social function (Rimé & Christophe, chapter 6, this volume), and to make attitudes more extreme toward past collective issues and the current society (Paez et al., chapter 7).

In Study 2, in order to analyze the relation between the manner in which veteran acquaintances talk about and explain the war, and the perception of the war by the subjects, the latter were asked a number of questions on the way in which veterans share, the affective impact of such sharing on the subjects and on the veterans' families, the subjects' attitudes toward the war, and the explanations of the war and the veterans' participation in it. A second-order factor analysis on questions about the impact of war as well as on the level and quality of social sharing yielded five core dimensions, according to which subjects organized their perceptions. These dimensions included:

1. Personal changes in the person and existence of family problems.
2. Social integration, participation in activities related to the war, friendships in the war, and absence of family problems.
3. Feeling at ease when they talk about the war and talking favorably about the war.
4. Receiving medical treatment and involvement in war violence.
5. Talking frequently about the war, in general, and in the family.

Participants also answered one question about the frequency with which they heard someone talking about the war and one question about the level of closeness to the person talking about the war. These last two questions showed a coherent correlational pattern with the last dimension ($r = .58$, $p < .001$, and $r = .35$, $p < .001$, for frequency and closeness, respectively). This result indicates that social sharing is related to these two variables. In addition, the more subjects heard about the war, the more they reported a negative mood ("unhappy," "worried," "sad," "anxious") in the veteran ($r = .19$, $p < .05$, one-tailed) when he shared about the war. A similar phenomenon occurred with respect to the perception of the veteran's family climate: The more they heard about the war, the more they perceived the family climate to be a negative one ($r = .38$, $p < .01$, for veteran's family negative climate; see Table 13.3). In the same vein, the subjects' emotional appraisal of the war varied as a direct function of the frequency with which they heard the person talk about the war ($r = .18$, $p < .05$, for "sadness," "fear," "anxiety," and "embarrassment"; $r = .21$, $p < .05$ for "disgust," "anger," and "contempt"). Finally, a higher frequency of hearing about war was related to a negative attitude toward this historical event ($r = .35$, $p < .01$, for "injustice," "massacre," "an evil to the country"; $r = .24$, $p < .01$, for "unimportant," "meaningless," "mistake"; $r = -.15$, $p < .10$, for "a good thing for the country," "important," "necessary"). Frequency of hearing was related with Dimensions 4 and 2 ($r = .18$, $p < .05$, and $r = .19$, $p < .05$, respectively). That is, the perception of personal changes and problems, as well as of social integration, increases with social sharing. The latter result may explain why a higher frequency of hearing about the war was also related to a relatively positive emotional appraisal of the war ($r = .43$, $p < .001$, for "joy," "surprise," and "interest").

The results indicate that whereas a majority of veterans talk very little or not at all, and, when they do, in a negative way, a minority talks much more frequently and in a positive way. Clearly, there is a direct relation between the frequency and the tone with which veterans speak about the war and the

TABLE 13.3
Main Results Obtained in the Portuguese Study

Dimensions and Factors	Questionnaire Items
Dimension 1. (Negative) Emotional Climate	
a. Mood depicted by the veteran when talking about the war	Unhappy, sad, anxious, worried
b. Perceived negative family climate when the veteran went to the war	Unhappy, worried, sad, fearful
c. Emotions felt by the subject when thinking about the war	Anxious, fearful, embarassment, sadness
d. Emotions felt by the subject when thinking about the war	Disgust, contempt, anger
Dimension 2. Positive Content Social Sharing	
a. Social sharing 1	Veteran frequently talking about the war in general and in the family
b. Social sharing 2	Veteran speaking frequently and at ease about the war
	Veteran speaking positively about the war
	Subject frequently listening about the war
Dimension 3. (Negative) Attitude Toward the War	
a. Subject's attitude toward the war 1	Injustice, massacre, a bad thing for the country
b. Subject's attitude toward the war 2 (inverted load)	A bad thing for the country, unnecessary, unimportant
c. Subject's attitude toward the war 3	Meaningless, a mistake
Dimension 4. Perceptions of the Veterans	
a. Perception of problems and changes in the veteran	Changes in personality and ways of reacting, and existence of family problems
b. Impact of the war in the veteran	Medical treatment and participation in war violence
c. Causal attributions for the veteran's participation in the war (naive patriotism)	To defend the country, candid, believing that the colonies should remain Portuguese
Dimension 5. Explanations of the War	
a. Causal explanation of the colonial war (dispositional explanations)	Violence of the Portuguese and Africans; there has always been wars; the Portuguese are puffed-up with pride; the population of the colonies didn't know what was best for them
b. Causal attributions for the veteran's participation in the war (psychosocial vulnerability)	Driven by family, social, and economic problems; trigger-happy; racist; being a soldier's son; being afraid to desert

frequency with which subjects hear about it. However, the effects of social sharing seem to be, to some degree, ambivalent: The more the veterans talk about the war, the more the subjects perceive them as having been success- fully integrated in their army social environment; still, subjects also perceive more personal changes and more problems in the veteran's family in this case. More generally speaking, the frequency and tone with which veterans talk about the war and the frequency with which subjects listen about the war are not straightforward determinants of the subjects' image of both the veteran and the war. Indeed, the former variables seem to be less important than is the frequency with which subjects hear about the war in generating a negative image of both the veteran and the war.

The fact that the frequency of hearing about the war was related to a perception of social integration and positive experience during the war suggests that some form of positive reconstruction of the war was present in some instances of social sharing. As was pointed out earlier, not only is forgetting and silence something usual when confronted with traumatic events, there is also an active construction of meaning. For instance, sub- jects in Study 1 reported that they share more ($M = 4.29$), they confront more by reevaluation ($M = 3.62$) than they avoid ($M = 2.41$), or suffer ruminations ($M = 2.28$) about traumatic political and war-related events when the acquaintance lived through these events as victims (all ts are significant at least at the $p < .05$ level, with the exception of the comparison between avoidance and rumination).

In this process, and from the point of view of those directly involved in the situation, three mechanisms may be distinguished. First, it is quite normal for individuals to blame themselves either due to their own behav- iors or to their personality traits. Janoff-Bulman (1992) stated that this is a form of reconstructing the belief in a just world. If an individual is in part responsible (behavioral self-blaming) for what has happened, then that person can also, in some way, control the event now or in the future. Social comparison with those who are worse off is also quite normal among victims of traumatic events. It is also usual for these individuals to believe that they confront negative events better than other people do (Janoff- Bulman, 1992). A third form of reconstructing the meaning of the trau- matic event is to reevaluate it under the light of some positive aspect. These individuals see it as a sacrifice or as a way of learning more about life (the "real" priorities) and about themselves (see what you really can do; Janoff-Bulman, 1992).

Of all the aforementioned coping mechanisms, the third seems to be the most adaptive. Indeed, a research project comparing World War II veterans with and without PTSD showed that those who had fewer symp- toms used as their main coping device of war memories that of stressing the positive aspects of the situations they had lived through during the war. They also thought that the memories were less stressful and more controllable than those veterans who did suffer from PTSD. Those who showed stronger symptomatology isolated themselves as their main coping mechanism, blaming themselves for what had happened, fantasizing about dreams coming true, and seeking emotional support in order to confront war memories (Fairbank, Hansen, & Fitterling, 1991). This confirms that self-blaming, avoidance or inhibition, and simple social sharing (i.e., talking about negative past events) reinforce psychological distress. Table 13.3 presents a summary of the relations between the five most important dimensions, and the factors comprised by these dimensions, as extracted from the second-order factor analysis in Study 2.

Of particular importance in Table 13.3 are the results relative to Dimensions 1 and 2. These results show a reconstruction effect, so that those who frequently talk about the war are judged to do it under a favorable light. On the other hand, when individuals perceive a negative mood on the part of the veteran, they also report that the veteran has a more negative family climate and apparently depict a contagion effect, which is expressed by negative personal emotions. This general result shows a parallel between subjects' perceptions and the veterans' actual responses. Previous research (e.g., Fairbank et al., 1991) has shown that World War II veterans with better affective balance emphasized the positive aspects of their participation in that war when remembering their experiences.

Emphasis on the positive aspects of participation in the war also emerges from the subjects' reports as regards those veterans who talk frequently, in general, and in the family (cf. Dimension 2a in Table 13.3). In this case, subjects depict a more positive image of the veteran. Indeed, they dismiss dispositional explanations of the war (Dimension 5a: $r = -.20$, $p < .05$) as well as psychosocial vulnerabilities (Dimension 5b: $r = -.21$, $p < .05$) in their attributions of the veterans' participation in the war. Similarly, Dimension 2b indicates that, when veterans talk voluntarily and at ease about the war, subjects dismiss more external social-political explanations of the colonial war ("uprising of the African population," "the Portuguese did not want to abandon Africa," "cultural conflict," "the Portuguese dictatorship"; $r = -.19$, $p < .05$). Dimensions 2a and 2b are negatively correlated with situational individualistic explanations given by subjects for the veterans' participation in the war ("the person was forced," "he was in service when the war started," "he had to go in order to avoid problems," "he didn't have people pulling strings for him"; $r = -.17$, $p < .05$, and $r = -.28$, $p < .01$, respectively). This phenomenon is akin to the positive emphasis put by semiotic devices (movies, narratives, monuments, etc.) on the same subject (Igartua & Paez, chapter 4, this volume): The positive aspects of individual participation, like group solidarity, heroism, altruism, and so on, are stressed to the detriment of the social-political causes of the war.

Probably, the positive side of participation in the war does not appear clearly from these responses, due to the fact that this point of view would be negatively valued in the present social-political context.

Table 13.3 displays another aspect that renders the colonial war similar to the Vietnam War. As reported by participants, there is a dominant negative attitude toward the war (means are 4.61 for "injustice, bad thing, massacre"; 4.19 for "meaningless, mistake"; and 3.01 for "good thing, important," 1 = disagree and 7 = agree; both ts, 97 df, are significant at least at the $p < .02$ level). In addition, personal changes showed by veterans are generally associated with physical and mental health problems. Interestingly, explanations given for their participation in the war are mainly based on what we called *naive patriotism*, a result that parallels many recent popular accounts of North American veterans' participation in the war, from which Oliver Stone's *Born on the 4th of July* is but one striking example. Naive patriotism explanations show a higher mean than explanations based on psychosocial vulnerability (means are, respectively, 4.00 and 2.27; $t(97)$ = 9.71, $p < .001$). However, situational individualistic explanations were the most important ones ($M = 4.81$), as compared to psychosocial vulnerability ($t(97) = 12.58$, $p < .001$), and to naive patriotism ($t(97) = 4.05$, $p < .001$), which is also a commonsense account for mobilization (e.g., Robert Zemeckis' movie *Forrest Gump*).

Labeling and Explanations for the War

In order to examine how the social labeling of the past allows individuals to assign different meanings to the war, and, particularly, how this process mobilizes different causal explanations of it, an experimental study was conducted. In the old dictatorship, referring to the African war as a "colonial war" was forbidden. The official designation was "overseas war," because, according to the regime, the colonies had the status not of colonies but rather of "overseas provinces." After the 1974 revolution, and following the term that had never been abandoned by the clandestine left-wing movement, the war became to be referred to as a "colonial war." Therefore, whereas the former term has a clearly conservative and even imperialist nature, the latter became more generally employed, although it still very much presents a left-wing connotation. Therefore, it was reasoned that the semantic, ideological content induced by the use of each alternative term, could trigger different explanations, particularly in the case of youths who did not live through the war and do not have a very structured political stance.

As part of Study 2, participants were randomly divided into two conditions, according to whether they received a version of the questionnaire "on the Portuguese colonial war" ($n = 48$ Ss) or "on the Portuguese overseas war" (n

= 49 Ss). These two groups did not differ in terms of political opinions (50% moderate left, 50% right, in the total sample), religiousness, frequency with which they heard about the war, and closeness to veteran personal acquaintances. There was, however, a marginal tendency for subjects to differ according to the amount of talk about the war given by veteran acquaintances. This variable was used as a covariate in all subsequent analyses.

A multivariate analysis of variance (MANOVA) on the causal explanations about the war and the veterans' participation in it showed a marginally significant effect of the "colonial versus overseas" labeling, $F(6, 89) = 1.86$, $p < .10$. Means and univariate F tests are depicted in Table 13.4.

The results suggest that when the war was labeled with the conservative and legitimizing "overseas" tag, subjects emphasized external factors, like "the influence of other countries" (e.g., USSR, People's Republic of China, Cuba). Simultaneously, under this tag, subjects attribute the veteran's participation in the war more to explanations relating to naive patriotism (see Table 13.3). Instead, subjects who received the "colonial" tag agreed less with the external attribution of the war and dismiss a causal explanation of individual participation in the war based on naive patriotism.

Regardless of the effects of the "colonial versus overseas" induction, it was found that other interesting results by means of a correlational analysis of explanations and attitudes toward the war. This analysis showed that, not only labeling, but also different explanations may legitimize or undermine the social meaning of the war. After reversing positively oriented scores, an overall index of negative attitude toward the war was computed, as the averaged sum of subjects' raw scores to attitudinal questions. This score was then correlated with causal explanations of war and veteran participation. Positive attitudes toward the war were related to explanations based on human nature and social factors ($r = -.13$, $p < .10$). Negative attitudes toward the war were associated with external explanations ($r = .13$, $p < .10$). In addition, positive attitudes toward the war were associated with explanations of the veteran's participation based on psychosocial vulnerability ($r = -.19$, $p < .05$) and naive patriotism ($r = -.14$, $p < .10$). Finally, a critical attitude

TABLE 13.4
Means and Standard Deviations of Explanations Given by the
Subjects as a Function the "Colonial versus Overseas" Labeling

	Colonial (N = 48)		Overseas (N = 49)			
	M	SD	M	SD	F(1, 89)	p
Causal attributions of the veteran's participation in the war (naive patriotism)	3.76	1.61	4.23	1.37	3.73	< .06
External sociopolitical explanations	4.53	1.18	4.97	1.05	4.05	< .05

toward the war was related to the perception of forced participation on the part of the veteran's acquaintance ($r = .21$, $p < .05$). A marginally significant ($-.12$) correlation was also found between political opinion (1 = right wing; 5 = left wing) and depreciation of the war, such that right-wing participants showed a more positive attitude toward the war. This phenomenon is congruent with the previous discussion. To contrast the simultaneous effect of political opinion and explanations, on the subjects' expressed attitudes toward the war, a multiple regression analysis was performed showing that those subjects who believed that the veterans' participation in the war was forced were also those who had a more negative attitude toward the war.

The correlational nature of the present data prevents us from ascertaining the causal direction of the attitude–explanation relation. Indeed, it may either stand as an effect of the reconstructive nature of memory, in which case (as suggested by Halbwachs, 1950/1968) attitudes would be the causal factor, serving as a framework for such reconstruction. Conversely, it may be that social sharing acts as a way of transmitting facts and critical explanations of the past collective event—that is, the colonial war—therefore forming the subjects' attitudes. This would be in line, both with Freud's notion of the return of the repressed, and with Halbwachs' idea according to which collective memory acts as a normative process of construction of individual attitudes and identities. Nevertheless, all the results obtained for the association between hearing about the war and perceiving in the veterans and also reporting personal negative feelings, as well as the relation between social sharing and a negative attitude toward the war reinforce the latter alternative explanation. Partially reinforcing the previous explanation is the fact that measures of personal mood in Study 1 were not related to the amount of collective traumatic events recalled by the subjects.

CONCLUSIONS

The two studies summarized in this chapter yield what appears to be valuable data on the social concomitants of a collective trauma, on an informational, emotional, attitudinal, and reconstruction level. On an informational level, 51% of young school pupils report that their family members or acquaintances suffered the war or torture. In addition, those pupils who indicated that their acquaintances suffered from war- and torture-related problems, show the highest tendencies to engage in social sharing and reevaluation processes about this topic. Most students reported that their veteran acquaintances talk very little about the war. Key informants belonging to the Portuguese association of disabled war veterans (ADFA) corroborated this fact: Veterans attempt to forget and it is hard for them to speak about their negative experiences at war; those who are strongly disturbed have the tendency to avoid sharing and to ruminate.

On the emotional-attitudinal level, the results indicate that the more individuals share past traumatic collective episodes, the more negative are their views of current society and the war. Namely, the more they hear about the war, the more negatively they perceive the veteran's mood, the more they perceive the veteran's family climate to be a negative one, and the more their personal appraisal of the war is fearful and hostile. These results, even if their retrospective and self-reporting origins suggest caution about the conclusions, indicate the existence of a general emotional climate marked by anxiety, fear, disgust, contempt, and anger. Moreover, the results show that this was the most important organizer of the perceptions about the Portuguese colonial war (see Table 13.3, Dimension 1).

On the reconstruction level, the data showed that the minority of veterans who frequently talk about the war are perceived to do so in a favorable mood (joyful, pleased, interested, at ease). This allows the subjects to hold a positive image of the veteran, as shown by the subjects' dismissal of explanations based on psychosocial vulnerability (social and psychological problems) and situational individualistic explanations (he was forced) to address the veteran's participation in the war. Simultaneously, subjects scoring higher in the positive content social-sharing dimension (Table 13.3) rejected more external social-political explanations of the colonial war as well as naturalistic dispositional explanations. In brief, these people hold a more positive image of veterans, reject more the human and social-political constraints of the war than do subjects whose acquaintances speak less frequently and/or more negatively about the war.

With regard to the relation between social reconstruction and labeling, the data support the idea that, when the war was labeled as an "overseas war," individuals emphasized external and conjunctural factors as explanations of the war. In this case, veterans' participation was explained in light of naive patriotism. These explanations somehow appear to be a "better" justification of Portugal's engagement in the war in this condition than in the "colonial war" condition. These latter subjects rejected more the aforementioned explanations. Because "overseas war" was the official term used in the African struggle, this fact clearly indicates that social labeling is not a neutral process and it may have ideological, justification, and behavioral effects that go beyond the mere status of a semantic artifact. Finally, a less negative view of the war was related to explanations based on "human nature" and global factors as well as to the naive patriotism explanation for veteran participation. This would be a way to depict war, as well as individual participation in it, under a somewhat more positive light. Conversely, negative attitudes toward the war were related to conjunctural and external explanations and to veterans' forced participation.

This is a social psychological context that gives veterans the double role of actors and victims of war violence. As soldiers, they probably were victimizers of, at least, part of the African population. But, as participants in a war that was lost and perceived as illegitimate by many, both before and after the fall of the regime, they can be conceived of as victims. With important differences, this situation is analogous, in some aspects, to that of the German soldiers after World War II. In this vein, analyzing the German case, A. Mitscherlicht and M. Mitscherilicht (1972) suggested that victimizers (i.e., those who commit an abuse) generally build or create a defensive meaning for the event. In the case analyzed by these authors, German respondents used as a collective defensive mechanism that of an affective dis-inversion of the past, namely, they forgot about their support for the Nazi party, despite the fact that in the election held just before World War II nearly 90% of the population voted for Hitler—even in areas where the Nazis did not have total control. After the war, not talking about it or not accepting the possibility of being judged for their past was the predominant attitude. A. Mitscherlicht and M. Mitscherlicht stated that out of a total number of 4,000 files obtained from the psychosomatic clinic in Heidelberg, not even one patient established the relationship between their symptoms and the events that took place during the Nazi era. These results suggest a systematic silence in relation to this era. There may be another parallel with the Portuguese case, as shown by the general silence about eventual active participation in the past regime (e.g., by some of those military who made the revolution, or by public figures).

Another important attitude was that of denying defeat and identifying with the "winner." This is the most predominant attitude in present days, as we can see by the fact that in interviews conducted on the topic of D-Day, 69% of the German population think that the end of World War II and having defeated Nazism was a liberation for the German people. Only 13% see it as a defeat and 14% have an ambiguous stance toward it (Comas, 1994). This attitude may be described as "identification with the winner" (A. Mitscherlicht & M. Mitscherlicht, 1972). In Italy, a very popular joke says that the night Mussolini was led to resign, Italians went to bed as fascists, and, the next day, they woke up as antifascists. Another joke in Portugal says that the Portuguese are the only people who can "pull down" a bridge much like San Francisco's Golden Gate and build a new one overnight: The day before the revolution, they had "Salazar bridge" (named after the main figure of the old regime); the next day, they had an "April 25" (the revolution day) bridge. This latter bridge still exists. The identification with the winner is also a predominant strategy in Portugal which is used by most of the population. Specifically, the fact that the military, who were engaged in the war, played the crucial role in the revolution helps in understanding why they acquired a very positive image, at least during the first years after the revolution.

Another way of creating a positive meaning for traumatic events is to generate attributions blaming the victims. Although this phenomenon does not seem to have emerged in Portugal, this seems to be a psychologically useful process in maintaining a belief in a just and meaningful world. As a case in point, one third of the Germans, and the most of those are over 40 years old, are in total or partial agreement with the idea that "it is the Jews' own fault if they have been persecuted for centuries" (Martí-Font, 1992). The wife of a Russian civil servant who worked in concentration camps stated (even in 1989) this belief in a just world in relation to the gulag: "There were innocents who were unjustly jailed, that is true, but the rest, the majority, those were bandits" (Potel, 1992, p. 402).

The effort to provide a traumatic event with meaning is a normal feature, although it is not always possible to do so (Janoff-Bulman, 1992). But, in more appropriate social-political circumstances, the strife against forgetting and the existence of testimonial commemorations are mechanisms that allow people to give individual intrusive memories of collective traumatic events a social meaning (Jodelet, 1993), while also decreasing symptomatology (Becker & Lira, 1989). As stated by one key informant of the Portuguese disabled veterans' association, attempts to discuss the African war were poorly received by society. Even members of this association decreased in their efforts toward fostering this debate.

Faced with traumatic events that divide a society, those rituals aimed at remembering do not have a unifying normative nature as Halbwachs thought. For the victims and those who are close to them, commemorating a collective catastrophe may give it a positive meaning: Remember as a way of recognizing that it happened, that it was unjust and it should not happen again (Jodelet, 1993). For those responsible for the catastrophe, avoiding that memory or conventionalizing it has the same function although its contents may be different. In the Portuguese case, the recent construction of a monument to the African war veterans in Lisbon provoked public debates. Some sectors of the Portuguese society thought this monument was a recognition of the Portuguese soldiers' heroism. But, for others, it was no more than the mystification of the real status of war veterans: that of normal people having been victims of an illegitimate war.

ACKNOWLEDGMENTS

This chapter is part of a research project on "social memory and collective traumas" conducted by the Center of Psychology of the University of Porto, Portugal (JNICT Unit no. 50/94), in which the first author is a researcher and the second author is a consultant. The writing of this chapter and some of the research reported herein was partially supported by grant PB

MARQUES, PAEZ, SERRA

94-0475-CO2 from the Ministry of Education and Science. The authors are grateful to the ADFA, Portugal, for its valuable cooperation.

REFERENCES

Alameda, S. (1994). Jorge Semprún. *El País, 172,* 69–76.

Albuquerque, A. (1992). Tratamiento del estrés post-traumático en ex-combatientes [Treatment of posttraumatic stress in war veterans]. In E. Echeburua (Ed.), *Avances en el tratamiento psicológico de los trastornos de ansiedad.* Madrid: Pirámide.

Bartlett, F. C. (1973). Los factores sociales del recuerdo [Social factors of memory]. In H. Proshansky & B. Seidenberg (Eds.), *Estudios básicos de psicología social.* Madrid: Tecnos. (Original work published 1932)

Becker, D., & Lira, E. (1989). *Derechos humanos: Todo es según el dolor con que se mire* [Human rights: Differing perspectives on human pain]. Santiago: ILAS.

Brossart, A. (1992). URSS/Polonia/RDA. El quincuagésimo aniversario del pacto germano-soviético [The 50th anniversary of the German-Soviet pact]. In A. Brossart, S. Combe, J. Y. Potel, J. Ch. Szurek (Eds.), *En el Este, la memoria recuperada.* Valencia: Alfons el Magnánim.

Brossart, A., Combe, S., Potel, J. Y., & Szurek, J. Ch. (Eds.). (1992). *En el Este, la memoria recuperada* [In the East: Recovered memory]. Valencia: Alfons el Magnánim.

Comas, J. (1994). Un mal sabor de boca que mira al pasado [The bitter taste of looking back]. *El País, 6,* 4.

Davidson, L. M., & Baum, D. (1986). Implications of post-traumatic stress for social psychology. *Journal of Applied Social Psychology, 6,* 207–233.

Davidson, J. T., & Foa, E. A. (1991). Diagnostic issues in posttraumatic stress disorder. *Journal of Abnormal Psychology, 100,* 346–355.

Echeburúa, E. (1992). *Avances en el tratamiento psicológico de los trastornos de ansiedad* [Advances in the psychological treatment of anxiety disorders]. Madrid: Pirámide.

El País (1994). Dentro de 50 años [editorial] [Within 50 years]. *El País, 20,* 14.

Erdelyi, M. H. (1990). Repression, reconstruction and defense: History and integration of the psychoanalytic and experimental frameworks. In J. L. Singer (Ed.), *Repression and dissociation* (pp. 1–31). Chicago: University of Chicago Press.

Fairbank, J. A., Hansen, D. J., & Fitterling, J. M. (1991). Pattern of appraisal and coping across different stressor conditions among former prisoners of war with and without posttraumatic stress disorder. *Journal of Consulting and Clinical Psychology, 59,* 274–281.

Faúndez, H., Hering, M., & Balogi, S. (1990). Vivir en pareja: Vivencia y elaboración de los traumas [Living in pairs: Living with and working through traumas]. In CODEPU (Ed.), *Tortura: Aspectos médicos, psicológico y sociales.* Santiago: CODEPU.

Guerra, J. P. (1994). *Memória das guerras coloniais* [Recollections of the colonial wars]. Lisbon: Edições Afrontamento.

Halbwachs, M. (1968). *La mémoire collective* [Collective memory]. París: PUF. (Original work published 1950)

Horowitz, M. (1986). *Stress response syndrome.* Northvale, NJ: Aronson.

Janoff-Bulman, R. (1992). *Shattered assumptions: Towards a new psychology of trauma.* New York: The Free Press.

Jodelet, D. (1993). El lado moral y afectivo de la historia. Un ejemplo de la memoria de masas: El proceso de K. Barbie "el carnicero de Lyon" [The moral side and the effects of history. An example of collective memory: The case of K. Barbie—"the butcher of Lyon"]. *Revista de Psicología Política, 6,* 53–72.

Marti-Font, J. M. (1992). Uno de cada tres alemanes cree que Hitler "tuvo sus cosas buenas" [One in three Germans believe that Hitler "had some good qualities"]. *El País, 7,* 2.

Mitscherlicht, A., & Mitscherlicht, M. (1972). *Le Deuil impossible: Les fondements du comportement collectif* [The impossible grief: The foundations of collective behavior]. París: Payot.

Modell, J., & Haggerty, T. (1991). The social impact of war. *Annual Review of Sociology, 17,* 205–224.

Padilla, A., & Comas-Díaz, A. (1986). Un estado de miedo [The state of fear]. *Psychology Today Español, 3,* 30–34.

Pennebaker, J. W. (1990). *Opening up.* New York: Morrow.

Pennebaker, J. W. (1993). Creación y mantenimiento de las memorias colectivas [Creation and maintenance of collective memories]. *Revista de Psicología Política, 6,* 35–51.

Potel, J. Y. (1992). URSS. Irkutsk, puerta del exilio siberiano [Irkutsk, USSR: Port of the Siberian exile]. In A. Brossat, S. Combe, J. Y. Potel, & J. Ch. Szurek (Eds.), *En el este, la memoria recuperada.* Valencia: Alfons el Magnánim.

Sichrowsky, P. (1987). Nacer culpable, nacer víctima [Born guilty, born victim]. Nota bibliográfica. *Memoria, 3,* 56–57.

Steinglass, D., & Gerrity, E. (1990). Natural disasters and post-traumatic stress disorder. *Journal of Applied Social Psychology, 20,* 1746–1754.

Taylor, S., & Brown, J. (1988). Illusion and well-being. *Psychological Bulletin, 103,* 193–210.

Thompson, P. (1988). *La voz del pasado* [The voice of the past]. Valencia: Alfons el Magnánim.

Unzueta, P. (1994). Biografía política [Political biography]. *El País, 10,* 18.

Wortman, C., & Silver, R. C. (1989). The myths of coping with loss. *Journal of Consulting and Clinical Psychology, 57,* 344–357.

Chapter 14

Distortions of Collective Memory: How Groups Flatter and Deceive Themselves

Roy F. Baumeister
Stephen Hastings
Case Western Reserve University

Like individuals, social groups have important memories that help them define themselves, understand the world, and structure their motivations. Also like individuals, social groups may often find that a literal, objective record of the facts is not always the most helpful way of satisfying those interpretive needs. As a result, social groups (again like individuals) will sometimes gradually distort their memories in systematic ways.

This chapter intends to provide some empirically based theorizing about patterns of distortion in collective memories. At a minimum, the selection of particular memories may serve one's goals and needs. At the other extreme, severely distorted memory can be a potent tool for self-deception. Self-deception is of particular interest to us, and so we focus on how group memory can be manipulated for the sake of collective self-deception.

Most groups, like most individuals, try to maintain a positive image of self. Because the reality of events does not always fit that desired image, it is necessary to choose between revising the image and revising the meaning of events. The latter choice is the one of self-deception, and so it is the one discussed here. But this does not mean groups never revise their self-appraisals in light of the facts.

Indeed, there are examples where groups have acknowledged guilt or wrongdoing. As this chapter was being prepared, the Baptist church issued a statement apologizing for its past support of slavery and oppression against African Americans, and the Pope issued an apology for the Catholic Christian church's record of oppressing women. Some acknowledgments go beyond mere apologies. In recent decades, Germany has maintained one of the world's most liberal immigration and asylum policies and has also followed constitutional restrictions that prohibit military involvement outside its own borders, both of which presumably derive from recognizing the military aggression and mistreatment of other peoples earlier this century. In a similar fashion, the civil rights and affirmative action laws of the United States have often been justified by the need to make up for past oppression, discrimination, and other mistreatment of African Americans and women.

Self-deception is a notoriously difficult topic to study (see, e.g., Gur & Sackeim, 1979). By studying how shared memories differ from objective facts, it may be possible to gain valuable insights into the mechanisms by which groups (as well as individuals) set about constructing a worldview that fits their preferred self-interpretations (cf. Baumeister & Newman, 1994; Greenwald, 1980; Taylor & Brown, 1988).

This chapter consists of empirically based speculations. We have searched various literatures for good examples of motivated distortions in collective memory. These are used as case studies to provide a basis for theorizing about collective self-deception techniques. We take it as axiomatic that most social groups wish to maintain a positive image of themselves. Errors in collective memory that end up presenting a more positive image of the group than the truth would entail are therefore the focus. We infer that most such errors are indeed motivated forms of collective self-deception.

This way of proceeding runs the risk of overinterpretation. After all, memories are generally imperfect, and some errors would be expected even if no motivations were at work. Still, if memories were merely the random result of imperfect cognitive processes, then there should be as many errors that make a group seem worse than it is than errors that make the group look good. (Indeed, assuming most groups are relatively benign, and assuming regression to the mean, it can be predicted that the majority of errors would tarnish rather than enhance a group's image.) Yet errors that systematically make an individual's own group look worse are relatively rare. The asymmetry in errors—that is, the tendency for the majority of errors to enhance rather than diminish the group's positive image—suggests that they are motivated.

How common are these? There is no simple answer. Today's United States enjoys a long tradition of free speech, free press, and license to criticize any public official. This tradition may be taken for granted, whereas other countries have offered far less scope. Such a tradition will clearly make it difficult for a government to impose its own preferred view of history by suppressing contrary facts. Thus, if there is any distortion in collective memory of the United States, this must be regarded as quite important, because societies that have lacked the tradition of free press and free speech probably have much greater distortions.

Of course, the very tradition of free speech allows people to speak falsehoods as well. Many informed Americans have probably been exposed to speakers and writers who deny that 6 million Jews were murdered by the Nazi Germany system during World War II. People are free to express such views even if they are demonstrably false.

In contrast, other countries sometimes have passed laws prohibiting people from denying such facts. Shigeto Nagano, the justice minister of Japan, said in an interview published in May 1994 that Japan was not an aggressor in World War II. He was a veteran of that war and later was army chief of staff. He said the 1937 "Rape of Nanking" was a fabrication. International outrage over his remarks prompted his resignation as justice minister a few days later (Associated Press, 1994). Another 1994 news report said that a German who denied the reality of the Holocaust was sentenced to 2 years in prison for those remarks, and indeed German law forbids the voicing of such an opinion.

For the most part, however, laws do not enforce the memory of disagreeable facts. In some societies, laws prevent criticism of the state and nation, including any discussion of shameful or embarrassing history. In others, the unwelcome past is buried more by tacit agreement and social pressures, but the result may be quite similar. Thus, for example, various Japanese officials recently sought to apologize for acts of aggression and oppression committed during World War II, but these efforts were met with protests, demonstrations, and threats (e.g., "Japan and the War," 1995; Powell, 1995).

GENERATIONAL PATTERNS

Collective self-deception observes generational patterns and effects. Such effects involve beliefs held by people that exert a decisive influence on the later actions and attitudes of those same people (Schuman & Scott, 1989). Young adulthood (approximately 17 to 25 years of age) is the time when these effects appear. This fact has been shown on both individual and collective levels. On the individual level, Duncan and Agronick (1995) demonstrated that social events coinciding with early adulthood are exceptionally meaningful to individuals. On the collective level, Schuman and Scott (1989) showed that major collective memories of social and political events are structured by age. That is, major events that occurred during people's adolescence or early adulthood are more predictive of their later behaviors and opinions than are events from other periods in life.

Groups hold their beliefs in high regard and will strive hard to defend them, and such strivings include resorting to collective self-deception. When a group analyzes some of the actions of its ancestors in the context of its new generational effects, it may selectively distort the memory of those events in order to fit them into the current set of beliefs. Slavery is a good example. Centuries ago, slavery was regarded as a representation of power and wealth in many different societies (e.g., Patterson, 1982). Most people felt little or no shame about owning slaves. In modern Western society, however, slavery is considered one of the worst kinds of evil, and many people would prefer to forget or conceal their ancestors' slave ownership.

What do generational effects reveal about the nature of collective self-deception? Each generation holds certain beliefs. Most of the beliefs remain relatively constant across generations, but each generation develops some new opinions and attitudes based on what events shaped the social and political environment during early adulthood. It is these new beliefs that seem especially prone to produce collective self-deception, because people may want to protect themselves by distorting certain facts to fit in with the new beliefs.

Generational effects are not wholly new systems of moral thought. They are typically subtle changes in beliefs from one generation to the next. As a result, the collective self-deceptions they spawn are likely to appear gradually over time rather than to pop up abruptly.

Generational effects are not necessarily consistent across different groups within a society. Different groups of people experience different social and political events, and even world political events may affect different groups in different ways. World War II, to use an extreme example, affected different countries in quite different ways: Some were conquered, some were bombed, some were untouched but suffered combat losses, some had lasting political or economic changes, and others were only minimally affected.

STRATEGIES AND MECHANISMS

Selective Omission

Probably the easiest and most obvious way to distort collective memory involves the selective omission of disagreeable facts. Events that make one's social group look bad can often be ignored or expunged from its memory. To the extent that a group can succeed in deleting the bad side of its past, what remains will be mostly positive, and this will provide a good foundation for a positive collective self-image.

For example, nearly every school course in American history mentions the Dutch purchase of Manhattan island for $24 from the Native Americans. People laugh and shake their heads over the story, especially because it seems amazing that the Indians were so naive as to utterly fail to appreciate the land's value. The sellers were perhaps not so naive, however, as is suggested by a relevant fact that most histories omit: The Dutch actually paid the wrong tribe for the island. The Canarsees lived in what is now Brooklyn, and so they may have felt they made a good deal selling land they did not own. The Weckquaesgeeks lived on and owned the island but were not party to the transaction (Loewen, 1995).

The omission is presumably not motivated by a simple wish to preserve the belief in the naiveté of the Native Americans. It was the greed of the White settlers that led them to do whatever they felt was necessary to get the land they wanted, and so they deliberately paid the wrong tribe for it. Viewed in its proper light, the deal was an utter swindle, but by presenting it as a great bargain the dishonesty of our forefathers is greatly concealed.

Selective omission can also occur as values change. Slavery was once practiced without much question or controversy through much of the civilized world. Even in North America it was accepted for many decades before an organized opposition began. Now that it is considered morally repugnant and is linked with a problematic network of grievances and entitlements that complicate American race relations, the formerly moderate positions of compromise and partial tolerance are unacceptable. Hence any pro-slavery acts or opinions of favorite American historical figures are leading candidates for selective omission.

Several such omissions have been noted by Loewen (1995). Thomas Jefferson, who wrote in the Declaration of Independence that "all men are created equal," owned many slaves and advocated extending slavery into the western territories. Abraham Lincoln, the president who freed the slaves, had been heard to remark that he would prefer to save the Union without freeing the slaves because the likelihood of eventual equality between Blacks and Whites was small. Most dramatically, perhaps, Patrick Henry's famous libertarian assertion "Give me liberty or give me death" is well remembered, but little mention is made of his subsequent command to prevent Virginia slaves from accepting the British offer of freedom if they joined the British side.

Fabrication

The logical complement to a strategy of denying something that did happen is to affirm something that did not—in other words, to invent a false memory. Despite the seeming appeal of such myths, few examples of complete fabrication can be found.

One such apparent fabrication involves Betsy Ross. Everyone has heard the story, although history books do not generally tell it. According to such accounts, George Washington asked Betsy Ross to create a new flag for the new nation. Although Ross actually existed, she did not sew the first American flag. The story was invented in 1876 by some of her descendants in order to create a tourist attraction in Philadelphia.

Still, it seems that by and large outright fabrication of collective memory is rare. The implication may be that collective memories are to some extent constrained by the facts. Facts may be deleted, altered, shaded, reinterpreted, exaggerated, and placed in favorable contexts, but wholesale fabrication seems to lie beyond what most groups can accomplish. Presumably, a thorough historical search would eventually uncover an example or two of fabrication, but these would be extreme exceptions. Fabrication is thus not one of the standard techniques of altering collective memory for self-serving ends.

Exaggeration and Embellishment

Although it is apparently rare and difficult to fabricate a wholly spurious group memory, it is relatively easy and common to take some shreds of historical truth and blow them up into a major, important myth for the group. Social groups exaggerate the importance and positivity of the deeds of their ancestors.

The recent 50-year anniversary of the end of World War II led to several reassessments of the collective memories about that conflict. One theme that repeatedly emerges is that Britain and the United States have exaggerated the role their troops played in defeating the Germans. Although British and American troops did certainly make important contributions to the victory, the revisionists generally point out that the Red Army bore the brunt of the war and were by far the most important force in bringing about the victory. Germany's best forces were on the Russian front, and it was there that the war was decided. The *Economist* recently concluded that the Normandy invasion and the American attack into Germany was "almost a sideshow" in comparison with the eastern conflict. Yet in the American collective memory—especially as sustained in movies, television shows, and other mass media—the war was fought and won mainly by American soldiers.

The very discovery of the American hemisphere has long been subject to self-serving embellishments. It is well known that Christopher Columbus landed in the New World in 1492, and his voyage is generally credited with the discovery. There are, however, ample claims of earlier discoveries (i.e., by Vikings). These have received some grudging acknowledgment in history texts. Recent evidence suggests that Afro-Phoenicians may have arrived here as early as 1000 B.C. and stayed for a good length of time, but these are largely neglected, possibly because the Eurocentric historians are loath to give credit for such a major discovery to a different race and continent (Loewen, 1995). Of course, some might question whether there is any meaningful way to speak of "discovering" a place that was already inhabited by 60 million people.

Probably the most common form of exaggeration is to glorify one's past. Most groups presumably have some positive accomplishments in their past, and by emphasizing and embellishing them the group can give itself a compelling basis for being proud of its heritage. Thus, for example, Becker (1985) described how the Khmer Rouge revived the brief history of the 14th-century Cambodian (Angkor) empire as a way of fueling Cambodian nationalistic pride. Cambodia's actual history consists mostly of alternating between being a sleepy rural backwater and being overrun by various powerful neighbors. To inspire the Cambodians to support their plan of expelling foreign influence and making the nation strong and self-sufficient, the Khmer Rouge embellished the one rather short period when their nation had been a formidable power.

The origins of the Thanksgiving holiday likewise involve embellishment and exaggeration. It is true that the Pilgrim settlers invited the Native Americans to join them at a festive meal to celebrate their first harvest, which the Native Americans had helped them plant. Still, this event was not noted or celebrated in the following years. Other cultures around the world had been holding autumnal harvest celebrations for centuries before the Pilgrims landed at Plymouth Rock. George Washington did set aside a national day of thanksgiving, but it had little or nothing to do with the collective memory of the Pilgrims' first harvest. The current Thanksgiving Day celebration was proclaimed by Abraham Lincoln in 1863 to bolster patriotism during the Civil War. The Pilgrims became associated with the holiday during the 1890s (Loewen, 1995).

Linking Versus Detaching

Thus far we have discussed the most obvious means of distorting collective memory: denying the truth, inventing false events, and embellishing minor achievements into glorious triumphs. Consider now some of the theoretically more interesting forms of distorting collective memory.

One fertile means of distorting collective memory is by manipulating associations. That is, whether events are linked or separate is often quite important. Often events are the products of multiple causes. By focusing on one cause and ignoring the others, one can severely bias an interpretation without actually altering the facts. Thus, this technique has the advantage of being strongly rooted in the truth (and therefore being relatively impervious to disconfirmation, unlike fabrication would be).

One example of considerable interest (and controversy) these days concerns the dropping of the atomic bomb on Hiroshima and Nagasaki. These two bombs killed millions of people, most of them civilians. The motives and consequences of these bombings have been interpreted in multiple contexts. They showed the Japanese that the Americans had a supreme

weapon. They also showed the Russians that the Americans had a supreme
weapon. They very likely accelerated the Japanese surrender, thereby saving
the lives of many American soldiers who would have died in an invasion
and perhaps also ending the conflict before the Soviet Union could enter
the conflict and lay eventual claim to a share of Japanese territory.

Apparently the biggest gap between Japanese and American views of
the atomic bombings concerns the link to Pearl Harbor. Most Americans
see the two events as inextricably linked. They attacked us, and so we
attacked them back. Seeing the American bombings as the natural result
of the unprovoked attack makes them look quite reasonable. To be sure,
one may regret the deaths of so many people, especially civilian noncombatants, but that is the inevitable aspect of the war started by Japan.

The Japanese, however, tend to see little or no relation between Pearl
Harbor and Hiroshima. Recent statements in the news by Japanese officials
have compared the atomic bombings to the Holocaust and other major
atrocities. "I think that the atomic bombings were one of the two greatest
crimes against humanity in the 20th century, along with the Holocaust,"
said Nagasaki's mayor Hitoshi Motoshima in March 1995. Reporting this,
the magazine *Newsweek* commented that Mayor Motoshima ignored the
crucial fact that the Jews had done nothing to deserve the murderous
treatment by the Nazis. *Newsweek*'s implication is clearly that the citizens
of Nagasaki had done something to deserve the bomb—namely, belong
to a country that started a total war against a country that was at peace.

Other news reports have commented on the Japanese attitudes. When
asked about Pearl Harbor, Japanese often deny any connection to the
atomic bombings, and if pressed they point out (correctly) that the bombing of Pearl Harbor was focused entirely on military targets and there were
almost no civilian casualties. (Americans might prefer to use the category
"noncombatant" rather than "civilian," however, because insofar as the
United States was not at war, all the casualties of the Pearl Harbor bombing
could be called noncombatants.) To them, Pearl Harbor was a battle between military units, and it had nothing to do with the destruction of a
civilian city.

The Nagasaki bombing is of particular interest. Some Japanese were
reported to have said that the Hiroshima bombing may have been understandable, but the destruction of a second city a few days later was atrocious
because it was unnecessary. To the Japanese, the point had been made
sufficiently by the first bombing. (Then again, Americans might reply, the
Japanese had not yet surrendered; the United States thought *that* was the
point.)

Thus, the degree of atrocity involved in the atomic bombings varies
widely depending on whether or not they are linked to other events. Many
people, especially Americans, see the bombings as a regrettable but prob-

ably necessary part of the causal chain leading from the Japanese attack on Pearl Harbor to the Japanese surrender. By not recognizing those links, the Japanese can see the bombings as cruel acts of terrorist atrocity. The difference in collective self-images is immense: Americans can see themselves as either cruel, terrorist monsters or as pragmatists defending themselves against unprovoked attack. Japanese can see themselves as innocent victims or as the authors of their own misfortune and downfall.

In a sense, both groups have manipulated the meaningful links between events to permit themselves to claim the role of victim. In the American view, the "day of infamy" attack on Pearl Harbor cast the United States in the role of victim for the duration of the war, and the atomic bombings were merely an understandable response to their victimization. To the Japanese, the atomic bombings were beyond the scope of fair warfare and entitle them to victim status.

Actually, Japanese have an additional claim to victim status. In their view, much of Asia had been exploited, conquered, and colonized by the decadent and imperialistic Western powers. The Japanese described their own conquests during World War II as liberations, in the sense that White colonial powers were defeated. To be sure, one may question whether the various conquered parties were really any more liberated under Japanese rule than they had been under, say, British, but the Japanese were able to treat themselves as champions of Asian rule against Western oppression. Even the attack on Pearl Harbor can be seen as a defensive response to Western imperialist conquests in general.

Similar patterns can sometimes be observed in the linking of self to past perpetrators and victims. In terms of the current ethnic conflict in the former Yugoslavia, both sides seem to have ample claims to victim status based on manipulating the historical time span. This is covered later, because of special interest in the manipulation of time perspective as a form of self-deception. For now, another example is presented, based on current racial politics in the United States.

Current discussions of race relations in the United States frequently involve references to slavery. Most African American U.S. citizens can trace at least part of their ancestry to people who were brought to this country as slaves. Although slavery ended over a century ago, slavery is still depicted as a crime perpetrated by Whites against African Americans, with the assumption being that today's White Americans are guilty and African Americans deserve compensation as victims.

It is undeniably true that in the antebellum South most slaves were African Americans and slaveowners White. Yet the implications for today's Americans are far more muddled and complex. For the moment, set aside the issue of whether people should be held responsible for the misdeeds of their ancestors, because such links seem to be commonly recognized by all concerned wherever it may serve their ends—even though, strictly speaking, modern concepts of justice do not blame descendants or other family members for a perpetrator's crime. Assume, therefore, that descendants of slaveowners should be blamed for slavery, even if they themselves never owned slaves and would abhor the practice.

Should White Americans feel guilty over slavery? Only a small minority are descended from slaveowners. Most of today's White Americans are descended from the great waves of European immigration after the Civil War ended. Even those whose ancestors were here earlier may not be descended from slaveowners. Only a few rich Southerners owned slaves, and most of the country never permitted slavery. (Not to mention the fact that millions of White Americans campaigned, fought, suffered, and even died to end slavery.)

Thus, the guilt or innocence of today's White Americans rides heavily on how they link themselves to their predecessors. If a law were instituted stipulating that the descendents of slaveowners had to pay restitution, most White Americans could probably make a legal argument for their own innocence. In contrast, if they simply identify themselves as White people and see slavery as a White crime against African Americans, then they are guilty.

The Black side of the argument is even more interesting. Most Black Americans have lighter skin than African Blacks, and the main reason for this is racial mixing. The most common form, perhaps, was White masters mating with Black slaves. The offspring of these interracial couplings have (by somewhat arbitrary convention) been widely classified as Black people, and so they were most likely to mate with other Black people. Given the relative lack of Black immigration to the United States since the Civil War, it must be concluded that the offspring of these interracial matings have probably disseminated their genes through the Black gene pool.

Thus, one must assume on a demographic basis that African Americans today are more likely than White Americans to be descended from slaveowners. Yet this is almost never acknowledged, particularly by today's African American citizens. Thus, a person who is descended from both a slaveowner and a slave may often identify strongly with the slave (victim) group while failing to acknowledge any link to the slaveowner (perpetrator) group.

A revealing example of this reasoning was furnished by McCall (1994). He noted that when he was in prison in Virginia, the African American prisoners would have lengthy discussions about slavery. One prisoner in particular asserted that the relatively light skin of today's African Americans was a direct result of White masters having sex with Black slaves. He drew the conclusion that White people recognized the inherent superiority of Black people, at least to the extent that White slaveowners were unable to resist the sexual appeal of Black slaves. Yet, he completely ignored the implication that light skin of modern American Blacks meant being descended from slaveowners.

If self-deception is indeed involved in such selective identification, then it is presumably a product of a culture that wishes to reward and compensate victims. A culture that did not hold similar views might exhibit the reverse pattern, in which descendants of master–slave matings would emphasize the link to the slaveowner and downplay or conceal the descent from the slave. Thus, in many slaveowning cultures, even freeborn descendants of slaves suffered from some stigma (Patterson, 1982).

Blaming the Enemy

An important form of memory distortion involves focusing on actual or presumptive misdeeds by one's enemies or opponents, to the extent that even one's own misdeeds can be minimized as mere responses to the enemy (see Baumeister, in press). The ultimate form of this allows one to attribute one's own misdeeds to one's enemies.

A rather deliberate form of this occurred during World War II. As surprising as this may seem today, most of warfare in Western history had been directed against enemy soldiers, not civilians. (The main historical exceptions involved sieges of cities, after which the inhabitants were often mistreated or even massacred as if they had all been combatants.) Even World War I, as shockingly brutal as it was on the battlefield, essentially spared civilians from being direct targets of attack.

According to the eminent British historian Keegan (1993), the transition came about somewhat by accident early in World War II. The German air force mistakenly bombed a city in Germany (Freiburg) instead of its intended military target. Unwilling to admit that their own troops had been so incompetent, the German propaganda machine blamed the Freiburg bombing on the French. The spurious "news" that the French had bombed a German city led to calls for retaliation. This was a crucial reason for switching the bombing targets during the Battle of Britain from the initial military targets (e.g., airfields) to civilian London itself. Later, when the Allies gained the upper hand, they likewise debated whether to attack civilian targets in Germany, but because the Germans had already targeted Allied civilians it seemed quite right and appropriate to do the same in reverse.

Another version of this strategy involves constructing a view about what the enemy was going to do. Thus, one's own aggression can be perceived as a necessary means of preventing disaster. This strategy has the advantage of being extra difficult to disprove, because in order to prove the account wrong one would have to demonstrate what would have happened under other circumstances.

A good example of this pattern of distorted memory can be found with regard to the German invasion of Soviet Russia in 1941, which in retrospect can be seen as one of the greatest military blunders of all time. Even when it occurred it was a remarkable breach of international law, given that Russia and Germany had signed a mutual nonaggression pact in 1939. Unsuspecting Russian cities suddenly found themselves under attack, and in the ensuing struggle Russia probably suffered more casualties (civilian and military) than any other country has ever suffered in any war.

During the 50-year anniversary of this invasion, it was the subject of a stream of retrospective books, symposia, and other treatments. One theme that surfaced repeatedly was the accusation that the Soviets had actually been preparing to attack the Germans, and so the German attack was a form of preemptive self-defense. Although this version of the memory would not entirely excuse the Germans for violating the treaty (and would certainly not justify the massacres and other harsh treatment of civilians), it would undoubtedly mean a significant reduction in the blameworthiness. To attack a giant enemy who is preparing to attack you is clearly much less reprehensible than to attack an innocent, unsuspecting quasi-ally.

The strong motivation to rationalize that attack cannot be denied. Germany violated a treaty that was scarcely 2 years old. They inflicted extensive and brutal violence on the Russians during the ensuing war, including illegal killings of prisoners of war and massacres of civilians. Their conduct in that war played a large part in creating the national stigma that persists today. Moreover, even apart from moral concerns, Germany's invasion of Russia brought disaster on itself; with peace in the East, it is doubtful that the American and British invasions of France and Italy could have succeeded. The Russian counterattack eventually destroyed the German empire, left millions of young men dead and women raped, turned their cities to rubble, and put a third of their country under foreign occupation for several decades. Despite the very respectable German efforts to face up to their past, the memory of the invasion of Russia would certainly cry out for some rationalization.

It is useful to examine the context in which the attack took place. In the first place, the 1939 nonaggression pact probably did not provide a guarantee of safety. Germany and Russia had been perennial enemies, and their troops had fought each other for centuries, most recently in World War I. Alongside the traditional, territorial animosity was a strong ideological one. The right-wing fascists who ran Germany considered the left-wing Communists to be their greatest enemies. The Germans had facilitated the Communist Russian Revolution in order to destabilize their enemy, and the Russians had supported a nearly successful Communist takeover in Germany. The nonaggression pact had surprised everyone because it came between the two seemingly most bitter of enemies.

Most historians believe that Russia was not preparing to attack Germany in 1939, although the reasons could also support a weaker version of the German rationalization. After the Communist party purges of the 1920s and early 1930s, Stalin had turned on the military and begun an exceptionally bloody purge of the officer corps, right up through the general staff. According to Conquest (1990), the Stalinist purge of the army killed more officers than died in the war with Germany. Because paranoid jealousies and concern about preserving power drove the purge, it focused heavily on the best and most capable officers, with the result that the Soviet military was effectively crippled. This was revealed in the war with Finland in the 1930s. It was apparent to all that the Soviet army was not currently capable of fighting a major war. Russian embarked on a rebuilding program.

The temporary incapacitation of the Red Army would have made an attack on Germany in 1941 absurd and doomed. The literal form of the German belief is therefore implausible. On the other hand, there was a military buildup going on (mainly to recover from the damage the purge had caused), which could have caused some worry. A Soviet attack on Germany several years later would have been plausible. This possibility, however, presented the Germans with a dilemma: If there was ever to be a war with Russia, they would be best off fighting it right away rather than after the Red Army regained its potency.

Thus, to a coldly rational German planner, the essential question was whether there was ever to be a war between Germany and the Soviet Union. Given the historical antagonism and the ideological opposition, one would probably have to predict that the odds of an eventual conflict would be greater than 50%. And on the basis of that supposition, an immediate attack would have made sense.

The distortion of collective memory thus takes the form of transforming an educated guess about an eventual conflict into an imminent reality. In other words, the possibility that the Russians would attack someday was exaggerated into a belief that they were preparing to attack right then.

A contemporary version of the strategy of blaming the enemy for one's misdeeds has been furnished in recent discussions of crime in the United States. The highest levels of violent crime today involve Black-on-Black crime, that is, crimes by African Americans against other African Americans. Yet many perpetrators explain even these activities as a direct response to oppression by the White establishment.

McCall's (1994) recollections of his violent youth emphasize the periodic rationalizations that all crimes and activities were justified because of past oppressive acts by White people against African Americans (see also Shakur, 1993). Violent acts and other crimes against White people therefore made perfect sense and seemed legitimate; in this respect, the rationalizations are no different from those used by perpetrators of all races and nationalities. What is especially ironic, however, is that the collective memory of victimization by White people somehow managed to serve as justification for crimes by African Americans against other African Americans. In a remarkable passage, McCall discussed how he and his fellow delinquents rationalized armed robbery, burglary, and rape of other African Americans, especially because he noted that their rape victims (African American women) came from one of the most oppressed and disadvantaged segments of any modern society. He said, however, that the young criminals told themselves that the White-dominated society was itself evil, and so anything that allowed them to live outside that society was acceptable. In other words, they regarded it as morally better to victimize their racial fellows than to accommodate themselves to a society dominated by another race.

Blaming Circumstances

If one cannot blame one's enemy or one's victim, then sometimes one can shift the blame off oneself by pointing to external circumstances. One's own responsibility for the suffering of others can thereby be minimized.

Possibly the best example of this is the popular attribution for the deaths of the indigenous peoples in the Americas. It is clear that diseases brought by European explorers and invaders killed millions of these people. Yet it is also clear that deliberate policies of genocide, subjection, and extermination also killed millions. In some cases these even overlapped, such as the cases in which the Whites sold the native "Indians" blankets that had been contaminated with smallpox (Stannard, 1992). The combination of deliberate killing, oppressive treatment, and epidemics of disease is estimated to have killed between 60 and 80 million natives by the end of the 16th century (p. 95).

How is this holocaust remembered by the White-dominated surviving culture? Not surprisingly, the popular view of history assigns the main weight of responsibility to disease. Stannard's (1992) history of the calamity concluded that the impact of disease has been wildly exaggerated in order to cover up the systematic patterns of murder and lethal oppression by the European intruders.

Contextual Framing

Most major historical events involve a highly complex web of causes, consequences, and corollaries. Perhaps inevitably, collective memory will reduce these to fairly simple explanations. By choosing which causal nexus to emphasize, people can cast an event in a particular context that can make the memory serve the group's self-image.

The American Civil War is a good illustration. No single explanation of the origins of the conflict is satisfactory, but collective memory tends to prefer to focus on one. Not surprisingly, Northern and Southern views diverge rather sharply about which one to emphasize. In today's northern states, most schoolchildren know the overriding fact that the war was about slavery: The North went to war to bring an end to an evil institution. In contrast, modern Southerners often reject the view that the war was about slavery. (Indeed, when the Public Broadcasting Service aired Ken Burns's 5-part documentary on the Civil War, the stations received many complaints from Southerners for the supposedly erroneous emphasis on slavery as a cause of the war.) To the South, the issue was the rights of Americans to live as their local values and culture preferred. The South did not go to war to defend slavery, in their view. States' rights and the survival of Southern culture as a whole were the crucial factors.

Collective memories of the Crusades offer a similar illustration of differential framing (cf. Maalouf, 1987; Runciman, 1951–1954). From the Christian side, the Crusades were a noble attempt to guarantee the rights of pilgrims to visit the Holy Land, as well as possibly a chance to recapture territory that was centrally important to Christendom but had been conquered by heathens centuries before. To the Arabs, however, the Crusades were an unprovoked invasion of territory that was, after all, equally sacred to them, and that they had held more or less peacefully for centuries.

The capture of Jerusalem in the First Crusade is a good example of these differential contexts. From the Christian view, the fall of the city was a sign of God's favor and hence a divine mandate to impose strict, thorough control, which they did with a certain excess of zeal. A less theologically inclined Western historian would note that the capture of Jerusalem was the culmination of the long Crusade that had included brutal battles, heartbreaking struggles with the elements, frequent brushes with starvation and other deprivations, and simply the utterly wearing process of walking the immense distance from central Europe to what is now Israel. Only the intense religious fanaticism could sustain these troops to carry on to victory, and so it is not surprising that at their moment of triumph they visited some of their accumulated frustrations and sufferings on the vanquished foes.

Arab historians, in contrast, compare the First Crusade's conquest of Jerusalem to its fall to Arab Moslem troops in the 6th century. The Arabs entered the city in disciplined order and left the inhabitants pretty much alone. The Christian patriarch invited the Arab leader to worship with him in the great church, but the Arab politely pointed out that wherever he first worshiped would likely become a shrine, and so to avoid having a Christian sanctuary forcibly converted to Islam he would perform his worship elsewhere. This respectful and considerate conquest makes a sharp contrast to the Crusaders' victory, which involved looting the city, massacring inhabitants, and burning down Moslem and Jewish places of worship (including those that were full of terrified refugees).

CONCLUSIONS

This survey has suggested that group memories are systematically distorted in a variety of ways to maintain a positive image of the group. Sometimes these distortions are initiated in a deliberate, intentional fashion, such as in the efforts by totalitarian regimes to rewrite history. Other times, perhaps, they result from well-meaning efforts to furnish a truthful account. The line between deliberate and unintentional distortion is inevitably a fuzzy one, because self-deception cannot succeed if it is recognized as such, by definition.

Whatever the motives and intentions of the people who start the distortions, one must also recognize the important role played by the people who listen, accept, and pass along these biased views. People want to think well of their social group, and so even if they are equally exposed to truthful and flattering versions of the past, they may find it easier to understand, remember, and repeat the flattering ones.

ACKNOWLEDGMENTS

Preparation of this chapter was facilitated by NIMH grants MH 43826 and MH 51482.

REFERENCES

Associated Press. (1994). Japanese minister quits over war gaffe. *Charlottesville Daily Progress,* May 8.
Baumeister, R. F. (in press). *Evil: Inside human violence and cruelty.* New York: Freeman.
Baumeister, R. F., & Newman, L. S. (1994). Self-regulation of cognitive inference and decision processes. *Personality and Social Psychology Bulletin, 20,* 3–19.
Becker, E. (1986). *When the war was over.* New York: Simon & Schuster/Touchstone.
Conquest, R. (1990). *The Great Terror: A reassessment.* New York: Oxford University Press.
Duncan, L. E., & Agronic, G. S. (1995). The intersection of life stage and social events: Personality and life outcomes. *Journal of Personality and Social Psychology, 69,* 558–568.
Greenwald, A. G. (1980). The totalitarian ego: Fabrication and revision of personal history. *American Psychologist, 35,* 603–618.
Gur, R. C., & Sackeim, H. A. (1979). Self-deception: A concept in search of a phenomenon. *Journal of Personality and Social Psychology, 37,* 147–169.
"Japan and the war: The Japan that cannot say sorry." (1995, August 12). *The Economist, 336*(7927), 31–33.
Keegan, J. (1993). *A history of warfare.* New York: Knopf.

Loewen, J. W. (1995). *Lies my teacher told me.* New York: New Press.

Maalouf, A. (1987). *The Crusades through Arab eyes* (J. Rothschild, Trans.). New York: Schocken.

McCall, N. (1994). *Makes me wanna holler: A young Black man in America.* New York: Random House.

Patterson, O. (1982). *Slavery and social death: A comparative study.* Cambridge, MA: Harvard University Press.

Powell, B. (1995, July 24). Who's sorry now? *Newsweek,* 38–39.

Runciman, S. (1951–1954). *A history of the Crusades* (3 vols.). Cambridge, England: Cambridge University Press.

Schuman, H., & Scott, J. (1989). Generations and collective memories. *American Sociological Review, 54,* 359–381.

Shakur, S. (1993). *Monster: The autobiography of an L.A. gang member.* New York: Atlantic Monthly Press.

Stannard, D. E. (1992). *American holocaust: Columbus and the conquest of the New World.* New York: Oxford University Press.

Taylor, S. E., & Brown, J. D. (1988). Illusion and well-being: A social psychological perspective on mental health. *Psychological Bulletin, 103,* 193–210.

Author Index

295

Subject Index